Rick

VENICE
2006

Rick Steves & Gene Openshaw

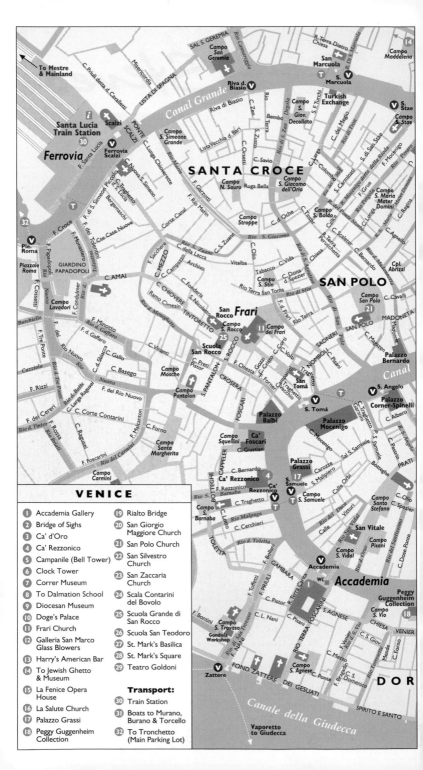

VENICE

1. Accademia Gallery
2. Bridge of Sighs
3. Ca' d'Oro
4. Ca' Rezzonico
5. Campanile (Bell Tower)
6. Clock Tower
7. Correr Museum
8. To Dalmation School
9. Diocesan Museum
10. Doge's Palace
11. Frari Church
12. Galleria San Marco Glass Blowers
13. Harry's American Bar
14. To Jewish Ghetto & Museum
15. La Fenice Opera House
16. La Salute Church
17. Palazzo Grassi
18. Peggy Guggenheim Collection

19. Rialto Bridge
20. San Giorgio Maggiore Church
21. San Polo Church
22. San Silvestro Church
23. San Zaccaria Church
24. Scala Contarini del Bovolo
25. Scuola Grande di San Rocco
26. Scuola San Teodoro
27. St. Mark's Basilica
28. St. Mark's Square
29. Teatro Goldoni

Transport:
30. Train Station
31. Boats to Murano, Burano & Torcello
32. To Tronchetto (Main Parking Lot)

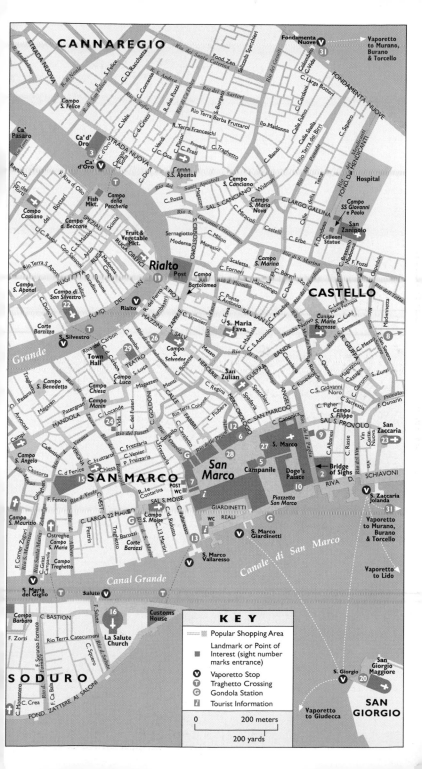

Rick Steves'®

VENICE
2006

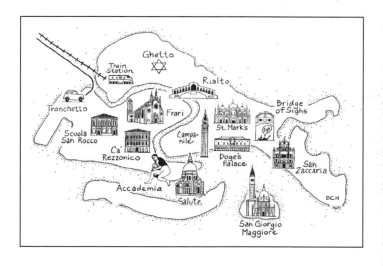

AVALON
TRAVEL

CONTENTS

Venice Overview

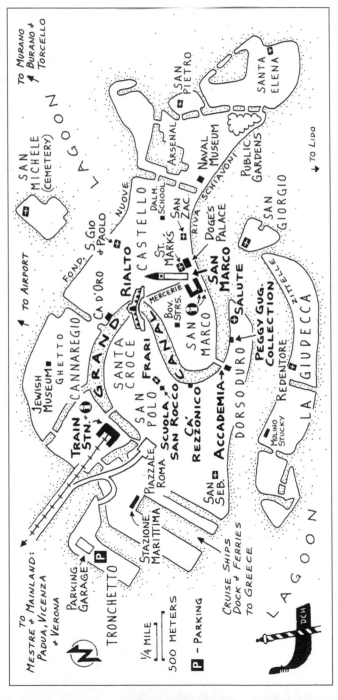

INTRODUCTION

Engineers love Venice—a completely man-made environment rising from the sea, with no visible means of support. Romantics revel in its atmosphere of elegant decay, seeing the peeling plaster and seaweed-covered stairs as a metaphor for beauty in decline. And first-time visitors are often stirred deeply, awaking from their ordinary lives to a fantasy world unlike anything they've ever seen before.

Those are strong reactions, considering that Venice today, frankly, can also be an overcrowded, prepackaged, and tacky tourist trap. But Venice is unique. Built on a hundred islands with wealth from trade with the East, its exotic-looking palaces are laced together by sun-speckled canals. The car-free streets suddenly make walkers feel big, important, and liberated.

By day, it's a city of museums and churches, packed with great art. Everything's within a half-hour walk. Cruise the canals on a vaporetto water-bus. Climb towers for stunning seascape views. Shop for local crafts (such as glass and lace), high fashions, or tacky souvenirs for your Uncle Eric. Linger over lunch, trying to crack a local crustacean with weird legs and antennae. Sip Valpolicella wine at a café on St. Mark's Square as the orchestra plays "New York, New York."

At night, when the hordes of day-trippers have gone, another Venice appears. Dance across a floodlit square. Glide in a gondola through quiet canals while music echoes across the water. Pretend it's Carnevale time, don a mask—or just a clean shirt—and become someone else for a night.

This Information Is Accurate and Up-to-Date

This book is updated every year. Most publishers of guidebooks can afford an update only every two or three years (and even then, it's often by e-mail or fax). Since this book is selective, we can update it in person each summer. The telephone numbers and hours of sights listed in this book are accurate as of mid-2005—but once you pin Italy down, it wiggles. Still, if you're traveling with the current edition of this book, we guarantee you're using the most up-to-date information available in print. For any updates, see www.ricksteves .com/update. Also at our Web site, you'll find a valuable list of reports and experiences—good and bad—from fellow travelers who have used this book (www.ricksteves.com/feedback).

Use this year's edition. People who try to save a few bucks by traveling with an old book are not smart. They learn the serious-ness of their mistake...in Europe. Your trip costs about $10 per waking hour. Your time is valuable. This guidebook saves lots of time.

About This Book

Rick Steves' Venice is a personal tour guide in your pocket. Better yet, it's actually two tour guides in your pocket: The co-author of this book is Gene Openshaw. Since our first "Europe through the gutter" trip together as high-school buddies almost 30 years ago, Gene and I have been exploring the wonders of the Old World. An inquisitive historian and lover of European culture, Gene wrote most of this book's self-guided museum tours and neighborhood walks. Together, Gene and I will keep this book up-to-date and accurate (though for simplicity, from this point "we" will shed our respective egos and become "I").

The book is organized this way:

Each **Orientation** includes tourist information and public transportation. The "Planning Your Time" section offers a sug-gested schedule with thoughts on how to best use your limited time.

Sights provide a succinct overview of the most important sights, arranged by neighborhood, with ratings: ▲▲▲—Don't miss; ▲▲—Try hard to see; ▲—Worthwhile if you can make it; no rating—Worth knowing about.

The **Self-Guided Tours** lead you through Venice's most important sights, with tours of the Grand Canal, St. Mark's Square, St. Mark's Basilica, Doge's Palace, Correr Museum, Accademia, Scuola San Rocco, Frari Church, Ca' Rezzonico (Museum of 18th-Century Venice), Peggy Guggenheim Collection, La Salute Church, San Giorgio Maggiore, and the islands in Venice's lagoon: Cimitero, Murano, Burano, and Torcello.

The **Self-Guided Walks** take you through Venice's back streets. The walk from St. Mark's to Rialto follows a less tour-isty route between these two major landmarks. The walk from Rialto to Frari Church leads from the Rialto Bridge to the Frari Church's exquisite art, with interesting stops (the Rialto Market, a local pub, and a mask-making shop) en route. The walk from St. Mark's to San Zaccaria explores the area behind the basilica, featuring an historic church and a seldom-seen view of the famous Bridge of Sighs.

Sleeping is a guide to my favorite of Venice's budget accommodations, conveniently located near St. Mark's Square, the Rialto Bridge, and the Accademia—all handy to the sights in this compact city.

Eating offers restaurants ranging from inexpensive eateries to splurges, with an emphasis on good value.

Venice with Children, Shopping, and **Nightlife** contain my best suggestions on those topics.

Transportation Connections covers connections by train, bus, and plane, laying the groundwork for your smooth arrival and departure.

Day Trips covers nearby destinations: Padua, Vicenza, Verona, and Ravenna.

Venetian History fills you in on the background of this fascinating city.

The **appendix** is a traveler's tool kit, with telephone tips, useful Italian phone numbers, a climate chart, a list of festivals, and a handy list of Italian survival phrases.

Throughout this book, when you see a ✪ in a listing, it means that the sight is covered in more detail in one of my self-guided tours. A page number will tell you where to find more information.

Browse through this book and choose your favorite sights. Then have a great trip! Traveling like a temporary local, you'll get the absolute most out of every mile, minute, and euro.

PLANNING

Trip Costs

Six components make up your trip costs: airfare, surface transportation, room and board, sightseeing/entertainment, shopping/miscellany, and gelato.

Airfare: Don't try to sort through the mess. Find and use a good travel agent. A basic, round-trip United States–Venice (or even cheaper, Milan) flight should cost $700–1,000, depending on where you fly from and when (cheapest in winter). Always consider saving time and money in Europe by flying "open jaw" (into one city and out of another).

Surface Transportation: Venice's sights are within walking distance of each other, but vaporetto boat rides are affordable ($4–6) and fun time-savers. For a one-way trip between Venice's airport and the city, allow about $3 by bus, $12 by speedboat, or $95 by water taxi (for details, see Transportation Connections, page 251).

The cost of round-trip, second-class train transportation to day-trip destinations is affordable (about $10 to Padua; about $10 to Vicenza; about $15 to Verona; and about $20 to Ravenna).

Room and Board: You can easily manage in Venice in 2006 on an overall average of $100 a day per person for room and board. This allows $10 for lunch, $5 for snacks, $20 for dinner, and $65 for lodging (based on 2 people splitting the cost of a $130 double room that includes breakfast). If you've got more money, I've listed great ways to spend it. Students and tightwads can enjoy Venice for as little as $50 a day ($25 for a bed, $25 for meals and snacks).

Sightseeing and Entertainment: Figure about $9–13 per major sight (Accademia, Doge's Palace), $3–6 for smaller ones (museums, climbing church towers), and $25 or more for splurge experiences (e.g., tours and concerts). A gondola ride costs $80–95 (by day) or $95–125 (at night); split the cost by going with a pal. An overall average of $30 a day works for most. Don't skimp here. After all, this category is the driving force behind your trip—you came to sightsee, enjoy, and experience Venice.

Shopping and Miscellany: Figure a minimum of $2 per postcard, coffee, soft drink, or gelato. Shopping can vary in cost from nearly nothing to a small fortune. Good budget travelers find that this category has little to do with assembling a trip full of lifelong, wonderful memories.

When to Go

Venice's best travel months (and busiest, most expensive months) are May, June, September, and October. Between November and April you can usually expect mild winter weather, some flooding (particularly March and Nov), and generally none of the sweat and stress of the tourist season (except during the Carnevale festival in mid–late-Feb).

Venice's summers are more temperate than Italy's scorching inland cities. Venetian temperatures hit the high 70s and 80s in summer and drop to the 30s and 40s in winter. Spring and fall can be cool, and many hotels do not turn on their heat until winter. Many mid-range hotels come with air-conditioning—a worthwhile splurge in the summer (usually only operates June–Sept). For specific temperatures, see the climate chart in the appendix.

Off-Season Travel: Here are several things to keep in mind if you visit Venice off-season.

- The orchestras in St. Mark's Square might stop playing at 18:00 (or not play at all in bad weather or for several days during their annual vacations).
- Vaporetto #82 (the Grand Canal fast boat) has surprisingly limited off-season hours: 9:30–16:30.

- Expect the occasional *acqua alta* (flooding), particularly at St. Mark's Square and along Zattere (southern edge of Venice, opposite Giudecca Island).

Venice has two main weather patterns: Wind from the southeast (Bulgaria) brings cold and dry weather. The scirocco wind from the south (Egypt) brings warm and wet weather, pushing more water into the lagoon and causing the *acqua alta*. This shouldn't greatly affect your sightseeing plans. Elevated wooden walkways are sometimes set up in the busier, more flooded squares to keep you above the water. And it's worth a trip to St. Mark's Square to see waiters in fancy tuxes and rubber boots.

Travel Smart

Many people travel through Italy thinking it's a chaotic mess. They feel that any attempt at efficient travel is futile. This is dead wrong—and expensive. Italy, which seems as orderly as spilled spaghetti, actually functions well. Only those who understand this and travel smart can enjoy Italy on a budget.

Buy a phone card, and use it for reservations and double-checking hours of sights. (I've included phone numbers for this purpose.) Enjoy the friendliness of the local people. Ask questions. Most locals are eager to point you in their idea of the right direction. Pack along a pocket-size notebook to organize your thoughts. Those who expect to travel smart, do.

Sundays have the same pros and cons as they do for travelers in the United States: Sightseeing attractions are generally open, though some churches in Venice are closed in the morning to sightseers. Banks, open-air produce markets, and many shops are closed. Rowdy evenings are rare on Sundays. Saturdays are virtually weekdays with earlier closing hours.

Museums and sights, especially large ones, usually stop admitting people 30–60 minutes before closing time.

Hotels in Venice are usually booked up on Carnevale (Feb 17–Feb 28), Easter (April 16 in 2006), April 25, May 1, November 1, and on Fridays and Saturdays year-round. Religious holidays and train strikes can catch you by surprise anywhere in Italy.

Really, this book can save you lots of time and money. But to have an A trip, you need to be an A student. Read the whole thing before your trip; note the time-saving tips and the days when museums are closed. If you save St. Mark's Basilica for Sunday morning (when it's closed), you'll miss the gondola. You can sweat in line at the Doge's Palace, or you can buy your Museum Card at the nearby Correr Museum and zip right though the Doge's Palace turnstile. Day-tripping to Verona or Vicenza on Monday, when most sights are closed, is bad news. A smart trip is a puzzle—a fun, doable, and worthwhile challenge.

RESOURCES

Tourist Offices in the United States

Venice has several tourist information offices (abbreviated **TI** in this book); for a list, see page 23.

Before your trip, contact the nearest Italian TI in the United States and briefly describe your trip and request information. You'll get the general packet and, if you ask for specifics (city map, calendar of festivals, etc.), an impressive amount of help. If you have a specific problem, they're a good source of sympathy.

Contact the office nearest you:

In New York: 630 Fifth Ave. #1565, New York, NY 10111, brochure hotline tel. 212/245-4822, tel. 212/245-5618, fax 212/586-9249, enitny@italiantourism.com.

In Illinois: 500 N. Michigan Ave. #2240, Chicago, IL 60611, tel. 312/644-0996, fax 312/644-3019, enitch@italiantourism.com.

In California: 12400 Wilshire Blvd. #550, Los Angeles, CA 90025, brochure hotline tel. 310/820-0098, tel. 310/820-4498, fax 310/820-6357, enitla@italiantourism.com.

Web Sites on Venice: www.turismovenezia.it (Tourist Board of Venice), www.veniceforvisitors.com, www.museiciviciveneziani.it (civic museums in Venice), www.venicexplorer.net (interactive maps), www.meetingvenice.it, and www.aguestinvenice.com.

Web Sites on Italy: www.italiantourism.com (Italian Tourist Board in the U.S.), www.museionline.it (museums in Italy), and www.trenitalia.com (train info and schedules).

Rick Steves' Guidebooks, Public Television Show, and Radio Show

The book *Rick Steves' Europe Through the Back Door* gives you budget-travel skills, such as minimizing jet lag, packing light, planning your itinerary, traveling by car or train, finding rooms, changing money, avoiding rip-offs, buying a mobile phone, hurdling the language barrier, staying healthy, taking great photographs, using a bidet, and much more. The book also includes chapters on 38 of my favorite "Back Doors."

Country Guides: These annually updated books offer you the latest on the top sights and destinations, with tips on how to make your trip efficient and fun. Here are the titles:

Rick Steves' Best of Europe	*Rick Steves' Great Britain*
Rick Steves' Best of Eastern Europe	*Rick Steves' Ireland*
	Rick Steves' Italy
Rick Steves' England (new in 2006)	*Rick Steves' Portugal*
	Rick Steves' Scandinavia
Rick Steves' France	*Rick Steves' Spain*
Rick Steves' Germany & Austria	*Rick Steves' Switzerland*

City and Regional Guides: Updated every year, these focus on Europe's most compelling destinations. Along with specifics on sights, restaurants, hotels, and nightlife, you'll get self-guided, illustrated tours of the outstanding museums and most characteristic neighborhoods.

Rick Steves' Amsterdam,
  Bruges & Brussels
Rick Steves' Florence
  & Tuscany
Rick Steves' London
Rick Steves' Paris

Rick Steves' Prague
  & the Czech Republic
Rick Steves' Provence
  & the French Riviera
Rick Steves' Rome
Rick Steves' Venice

Rick Steves' Phrase Books: In Italy, a phrase book is as fun as it is necessary. This practical and budget-oriented series covers Italian, French, German, Portuguese, Spanish, and French/Italian/German. You'll be able to ask the gelato man for a free little taste, chat with your cabbie, and make hotel reservations over the phone.

And More Books: *Rick Steves' Europe 101: History and Art for the Traveler* (with Gene Openshaw) gives you the story of Europe's people, history, and art. It's heavy on Italy's ancient, Renaissance, and modern eras. Written for smart people who were sleeping in their history and art classes before they knew they were going to Europe, *101* helps Europe's sights come alive.

Rick Steves' Easy Access Europe, geared for travelers with limited mobility, covers London, Paris, Bruges, Amsterdam, and the Rhine River.

Rick Steves' Postcards from Europe, my autobiographical book, packs 25 years of travel anecdotes and insights into the ultimate 2,000-mile European adventure (including Venice).

My latest book, *Rick Steves' European Christmas,* covers the joys, history, and quirky traditions of the holiday season in seven European countries.

Public Television Show: My series, *Rick Steves' Europe,* keeps churning out shows. Several of the more than 60 episodes feature sights covered in this book.

Radio Show: My new weekly radio show, which combines call-in questions (à la *Car Talk*) and interviews with travel experts, airs on public radio stations. For a schedule of upcoming topics, an archive of past programs, and details on how to call in, see www.ricksteves.com/radio.

Other Guidebooks

For most travelers, this book is all you need. But when you consider the improvements they'll make in your $2,000–3,000 vacation, $25 or $35 for extra maps and books is money well spent. The well-researched Access guide (which combines Venice and Florence) and the colorful Eyewitness guide (on Venice and the Veneto) are popular with travelers. Eyewitness is fun for its great, easy-to-grasp graphics and photos, and it's just right for people who want only factoids. But the Eyewitness books are relatively skimpy on content, and they weigh a ton. (Their *Top 10 Venice* book, which features top 10 lists, is lighter.) You can buy them in Venice (no more expensive than in the U.S.) or simply borrow them for a minute from other travelers at certain sights to make sure you're aware of that place's highlights. If you'll be traveling elsewhere in Italy, consider the 2006 editions of *Rick Steves' Italy, Rick Steves' Florence & Tuscany,* and *Rick Steves' Rome.*

In Venice, local guidebooks (sold at kiosks) are cheap and give you a map and a decent commentary on the sights.

Recommended Reading and Movies

To get the feel of Venice past and present, consider reading some of these books or seeing these films:

Non-Fiction: *A History of Venice* (John Julius Norwich), *Venice: A Maritime Republic* (Frederic C. Lane), *Venice: Lion City* (Garry Wills), *Venice Observed* (Mary McCarthy), *The World of Venice* (Jan Morris), *A Literary Companion to Venice* (Ian Littlewood), *Venice: A Cultural and Literary Companion* (Martin Garrett), *Venice: The Collected Traveler* (Barrie Kerper), and *My Venice* (Harold Brodkey).

For a look at more of Italy, consider *Italian Days* (Barbara Grizzuti Harrison), *Desiring Italy* (Susan Cahill), *The Italians* (Luigi Barzini), *Italian Neighbors* (Tim Parks), and *Travelers' Tales Italy* (Anne Calcagno). Gourmets like *The Marling Menu-Master for Italy.*

Fiction: *The Palace* (Lisa St. Aubin de Terán), *Dead Lagoon* (Michael Dibdin), *Serenissima* (Erica Jong), *Death at La Fenice* (Donna Leon), *Dirge for a Doge* (Elizabeth Eyre), *Stone Virgin* (Barry Unsworth), *Vaporetto 13* (Robert Girardi), and *Death in Venice* (Thomas Mann).

Flicks: *The Wings of the Dove, Dangerous Beauty, Bread and Tulips, The Merchant of Venice* (the 2004 version, with Al Pacino), *Death in Venice, The Italian Job* (the 2003 version), and *Only You.*

Maps

The black-and-white maps in this book, drawn by Dave Hoerlein, are concise and simple. Dave is well-traveled in Venice and Italy, and has designed the maps to help you orient quickly and get to where you want to go painlessly. In Venice, hotels give out free basic maps and the TI sells a cheapie. Better maps are sold at kiosks, newsstands, and bookstores. While maps sold for €3 are better than the TI map, the high-quality ones for €5 will save you lots of wandering. Take a look before you buy to be sure the map has the level of detail you want.

Begin your trip at www.ricksteves.com

At www.ricksteves.com, you'll find a wealth of **free information** on destinations covered in this book, including fresh European travel and tour news every month and helpful "Graffiti Wall" tips from thousands of fellow travelers.

While you're there, the **online Travel Store** is a great place to save money on travel bags and accessories designed by Rick Steves to help you travel smarter and lighter, plus it has a wide selection of guidebooks, planning maps, and DVDs.

Traveling through Europe by rail is a breeze, but choosing the right railpass for your trip—amidst hundreds of options—can drive you nutty. At www.ricksteves.com, you'll find **Rick Steves' Annual Guide to European Railpasses**—your best way to convert chaos into pure travel energy. Buy your railpass from Rick, and you'll get a bunch of free extras to boot.

Travel agents will tell you about mainstream tours of Europe, but they won't tell you about **Rick Steves' tours.** Rick Steves' Europe Through the Back Door travel company offers more than two dozen itineraries and 300 departures reaching the best destinations in this book...and beyond. You'll enjoy the services of a great guide, a fun bunch of travel partners (with group sizes in the twenties), and plenty of room to spread out in a big, comfy bus. You'll find trips to fit every vacation size, from week-long city getaways to longer cross-country adventures. For details, visit www.ricksteves.com or call 425/771-8303, ext 217.

PRACTICALITIES

Red Tape: You need a passport but no visa or shots to travel in Italy.

Time: In Venice—and in this book—you'll use the 24-hour clock. It's the same through 12:00 noon, then keep going—13:00, 14:00, and so on. For anything over 12, subtract 12 and add p.m. (14:00 is 2:00 p.m.). Italian time is generally six/nine hours ahead of the East/West Coast of the United States.

Business Hours: Traditionally, Italy uses the siesta plan. People work from about 8:00 to 13:00 and from 15:30 to 19:00, Monday through Saturday. Many businesses have adopted the government's recommended 8:00 to 16:00 workday. In tourist areas, shops are open longer.

Shopping: Shoppers interested in customs regulations and VAT refunds (the tax refunded on large purchases made by non-EU residents) can refer to page 243.

Discounts: Discounts for sights are not listed in this book, because they are generally limited to European residents and countries that offer reciprocal deals (the U.S. doesn't). Young people can get some price breaks in Venice by buying a "Rolling Venice" Youth Discount Pass (see page 25).

Watt's up? If you're bringing electrical gear, you'll need a two-prong adapter plug (sold cheap at travel stores in the U.S.) and a converter. Travel appliances often have convenient, built-in converters; look for a voltage switch marked 120V (U.S.) and 240V (Europe). If yours doesn't have a built-in converter, you'll have to buy an external one.

News: Americans keep in touch with the *International Herald Tribune* (published almost daily via satellite). Every Tuesday, the European editions of *Time* and *Newsweek* hit the stands with articles of particular interest to European travelers. Sports addicts can get their fix from *USA Today*. Good Web sites include www.europeantimes.com and http://news.bbc.co.uk.

MONEY

Banking

Bring plastic (ATM, credit, or debit cards) along with several hundred dollars in hard cash as an emergency backup. Traveler's checks are a waste of time and money.

To withdraw cash from a bank machine *(bancomat)*, you'll need a PIN code (numbers only, no letters on European keypads) and your bank card. Before you go, verify with your bank that your card will work and alert them that you'll be making withdrawals in Europe; otherwise, the bank might not approve transactions if it perceives unusual spending patterns. If you plan on getting cash advances with your regular credit card, be sure to ask the card company about fees before you leave.

It's smart to bring two cards in case one gets demagnetized or eaten by a temperamental machine. If your card doesn't work, try again, and request a smaller amount; some cash machines won't let you take out more than about €150 (don't take it personally). Also be aware that some ATMs will tell you to take your cash within 30 seconds, and if you aren't fast enough, your cash may be sucked back into the machine...and you'll have a hassle trying to get it from the bank.

Visa and MasterCard are more commonly accepted than American Express. Just like at home, credit or debit cards work easily at larger hotels, restaurants, and shops, but smaller businesses prefer payment in local currency. If you have lots of large bills, break them at a bank, especially if you like shopping at mom-and-pop places; they rarely have huge amounts of change.

Exchange Rate

1 euro (€) = about $1.20

To convert prices in euros to dollars, add 20 percent: €20 = about $24, €45 = about $54. Just like the dollar, one euro is broken down into 100 cents. You'll find coins ranging from €0.01 to €2, and bills ranging from €5 to €500.

Look carefully at any €2 coin you get in change. Some unscrupulous merchants are giving out similar-looking, gold-rimmed old 500-lire coins (worth $0) instead of €2 coins (worth $2.40). You are now warned!

Regular banks have the best rates for changing cash and traveler's checks. For a large exchange, it pays to compare rates and fees. Banks—not exchange offices—have the best rates for cashing traveler's checks. Banking hours are generally 8:30 to 13:30 and 15:30 to 16:30 Monday through Friday, but they can vary wildly. Banks are slow; simple transactions can take 15 to 30 minutes. Post offices and train stations usually change money if you can't get to a bank.

You should use a money belt (a pouch with a strap that you buckle around your waist like a belt and wear under your clothes). Thieves target tourists. A money belt provides peace of mind, allowing you to carry lots of cash safely.

Don't be petty about withdrawing money. You don't need to waste time every few days tracking down a cash machine. Change a week's worth of money, get big bills, stuff them in your money belt, and travel!

Tipping

Tipping in Italy isn't as automatic and generous as it is in the United States, but for special service, tips are appreciated, if not expected. As in the United States, the proper amount depends on your resources, tipping philosophy, and the circumstances, but some general guidelines apply.

Restaurants: Check the menu to see whether the service is included (*servizio incluso*—generally 15 percent); if not, a tip of 5–10 percent is fine (for details, see page 219), though Italians rarely tip.

***Traghetto*, Gondolas, and Water Taxis:** There's no need to tip on a cheap *traghetto* ride (a stand-up ride in a gondola across the Grand Canal); it'd be a little like tipping for a city bus ride. You also don't need to tip for a romantic gondola ride; you're already paying plenty. If you take a ride in a water taxi, round your fare up to the nearest euro. If the driver hauls your bags and zips you

Damage Control for Lost or Stolen Cards

If you lose your credit, debit, or ATM card, you can stop people from using your card by reporting the loss immediately to the respective global customer-assistance centers. Call these 24-hour U.S. numbers collect: Visa (tel. 410/581-9994), MasterCard (tel. 636/722-7111), and American Express (tel. 336/393-1111).

Have, at a minimum, the following information ready: the name of the financial institution that issued you the card, along with the type of card (classic, platinum, or whatever). Ideally, plan ahead and pack photocopies of your cards—front and back—to expedite their replacement. Providing the following information will allow for a quicker cancellation of your missing card: full card number, whether you are the primary or secondary cardholder, the cardholder's name exactly as printed on the card, billing address, home phone number, circumstances of the loss or theft, and identification verification (your birthdate, your mother's maiden name, or your Social Security number—memorize this, don't carry a copy). If you are the secondary cardholder, you'll also need to provide the primary cardholder's identification verification details. You can generally receive a temporary card within two or three business days in Europe.

If you promptly report your card lost or stolen, you typically won't be responsible for any unauthorized transactions on your account, although many banks charge a liability fee of $50.

to the airport to help you catch your flight, you might want to toss in a little more. But if you feel like you got on the slow boat to nowhere fast, skip the tip.

Special Services: It's thoughtful to tip a couple of euros to someone who shows you a special sight and who is paid in no other way (such as a man who shows you a private chapel or tower viewpoint that's usually off-limits). Tour guides at public sites sometimes hold out their hands for tips after they give their spiel; if I've already paid for the tour, I don't tip extra, though some tourists do give a euro or two, particularly for a job well done. I don't tip at hotels, but if you do, give the porter a euro for carrying bags and leave a couple of euros in your room at the end of your stay for the maid if the room was kept clean. In general, if someone in the service industry does a super job for you, a tip of a couple of euros is appropriate...but not required.

When in doubt, ask. If you're not sure whether (or how much) to tip for a service, ask your hotelier or the tourist information office; they'll fill you in on how it's done on their turf.

TRANSPORTATION

Your public transportation concerns in Venice are limited to vaporetto boats, covered in the Orientation chapter. For a private ride, you can hire a *traghetto* (gondola) or a pricey, speedy water taxi. For more information on boating, see "Getting Around Venice" in the Orientation chapter. If you have a car, stow it at a parking lot at Tronchetto (in Venice) or Mestre (on the mainland). For arrival and departure information, see the Transportation Connections chapter. For specifics on traveling throughout Italy by train or car, see *Rick Steves' Italy 2006*. For advice on travel agencies in Venice, see page 28.

COMMUNICATING

Telephones

Smart travelers learn the phone system and use it daily to reserve or reconfirm rooms, get tourist information, or phone home.

If you have to spell out your name on the phone when making a reservation, you might have trouble with *a* (pronounced "ah" in Italian), *e* (pronounced "ay"), and *i* (pronounced "ee"). Say "*a,* Ancona," "*e,* Empoli," and "*i,* Italia" to clear up that problem. If you plan to access your voice mail from Italy, be advised that you can't always dial extensions or secret codes once you connect (you're on vacation—relax).

Types of Phones

You'll encounter various kinds of phones in your European travels.

• Telecom **pay phones** are everywhere and take cards only (no coins). About a quarter of the phones are broken. The rest work reluctantly. Dial slowly and deliberately, as if the phone doesn't understand numbers very well. Often a recorded message in Italian will break in, brusquely informing you that the phone number does not exist *(non-esistente),* even if you're dialing your own home phone number. Check to make sure you're dialing the correct prefixes (see chart on page 324). Then dial again with an increasing show of confidence, in an attempt to convince the phone of your number's existence. If you fail, try a different phone. Repeat as needed.

• **Hotel room phones** are fairly cheap for local calls but pricey for international calls, unless you use an international phone card (see below).

• **American mobile phones** work in Europe if they're GSM-enabled, tri-band (or quad-band), and on a calling plan that includes international calls. With a T-Mobile phone, you can roam using your home number and pay $1–2 per minute for making or receiving calls.

• Some travelers buy a **European mobile phone** in Europe. For about $125, you can get a phone (called a MOH-bee-lay) that will work in most countries once you pick up the necessary chip (about $30) per country. You may also be able to buy a cheaper, "locked" phone that only works in the country where you purchased it (about $100, includes $20 worth of calls). If you're interested, stop by any European shop that sells mobile phones; you'll see prominent store window displays. You aren't required to (and shouldn't) buy a monthly contract—buy prepaid calling time instead (as you use it up, buy additional minutes at newsstands or mobile-phone shops). If you're on a budget, skip mobile phones and use international phone cards instead.

Paying for Calls

You can spend a fortune making phone calls in Europe...but why would you? Here's the skinny on different ways to pay, including the best deals.

Italian Phone Cards come in two types: official phone cards that you insert into a pay phone, and international phone cards that can be used from virtually any phone.

Insertable phone cards are used to make calls from pay phones. You can buy these Telecom cards (in denominations of €5 or €10) at *tabacchi* shops, post offices, and machines near phone booths (many phone booths indicate where the nearest phone-card sales outlet is located). Rip off the perforated corner to "activate" the card, then insert it into a slot in the pay phone. It displays how much money you have remaining on the card. Then just dial away to anywhere in the world. The price of the call is automatically deducted while you talk. These cards give you your best deal for calls within Italy, and are reasonable for international calls.

International phone cards are an even better deal for overseas calls (as cheap as 2 cents per minute to the United States). Unlike the official phone cards, an international phone card is *not* inserted into the phone. Instead, you dial the toll-free number listed on the card, reaching an automated operator. When prompted, you dial in a scratch-to-reveal code number, also written on the card. Then dial your number. You can use the cards to make local and domestic long-distance calls as well. Since they're not insertable, you can use them from any phone—including the one in your hotel room (if your phone is set to pulse, switch it to tone). Generally you'll get more minutes out of a card if you use it from your hotel room, rather than from a pay phone. (For a €5 card, for example, you may get 180 minutes from your hotel room phone, compared to 40 minutes from a pay phone.) Buy cards at small newsstand kiosks and hole-in-the-wall long-distance phone shops. Because there are so many brand names, simply ask for an international phone card (*carta telefonica prepagata internazionale,* KAR-tah teh-leh-FOHN-ee-kah pray-pah-GAH-tah in-ter-naht-zee-oh-NAH-lay). Tell the vendor where you'll be making most calls (*"per Stati Uniti"*—to America), and he'll select the brand with the best deal. Buy a lower denomination in case the card is a dud. I've had good luck with the Europa card, offering 180 minutes from Italy to the United States for €5. If you have time left on your card when you leave the country (as you likely will), simply give it to another traveler—anyone can use it.

Dialing direct from your hotel room without using an international phone card is usually quite expensive for international calls, but it's convenient. I always ask first how much I'll be charged. Keep in mind that you have to pay for local and occasionally even toll-free calls.

Receiving calls in your hotel room is often the cheapest way to keep in touch with the folks back home—especially if your family has an inexpensive way to call you (either a good deal on their long-distance plan, or a prepaid calling card with good rates to Europe). Give them a list of your hotels' phone numbers before you go. As you travel, send your family an e-mail or make a quick payphone call to set up a time for them to call you, and then wait for the ring.

Metered phones are sometimes available in bigger post offices. You can talk all you want, then pay the bill when you leave—but be sure you know the rates before you have a lengthy conversation.

Coin-operated phones, while rare, still exist in some areas. If making a call, have a bunch of coins handy—they go fast.

U.S. Calling Cards (such as the ones offered by AT&T, MCI, or Sprint) are the worst option. You'll nearly always save a lot of money by paying for your call in any of the other ways described above.

How to Dial

Calling from the United States to Italy, or vice versa, is simple—once you break the code. The European calling chart on page 322 will walk you through it. Remember that European time is six/nine hours ahead of the East/West Coast of the United States.

Dialing within Italy: Italy has a direct-dial phone system (no area codes). To call anywhere within Italy, just dial the number. For example, the number of one of my recommended Venice hotels is 041-528-5174. To call it from a Venice train station, dial 041-528-5174. If you call it from Florence, it's the same: 041-528-5174. Italian mobile phone numbers no longer start with zero (these are dialed direct like fixed phone numbers).

Italian phone numbers vary in length; a hotel can have, say, an 8-digit phone number and a 9-digit fax number.

Italy's toll-free numbers start with 800 (like U.S. 800 numbers, though in Italy you don't need to dial a "1" first). In Italy, these 800 numbers—called *freephone* or *numero verde* (green number)—can be dialed free from any phone without using a phone card or coins. Note that you can't call Italy's toll-free numbers from America, nor can you count on reaching America's toll-free numbers from Italy.

Dialing International Calls: When calling internationally, dial the international access code (00 if you're calling from Europe, 011 from the U.S. or Canada), the country code of the country you're calling (39 for Italy; see appendix for list of other countries), and the local number. Note that in most European countries, you have to drop the zero at the beginning of the local number—but in Italy, you dial it. So, to call the Venice hotel from the United States, dial 011 (the U.S. international access code), 39 (Italy's country code), then 041-528-5174. To call my office in Edmonds, Washington, from Italy, I dial 00 (Europe's international access code), 1 (the U.S. country code), 425 (Edmonds' area code), and 771-8303.

E-mail and Mail

E-mail: E-mail use among Italian hoteliers is common. Drab little Internet cafés are popular in big cities like Venice. Your hotelier can steer you to one near your hotel.

When you see a cluster of orange public phones in a room off a busy street, you might see several computers in the batch. With these, you can use your Italian phone card to access the Internet. You won't be comfortable (no seat), and you'll get cut off if your phone card runs out of time, but this can be a handy, quick way to check your e-mail.

Mail: Mail service in Italy has improved over the last few years, but even so, send nothing precious from Italy. If you need to receive mail while traveling, consider a few pre-reserved hotels along your route. Allow 14 days for United States-to-Italy mail delivery, but don't count on it. Federal Express makes pricey two-day deliveries. E-mailing and phoning are so easy that I've completely dispensed with mail stops.

TRAVELING AS A TEMPORARY LOCAL

We travel all the way to Italy to enjoy differences—to become temporary locals. You'll experience frustrations. Certain truths that we find "God-given" or "self-evident," such as cold beer, ice in drinks, bottomless cups of coffee, hot showers, and bigger being better, are suddenly not so true. One of the benefits of travel is the eye-opening realization that there are logical, civil, and even better alternatives. A willingness to go local ensures that you'll enjoy a full dose of Italian hospitality.

Send Me a Postcard, Drop Me a Line

If you enjoy a successful trip with the help of this book and would like to share your discoveries, please fill out the survey at www.ricksteves.com/feedback. I personally read and value all feedback.

If there is a negative aspect to the image that Italians have of Americans, it is that we are big, loud, aggressive, impolite, rich, and a bit naive. Europeans don't respond well to Americans complaining about being too hot or too cold. To encourage conservation, the Italian government limits when air-conditioning or central heating can be used. Bring a sweater in winter, and in summer, be prepared to sweat a little...like everyone else. Also, Americans tend to be noisy in public places, such as restaurants and trains. Our raised voices can demolish Europe's reserved and elegant ambience. Talk softly.

While Italians, flabbergasted by our Yankee excesses, say in disbelief, *"Mi sono cadute le braccia!"* ("I throw my arms down!"), they nearly always afford us individual travelers all the warmth we deserve.

Judging from all the happy postcards I receive from travelers who have used this book, it's safe to assume you'll enjoy a great, affordable vacation—with the finesse of an independent, experienced traveler.

Thanks, and *buon viaggio!*

BACK DOOR TRAVEL PHILOSOPHY
From *Rick Steves' Europe Through the Back Door*

Travel is intensified living—maximum thrills per minute and one of the last great sources of legal adventure. Travel is freedom. It's recess, and we need it.

Experiencing the real Europe requires catching it by surprise, going casual..."Through the Back Door."

Affording travel is a matter of priorities. (Make do with the old car.) You can travel—simply, safely, and comfortably—anywhere in Europe for $100 a day plus transportation costs. In many ways, spending more money only builds a thicker wall between you and what you came to see. Europe is a cultural carnival, and, time after time, you'll find that its best acts are free and the best seats are the cheap ones.

A tight budget forces you to travel close to the ground, meeting and communicating with the people, not relying on service with a purchased smile. Never sacrifice sleep, nutrition, safety, or cleanliness in the name of budget. Simply enjoy the local-style alternatives to expensive hotels and restaurants.

Extroverts have more fun. If your trip is low on magic moments, kick yourself and make things happen. If you don't enjoy a place, maybe you don't know enough about it. Seek the truth. Recognize tourist traps. Give a culture the benefit of your open mind. See things as different but not better or worse. Any culture has much to share.

Of course, travel, like the world, is a series of hills and valleys. Be fanatically positive and militantly optimistic. If something's not to your liking, change your liking. Travel is addictive. It can make you a happier American as well as a citizen of the world. Our earth is home to six billion equally important people. It's humbling to travel and find that people don't envy Americans. They like us, but, with all due respect, they wouldn't trade passports.

Globe-trotting destroys ethnocentricity. It helps you understand and appreciate different cultures. Regrettably, there are forces in our society that want you dumbed down for their convenience. Don't let it happen. Thoughtful travel engages you with the world—more important than ever these days. Travel changes people. It broadens perspectives and teaches new ways to measure quality of life. Many travelers toss aside their hometown blinders. Their prized souvenirs are the strands of different cultures they decide to knit into their own character. The world is a cultural yarn shop. And Back Door travelers are weaving the ultimate tapestry. Come on, join in!

ORIENTATION

The island city of Venice is shaped like a fish. Its major thorough-fares are canals. The Grand Canal winds through the middle of the fish, starting at the mouth where all the people and food enter, passing under the Rialto Bridge, and ending at St. Mark's Square (Piazza San Marco). Park your 21st-century perspective at the mouth and let Venice swallow you whole.

Venice is a car-less kaleidoscope of people, bridges, and odorless canals. The city has no major streets, and addresses are hopelessly confusing. There are six districts (see map on page 22): San Marco (most touristy), Castello (behind San Marco), Cannaregio (from the train station to the Rialto), San Polo (other side of the Rialto), Santa Croce, and Dorsoduro. Each district has about 6,000 address numbers.

To find your way, navigate by landmarks, not streets. Many street corners have a sign pointing you to *(per)* the nearest major landmark, such as San Marco, Accademia, Rialto, and Ferrovia (train station). Obedient visitors stick to the main thoroughfares as directed by these signs and miss the charm of backstreet Venice.

Planning Your Time

Venice is remarkably small. You can walk across it, from head to tail, in an hour-plus. Nearly all of your sightseeing is within a 20-minute walk of the Rialto Bridge or St. Mark's Square.

Two key considerations: Maximize your evening magic, and avoid the midday crowds around St. Mark's Basilica and the Doge's Palace. Note that Museum Card and the pricier Museum Pass cover the popular Doge's Palace and less-visited Correr Museum (both on St. Mark's Square). Because the Doge's Palace has longer lines, it makes sense to buy your Card or Pass at the Correr Museum (for more tips on crowd control, see "Daily Reminder" on page 20).

Daily Reminder

Need a calendar? See the appendix.

Sunday: The Church of San Giorgio Maggiore (on an island near St. Mark's Square) hosts a Gregorian Mass at 11:00. The Rialto open-air market consists mainly of souvenir stalls today (fish and produce sections closed). These sights are open only in the afternoon: Frari Church (13:00–17:00, closed Sun in Aug) and St. Mark's Basilica (14:00–16:00). It's a bad day for a pub crawl, as most pubs are closed.

Monday: All sights are open except for the Rialto fish market, Dalmatian School, the skippable Palazzo Mocenigo (textiles), and Torcello Museum (on Torcello island). The Accademia and Ca' d'Oro (House of Gold) close at 14:00. Don't side-trip to Verona or Vicenza today, as most sights in these towns are closed.

Tuesday: All sights are open except the Peggy Guggenheim Collection, Ca' Rezzonico (Museum of 18th-Century Venice), and the Lace Museum (on Burano island).

Wednesday: All sights are open except the Glass Museum (on Murano Island).

Thursday/Friday: All sights are open.

Saturday: All sights are open (Peggy Guggenheim Collection until 22:00 June–July) except the Jewish Museum.

Notes: The Accademia is open earlier (daily at 8:15) and closes

If you're heading from St. Mark's Square to the Frari Church via the Rialto Bridge, consider connecting two of my self-guided walks (St. Mark's to Rialto, and Rialto to Frari Church).

Remember that Venice itself is its greatest sight. Make time to wander, explore, shop, and simply be.

Venice in One (Busy) Day

9:00   Walk from St. Mark's Square to Frari Church (following 2 of my self-guided walks), and make time to enjoy the Rialto market action.

11:00   Tour Frari Church.

12:00   Lunch near the Frari, then catch the vaporetto (boat) back to St. Mark's to wander and shop.

14:30   Correr Museum.

15:30   St. Mark's Basilica.

16:30   Doge's Palace.

18:00   Go up the Campanile for city view.

18:30   Pub dinner (crawl, or stay put and munch).

20:00   Gondola ride.

later (19:15 Tue–Sun) than most sights in Venice. Some sights close earlier off-season (e.g., Doge's Palace, Correr Museum, Campanile, and St. Mark's Basilica).

Churches: Modest dress is recommended at churches and required at St. Mark's Basilica—no bare shoulders, shorts, or short skirts. Some churches are closed to sightseers on Sunday morning (e.g., St. Mark's Basilica and Frari Church), and many are closed from roughly 12:00 to 14:30 or 15:00 Monday through Saturday (e.g., La Salute and San Giorgio Maggiore).

Crowd Control: Crowds can be a serious problem at the Accademia (to minimize crowds, go early or late, or call 041-520-0345 to reserve tickets in advance); St. Mark's Basilica (try going early or late, or you can skip the line if you have a bag to check—see page 66); Campanile (go early or late—it's open until 21:00 July–Sept); and the Doge's Palace. For the Doge's Palace, you have three options for avoiding the ticket-sales line: Buy your Museum Card or Museum Pass at the Correr Museum (then step right up to the Doge's Palace turnstile, thus skipping the long line); visit the Doge's Palace at 17:00 (if it's April–Oct), when lines disappear; or book a "Secret Itineraries" tour (see page 85). All of the sights that have crowd problems (St. Mark's Basilica, Doge's Palace, and Accademia) get more crowded when it rains.

   21:00   Enjoy the dueling orchestras with a drink on St. Mark's Square.

Venice in Two Days
Day 1

    9:00   Walk from St. Mark's Square to Frari Church (connecting 2 of my self-guided walks). Stop along the way at the Rialto market to browse.

  11:00   Tour Frari Church.

  12:00   Tour Ca' Rezzonico (Museum of 18th-Century Venice) or Scuola San Rocco (if you prefer Tintoretto to Casanova).

  13:00   Lunch in Dorsoduro neighborhood, then take the vaporetto back to St. Mark's Square to wander and shop.

  15:00   Correr Museum.

  16:00   St. Mark's Basilica.

  17:00   Doge's Palace.

Venice's Districts

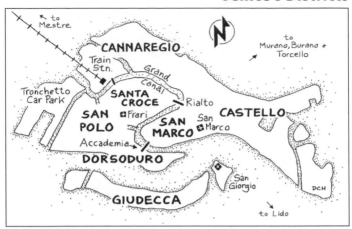

19:00 Go up the Campanile for city view (in Oct–June, the tower closes at 19:00; get here by 18:00, or skip the tower).

20:00 Dinner.

22:00 Enjoy the dueling orchestras with a drink on St. Mark's Square.

Day 2

9:00 Shopping or exploring.

11:00 Cruise Grand Canal.

13:00 Lunch (pizza near Accademia Bridge?).

14:00 Tour Accademia, explore Dorsoduro neighborhood, visit La Salute Church or Peggy Guggenheim Collection.

17:00 Commence pub crawl, eating dinner along the way.

20:00 Gondola ride.

Venice in Three (or Four) Days
Day 1

9:30 St. Mark's Basilica and Square.

11:00 Correr Museum.

12:00 Shop, wander, and have lunch in St. Mark's area.

16:00 Doge's Palace.

18:00 Ascend Campanile.

19:00 Gondola ride.

20:00 Dinner.

Day 2 *Sat*

9:00	Walk from St. Mark's Square to Frari Church (by linking my self-guided walks), allowing time to experience the Rialto market scene.
11:00	Tour Frari Church.
12:00	Tour Scuola San Rocco for Tintoretto.
13:00	Lunch.
14:00	Tour Ca' Rezzonico (Museum of 18th-Century Venice).
15:00	Explore Dorsoduro, the neighborhood around the Accademia.
17:00	Tour Accademia.
18:00	Cruise Grand Canal in vaporetto.

Day 3 *Sun*

9:00	Explore lagoon by vaporetto or tour boat, visiting Burano and Torcello.
15:00	Take my self-guided walk from St. Mark's to San Zaccaria, then catch a vaporetto to visit the Church of San Giorgio Maggiore for a superb view of Venice. *Closed*
17:00	Start pub crawl.
21:00	Savor a drink while listening to the dueling orchestras on St. Mark's Square.

Day 4

Side-trip to Padua and/or Verona.

OVERVIEW

Tourist Information

There are TIs at the **train station** (daily 8:00–18:30, crowded and hourly); at **St. Mark's Square** (daily 9:00–20:00; with your back to St. Mark's Basilica, it's in far left corner of square); and near the **St. Mark's Square vaporetto stop** on the lagoon (daily 10:00–18:00, sells vaporetto tickets, rents audioguides with a GPS system at €15 for self-guided walking tours—they work erratically, and when they do, they're boring). Smaller offices are at **Piazzale Roma** and the **airport** (daily 9:30–19:30). For a quick question, save time by phoning 041-529-8711. The TI's official Web site is www.turismovenezia.it.

At any TI, pick up the free bimonthly magazine **Leo**, which comes with an insert, *Leo Bussola*, that lists museum hours, exhibitions, and musical events (in Italian and English). Confirm your sightseeing plans. Ask for the fine brochures outlining three offbeat Venice walks.

The free periodical entertainment guide *Un Ospite di Venezia* (a monthly listing of events, nightlife, museum hours, train and vaporetto schedules, emergency telephone numbers, and so on) is available at the TI or fancy hotel reception desks (www.aguestinvenice.com).

Maps: Of all places, you'll need a good map in Venice. Hotels give away lousy freebies. The TI sells a simple one that isn't much better. Bookshops, newsstands, and postcard stands sell a wider range of maps; the €3 maps are pretty bad, but if you spend €5, you'll get a map that shows you everything. Invest in a good map and use it—this can be the best €5 you'll spend in Venice.

Arrival in Venice

For a rundown on Venice's train station and airport, see Transportation Connections, page 251.

Passes for Venice

To help control (and confuse?) its flood of visitors, Venice offers cards and passes that cover some museums and/or transportation. For most visitors, the simple Museum Card (the Doge's Palace/Correr Museum combo-ticket) or Museum Pass will do.

The **Museum Card** covers the museums of St. Mark's Square: Doge's Palace, clock tower *(torre dell'orologio)*, Correr Museum, and the two museums accessed from within the Correr—the National Archaeological Museum and the Monumental Rooms of Marciana National Library (€11, called *"Museum Card per i Musei di Piazza San Marco,"* valid for 3 months, 1 entry per museum; to bypass long line at Doge's Palace, purchase card at the Correr Museum, then enter Doge's Palace).

The pricier **Museum Pass** includes the St. Mark's Square museums listed above, plus Ca' Rezzonico (Museum of 18th-Century Venice), Mocenigo Palace museum (textiles and costumes), Casa Goldoni (home of the Italian playwright), and museums on the islands—Murano's Glass Museum and Burano's Lace Museum (€15.50, valid for 3 months, 1 entry per museum).

The **Chorus Pass** gives access to 15 of Venice's churches (including San Polo and the Frari, covered in this book) and their works of art (€8, or pay €2.50 per church). You'd need to visit four churches to save money.

Venice also (pointlessly) offers two other Museum Cards: €8 for the **museums of the 18th century** (called *"Museum Card per area del Settecento";* the museums are Ca' Rezzonico, Casa Goldoni, and Palazzo Mocenigo) and €6 for the **island museums** (called

"Museum Card per i musei delle isole," covering Murano's Glass Museum and Burano's Lace Museum).

No cards or passes cover these top attractions: Accademia, Peggy Guggenheim Collection, Scuola Grande di San Rocco, Campanile, and the three sights within St. Mark's Basilica that charge admission.

Venice Cards: These cards include Venice's public transportation, public toilets, and, if you get the "orange" version, some sights. Personally, I don't think these are worth the bother, but here's the information: The **Blue Venice Card** covers all your vaporetto rides, plus entry to public toilets (€11/1 day, €23/3 days, €41/7 days, cheaper for "Juniors" under 30). The **Orange Venice Card** includes transportation and toilets, as well as the museums covered by the Museum Pass—so it's like getting a Blue Venice Card and a Museum Pass (€26/1 day, €43/3 days, €58/7 days, cheaper for "Juniors" under 30). To order either card, book online at www.venicecard.com (tel. 041-2424). Better yet, if all you want is a vaporetto pass, you can get a 24-hour pass for €10.50 at any vaporetto dock; described under "Getting Around Venice," below.

"Rolling Venice" Youth Discount Pass: To those under age 30, this worthwhile €3 pass gives discounts on sights and transportation, plus information on cheap eating and sleeping. It is sold at kiosks at major vaporetto stops, including Ferrovia (train station), Rialto, Accademia, and San Marco/Vallaresso (St. Mark's Square).

Helpful Hints

Get Lost: Accept the fact that Venice was a tourist town 400 years ago. It was, is, and always will be crowded. While 80 percent of Venice is, in fact, not touristy, 80 percent of the tourists never notice. Hit the back streets. Venice is the ideal town to explore on foot. Walk and walk to the far reaches of the town. Don't worry about getting lost. Get as lost as possible. Keep reminding yourself, "I'm on an island, and I can't get off." When it comes time to find your way, just follow the directional arrows on building corners or simply ask a local, *"Dov'è San Marco?"* ("Where is St. Mark's?") People in the tourist business (that's most Venetians) speak some English. If they don't, listen politely, watch where their hands point, say, *"Grazie,"* and head off in that direction. If you're lost, pop into a hotel and ask for their business card—it comes with a map and a prominent "You are here."

Be Prepared to Splurge: Venice is expensive for locals as well as tourists. The demand is huge, supply is limited, and running a business is costly. Things just cost more here; everything must be shipped in and hand-trucked to its destination. Perhaps the best way to enjoy Venice is just to succumb to its charms and blow a lot of money.

Rip-offs, Theft, and Help: The dark, late-night streets of Venice are safe. Even so, pickpockets (often elegantly dressed) work the crowded main streets, docks, and *vaporetti* (wear your money belt and carry your daybag in front). Your biggest risk of pickpockets is actually inside St. Mark's Basilica. A service called Counter of Tourist Mediation handles complaints about local crooks, but does not give out information (tel. 041-529-8710, complaint@turismovenezia.it).

Take Breaks: Venice's endless pavement, crowds, and tight spaces are hard on the tourist. Schedule breaks in your sightseeing. Grab a cool place to sit down, relax, and recoup—meditate on a pew in an uncrowded church, or buy a cappuccino and a fruit cup in a café.

Etiquette: Walk on the right and don't loiter on bridges. Picnicking is technically forbidden (keep a low profile). Dress modestly. Men should keep their shirts on. (Women, too.) When visiting St. Mark's Basilica or other major churches, men, women, and even children must cover their knees and shoulders (or risk being turned away). Remove hats when entering a church.

Pigeon Poop: If bombed by a pigeon, resist the initial response to wipe it off immediately—it'll just smear into your hair. Wait until it dries and flake it off cleanly.

Public Toilets: There are handy public WCs near St. Mark's Square, the Rialto, and the Accademia Bridge. You'll find public pay toilets near most major landmarks. Use free toilets—in a museum you're visiting or a café you're eating in—when you can.

Water: Venetians pride themselves on having pure, safe, and tasty tap water piped in from the foothills of the Alps. You can actually see the mountains from Venice's bell towers on crisp, clear winter days.

Lingo: *Campo* means square, *campiello* is a small square, *calle* is street, *fondamenta* is the road running along a canal, *rio* is a small canal, *rio terra* is a street that was once a canal and has been filled in, and *ponte* is a bridge.

Services

Money: The plentiful ATMs are the easiest way to go. If you must exchange currency, be aware that bank rates vary. The American Express change desk

Tips for Tackling My Self-Guided Tours

Sightseeing can be hard work. The self-guided tours in this book are designed to help make your visits to Venice's finest museums meaningful, fun, fast, and painless. To get the most out of the tours, read the tour the night before your visit.

When you arrive at the sight, use the overview map to get the lay of the land and the basic tour route. Expect a few

changes—paintings can be on tour, on loan, out sick, or shifted at the whim of the curator. To adapt, pick up any available free floor plans as you enter, or ask an information person to glance at this book's maps to confirm they're current. If you can't find a particular painting, just ask any museum worker. Point to the photograph in this book and ask, *"Dov'è?"* (doh-vay, meaning "Where?").

The tours cover the highlights. You might want to supplement with an audioguide, a dry-but-useful recorded description in English (about $5).

Museums have their rules. For security reasons, you're often required to check even small bags. Every museum has a free checkroom at the entrance. They're safe. If you have something you can't bear to part with, be prepared to stash it in a pocket or purse. Cameras are normally permitted in museums, but no flashes or tripods (without special permission). Video cameras are usually allowed. Many sights have "last entry" times 30–60 minutes before closing. Guards usher people out before the official closing time.

At the museum bookshop, thumb through a guidebook to be sure you haven't overlooked something of particular interest to you. If there's an on-site cafeteria, it's usually a good place to rest and have a snack or light meal. Museum WCs are free and generally clean.

And finally, every sight or museum offers infinitely more than the few stops I cover. Use these tours as an introduction—not the final word.

---

is just off St. Mark's Square (see "Travel Agencies," below). Non-bank exchange bureaus, such as Exacto, will charge you $10 more than a bank for a $200 exchange.

Internet Access: You'll find handy little Internet places all over town. They're all equally good.

Post Office: A large post office is just outside the far end of St. Mark's Square (the end farthest from the basilica; Mon–Fri 8:30–14:00, Sat 8:30–13:00, closed Sun, shorter hours off-season). The main P.O. is near the Rialto Bridge (on St. Mark's side, Mon–Fri 8:10–13:30, Sat 8:10–12:30, closed Sun). Use post offices only as a last resort, as simple transactions can take 45 minutes if you get in the wrong line. You can buy stamps from tobacco shops and mail postcards from any of the red postboxes around town.

Bookstores: Libreria Studium stocks all the English-language guidebooks (including mine for Venice, Florence, and Rome) just a block behind St. Mark's Basilica (daily 9:00–19:30, Calle de la Canonica, tel. 041-522-2382).

Laundry: I list several laundry options below, but your hotelier can direct you to one nearest your hotel. A modern **self-service** *lavanderia* is near St. Mark's Square on Ruga Giuffa at #4826 (daily 8:30–23:00, next to recommended Hotel al Piave—see page 211, tel. 393-760-7499, run by Massimo). **Lavanderia Gabriella** is also near St. Mark's Square (€14/load wash and dry, Mon–Fri 8:00–12:30, closed Sat–Sun; Rio Terra Colonne 985, from San Zulian Church go over Ponte dei Ferali, then take first right down Calle dei Armeni; tel. 041-522-1758). A **self-service launderette** near the train station is a few steps from the recommended hotel Albergo Marin—see page 216 for directions (daily 7:30–22:30, Campiello delle Muneghe 665a/b, San Polo, tel. 348-301-7457).

Travel Agencies: If you need to get train tickets, pay supplements, make reservations, or arrange a *cucetta* (*koo-CHET-tah*—a berth on a night train), avoid the time-consuming trip to the crowded train station by using a downtown travel agency. While American Express charges railpass holders a €3 service fee for reservations, the other agencies do basically everything the train station does for the same price with no fee. All can give advice on cheap flights. Note that you'll get a far better price if you're able to book at least a week in advance. Consider booking flights for later in your trip while you're here (and the good news is that in Europe, you don't have to buy a round-trip ticket to get the best price).

Kele & Teo Viaggi e Turismo is reliable and handy, selling train tickets with no fees (Mon–Fri 8:30–18:00, Sat 9:00–12:00, closed Sun, at Ponte dei Bareteri on the Mercerie midway between Rialto and St. Mark's Square, tel. 041-520-8722, www.keleteo.com, incoming@keleteo.com).

Oltrex, just one bridge past the Bridge of Sighs, is a great little agency. They sell train and plane tickets and happily book train reservations for no extra fee (daily 9:00–19:00, Riva Degli Schiavoni, tel. 041-524-2828).

American Express books flights, sells train tickets, and makes train reservations for a €3 fee (Mon–Fri 9:00–17:30, closed Sat–Sun, about 2 blocks off St. Mark's Square en route to Accademia at 1471 San Marco, tel. 041-520-0844).

Church Services: The **San Zulian Church** (the only church in Venice that you can actually walk around) offers a Mass in English at 9:30 on Sunday (May–Sept, 2 blocks toward Rialto off St. Mark's Square). Gregorians enjoy the sung Gregorian Mass on Sundays at 11:00 (plus Mon–Sat at 8:00) at the **Church of San Giorgio Maggiore** (on island of San Giorgio Maggiore, visible from Doge's Palace, see page 171). Call 041-522-7827 to confirm times.

Haircuts: I've been getting my hair cut at Coiffeur Benito for 15 years. Benito has been keeping local men and women trim for 25 years. He's an artist—actually a "hair sculptor"—and a cut here is a fun diversion from the tourist grind (€19.50 for women, €16.50 for men, Tue–Sat 8:30–13:00 & 15:30–19:30, closed Sun–Mon, behind San Zulian Church near St. Mark's Square, Calle S. Zulian Gia del Strazzariol 592a, tel. 041-528-6221).

Getting Around Venice

By Vaporetto: The public transit system is a fleet of motorized bus-boats called *vaporetti*. They work like city buses except that they never get a flat, the stops are docks, and if you get off between stops, you might drown.

For most travelers, only two lines matter: #1 is the slow boat, which takes 45 minutes to make every stop along the entire length of the Grand Canal (leave every 10 min); #82 is the fast boat that zips down the Grand Canal in 25 minutes (leaves every 20 min),

stopping mainly at Tronchetto (parking lot), Piazzale Roma (bus station), Ferrovia (train station), Rialto Bridge, San Tomà (Frari Church), the Accademia Bridge, and St. Mark's Square (specifically, the San Marco/Vallaresso dock). Some #82 boats go only as far as Rialto *(solo Rialto)*—check with the conductor before boarding.

It's a simple system, but there are a few quirks. Some stops have just one dock for boats going in both directions, while others have docks across the canal from each other—one side of the canal if you're going upstream, the other side for downstream. Electric reader boards on busy docks indicate which boats are coming next and when. Signs on board indicate upcoming stops.

Some lines don't run early or late. For example, the #82 fast vaporetto often doesn't leave the San Marco/Vallaresso stop (at

St. Mark's Square) until 9:30; if you're trying to get from St. Mark's Square to the train station to catch an early train, you'd need to take slow #1 instead. If there's any doubt, ask a ticket-seller or conductor. If you plan to ride a lot of *vaporetti*, consider picking up the most current ACTV timetable (€0.60, in English and Italian, www.actv.it).

Tickets are €5 to travel up or down the Grand Canal, and €3.50 for other routes. They're good for 90 minutes in one direction (you can hop on and off during that time). Technically, you're not allowed a round-trip, even if you can do it within the 90-minute span. Buy tickets at the dock from ticket booths or from a conductor on board (do it before you sit down, or you risk being fined).

A 24-hour pass (€10.50) saves money after two trips. Also consider the 72-hour pass (€22). It's fun to be able to hop on and off spontaneously. There are also two round-trip tickets available: one for €6 (good for any route that doesn't go on the Grand Canal) and another for €7 (includes 1 trip on the Grand Canal). Technically, luggage costs the same as dogs—€3.50—but I've never been charged for either.

To avoid a fine, make sure your ticket is stamped with a time before boarding. Tickets come already stamped unless you specify otherwise; if for whatever reason, your ticket lacks a stamp, stick it into the time-stamping yellow machine before boarding. A 24- or 72-hour pass must be stamped before the first use. Riding free? There's a one-in-10 chance a conductor will fine you €23.

For vaporetto fun, take the Grand Canal Cruise (see page 46). During rush hour (about 9:00 from the Tronchetto parking lot and train station toward St. Mark's, about 17:00 in the other direction), boats are jam-packed. If you like joyriding on *vaporetti*, ride a boat around the city and out into the lagoon, then over to the Lido, and back. Ask for the circular route—*circulare* (cheer-koo-LAH-ray). It's usually the #51 or #52, leaving from the San Zaccaria vaporetto stop (near the Doge's Palace) and from all the stops along the perimeter of Venice.

By *Traghetto*: Only three bridges cross the Grand Canal, but *traghetti* (gondolas) shuttle locals and in-the-know tourists

across the Grand Canal at several handy locations (see map on page 34; routes also marked on pricier maps sold in Venice). Take advantage of these time-savers—they can also save money. For instance, while most tourists take the €5 vaporetto to connect St. Mark's with La Salute

Church, a €0.50 *traghetto* does the job just as well. Most people stand while riding (generally run 6:00–20:00, sometimes until 23:00, tel. 041-2424 for schedule).

By Water Taxi: Venetian taxis, like speedboat limos, hang out at most busy points along the Grand Canal. Prices, which average €50 (about €90 to the airport, €50 to the train station, with extra fees for very early or late runs), are a bit soft. Negotiate and settle before stepping in. For travelers with lots of luggage or small groups who can split the cost, taxi rides can be a worthwhile and time-saving convenience—and skipping across the lagoon in a classic wooden motorboat is a cool indulgence. For €80 an hour, you can have a private taxi boat tour.

By Gondola: To hire a gondolier for your own private cruise, see the Nightlife chapter, page 245.

TOURS

Venice Walks and Tours—This company offers a selection of historic and entertaining walks, including the basic St. Mark's Square introduction (daily at 11:00), Cannaregio and the Jewish Ghetto, San Polo and Dorsoduro, Ghosts and Legends, Casanova, and Secret Gardens (€20 per person, cheaper for returnees and students, €5 discount with this book through 2006, group size 8–20,

English language only—guides are native-speaking expats, 2 hours each, rain or shine, also day trips into the mainland; tel. 041-520-8616, mobile 340-050-2444, www.tours-italy.com, Monica or Jonathan).

Their 75-minute Grand Canal boat tour, offered daily at 16:30 and 17:30 (€40), is good. Tours are limited to about eight passengers (sitting awkwardly in a taxi not designed for sightseeing). You'll enjoy a fascinating, relaxing look at the wonders of the Grand Canal as well as the intimate back canals with a motor-mouthed (and interesting) guide. Departures are timed to give photographers the best possible light.

Classic Venice Bars Tour—Debonair local guide Alessandro Schezzini is a connoisseur of Venetian *bacari*—classic old bars serving traditional *cicchetti* (local munchies). He offers evening tours that involve sampling a snack and a glass of wine at three different *bacari*. The fee—about €30 per person—includes wine, *cicchetti*, and a chat with Alessandro, who will answer all of your questions about Venice (April–Oct Wed and Sat at 18:00, other evenings and off-season by request and with demand, 6–8 per group, tours must have at least 6, call or e-mail a day or two in advance to confirm, meet at top of Rialto Bridge, tel. & fax 041-534-5367, mobile 335-530-9024, venische@tiscalinet.it).

Venicescapes—Michael Broderick's private theme tours of Venice are intellectually demanding and beyond the attention span of most mortal tourists. Rather than a "sightseeing tour," consider your time with Michael a rolling, graduate-level lecture. Michael's challenge: To help visitors gain a more solid understanding of Venice. For a description of his various itineraries, see www.venicescapes .org (book well in advance, 4–6-hr tour: €275 for 2, €50 per person after that, plus admissions and transportation, tel. 041-520-6361, info@venicescapes.org).

Local Guides—Licensed guides are carefully trained and love explaining Venice to visitors. The following companies and guides give excellent tours to individuals, families, and small groups. If you organize a small group from your hotel at breakfast to split the cost (€65/hour with 2-hour minimum), the fee becomes quite reasonable.

Elisabetta Morelli is reliable, personable, and informative, giving good insight into daily life in Venice (€60/hr for Rick Steves' readers, usually 2–3-hour tours, tel. 041-526-7816, mobile 328-753-5220, bettamorelli@inwind.it). **Venice With A Guide** is a co-op of 10 equally good guides (www.venicewithaguide.com). **Walks Inside Venice** is a group of three women who are enthusiastic about their teaching (Roberta Curiel, tel. 041-524-1706, mobile 347-253-0560, www.walksinsidevenice.com, info@walksinsidevenice.com).

Alessandro Schezzini isn't a licensed Italian guide (and is therefore unable to take you into actual sights), but he does a great job getting you beyond the clichés and into offbeat Venice (€90, 2.5 hrs, listed above in "Classic Venice Bars Tour"). He also does Ghost Tours for spooky evening fun.

SIGHTS

Venice's greatest sight is the city itself. As well as seeing world-class museums and buildings, make time to wander narrow lanes, linger over a meal, or enjoy evening magic on St. Mark's Square.

In this chapter, don't judge a listing by its length. Some of Venice's most important sights have the shortest listings and are marked with a ✪ (and page number). These sights are covered in greater detail in one of the tours included in this book.

One of Venice's most delightful experiences—a gondola ride, worth ▲▲▲—is covered under Nightlife (see page 245).

San Marco District

▲▲▲**St. Mark's Square (Piazza San Marco)**—This grand square is surrounded by splashy, historic buildings and sights (each one described in more detail below): St. Mark's Basilica, the Doge's Palace, the Campanile (bell tower), and the Correr Museum. The square is filled with music, lovers, pigeons, and tourists by day, and is your private rendezvous with the Venetian past late at night, when Europe's most magnificent dance floor is *the* romantic place to be.

For a slow and pricey evening thrill, invest about €15 (including the cover charge for the music) in a glass of wine or coffee at one of the elegant cafés with the dueling orchestras (see "Cafés on St. Mark's Square" sidebar, page 60). For an unmatched experience that offers the best people-watching, it's worth the small splurge. But if all you have is €1, buy a bag of pigeon feed and become popular in a flurry. (To control the poopulation, the city adds bird birth control to the feed.) To get the flock airborne, toss your sweater in the air.

The **clock tower** *(torre dell'orologio)*, built during the Renaissance in 1496, marks the entry to the main shopping drag, called the

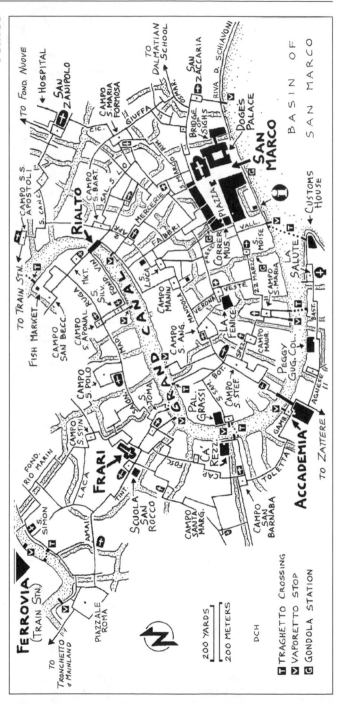

Mercerie, which connects St. Mark's Square with the Rialto. From the piazza, you can see the bronze men (Moors) swing their huge clappers at the top of each hour. In the 17th century, one of them knocked an unsuspecting worker off the top and to his death—probably the first-ever killing by a robot. Notice one of the world's first "digital" clocks on the tower facing the square (with dramatic flips every 5 min). The clock tower, which opens for visitors in 2006, is included in the Museum Card and the pricier Museum Pass (both cover the museums of St. Mark's Square—see page 24).

Venice's best TI is in the far left corner of the square (daily 9:00–20:00), and a €0.50 WC is 30 yards beyond St. Mark's Square (see *Albergo Diorno* sign marked on pavement, WC open daily 9:00–17:30). The other TI is on the lagoon (daily 10:00–18:00, walk toward the water by the Doge's Palace and go right, pay WCs nearby).

✪ For more about the square, see my St. Mark's Square Tour, page 55.

▲▲▲**St. Mark's Basilica**—Built in the 11th century to replace an earlier church, this basilica's distinctly Eastern-style architec-

ture underlines Venice's connection with Byzantium (which protected it from the ambition of Charlemagne and his Holy Roman Empire). It's decorated with booty from returning sea captains—a kind of architectural Venetian trophy chest. The interior glows mysteriously with gold mosaics and colored marble. Since about A.D. 830, the saint's bones have been housed on this site.

Cost, Hours, Information: Basilica entry is free, open Mon–Sat 9:30–17:30, until 16:30 off-season, Sun 14:00–16:00. Lines can be long, the dress code is strictly enforced, and bag check is mandatory and free; for details, see page 66. No photos are allowed inside. Three separate exhibits inside each charge admission: the **Treasury** (€2, includes audioguide, same hours as church), the **Golden Altarpiece** (€2, same hours as church), and the **San Marco Museum** (€3, Mon–Sat 9:45–16:30, Sun 9:45–16:00). The San Marco Museum has the original bronze horses, a balcony offering a remarkable view over St. Mark's Square, and various works related to the church. ✪ See my St. Mark's Basilica Tour, page 65.

▲▲▲**Doge's Palace (Palazzo Ducale)**—The seat of the Venetian government and home of its ruling duke, or doge, this was the most powerful half-acre in Europe for 400 years. The Doge's Palace was built to show off the power and wealth of the Republic. The doge lived with his family on the first floor near the halls of power.

Venice at a Glance

▲▲▲**St. Mark's Square** Venice's grand main square. **Hours:** Always open.

▲▲▲**St. Mark's Basilica** Cathedral with mosaics, saint's bones, treasury, museum, and viewpoint of square. **Hours:** Basilica open to tourists Mon–Sat 9:30–17:30, until 16:30 off-season, Sun 14:00–16:00; San Marco Museum open Mon–Sat 9:45–16:30, Sun 9:45–16:00.

▲▲▲**Doge's Palace** Art-splashed palace of former rulers, with prison accessible through Bridge of Sighs. **Hours:** Daily April–Oct 9:00–19:00, Nov–March 9:00–17:00.

▲▲▲**Rialto Bridge** Distinctive bridge spanning the Grand Canal, with a market nearby for locals and tourists. **Hours:** Bridge—always open; market—souvenir stalls open daily, produce market closed Sun, fish market closed Sun–Mon.

▲▲**Correr Museum** Venetian history and art. **Hours:** Daily April–Oct 9:00–19:00, Nov–March 9:00–17:00.

▲▲**Accademia** Venice's top art museum. **Hours:** Mon 8:15–14:00, Tue–Sun 8:15–19:15, shorter hours off-season.

▲▲**Peggy Guggenheim Collection** Popular display of 20th-century art. **Hours:** Wed–Mon 10:00–18:00, June–July open until 22:00 on Sat, always closed Tue.

▲▲**Frari Church** Franciscan church featuring Renaissance masters. **Hours:** Mon–Sat 10:00–18:00, Sun 13:00–17:00 (closed Sun in Aug).

▲▲**Scuola Grande di San Rocco** "Tintoretto's Sistine Chapel." **Hours:** Daily April–Oct 9:00–17:30, Nov–March 10:00–16:00.

▲**Campanile** Dramatic bell tower on St. Mark's Square with elevator to top. **Hours:** Daily July–Sept 9:00–21:00, Oct–June 9:00–19:00.

▲**Bridge of Sighs** Famous enclosed bridge, part of Doge's Palace, near St. Mark's Square. **Hours:** Always viewable.

▲**San Giorgio Maggiore** Island across the lagoon featuring church with Palladio architecture, Tintoretto paintings, and fine views back on Venice. **Hours:** Daily May–Sept 9:30–12:30 & 14:30–18:30, Oct–April 9:30–12:30 & 14:30–16:30, closed Sun to sightseers during Mass.

▲**La Salute Church** Striking church dedicated to the Virgin Mary. **Hours:** Daily 9:00–12:00 & 15:00–18:00,

▲**Ca' Rezzonico** Posh Grand Canal palazzo with 18th-century Venetian art. **Hours:** April–Oct Wed–Mon 10:00–18:00, Nov–March Wed–Mon 10:00–17:00, closed Tue.

Church of San Zaccaria Final resting place of St. Zechariah (San Zaccaria), plus a Bellini altarpiece. **Hours:** Mon–Sat 10:00–12:00 & 16:00–18:00, Sun 16:00–18:00 only.

Church of San Polo Ninth-century church with works by Tintoretto, Veronese, and Tiepolo. **Hours:** Mon–Sat 10:00–17:00, Sun 10:00–13:00.

Jewish Ghetto Neighborhood and Jewish Museum. **Hours:** June–Sept Sun–Fri 10:00–19:00, Oct–May Sun–Fri 10:00–17:30, closed Sat and Jewish Holidays.

Ca' d'Oro Venetian Gothic palace with temporary exhibits, fronting the Grand Canal. **Hours:** Mon 8:15–14:00, Tue–Sun 8:15–19:15.

Dalmatian School Exquisite Renaissance meeting house. **Hours:** Tue–Sat 9:30–12:30 & 15:30–18:30, Sun 9:30–12:30, closed Mon.

Santa Elena 100-year-old neighborhood with few tourists. **Hours:** Always open.

Murano Island famous for glass factories and glassmaking museum. **Hours:** Museum—April–Oct Thu–Tue 10:00–17:00, Nov–March Thu–Tue 10:00–16:00, closed Wed.

Burano Sleepy lacemaking island with lace museum. **Hours:** Museum—April–Oct Wed–Mon 10:00–17:00, Nov–March Wed–Mon 10:00–16:00, closed Tue.

Torcello Near-deserted island with old church and museum. **Hours:** Church—daily 10:30–17:30; museum—Tue–Sun 10:30–17:30, closed Mon.

From his once-lavish (now sparse) quarters, you'll follow the one-way tour through the public rooms of the top floor, finishing with the Bridge of Sighs and the prison. The place is wallpapered with masterpieces by Veronese and Tintoretto. Don't worry much about the great art. Enjoy the building.

Cost and Hours: €11 for Museum Card, includes admission to the Correr Museum (also covered by €15.50 Museum Pass). If the line is long at the Doge's Palace, buy your ticket at the Correr Museum across the square. With that, you can go directly through the Doge's turnstile without waiting in the long line. Open daily April–Oct 9:00–19:00, Nov–March 9:00–17:00, last entry 1 hour before closing.

Tours: Consider the €5.50 audioguide (high-tech device, dry but informative) or the "Secret Itineraries Tour," which takes you into palace rooms otherwise not open to the public (€12.50, in English at 9:55, 10:45 and 11:35, 75 min, call 041-291-5911 to reserve tour same day or a day in advance or call 041-520-9070 if more than 2 days in advance). ✪ See Doge's Palace Tour, page 83.

▲▲**Correr Museum (Museo Civico Correr)**—The uncrowded museum gives you a good overview of Venetian history and art. The doge memorabilia, armor, banners, statues (by Canova), and paintings (by the Bellini family and others) re-create the festive days of the Venetian Republic. There are English descriptions and breathtaking views of St. Mark's Square throughout (€11 Museum Card also includes the Doge's Palace, daily April–Oct 9:00–19:00, Nov–March 9:00–17:00, last entry 70 min before closing, enter at far end of square directly opposite church, tel. 041-240-5211). ✪ See Correr Museum Tour, page 98.

▲**Campanile (Campanile di San Marco)**—This dramatic bell tower replaced a shorter lighthouse, once part of the original fortress/palace that guarded the entry of the Grand Canal. The lighthouse crumbled into a pile of bricks in 1902, a thousand years after it was built. Ride the elevator 300 feet to the top of the reconstructed bell tower for the best view in Venice. For an ear-shattering experience, be on top when the bells ring (€6, daily July–Sept 9:00–21:00, Oct–June 9:00–19:00). The golden angel at the top always faces into the wind. Lines are longest at midday; beat the crowds and enjoy crisp morning air at 9:00, or try in the early evening (around 18:00). ✪ For more on the Campanile, see page 59.

Behind St. Mark's Basilica
Diocesan Museum (Museo Diocesano)—This little-known museum circles a peaceful Romanesque courtyard immediately behind the basilica (just before the Bridge of Sighs). It's filled with plunder from the Venetian Empire that never found a place in St. Mark's. While free and in a state of disarray in 2005, it expects to

be presentable and worth an admission charge in 2006 (Mon–Sat 10:00–12:30, closed Sun).

▲**Bridge of Sighs**—Connecting two wings of the Doge's Palace high over a canal, this enclosed bridge was popularized by travelers in the Romantic 19th century. Supposedly, a condemned man would be led over this bridge on the way to the prison, take one last look at the glory of Venice, and sigh. While overhyped, the bridge is undeniably tingle-worthy—especially after dark, when the crowds have dispersed and it's just you and floodlit Venice. It's around the corner from the Doge's Palace: Walk towards the waterfront, turn left along the water, and look up the first canal on your left. ✪ See St. Mark's to San Zaccaria Walk, page 197. You can cross the bridge by visiting the Doge's Palace. ✪ See Doge's Palace Tour, page 83.

Church of San Zaccaria—This historic church is home to a sometimes-waterlogged crypt, a Bellini altarpiece, Tintoretto painting, and the final resting place of St. Zechariah, the father of John the Baptist (free, €1 to enter crypt, €0.50 coin to light up Bellini's altarpiece, Mon–Sat 10:00–12:00 & 16:00–18:00, Sun 16:00–18:00 only, 2 canals behind St. Mark's Basilica). ✪ See St. Mark's to San Zaccaria Walk, page 197.

Across the Lagoon from St. Mark's Square

▲**San Giorgio Maggiore**—This is the dreamy island you can see from the waterfront by St. Mark's Square. The striking church, designed by Palladio, features art by Tintoretto and good views of Venice (free entry to church, daily May–Sept 9:30–12:30 & 14:30–18:30, Oct–April 9:30–12:30 & 14:30–16:30, closed Sun to sightseers during Mass, Gregorian Mass sung Mon–Sat at 8:00, Sun at 11:00). The church's bell tower, which usually provides oh-wow views over Venice, will be closed for restoration through 2006 (when it's open, it costs €3 and is accessible by elevator until 30 min before church's closing time). To reach the island from St. Mark's Square, take the five-minute vaporetto ride on #82 from the San Zaccaria Jolanda stop, just past the Bridge of Sighs, closest to the big statue. ✪ See San Giorgio Maggiore Tour, page 171.

Dorsoduro District

▲▲**Accademia (Galleria dell' Accademia)**—Venice's top art museum, packed with highlights of the Venetian Renaissance, features paintings by the Bellini family, Titian, Tintoretto, Veronese, Tiepolo, Giorgione, Canaletto, and Testosterone. It's just over the wooden Accademia Bridge. Expect long lines in the late morning because they allow only 300 visitors in at a time; visit early or late to miss crowds, or call 041-520-0345 to book tickets at least a day in advance (€7.50, Mon 8:15–14:00, Tue–Sun 8:15–19:15,

Floods and a Dying City

Venice floods about 100 times a year—normally in March and November, when the wind blowing from the south (Egypt) and high barometric pressure on the lower Adriatic Sea are most likely to combine to push water up to this top end of the sea. (The lunar tide in the Mediterranean is miniscule.)

Floods start in St. Mark's Square. The entry of the church is nearly the lowest spot in town. You might see stacked wooden benches; when the square floods, these are placed end to end to make elevated sidewalks. If you think the square is crowded now, in times of floods it turns into total gridlock, as everyone jostles for space on the wooden walkways.

The measuring devices at the outside base of the Campanile (near the exit, facing St. Mark's Square) show the current sea level *(livello marea)*. When the water level rises one meter, a warning siren sounds. It repeats if a serious flood is imminent. Find the mark that shows the high-water level from the terrible floods of 1966 (waist-level, on right). Imagine being a Venetian

shorter hours off-season, last entry 45 min before closing, no photos allowed, tel. 041-522-2247). The dull audioguide doesn't let you fast-forward to the works you want to hear about; you have to listen to the whole spiel for each room (€4/person, €6/double set, or €6/PalmPilot). ○ See Accademia Tour on page 112.

At the Accademia Bridge, there's a decent canalside pizzeria (Pizzeria Accademia Foscarini—see page 230) and a public WC at the base of the bridge.

▲▲**Peggy Guggenheim Collection**—The popular museum of far-out art, housed in the American heiress' former retirement palazzo, offers one of Europe's best reviews of the art of the first half of the 20th century. Stroll through styles represented by artists whom Peggy knew personally—Cubism (Picasso, Braque), Surrealism (Dalí, Ernst), Futurism (Boccioni), American Abstract Expressionism (Pollock), and a sprinkling of Klee, Calder, and Chagall (€10, Wed–Mon 10:00–18:00, closed Tue, June–July open until 22:00 on Sat, audioguide-€5, guidebook-€18, free and mandatory baggage check, pricey café, photos allowed only in garden and terrace—a fine and relaxing perch overlooking Grand Canal, free concerts in summer in garden—see ticket counter or www.guggenheim-venice.it for schedule, near Accademia, and hearing the alarm. You rush home to remove your carpets and raise your furniture above the (salt) water level. Many doorways have three-foot-tall wooden or metal barriers to fight the *acqua alta,* but the seawater still seeps through floors and drains, rendering the barriers nearly useless. After the water recedes, you have to carefully clean everything it touched to minimize the damage caused by the corrosive salt water.

In 1965, Venice's population was more than 150,000. Since the flood of 1966, the population has been shrinking. Today the population is about 65,000...and geriatric. Sad, yes, but imagine raising a family here: The fragile nature of the city means piles of regulations (for example, no biking), and costs are high—even though the government is now subsidizing rents to keep people from moving out. You can easily get glass and tourist trinkets, but it's hard to find groceries. And floods and the humidity make house maintenance an expensive pain.

You might notice construction work going on along the waterfront near St. Mark's Square. They're raising the entire level of the square by bringing up the pavement stones, adding a layer of sand, and replacing the stones. If the columns along the ground floor of the Doge's Palace look stubby, it's because this process has been carried out many times over the centuries.

tel. 041-240-5411). The place is staffed by international interns working on art-related degrees. ✪ See Peggy Guggenheim Collection Tour, page 153.

▲**La Salute Church (Santa Maria della Salute)**—The impressive church with a crown-shaped dome was built and dedicated to the Virgin Mary by grateful survivors of the 1630 plague (free, daily 9:00–12:00 & 15:00–18:00, tel. 041-522-5558 to confirm). It's a 10-minute walk from Accademia Bridge, or a vaporetto ride (stop: Salute), or an inexpensive *traghetto* crossing from near St. Mark's Square—catch it on the lagoon next to the TI and Harry's Bar. ✪ See La Salute Tour, page 166.

▲**Ca' Rezzonico (Museum of 18th-Century Venice)**—This grand Grand Canal palazzo offers the best look in town at the life of Venice's rich and famous in the 1700s. Wander under ceilings by Tiepolo, among furnishings from that most decadent century, enjoying views of the canal and paintings by Guardi, Canaletto, and Longhi (€6.50, covered by Museum Pass, April–Oct Wed–Mon 10:00–18:00, Nov–March Wed–Mon 10:00–17:00, closed Tue, last entry 1 hr before closing, audioguide-€4/person or €6/double set, located at Ca' Rezzonico vaporetto stop, tel. 041-241-0100). ✪ See Ca' Rezzonico Tour, page 142.

Santa Croce District

▲▲▲Rialto Bridge—One of the world's most famous bridges, this distinctive and dramatic stone structure crosses the Grand Canal with a single confident span. The arcades along the top of the bridge help reinforce the structure...and offer some enjoyable shopping diversions, as does the **market** surrounding the bridge (souvenir stalls open daily, produce market closed Sun, fish market closed Sun–Mon). ✪ See St. Mark's to Rialto Walk, page 184; also Rialto to Frari Church Walk, page 191.

San Polo District

▲▲Frari Church (Chiesa dei Frari)—My favorite art experience in Venice is seeing art in the setting for which it was designed—as it is at the Frari Church. The Franciscan "Church of the Brothers" and the art that decorates it is warmed by the spirit of St. Francis. It features the work of three great Renaissance masters: Donatello, Giovanni Bellini, and Titian—each showing worshippers the glory of God in human terms (€2.50, covered by €8 Chorus Pass, Mon–Sat 10:00–17:00, Sun 13:00–17:00, closed Sun in Aug, last entry 15 min before closing, audioguides-€1.60/person or €2.60/double set, modest dress recommended, tel. 041-272-86118). ✪ See Frari Church Tour, page 135; if you'll be walking to the church from the Rialto Bridge, see Rialto to Frari Church Walk, page 191.

▲▲Scuola Grande di San Rocco—Sometimes called "Tintoretto's Sistine Chapel," this lavish meeting hall (next to the Frari Church) has some 50 large, colorful Tintoretto paintings plastered to the walls and ceilings. The best paintings are upstairs, especially the *Crucifixion* in the smaller room. View the neck-breaking splendor with one of the mirrors *(specchio)* available at the entrance (€5.50, includes free and informative audioguide, daily April–Oct 9:00–17:30, Nov–March 10:00–16:00, last entry 30 min before closing, or see a concert here and enjoy the art as an evening bonus, www.scuolagrandesanrocco.it). ✪ See Scuola San Rocco Tour, page 125; also Rialto to Frari Church Walk, page 191.

Church of San Polo—This nearby church, which pales in comparison to the two sights listed above, is worth a visit for art-lovers. One of Venice's oldest church (from the 9th century), San Polo features works by Tintoretto, Veronese, and Tiepolo and son (€2.50, covered by €8 Chorus Pass, Mon–Sat 10:00–17:00, Sun 10:00–13:00, last entry 15 min before closing). ✪ See Rialto to Frari Church Walk, page 191.

Cannaregio District

Jewish Ghetto—In medieval times, Jews were grudgingly allowed to do business in Venice, but only in 1385 were they allowed to live there (subject to strict laws and special taxes). Anti-Semitic forces

San Polo District

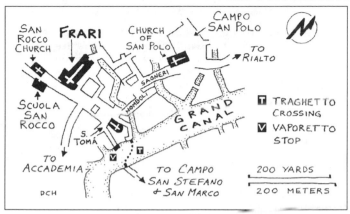

tried to oust them from the city, but in 1516, the doge compromised by restricting Jews to a special (undesirable) neighborhood. It was located on an easy-to-isolate island near the former foundry *(geto)*, coining the word "ghetto" for a segregated neighborhood.

The population swelled with immigrants from Germany, reaching 5,000 in the 1600s, the Golden Age of Venice's Jews. Restricted within their tiny neighborhood (the Ghetto Nuovo, or "New Ghetto"), they expanded upward, building six-story "skyscrapers" which stand today. The community's five synagogues were built atop the high-rise tenements. (As space was very tight and you couldn't live above a house of worship, this was the most practical use of precious land.) Only two synagogues are still active. You can spot them (with their 5 windows) from the square, but you can visit them only with a tour booked through the Jewish Museum (listed below).

The island's two bridges were locked up at night, when only Jewish doctors—coming to the aid of Venetians—were allowed to come and go. Eventually the ghetto community outgrew its original island, and the ghetto spread to adjacent blocks.

The main square, Campo di Ghetto Nuovo, must have been quite a scene, with 70 shops ringing it and all of Venice's Jewish commerce compressed onto this one spot. As late as the 1930s, 12,000 Jews called Venice home, but today there are only 200—and only a handful live in the actual Ghetto. Today the square, with its three cistern wells, is quiet. Facing it is the city's only kosher hotel (Locanda del Ghetto), in addition to a senior center and a Holocaust memorial by the Lithuanian artist Arbit Blatas (under the evocative barbed wire).

The **Jewish Museum** (Museo Ebraico) offers a humble two-room collection of silver and cloth worship aids and artifacts of the old community (€3, June–Sept Sun–Fri 10:00–19:00, Oct–May

Water, Water Everywhere, but...

As you explore Venice, notice the wells that grace nearly every square. Well water in the middle of the sea? Venice, while surrounded by water, originally had no natural source of drinking water. For centuries, locals collected water from the mainland with much effort and risk. Eventually, in the ninth century, they devised a way to collect rainwater by using town squares as catchment systems. The rain falls into the square, flows down through the slightly sloped pavement, drains through the marble grates, and filters through sand into a large clay tub under the pavement. Citizens could drop their buckets down the "well" to draw up fresh rainwater. (In actual fact, Venice's wealthiest always bought bottled water imported from the mainland.) With a safe local source of drinking water, Venice's population began to grow. Several thousand of these cisterns provided lagoon communities with drinking water right up until 1886, when an aqueduct was built (paralleling the railroad tracks across the lagoon) to bring in water from nearby mountains. Since then, the clay tubs have rotted out and the wells have been capped. Now, with a high tide, the floods show first on these marble grates, which mark the low point of each town square.

Sun–Fri 10:00–17:30, closed Sat and Jewish holidays, Campo di Ghetto Nuovo, tel. 041-715-359). Synagogue tours in English are offered hourly (€8, 30 min, Sun–Fri 10:30–17:30, until 16:30 in winter, contact museum for details).

Ca' d'Oro—This "House of Gold" palace, fronting the Grand Canal, is quintessential Venetian Gothic (Gothic seasoned with Byzantine and Islamic accents). Inside, there's little to see aside from special exhibitions (€5, Mon 8:15–14:00, Tue–Sun 8:15–19:15, free peek through hole in door of courtyard, Cannaregio 3932). ✪ See Grand Canal Cruise, page 46.

Castello District

Dalmatian School (Scuola Dalmata di San Giorgio)—This "school" (which means "meeting place") is a reminder that Venice was Europe's most cosmopolitan place in its heyday. It was here that the Dalmatians (from the present-day country of Croatia) worshipped in their own way, held neighborhood meetings, and worked to preserve their culture. The chapel on the ground floor happens to have the most exquisite Renaissance interior in Venice, with a cycle of paintings by Carpaccio ringing the room (€3, Tue–Sat 9:30–12:30 & 15:30–18:30, Sun 9:30–12:30, closed Mon, between St. Mark's Square and Arsenale, on Calle dei Furlani, 3 blocks southeast of Campo San Lorenzo, tel. 041-522-8828).

Santa Elena—For a pleasant peek into a completely non-touristy, residential side of Venice, walk or catch vaporetto #1 from St. Mark's Square to the neighborhood of Santa Elena (at the fish's tail). This 100-year-old suburb lives as if there were no tourism. You'll find a kid-friendly park, a few lazy restaurants, and beautiful sunsets over San Marco.

The Biennale—Every odd year (next in 2007), Venice hosts a world's fair of contemporary art. Countries from around the world send their best and most outrageous art to be displayed in buildings and pavilions scattered over the Giardini park and the Arsenale. Some artists convert entire buildings into a single installation, creating a weird wonderland of colors, video images, stage fog, laser lights, and piped-in sound. The festival is an excuse for temporary art exhibitions, concerts, and other cultural events around the city (June–Oct 2007, take vaporetto #1 or #82 to Giardini/Biennale; for the latest, see www.labiennale.org).

Venice's Lagoon

With more time, venture to some nearby islands in Venice's lagoon. While still somewhat touristy, they offer you an escape from the crowds, a chance to get out on a boat, and some enjoyable museums for fans of glassmaking and lace. ☉ See Venice's Lagoon Tour on page 176.

Murano—This island, famous for its glassmaking, is home to several glass factories and the **Glass Museum** (Museo Vetrario), which traces the history of this delicate art (€4, covered by €15.50 Museum Pass, April–Oct Thu–Tue 10:00–17:00, Nov–March Thu–Tue 10:00–16:00, closed Wed, last entry 30 min before closing, tel. 041-739-586).

Burano—The island's claim to fame is lacemaking, and the easiest one-stop opportunity to learn more is at the **Lace Museum** (Museo del Merletto di Burano, €4, covered by €15.50 Museum Pass, April–Oct Wed–Mon 10:00–17:00, Nov–March Wed–Mon 10:00–16:00, closed Tue, tel. 041-730-034).

Torcello—This sparsely populated island features what's claimed to be Venice's oldest church. With impressive mosaics, a climbable bell tower, and a modest museum of Roman sculpture and medieval sculpture and manuscripts, the church is worth a wander (€6 combo-ticket gets you into all the sights, or pay €2 apiece, most open daily 10:30–17:30, museum closed Mon, tel. 041-730-761).

GRAND CANAL CRUISE

Take a joyride and introduce yourself to Venice by boat. Cruise the Canal Grande from Tronchetto (parking lot) or Ferrovia (train station) all the way to San Marco.

If it's your first trip down the Grand Canal, you might want to stow this book and just take it all in—Venice is a barrage on the senses that hardly needs a narration. But these notes give the cruise a little meaning and help orient you to this great city.

ORIENTATION

Cost: €5 for a vaporetto ticket or €10.50 for a 24-hour pass.

Hours: Enjoy the best light and the fewest crowds by riding early or late. Sunset bathes the buildings in gold. Twilight is magic. After dark, chandeliers light up building interiors.

Getting There: From Tronchetto (the bus and car park) or the Santa Lucia train station (Ferrovia), catch vaporetto #1, which is ideal because it's slow (45 min). Although vaporetto #82 does the same route, it's too fast (25 min) to follow this tour comfortably. When catching either boat, confirm that you're on a "San Marco via Rialto" boat (some boats finish at the Rialto Bridge, others take a non-scenic outside route). The conductor announces *"Solo Rialto!"* for boats going only as far as Rialto, or *"Piazzale Roma!"* for boats terminating their route there. Note that the San Marco vaporetto stop is actually called San Marco/Vallaresso. The best seats are in the open air—in the front (you must stay seated), at the stern, or standing along the railing.

Information: Some city maps (on sale at postcard racks) have a handy Grand Canal map on the back.

Grand Canal

Length of This Tour: Allow 45 minutes on vaporetto #1 or 25 minutes on vaporetto #82.

Starring: Palaces, markets, boats, bridges—Venice.

THE TOUR BEGINS

Start at the **train station** or **Tronchetto** parking lot. We'll orient by the vaporetto stops.

Venice's main thoroughfare is busy with all kinds of **boats:** taxis, police boats, garbage boats, ambulances, construction cranes, and even brown-and-white UPS boats. Venice's sleek, black, graceful **gondolas** are a symbol of the city. While used gondolas cost

Palaces Rising from the Sea

The Grand Canal is Venice's "Main Street." At more than two miles long, nearly 150 feet wide, and nearly 15 feet deep, it's the biggest canal with the most impressive palaces. The canal is the remnant of a river that once spilled from the mainland into the Adriatic. The sediment it carried formed barrier islands that cut off the sea, forming a lagoon.

Venice was built on the marshy islands of the former delta, sitting on pilings driven nearly 15 feet into the clay (alder wood worked best). About 25 miles of **canals** drain the city, dumping like streams into the Grand Canal. Technically, there are only three canals: Grand, Giudecca, and Cannaregio. The other 45 "canals" are referred to as rivers (e.g., Rio Nuovo).

about €10,000, new ones run up to €35,000 apiece. Today, with more than 400 gondoliers joyriding amid the churning *vaporetti*, there's a lot of congestion on the Grand Canal. Watch your vaporetto driver curse the better-paid gondoliers.

Ferrovia (vaporetto stop)

The **Santa Lucia train station** (on the left bank of the canal), one of the few modern buildings in town, was built in 1954. It's been the gateway into Venice since 1860, when the first station was built. "F.S." stands for "Ferrovie dello Stato," the Italian state railway system. The **bridge** at the station is the first of only three that cross the Grand Canal.

Over 20,000 a day commute in from mainland, making this the busiest part of Venice during each rush hour. To alleviate some of the congestion and make the commute easier, a new, fourth bridge over the Grand Canal (made of glass) is being

Venice is a city of **palaces,** dating from the days when Venice was the world's richest city. The most lavish palaces formed a grand chorus line along the Grand Canal. Once frescoed in reds and blues, with black-and-white borders and gold-leaf trim, they made Venice a city of dazzling color. This cruise is the only way to really appreciate the palaces, approaching them at water level, where their main entrances were located. Today, strict laws prohibit any changes in these buildings, so while landowners gnash their teeth, we can enjoy Europe's best-preserved medieval city—slowly rotting. Many of the grand buildings are now vacant. Others harbor chandeliered elegance above mossy, empty ground floors.

built between the train station and Piazzale Roma (bus station).

Opposite the train station, atop the green dome of **San Simeone Piccolo** church, Saint Simon waves *ciao* to whoever enters or leaves the "old" city.

Riva di Biasio

Just past the Riva di Biasio stop, look left down the broad **Cannaregio Canal.** The twin, pale-pink, six-story "skyscrapers" are reminders of how densely populated the world's original **ghetto** was. Set aside as the local Jewish quarter in 1516, the area (located behind the San Marcuola stop) became extremely crowded. This urban island developed into one of the most closely knit business and cultural quarters of all the Jewish communities in Italy and gave us our word ghetto (from *geto,* the copper foundry located here). For more information, visit the Jewish Museum in this neighborhood (see page 43).

San Marcuola

The gray **Turkish "Fondaco" Exchange** (right side, opposite San Marcuola vaporetto stop) is considered the oldest house in Venice. Its horseshoe arches and roofline of triangles-and-dingleballs are reminders of its Byzantine heritage. Turkish traders in turbans docked here, unloaded their goods into the warehouse on the bottom story, then went upstairs for a home-style meal and a place to sleep. Venice in the 1500s was very cosmopolitan, welcoming every religion and ethnicity, so long as they carried cash.

Venice's **Casino** (left-hand side) is housed in the palace where German composer Richard *(The Ring)* Wagner died in 1883. See his distinct, strong-jawed profile in the white plaque on the brick wall. In the 1700s, Venice was Europe's Vegas, with casinos and prostitutes everywhere. Today, this elegant Casino welcomes men in ties and ladies in dresses. "Casinos" (literally "little houses") have long provided Italians with a handy escape from daily life.

San Stae

Opposite the San Stae stop, look for the **faded frescoes** (left bank, on lower story). Imagine the facades of the Grand Canal at their finest. As colorful as the city is today, it's still only a sepia-toned snapshot of a long-gone era of lavishly decorated and brilliantly colored palaces.

Ca' d'Oro

The lacy **Ca' d'Oro,** or "House of Gold," (left bank, just before the vaporetto stop) is the best example of "Venetian Gothic" on the canal. Its three stories offer dif-ferent variations on balcony design, topped with a spiny white roofline. Venetian Gothic mixes traditional Gothic (pointed arches and round medallions stamped with a four-leaf clover) with Byzantine styles (tall, narrow arches atop thin columns), filled in with Islamic frills. Like all the palaces, this was originally painted and gilded to make it even more glorious than it is now. *"Ca'"* means "house." Because only the house of the doge (Venetian ruler) could be called a palace *(palazzo),* all other palaces are technically *"Ca'."*

Today the Ca' d'Oro is a museum, but, other than temporary exhibits, there's little to see inside (€5, Mon 8:15–14:00, Tue–Sun 8:15–19:15, free peek through hole in door of courtyard).

Farther along, on the right, the outdoor arcade of the **fish and produce market** bustles with people in the morning but is quiet the rest of the day. This is a great scene to wander through—even though European hygiene standards recently required a less-colorful remodeling

job. Find the *traghetto* gondola ferrying shoppers back and forth, standing like Washington crossing the Delaware.

The huge **post office** (left side, just before the Rialto Bridge), with *servizio postale* boats moored at its blue posts, was the German Exchange in the early 1500s, the trading center for German metal merchants. The building's top story has a rare sight in frilly Venice—square windows. Rising above the post office, you can see in the distance the golden angel of the Campanile (bell tower) at St. Mark's Square, where this tour will end.

As the canal bends, we pass beneath the impressive Rialto Bridge. Singing gondoliers love the acoustics here: *"O sole mio..."*

Rialto

A major landmark of Venice, the **Rialto Bridge** is lined with shops and tourists. Constructed in 1588, it's the third bridge built on this spot. With a span of 160 feet and foundations stretching 650 feet

on either side, the Rialto was an impressive engineering feat in its day. Earlier Rialto Bridges could open to let big ships in, but not this one. When this new bridge was completed, much of the Grand Canal was closed to shipping and became a canal of palaces.

Rialto, a separate town in the early days of Venice, has always been the commercial district, while San Marco was the religious and governmental center. Today, a winding street called the Mercerie connects the two, providing travelers with human traffic jams and a mesmerizing gauntlet of shopping temptations. The restaurants that line the canal feature great views, midrange prices, and low-quality food.

San Silvestro

On the left side, opposite the vaporetto stop, **two palaces stand side by side,** with stories the same height, creating the effect of one long balcony.

We now enter a long stretch of important **merchants' palaces**, each with proud and different facades. Since ships couldn't navigate beyond the Rialto Bridge to reach the section of the Grand Canal you just came from, the biggest palaces—with the major shipping needs—lie ahead.

Palaces like these were multifunctional: ground floor for the warehouse, offices and showrooms upstairs on the "noble floor" (with big windows designed to allow maximum light in), and living quarters on the top.

Sant'Angelo

Just past the Sant'Angelo stop (ahead on the right, with twin obelisks on the rooftop) stands the **palace of a 15th-century captain
general** of the sea. These Venetian equivalents of five-star admi-
rals were honored with twin obelisks decorating their palaces.
This palace flies three flags: those of Italy (green-white-red), the
European Union (blue with ring of stars), and Venice (the lion).

Notice how many buildings have a foundation of waterproof
white stone *(pietra d'Istria)* upon which the bricks sit high and dry.
Many canal-level floors are abandoned; the rising water level takes
its toll. The **posts**—historically painted gaily with the equivalent
of family coats of arms—don't rot under water. But the wood at
the waterline does.

In this city of masks, notice how the rich marble facades
along the Grand Canal mask what are generally just simple, no-
nonsense brick buildings. Look up at the characteristic **funnel-
shaped chimneys.** These forced embers through a loop-the-loop
channel until they were dead—required in the days when stone
palaces were surrounded by humble, wooden buildings, and a live
spark could make a merchant's workforce homeless.

Take a deep whiff of Venice. What's all this nonsense about
stinky canals? All I smell is my shirt. By the way, how's your captain? Smooth dockings? To get to know him, stand up in the bow
and block his view.

San Tomà

After the San Tomà stop, look down the side canal (on the right,
before the bridge) to see the traffic light, the **fire station,** and the
fireboats ready to go.

We now prepare to round the corner and double back toward
St. Mark's. The impressive **Ca' Foscari** (right side) dominates the
bend in the canal. Its four stories get increasingly ornate as they
rise from the water—from simple Gothic arches at water level, to
Gothic with a point, to Venetian Gothic arches topped with four-
leaf clovers, to still more medallions and laciness that look almost
Moorish. Wow.

These days, when buildings are being renovated, huge
murals with images of the building mask the ugly scaffolding.
Corporations sponsor these multistory covers, hiding the scaffolding for the goodwill—and the publicity.

Ca' Rezzonico

The grand, heavy, white **Ca' Rezzonico,** directly at the stop of the
same name, houses the Museum of 18th-Century Venice. ✪ See
Ca' Rezzonico Tour, page 142. Across the canal is the cleaner and

leaner **Palazzo Grassi,** the last major palace built on the canal, erected in the late 1700s. Today it showcases special exhibitions.

Accademia

The wooden **Accademia Bridge** crosses the Grand Canal and leads to the **Accademia** art museum (right side), filled with the best Venetian paintings. ✪ See Accademia Tour, page 112. The bridge was put up in 1932 as a temporary one. Locals liked it, so it stayed. Cruising under the bridge, you'll get a classic view of the domed La Salute Church ahead.

The low white building among greenery (on the right, between the bridge and the church) is the **Peggy Guggenheim Collection.** The American heiress "retired" here, sprucing up the palace that had been abandoned in mid-construction; the locals call it the "*palazzo non finito.*" Peggy willed the city her fine collection of modern art. ✪ See Peggy Guggenheim Collection Tour, page 153.

Next door, notice the early Renaissance building's flat-feeling facade with "pasted-on" Renaissance motifs. The Salviati building (with the fine mosaic and traditional chimneys) is a glass factory.

Salute

A crown-shaped dome supported by scrolls stands atop **La Salute**

Church (daily 9:00–12:00 & 15:00–18:00). ✪ See La Salute Church Tour, page 166. This Church of Saint Mary of Good Health was built to thank God for delivering Venetians from the devastating plague of 1630 (which had killed about a third of the city's population).

La Salute, like Venice itself, rests upon pilings. To build the foundation for the city, more than a million trees were piled together, reaching below the mud to the solid clay. Much of the surrounding countryside was deforested by Venice. Trees were exported and consumed locally to fuel the furnaces of Venice's booming glass industry, to build Europe's biggest merchant marine, and to prop up this city in the mud.

Across the canal (left side), several **fancy hotels** have painted facades that hint at the canal's former glory.

As the Grand Canal opens up into the lagoon, the last building on the right with the golden ball is the 16th-century **Customs House** (Dogana da Mar, not open to the public). Its two bronze Atlases hold a statue of Fortune riding the ball. Arriving ships stopped here to pay their tolls.

As you prepare to disembark at the San Marco/Vallaresso stop, look from left to right out over the lagoon. On the left, a wide harborfront walk leads past the town's most elegant hotels to the green area in the distance. This is the public garden, the largest of Venice's few parks, which hosts the Biennale art show. Farther in the distance is the **Lido,** the island with Venice's beach. It's tempting, with sand and casinos, but its car traffic breaks into the medieval charm of Venice.

The ghostly white church that seems to float is the architect Andrea Palladio's **San Giorgio Maggiore.** It's just a vaporetto ride away (#82 from the San Zaccaria Jolanda stop, just past the Bridge of Sighs). ✪ See San Giorgio Maggiore Tour, page 171. Across the lagoon (to your right) is a residential island called **Giudecca.**

San Marco/Vallaresso

Get off at the San Marco/Vallaresso stop. Directly ahead is **Harry's Bar.** Hemingway drank here when it was a characteristic no-name *osteria* and the gondoliers' hangout. Today, of course, it's the over-priced hangout of well-dressed Americans who don't mind paying triple for their Bellinis (peach juice with Prosecco—a sparkling white wine) to make the scene. While Harry's Bar is a non-sight, one of Europe's great experiences—St. Mark's Square—is just a long block up the waterfront.

ST. MARK'S SQUARE TOUR

(Piazza San Marco)

Venice was once Europe's richest city, and the Piazza San Marco was its center. As middleman in the trade between Asia and Europe, Venice reaped wealth from both sides. In 1450, Venice had 180,000 citizens (far more than London) and a gross "national" product that exceeded that of entire countries.

The rich Venetians taught the rest of Europe the good life—silks, spices, and jewels from the East, crafts from northern Europe, good food and wine, fine architecture, music, theater, and laughter. Venice was a vibrant city full of painted palaces, glittering canals, and impressed visitors. Five centuries after its power began to decline, Venice is all of these still, with the added charm of romantic decay. In this tour, we'll spend an hour in the heart of this Old World superpower.

ORIENTATION

Cost and Hours: If you ascend the Campanile (bell tower), it'll cost you €6 (daily July–Sept 9:00–21:00, Oct–June 9:00–19:00).

Getting There: Signs all over town point to *San Marco*—both the square and the basilica, located where the Grand Canal spills out into the lagoon. Vaporetto stop: San Marco/Vallaresso.

Information: There are two TIs. One is in the southwest corner of the square; the other is along the waterfront at the San Marco/Vallaresso vaporetto stop. In any given year, expect a famous building to be covered with scaffolding. Restoration is an ongoing process.

Cuisine Art: Cafés with live music are on St. Mark's Square; cheaper places are just off the square (see page 60). The Correr Museum (far end of the square, opposite the basilica) has a quiet coffeeshop overlooking the crowded square.

Starring: Byzantine domes, Gothic arches, Renaissance arches... and the wonderful space they enclose.

THE TOUR BEGINS

• *For an overview of this grand square and the buildings that surround it, view it from the far end of the square (away from St. Mark's Basilica).*

The Piazza—Bride of the Sea

St. Mark's Basilica dominates the square with its Byzantine-style onion domes and glowing mosaics. Mark Twain said it looked like "a warty bug taking a meditative walk." To the right of the basilica is its 300-foot-tall Campanile. Between the basilica and the Campanile, you can catch a glimpse of the pale-pink Doge's Palace. Lining the square are the former government offices that administered the Venetian empire's vast network of trading outposts, which stretched all the way to Turkey.

The square is big, but it feels intimate with its cafés and dueling orchestras. By day, it's great for people-watching and pigeon-chasing. By night, under lantern light, it transports you to another century, complete with its own romantic soundtrack. The Piazza draws Indians in saris, English nobles in blue blazers, and Nebraskans in shorts. Napoleon called the Piazza "the most beautiful drawing room in Europe." Napoleon himself added to the intimacy by building the final wing, opposite the basilica, that encloses the square.

For architecture buffs, here are three centuries of styles, bam, side by side, *uno-due-tre,* for easy comparison:

1. On the left side (as you face the basilica) are the "Old" offices, built in about 1500 in solid, column-and-arch Renaissance style.

2. The "New" offices (on the right), in a High Renaissance style from a century later (c. 1600), are a little heavier and more ornate. This wing mixes arches, the three orders of columns from bottom to top—Doric, Ionic, and Corinthian—and statues in the Baroque style.

3. Napoleon's wing is neoclassical (c. 1800)—a return to simpler, more austere classical columns and arches. Napoleon's architects tried to make his wing bridge the styles of the other two. But it turned out a little too high for one side and not enough for the other. Nice try.

St. Mark's Square

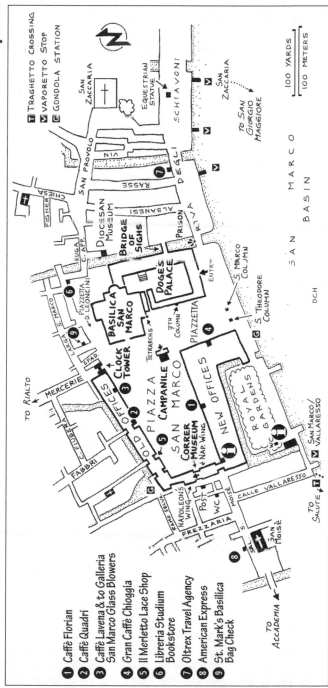

1 Caffè Florian
2 Caffè Quadri
3 Caffè Lavena & to Galleria San Marco Glass Blowers
4 Gran Caffè Chioggia
5 Il Merletto Lace Shop
6 Libreria Studium Bookstore
7 Oltrex Travel Agency
8 American Express
9 St. Mark's Basilica Bag Check

Imagine this square full of water, with gondolas floating where people now sip cappuccinos. That happens every so often at very high tides *(acqua alta),* a reminder that Venice and the sea are intertwined.

Venice became Europe's richest city from its trade with northern Europeans, Turkish Muslims, and Byzantine Christians. Here in St. Mark's Square, the exact center of this East–West axis, we see both the luxury and the mix of Eastern and Western influences.

Watch out for pigeon speckle. The pigeons are not indigenous to Venice (they were imported by the Hapsburgs) nor loved by the locals. In fact, Venetians love seagulls because they eat pigeons. Vermin are a problem on this small island, where it's said that each Venetian has two pigeons and four rats. (The rats stay hidden except when high tides flood their homes.)

• *The TI is nearby, in the corner of Napoleon's Wing. With Venice's inconsistent opening hours, it's wise to confirm your sightseeing plans here. Behind you (southwest of the Piazza), you'll find the public WC, a post office, and the American Express office.*

Now approach the basilica. If it's hot and you're tired, grab a shady seat at the foot of the Campanile.

St. Mark's Basilica—Exterior

The facade is a crazy mix of East and West. There are round, Roman-style arches over the doorways, golden Byzantine mosaics, a roofline ringed with pointed French Gothic pinnacles, and Muslim-shaped onion domes (wood, covered with lead) on the roof. The brick-structure building is blanketed in marble that came from everywhere—columns from Alexandria, capitals from Sicily, and carvings from Constantinople. The columns flanking the doorways show the facade's variety—purple, green, gray, white, yellow, some speckled, some striped horizontally, some vertically, some fluted, all topped with a variety of different capitals.

What's amazing isn't so much the variety as the fact that the whole thing comes together in a bizarre sort of harmony. St. Mark's remains simply the most interesting church in Europe, a church that (paraphrasing Goethe) "can only be compared with itself."

For more on the basilica, inside and out, see ✪ St. Mark's Basilica Tour, page 65.

• *Facing the basilica, turn 90 degrees to the left to see...*

The Clock Tower (Torre dell'Orologio)

Two bronze Moors (African Muslims) stand atop the clock tower. (They only gained their ethnicity when the metal darkened over the centuries.) At the top of each hour they swing their giant clappers.

The clock dial shows the 24 hours, the signs of the zodiac, and, in the blue center, the phases of the moon. Above the dial is the world's first digital clock, which changes every five minutes. The clock tower retains some of its original coloring of blue and gold, a reminder that, in centuries past, this city glowed with color.

An alert winged lion, the symbol of St. Mark and the city, looks down on the crowded square. He opens a book that reads *"Pax Tibi Marce"* or "Peace to you, Mark." As legend goes, these were the comforting words that an angel spoke to the stressed evangelist, assuring him he would find serenity during a stormy night that the saint spent here on the island. Eventually, St. Mark's body found its final resting place inside the basilica, and now his lion symbol is everywhere. (Find four in 20 seconds. Go.)

Venice's many lions express the city's various mood swings through history—triumphant after a naval victory, sad when a favorite son has died, hollow-eyed after a plague, and smiling when the soccer team wins. The pair of lions squatting between the clock tower and basilica have probably been photographed being ridden by every Venetian child born since the dawn of cameras.

The Campanile

The original Campanile (cam-pah-NEE-lay), or bell tower, was a lighthouse and a marvel of 10th-century architecture until the 20th century (1902), when it toppled into the center of the Piazza. It had groaned ominously the night before, sending people scurrying from the cafés. The next morning...crash! The golden angel on top landed right at the basilica's front door, standing up.

The Campanile was rebuilt 10 years later complete with its golden angel, which always faces the breeze. You can ride a lift to the top for the best view of Venice. It's crowded at peak times, but well worth it.

Notice the tide gauges on the side of the bell tower. Since St. Mark's Square is the first place in town to start flooding, it's an obvious place to take tidal measurements. Three factors

Cafés on St. Mark's Square

Cafés line the square. All three café orchestras feature similar food, prices, and a three- or four-piece combo playing a selection of classical and pop hits, from Brahms to "Bésame Mucho." If you get just a drink, expect to pay about €15, including the cover charge. It's perfectly acceptable to nurse a cappuccino for an hour, since you're paying for the music with the cover charge.

Caffè Florian (on the right as you face the church) is the most famous Venetian café and one of the first places in Europe to serve coffee. It's been a popular spot for a discreet rendezvous in Venice since 1720. The orchestra plays a more classical repertoire than the other cafés. The outside tables are the main action, but do walk inside through the richly decorated, 18th-century rooms where Casanova, Lord Byron,  Charles Dickens, and Woody Allen have all paid too much for a drink (reasonable prices at bar in back).

Caffè Quadri, exactly opposite the Florian, has an equally illustrious history of famous clientele, including the writers Stendhal and Dumas, and composer Richard Wagner. **Caffè Lavena,** near the clock tower, is newer and less prestigious.

Gran Caffè Chioggia, on the Piazzetta facing the Doge's Palace, charges slightly less, with one or two musicians playing cocktail jazz.

cause high water: low pressure, a full moon, and a wind from the south (called a "sirocco wind"). When these come together, Venice floods. The puddles appear first around round, white pavement stones like the one next to the Campanile. If the tide is mild, the water merely seeps up through the drains. But when there's a strong tide, it looks like someone's turned a faucet on down below. The water bubbles upward and flows like a river to the lowest points in the square, which can quickly be covered with a few inches of water in an hour or so. Check out the stone plaque showing the high-water line from the disastrous floods of 1966 (caused by 3 straight days of a strong sirocco).

• *The small square between the basilica and the water is...*

The Piazzetta

This "Little Square" is framed by the Doge's Palace on the left, the Library on the right, and the waterfront of the lagoon. In

former days, the Piazzetta was closed off to the public for a few hours a day so that government officials and bigwigs could gather in the sun to strike shady deals.

The pale-pink Doge's Palace is the epitome of the style known as Venetian Gothic. Columns support traditional, pointed Gothic arches, but with a Venetian flair—they're curved to a point, ornamented with a trefoil (three-leaf clover), and topped with a round medallion of a quatrefoil (four-leaf clover). The pattern is found on buildings all over Venice, but nowhere else in the world (except Las Vegas).

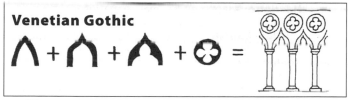

Venetian Gothic

The two large 12th-century columns near the water were looted from Constantinople. Mark's winged lion sits on top of one. The lion's body (nearly 15 feet long) predates the wings and is more than 2,000 years old. The other column holds St. Theodore (battling a crocodile), the former patron saint who was replaced by Mark. I

guess stabbing crocs in the back isn't classy enough for an upwardly mobile world power. These columns were used to execute criminals in hopes that the public could learn its lessons vicariously.

Venice was the "Bride of the Sea" because she was dependent on sea trading for her livelihood. This "marriage" was celebrated annually by the people. The doge, in full regalia, boarded a ritual boat (his Air Force One equivalent) here at the edge of the Piazzetta and sailed out into the lagoon. There a vow was made, and he dropped a jeweled ring into the water to seal the marriage. (I always think of that image whenever the café orchestras play the theme from *Titanic*.)

In the distance, on an island across the lagoon, is one of the grandest scenes in the city, the Church of San Giorgio Maggiore. With its four tall columns as the entryway, the church, designed by the late-Renaissance architect Andrea Palladio, influenced future

---

Escape from St. Mark's Square

Crowds getting to you? Here are some relatively quiet areas near St. Mark's Square.

Correr Museum: Sip a cappuccino in the café of this uncrowded history museum in a building that overlooks St. Mark's Square (enter at the far end of the Piazza). ◎ See Correr Museum Tour, page 98.

Giardinetti Reali: A small park along the waterfront west of the Piazzetta (facing the water, turn right—it's next to the TI).

Isle of San Giorgio Maggiore: The fairy-tale island you see from the Piazzetta (catch vaporetto #82 from the San Zaccaria Jolanda stop, past the Bridge of Sighs). ◎ See San Giorgio Maggiore Tour, page 171.

Il Merletto: A lace shop in a small chapel (near northwest corner of St. Mark's Square, on Sotoportego del Cavalletto).

La Salute Church: This cool church in a quiet neighborhood is a five-minute ride by vaporetto #1 or *traghetto*—both leave from the San Marco/Vallaresso stop. ◎ See La Salute Tour, page 166.

Caffè Florian: The plush interior of this luxurious 19th-century café, located on St. Mark's Square, is generally quiet and nearly empty. An expensive coffee here can be a wonderful break (see "Cafes on St. Mark's Square" sidebar, page 60).

government and bank buildings around the world.

Speaking of architects, I will: Sansovino. Around 1530, Jacopo Sansovino designed the Library (here in the Piazzetta) and the delicate Loggetta at the base of the Campanile (it was destroyed by the collapse of the tower in 1902 and was pieced back together as much as possible).

The Tetrarchs and the Doge's Palace's Seventh Column

Where the basilica meets the Doge's Palace is the traditional entrance to the palace, decorated with four small Roman statues—the Tetrarchs. While no one knows for sure who they are, I like the legend that says they're the scared leaders of a divided Rome during its fall—holding their swords and each other as all hell breaks loose around them. Whatever the legend, these statues—made of precious purple porphyry marble—are symbols of power. They

were looted from Constantinople, then placed here proudly as spoils of war. How old are they? They've guarded the doge's entrance since the city first rose from the mud.

The Doge's Palace's seventh column (the seventh from the water) tells a story of love, romance, and tragedy in its carved capital: (1) In the first scene (the carving facing the Piazzetta), a woman on a balcony is wooed by her lover, who says, "Babe, I want *you*!" (2) She responds, "Why, little old *me*?" (3) They get married. (4) Kiss. (5) Hit the sack—pretty racy for 14th-century art. (6) Nine months later, guess what? (7) The baby takes its first steps. (8) And as was all too common in the 1300s, the child dies.

The pillars along the Doge's Palace look short—a result of the square being built up over the centuries. It's happening again today. The stones are taken up, sand is added, and the stones are replaced, buying a little more time as the sea slowly swallows the city.

• *At the waterfront in the Piazzetta, turn left and walk (east) along the water. At the top of the first bridge, look inland at...*

The Bridge of Sighs

In the Doge's Palace (on your left), the government doled out justice. On your right are the prisons. (Don't let the palatial facade fool you—see the bars on the windows?) Prisoners sentenced in the palace crossed to the prisons by way of the covered bridge in front of you. This was called the Prisons' Bridge until the Romantic poet Lord Byron renamed it in the 19th century. From this bridge (according to romantic—and false—legend), the convicted got their final view of sunny, joyous Venice before entering the black and dank prisons. They sighed.

Venice has been a major tourist center for four centuries. Anyone who ever came here has stood on this very spot, looking at the Bridge of Sighs. Lean on the railing leaned on by everyone from Casanova to Byron to Hemingway.

I stood in Venice, on the Bridge of Sighs,
a palace and a prison on each hand.
I saw, from out the wave, her structures rise,
as from the stroke of the enchanter's wand.
A thousand years their cloudy wings expand
around me, and a dying glory smiles
o'er the far times, when many a subject land
looked to the Winged Lion's marble piles,
where Venice sat in state, throned on her hundred isles!
　　　　　　　　—from Lord Byron's *Childe Harold's Pilgrimage*

• *Sigh.*

ST. MARK'S BASILICA TOUR

(Basilica di San Marco)

Among Europe's churches, St. Mark's is peerless. From the outside, it's a riot of domes, columns, and statues, completely unlike the towering Gothic churches of the north. Inside, the decor of mosaics, colored marbles, and oriental treasures is rarely seen elsewhere. Even the Christian symbolism is unfamiliar to Western eyes, done in the style of icons and even Islamic designs. Older than most of Europe's churches, it feels like a remnant of a lost world.

This is your best chance (outside of Istanbul or Ravenna) to glimpse a forgotten and somewhat mysterious part of the human story—Byzantium.

ORIENTATION

Cost: While entering the church is free, I'd pay for each of its three separate admissions inside: the Treasury (€2, includes informative audioguide—free for the asking), Golden Altarpiece (€2), and San Marco Museum (€3, enter museum from atrium either before or after you tour church).

Hours: The church (including the Treasury and Golden Altarpiece) is open Mon–Sat 9:30–17:30 (until 16:30 off-season), Sun 14:00–16:00. The San Marco Museum is open Mon–Sat 9:45–16:30, Sun 9:45–16:00. To enjoy the gilded, mosaic-covered church in all its medieval glory, see it when it's lit up (unpredictable schedule, usually Mon–Sat 11:30–12:30, all day Sun).

Getting There: Signs throughout Venice point to *San Marco*, meaning the square and the church. It's on St. Mark's Square (Piazza San Marco), near the end of the Grand Canal. Vaporetto stop: San Marco/Vallaresso.

Lines: There's almost always a long line to get into St. Mark's. To deal with the relentless crowds, the church interior is roped off. You just have to shuffle through on a one-way system. It's best to read this chapter before you go...or while standing in line (bring a small flashlight to illuminate the text). Those checking a bag can skip to the front of the line—see "Bag Check," below.

Dress Code: To enter the church, modest dress is required even of kids (no shorts or bare shoulders). People who ignore the dress code hold up the line while they plead fruitlessly with the dress-code police.

Bag Check: While small purses are allowed inside the church, larger bags and backpacks are not. Check them for free at the nearby Ateneo S. Basso, a former church (open roughly Mon–Sat 9:30–17:30, Sun 14:00–16:30; from Piazzetta dei Leoncini to the left of basilica, head down Calle S. Basso, 2nd door on your right).

Those with a bag to check actually get to skip the line. Here's how it works: Drop by Ateneo S. Basso. (Consider watching the free 12-min intro video about St. Mark's Basilica.) Leave your bag and pick up the tag. Two people per tag are allowed to go to the basilica's gatekeeper and scoot directly in (ahead of the line). After touring the church, come back and pick up your bag.

Theft Alert: St. Mark's Basilica is the most dangerous place in Venice for pickpocketing—inside, it's always a crowded jostle.

Information: Tel. 041-522-5205. Guidebooks are sold in the bookstand in the basilica's atrium.

Services: There's a public pay WC just beyond the far end of St. Mark's Square. Another one is around the corner of the Piazzetta, near the Royal Gardens (Giardinetti Reali) and TI on the lagoon. Yet another WC is inside the San Marco Museum.

Tours: In the atrium, see the schedule board that lists free English-language guided tours (schedules vary, but generally May–Oct Tue, Wed, and Thu at 11:00, 1 hr, meet guide just to the right of main doors, tel. 041-270-2421).

Length of This Tour: Allow one hour.

Cuisine Art: Pricier cafés offering live music are on St. Mark's Square; less expensive bars are just off the square (see page 60).

Photography: Not allowed.

Starring: St. Mark, Byzantium, mosaics, and ancient bronze horses.

THE TOUR BEGINS

A complete visit to St. Mark's includes the church (free), plus three separate museums inside (with admission fees)—all described in this chapter.

St. Mark's Basilica

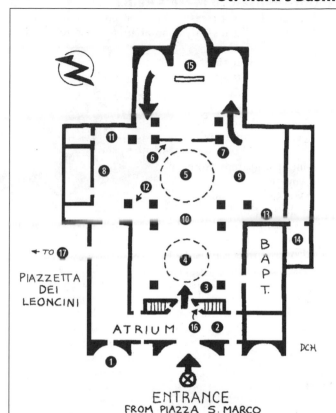

1. Exterior – Mosaic of Mark's Relics

2. Atrium – Mosaic of Noah's Ark and the Great Flood

3. Nave – Mosaics and Greek Cross Floor Plan

4. Pentecost Mosaic

5. Central Dome – Ascension Mosaic

6. Rood Screen

7. Doge's Pulpit

8. Tree of Jesse Mosaic

9. Last Supper Mosaic

10. Crucifixion Mosaic

11. Nicopeia Icon

12. Rifle on Pillar

13. Discovery of Mark Mosaic

14. Treasury

15. Golden Altarpiece

16. Stairs up to Loggia: San Marco Museum & Bronze Horses

17. To Ateneo S. Basso Bag Check across Square

Exterior—Mosaic of Mark's Relics

St. Mark's Basilica is a treasure chest of booty looted during Venice's glory days. That's only appropriate for a church built on the bones of a stolen saint.

The **mosaic over the far left door** shows the theft that put Venice on the pilgrimage map. Two men (in the center, with crooked staffs) enter the church bearing a coffin with the body of St. Mark, who looks somewhat grumpy from the long voyage.

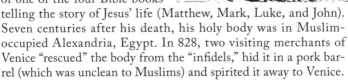

St. Mark was the author of one of the four Bible books telling the story of Jesus' life (Matthew, Mark, Luke, and John). Seven centuries after his death, his holy body was in Muslim-occupied Alexandria, Egypt. In 828, two visiting merchants of Venice "rescued" the body from the "infidels," hid it in a pork barrel (which was unclean to Muslims) and spirited it away to Venice.

The merchants presented the body—not to a pope or bishop—but to the doge (with white ermine collar, on the right) and his

wife, the dogaressa (with entourage, on the left), giving instant status to Venice's budding secular state. They built a church here over Mark's bones and made him the patron saint of the city. You'll see his symbol, the winged lion, all over Venice.

The original church burned down in 976. Today's structure was begun in 1063. The mosaic, from 1260, shows that the church hasn't changed much since then—you can see the onion domes and famous bronze horses on the balcony.

The St. Mark's you see today, mostly from the 11th century, was modeled after a sixth-century church in Constantinople. Venice needed roots. By building a retro church, the city could imply that it had been around for longer than it actually was. (Throughout European history, upstarts loved to fake deep roots this way. Germany embraced mystic, medieval lore as it emerged as a modern nation in the 19th century, England cooked up the King Arthur legend, and so on.)

In subsequent centuries, the church was encrusted with materials looted from buildings throughout the Venetian empire. Their prize booty was the four bronze horses that adorn the balcony,

---

St. Mark's...Cathedral, Church, or Basilica?

All three are correct. The church is also a cathedral, because it's the home church of the local bishop. It's a basilica, because it's the home of a patriarch and because the meaning of "basilica" evolved into an honorary title conferred on select churches by the pope. Coincidentally, it's also a basilica in the architectural sense. Its floor plan (if you ignore the transepts) has a central nave with flanking side aisles, a layout patterned after the ancient Roman law buildings called "basilicas." The transepts turn the basilica plan into a cross—in this case, a Greek cross, since it has four equal arms.

---

stolen from Constantinople during the Fourth Crusades (these are copies, as the originals are housed inside the church museum). The architectural style of St. Mark's has been called "Early Ransack."

• *Enter the atrium (entrance hall) of the basilica, past the guard who makes sure all who enter have covered legs and shoulders. The door is a sixth-century, bronze-paneled, Byzantine job.*

Immediately after entering the first door (crowd flow permitting), peel off to the right, and look overhead into an archway (not a dome) decorated with fine mosaics.

Atrium—Mosaic of Noah's Ark and the Great Flood

St. Mark's famous mosaics, with their picture symbols, were easily

understood in medieval times, even by illiterate masses. Today's literate masses have trouble reading them, so let's practice on these, some of the oldest (13th century), finest, and most accessible mosaics in the church.

Turn around and face the door you just came through, and to your left you'll see (on top of the arch) scenes from the story of Noah's Ark. Venetians—who were great ship builders—related to the Ark. At it's peak, Venice's Arsenale warship building plant employed several thousand. Nearby, the mosaic of the tower of Babel looks just like the Campanile tower outside. The mosaics show the Venetian view of the world in the 12th century. They saw things on their terms, from their perspective.

Take a closer look at the Ark scenes. Noah and sons are sawing logs to build the boat. Below that are three scenes of Noah putting all species of animals into the Ark, two by two. (Who's at the head of the line? Lions.) Turning around and facing the church interior, you'll see the Flood in full force, drowning the wicked. Noah sends out a dove twice to see whether there's any dry land where he can dock. He finds it, leaves the Ark with a gorgeous rainbow overhead, and offers a sacrifice of thanks to God. Easy, huh?

• *Now that our medieval literacy rate has risen, rejoin the slow flow of people. As you inch along, remember you're stepping on marble mosaics that were "inherited" from Constantinople. Notice the entrance to the San Marco Museum* (Loggia dei Cavalli), *which you can visit later. Glance above the door at the golden mosaic of Mark who opens his arms to say, "Welcome to my church." Now climb seven steps, pass through the doorway, and enter the nave. Loiter somewhere just inside the door (crowd flow permitting) and let your eyes adjust.*

The Nave—Mosaics and Greek Cross Floor Plan

The initial effect is dark and unimpressive (unless they've got the floodlights on). But as your pupils slowly unclench, you'll notice

that the entire upper part is decorated in mosaic—4,750 square yards (imagine paving a football field with contact lenses). These golden mosaics are in the Byzantine style, though many were designed by artists from the Italian Renaissance and later. The often-overlooked lower walls are covered with green-, yellow-, purple-, and rose-colored marble slabs, cut to expose the grain, and laid out in geometric patterns. Even the floor is mosaic, mostly geometrical designs. It rolls like the sea. Venice is sinking and shifting, creating these cresting waves of stone.

The church is laid out with four equal arms, topped with domes, radiating out from the center to form a Greek Cross (+). Those familiar with Eastern Orthodox churches will find familiar elements in St. Mark's—a central floor plan, domes, mosaics, and iconic images of Mary and Christ as Pantocrator. As your eyes adjust, the mosaics start to give off a "mystical, golden luminosity," the atmosphere of the Byzantine heaven. The air itself seems almost visible, like a cloud of incense. It's a subtle effect, one that grows on you as the filtered light changes. There are more beautiful, bigger, more overwhelming, and even holier churches, but none is as stately.

• *Find the chandelier near the entrance doorway (in the shape of a Greek Cross cathedral space station), and run your eyes up the support chain to the dome above.*

Mosaics

St. Mark's mosaics are designs or pictures made with small cubes of colored stone or glass pressed into wet plaster. Ancient Romans paved floors, walls, and ceilings with them. When Rome "fell," the art form died out in the West but was

carried on by Byzantine craftsmen. They perfected the gold background effect by baking gold leaf into tiny cubes of glass called *tesserae* (tiles). The uneven surfaces of the tiles give off a shimmering effect. The reflecting gold mosaics helped to light thick-walled, small-windowed, lantern-lit Byzantine churches, creating a golden glow that symbolized the divine light of heaven.

St. Mark's mosaics tell the entire Christian history from end to beginning. Entering the church, you're greeted with scenes from the end of the world (Apocalypse) and the Pentecost. As you approach the altar, you walk backward in time to the source, experiencing Jesus' Passion and crucifixion, his miraculous life, and continuing back to his birth and Old Testament predecessors. Over the altar at the far end of the church (and over the entrance door at the near end) are images of Christ—the beginning and the end, the Alpha and Omega of the Christian universe.

Pentecost Mosaic

In a golden heaven, the dove of the Holy Spirit shoots out a pin-

wheel of spiritual lasers, igniting tongues of fire on the heads of the 12 apostles below, giving them the ability to speak other languages without a Rick Steves phrase book. You'd think they'd be amazed, but their expressions are as solemn as... icons. One of the oldest mosaics in the church (c. 1125), it has distinct "Byzantine" features: a gold background and apostles with halos, solemn faces, almond eyes, delicate blessing hands, and rumpled robes, all facing forward.

This is art from a society still touchy about the Bible's commandment against making "graven images" of holy things. Byzantium had recently emerged from two centuries of

Byzantium

The Byzantine Empire was the eastern half of the ancient Roman Empire that *didn't* "fall" in A.D. 476. It remained Christian, Greek-speaking, and enlightened for another thousand years.

In A.D. 330, Constantine, the first Christian emperor, moved the Roman Empire's capital to the newly expanded city of Byzantium, which he humbly renamed Constantinople (modern Istanbul). With him went Rome's best and brightest. When the city of Rome decayed and fell, plunging western Europe into its "Dark Ages," Constantinople lived on as the greatest city in Europe.

Venice had strong ties with Byzantium from its earliest days. In the sixth century, Byzantine Emperor Justinian invaded northern Italy, briefly reuniting East and West, and making Ravenna his regional capital. In 800, Venetians asked the emperor in Constantinople to protect them from Charlemagne's marauding Franks.

Soon Venetian merchants were granted trading rights to Byzantine ports in the Adriatic and eastern Mediterranean. They traded raw materials from western Europe for luxury goods from the East.

When Muslim Turks threatened Christian Byzantium, the Venetians joined the Crusades, the series of military expeditions that were designed to "save" Jerusalem and Constantinople. Venetians grew rich renting ships to the Crusaders in exchange for money, favors, and booty.

During the Fourth Crusade (1202–1204), which went horribly awry, the Crusaders—led by the Venetian doge Dandolo—sacked

"Iconoclasm," in which statues and paintings were broken and burned as sinful "false gods." The Byzantine style emphasizes otherworldliness rather than literal human detail. The poet W. B. Yeats stood here and described what he saw: "O sages standing in God's holy fire as in the gold mosaic of a wall, come from the holy fire...and be the singing-masters of my soul."

• *Shuffle along with the crowds up to the central dome.*

Central Dome—Ascension Mosaic

Gape upward to the very heart of the church. Christ—having lived his miraculous life and having been crucified for man's sins—ascends into the starry sky on a rainbow. He raises his right hand and blesses the universe. This isn't the dead, crucified, mortal Jesus featured in most churches, but a powerful, resurrected god, the Ruler of All the Cosmos (Greek "Pantocrator").

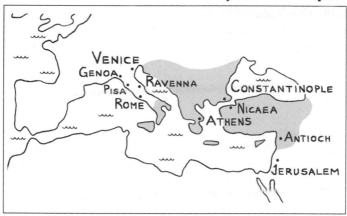

The Byzantine Empire

Constantinople, a fellow Christian city. This was, perhaps, the lowest point in Christian history, at least until the advent of TV evangelism. The Venetians carried home the bronze horses, the Pala d'Oro enamels, the Treasury's treasures, the Nicopeia icon, and much of the marble that now covers the (brick) church.

Venice rose while Byzantium faded. Then both civilizations nosedived when Constantinople finally fell to the Turks in 1453.

Today, we find hints of Byzantium in the Eastern Orthodox Church, in mosaics and icons, and in the looted treasures shipped back to Venice.

Christ's blessing radiates out, rippling down to the ring of white-robed apostles below. They stand amid the trees of the Mount of Olives, waving good-bye as Christ ascends. Mary is with them, wearing blue with golden Greek crosses on each shoulder and looking ready to play pattycake. From these saints, goodness descends, creating the Virtues that ring the base of the dome between the windows. In Byzantine churches, the window-lit dome represented heaven, while the dark church below represented Earth—a microcosm of the hierarchical universe.

Beneath the dome at the four corners, the four Gospel writers ("Matev," "Marc," "Luca," and "Ioh") thoughtfully scribble down the heavenly events. This wisdom flows down like water from the symbolic Four Rivers below them, spreading through the church's four equal arms (the "four corners" of the world), and baptizing the congregation with God's love. The church building is a series of perfect circles within perfect squares—the cosmic order—with

Christ in the center solemnly blessing us. God's in his heaven, saints are on Earth, and all's right with the world.

Under the Ascension Dome— The Church as Theater

Look around at the church's furniture and imagine a service here. The **rood screen** topped with 14 saints separates the congregation from the high altar, heightening the "mystery" of the Mass. The **pulpit on the right** was reserved for the doge, who led prayers and made important announcements. Mosaics were visual aids for the priest, telling the whole story of Jesus, from his ancestors perched in the **Tree of Jesse** (in the north transept; facing the altar, turn 90-degrees left, and it's on the far north wall), to the **Last Supper** (in the arch leading to the south transept), to the **Crucifixion** (in the west arch).

The Crucifixion mosaic features a stick-figure Christ, emphasizing the symbolic solemnity of the moment, not its Mel Gibson gruesomeness. In fact, there aren't very many crucifixes at all in the church, giving it an Eastern Orthodox flavor. While Western Christianity focuses on the death of Jesus, to Orthodox believers, Christ's death is just the tragic Act I. Other scenes in the arch show the rest of the story, Christ's triumphant Resurrection and post-death miracles, leading to the climax, his Ascension (in the central dome).

The Venetian church service is a theatrical multimedia spectacle, combining words (prayers, biblical passages, Latin and Greek phrases), music (chants, a choir, organ, horns, strings), costumes and props (priests' robes, golden reliquaries, candles, incense), set design (the mosaics, rood screen, Golden Altarpiece), and even stage direction (processionals through the crowd, priests' motions, standing, sitting, kneeling, crossing yourself). The symmetrical church is itself part of the set design. The Greek-cross floor plan symbolizes perfection, rather than the more common Latin cross of the crucifixion (emphasizing man's sinfulness). Coincidentally or not, the first modern opera—also a multimedia theatrical experience—was written by St. Mark's *maestro di cappella,* Claudio Monteverdi (1567–1643).

North Transept

In the north transept (the arm of the church to the left of the altar), today's Venetians pray to a painted wooden icon of Mary and baby Jesus known as **Nicopeia,** or "Our Lady of Victory" (on the east wall of the north transept). Supposedly painted personally by the evangelist Luke, it was once enameled with bright paint and precious stones, and Mary was adorned with a crown and necklace of gold and jewels (now on display in the Treasury). This Madonna

Christ as Pantocrator

Most Eastern Orthodox churches have at least one mosaic or painting of Christ in a standard pose—as "Pantocrator," a Greek word meaning "Ruler of All." St. Mark's features several Pantocrators, including the central dome, over the altar, and over the entrance door. The image, so familiar to Orthodox Christians, is a bit foreign to Protestants, Catholics, and secularists.

As King of the Universe, Christ sits (usually on a throne) facing directly out, with penetrating eyes. He wears a halo divided with a cross, worn only by the Trinity. In his left hand is a Bible, while his right hand blesses, with the fingers forming the Greek letters Chi and Rho, the first two letters of "Christos." The thumb touches the fingers, symbolizing how Christ unites both his divinity and his humanity. On either side of Christ's head are the Greek letters "IC XC," short for "IesuC XristoC."

has helped Venice persevere through plagues, wars, and crucial soccer games. When Mary answers a prayer, grateful Venetians give her offerings, like the old **rifle** that hangs on a pillar (as you approach the north transept). A wife prayed to the Madonna for her husband's safe return from war with Austria in 1848. When he came home alive, she gave his rifle to the Virgin in thanks.

• *In the south transept (to right of main altar), find the dim mosaic on the west wall.*

Discovery of Mark Mosaic

Not a biblical scene, this mosaic depicts the miraculous event that capped the construction of the present church.

It's 1094, the church is nearly complete (see the domes shown in cutaway fashion), and they're all set to re-inter Mark's bones under the new altar. There's just one problem: During the decades of construction, they forgot where they'd stored his body!

So (in the left half of the mosaic), all of Venice gathers inside the church to bow down and pray for help finding the bones. The doge (from the Latin "dux") leads them. Soon after (the right half), the patriarch (far right) is inspired to look inside a hollow column where he finds the relics. Everyone turns and applauds, including the womenfolk (left side of scene), who stream in from the upper-floor galleries. The relics were soon placed under the altar in a ceremony that inaugurated the current structure.

The south transept also features horseshoe arches atop slender columns, giving the transept the exotic flavor of a Muslim mosque. The door under the rose window leads directly from the Doge's

Palace. On important occasions, the doge entered the church through here, ascended the steps of his pulpit, and addressed the people.

ST. MARK'S THREE MUSEUMS

Inside the church are three sights, each requiring a separate admission. The Treasury and Golden Altarpiece are viewable during the church's opening hours; the San Marco Museum is open Mon–Sat 9:45–16:30, Sun 9:45–16:00. None is a must-see, but they're your best chance (outside of Istanbul or Ravenna) to soak up Byzantine ambience.

Treasury (Tesoro)

• *The Treasury is in the south transept. Admission is €2 (includes audio-guide when available—ask for it). The collection is housed in three tiny rooms.*

You'll see Byzantine chalices, silver reliquaries, monstrous monstrances (for displaying the Communion wafer), and icons done in gold, silver, enamels, gems, and semiprecious stones. Some pieces represent the fruit of labor by different civilizations over a thousand-year period. For example, an ancient rock-crystal chalice made by the Romans might be decorated centuries later with Byzantine enamels, and then finished still later with gold filigree by Venetian goldsmiths. This is marvelous handiwork, but all the more marvelous for having been done when western Europe was still rooting in the mud. Here are some highlights.

Entryway: The so-called Throne of St. Mark, just as you enter, is one of the church's oldest Christian objects (around A.D. 550). Created when Europe was being overrun by pagan hordes (and early Venetians were hiding in the marshes), its sheer bulk and carved Tree of Life offered Christians an image of stability.

• *We'll tour the main room counterclockwise. But first, start at the glass case in the center of the room.*

Main Room: The glass case in the center of the room holds the most precious Byzantine objects. The hanging lamp with the protruding fish features fourth-century Roman rock-crystal framed in 11th-century Byzantine metalwork. Just behind it, a purple bucket, carved with scenes of satyrs chasing nymphs, epitomizes the pagan world that was fading as Christianity triumphed. Also in the case are blue-and-gold lapis lazuli icons of the Crucifixion and of the Archangel Michael featuring a Byzantine specialty—enamel work (more on that craft at the Golden Altarpiece). See various chalices (cups used for the bread and wine during Mass) made of onyx, agate, and rock crystal, and an incense burner shaped like a domed church.

The Legend (Mixed with a Little Truth) of Mark and Venice

Mark (died c. A.D. 68) was a Jewish-born Christian, and he might have actually met Jesus. (The Bible mentions a "Mark" and a "John Mark" who may have been him.) He traveled with fellow convert Paul, eventually settling in Alexandria as the city's first Christian bishop. On a trip to Rome, Peter—Jesus' right-hand man—asked him to write down the events of Jesus' life that became the Gospel of Mark.

During his travels, Mark stopped in the lagoon (in Aquileia on the north coast), where he dreamed of a Latin-speaking angel who said, *"Pax tibi Marce, evangelista meus"* ("Peace to you, Mark, my evangelist"), promising him rest after death. Back in Alexandria, Mark was attacked by an anti-Christian mob. They tied him with ropes and dragged his body through the streets until he died.

Eight centuries later, his body lay in an Alexandrian church about to be vandalized by Muslim fanatics. Two Venetian traders on a business trip saved the relics from desecration by hiding them in a basket of pork—a meat considered unclean by Muslims—and quickly setting sail. The perilous voyage home was only completed after many more miracles. The doge received the body and, in 828, they built the first church of St. Mark's to house it. During construction of the current church (1094), Mark's relics were temporarily lost, and it took another miracle to find them, hidden inside a column. Today, Venetians celebrate Mark on the traditional date of his martyrdom, April 25.

The events of Mark's life are portrayed vividly in many frescoes throughout the Basilica. Unfortunately, most of them are either off-limits to tourists or in the dim reaches of the church. Enjoy them by buying a St. Mark's guidebook with photos.

Along the walls, find the following displays (working counterclockwise around the room): In a glass case, find several objects made by Muslims, Venice's other trading partners to the east. Next comes the Urn of Artaxerxes I (middle of the right wall), an Egyptian-made object that once held the ashes of the great Persian king who ruled 2,500 years ago (r. 465–425 B.C.). The next glass case has bishops' robes and a 600-year-old crosier (ceremonial shepherd staff) still used today by the chief priest on holy days.

Next is the Ciborio di Anastasia (far left corner), a small marble canopy that once arched over the blessed communion wafer during Mass. The object may be a gift from "Anastasia," the name carved on it in Greek. She was a lady-in-waiting in the court of the emperor Justinian (483–565). Christian legend has it that she was so beautiful that Justinian (a married man) pursued her amorously and so she had to dress like a monk and flee to a desert monastery.

As you leave, notice the granite column that extends below current floor level—you can see how the floor has risen as things have settled in the last 1,000 years.

Relics/Sanctuary Room: Straight ahead, the glass case over the alabaster altar contains elaborate golden reliquaries holding relics of Jesus' Passion—his torture and execution. For example, the reliquary in the center (from 1125), showing Christ being whipped, holds a stone from the column he was tied to. You may scoff, but of all of Europe's "Pieces of the True Cross" and "Crown of Thorns," these have at least some claim of authenticity. Legend has it that Christ's possessions were gathered up in the fourth century by Constantine's mother and taken to Constantinople. During the Crusade heist of 1204, Venetians brought them here. They've been paraded through the city every Good Friday for 800 years.

Immediately to the left of the room's entrance is a reliquary with the bones of Doge Orseolo (r. 976–978), who built the church that preceded the current structure, and those of St. George, legendary dragon slayer.

Golden Altarpiece (Pala d'Oro)

• *The Golden Altarpiece is located behind the main altar. The admission is €2.*

Under the stone canopy sits the high altar. Inside the altar is an urn (not visible) with the mortal remains of Mark, the Gospel writer. (Look through the grate of the altar to read, *"Corpus Divi Marci Evangelistae,"* or Body of the Evangelist Mark.) He rests in peace, as an angel had promised him. Shh.

As you shuffle along, notice the marble canopy's support columns carved with New Testament scenes in the 13th century. (On the right-hand pillar closest to the altarpiece, fourth row from the bottom: Is that a genie escaping from a bottle while someone tries to stuff him back in?)

The Golden Altarpiece is a stunning golden wall made of 250 blue-backed enamels with religious scenes, all set in a gold frame and studded with 15 hefty rubies, 300 emeralds, 1,500 pearls, and assorted sapphires, amethysts, and topaz. The Byzantine-made enamels (c. 1100) were part of the Venetians' plunder of 1204, subsequently pieced together by Byzantine craftsmen specifically

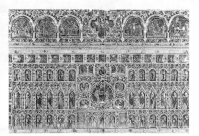

for St. Mark's high altar. It's a bit much to take in all at once, but get up close and find several details you might recognize:

In the center, Jesus as Ruler of the Cosmos sits on a golden throne, with a halo of pearls and jewels. Like a good Byzantine Pantocrator, he dutifully faces forward and gives his blessing while stealing a glance offstage at Mark ("Marcus") and the other saints.

Along the bottom row, Old Testament prophets show off the Bible's books they've written. With halos, solemn faces, and elaborately creased robes, they epitomize the Byzantine icon style.

Follow Mark's story in the panels along the sides. In the bottom left panel, Mark meets Peter (seated) at the gates of Rome. It was Peter (legend has it) who gave Mark the eyewitness account of Jesus' life that Mark wrote down in his Gospel. Mark's story ends in the bottom right panel with the two Venetian merchants returning by ship, carrying his coffin here to be laid to rest.

Byzantium excelled in the art of *cloisonné* enameling. A piece of gold leaf is stamped with a design, then filled in with pools of enamel paint, which are baked on. Look at a single saint to see the detail work: The gold background around the saint is the gold-leaf medallion that gets stamped. The golden folds in the robe are the raised edges of the impression. The different colors of the robe are different-colored paints in the recessed areas, each color baked on in a separate firing. Some saints even have pearl crowns or jewel collars pinned on. This kind of craftsmanship—and the social infrastructure that could afford it—made Byzantium seem like an enchanted world during Europe's dim Middle Ages.

Once you've looked at some individual scenes, back up as far as this small room will let you and just let yourself be dazzled by the "whole picture"—this "mosaic" of Byzantine greatness. This magnificent altarpiece sits on a swivel (notice the mechanism at its base) and is swung around on festival Sundays so the entire congregation can enjoy it.

San Marco Museum (Museo di San Marco)— Bronze Horses, View of the Piazza, and More

• *This is the one sight certainly worth the admission price, if only for the views of St. Mark's Square, the Piazzetta, and the interior of the church from above. The staircase up to the museum is in the atrium near the main entrance. The sign says* Loggia dei Cavalli, Museo. *The museum costs €3. Once upstairs, belly up to the center of the stone balustrade to survey the interior.*

View of Church Interior

Take a closer look at the Pentecost Mosaic (first dome above you, described earlier). The unique design at the very top signifies the Trinity: throne (God), Gospels (Christ), and dove (Holy Spirit). The couples below the ring of apostles are the people of the world (I can find Asia, Judaea, and Cappadocia), who, despite their different languages, still understood the Spirit's message.

If you were a woman in medieval Venice, you'd enjoy this same close-up view, because in the Middle Ages, women did not worship on the floor level. They climbed the same stairs you just did and found a spot along the balconies at your feet. The church was divided into three realms—the balcony for women, the nave for men, and the altar for the priests. Back then the rood screen (the fence with the 15 figures on it) separated the priest from the public, and he officiated with his back to the people.

From here you can appreciate the patterns of the mosaic floor—one of the finest in Italy—that covers the floor like a Persian carpet.

• *From here, the museum loops you to the far (altar) end of the church, then back to the bronze horses. Along the way, you'll see...*

Mosaic Fragments (Cassine)

These mosaics once hung in the church but when they became damaged or aesthetically old-fashioned, they were replaced by new and more fashionable mosaics. These few fragments avoided the garbage can. You'll see mosaics from the church's earliest days (and most "Byzantine" style, c. 1070) to the more recent (1700s) with realistic Renaissance detail.

The mosaics—made from small cubes of stone or colored glass pressed into wet clay—were assembled on the ground, then cemented onto the walls. Artists draw the pattern on paper, lay it on the wet clay, and slowly cut the paper away as they replace it with cubes. The first mosaic on your left as you enter shows a reproduction of a paper "cast" of a mosaic.

• *Continuing on, you'll see other artwork and catch glimpses of the interior of the church from the north transept. Descend the staircase to the next room, Sala Ongania (WCs to the right of entrance), which features drawings and watercolors made for the works of the basilica. Around the corner is a large room filled with displays.*

Sala dei Banchetti

The ornate room is filled with religious objects, tapestries, carpets that once carpeted the church, Burano lace, music manuscripts, a doge's throne, and much more.

Try reading some music. The manuscripts date from the 16th century—before the age of treble and bass clefs. You'll see a C clef (which could slide along the staff to locate middle C). From this, you could chant notes in proper relationship to each other according to the rhythm indicated.

The most prestigious artwork is the basilica's workaday altarpiece, the Pala Feriale, by Paolo Veneziano (1345). On ordinary workdays, these 14 scenes painted on wood covered the golden Pala d'Oro—seven saints above (including crucified Christ) and seven episodes in Mark's life below. The panel of the sailboat tells the story of the Venetian merchants' trip home with Mark's relics. A storm at sea billows their sails, ripples the flag, churns the waves, and scares the crew as the ship heads toward the rocks. But then Mark himself appears miraculously at the stern and calms the storm, bringing the ship (and his own body) safely to Venice. Paolo proudly signed his name (along the bottom) and the names of his two assistants, his sons Luca and Giovanni. The second half of the altarpiece (nearer to the exit of the room) is done in later Renaissance style by Matteo Verona (1614).

• *Now double back through displays of stone fragments from the church, finally arriving at*

The Bronze Horses (La Quadriga)

Stepping lively in pairs and with smiles on their faces, they exude energy and exuberance. Art historians don't know how old they are—they could be from ancient Greece (4th century B.C.) or ancient Rome during its Fall (4th century A.D.). They look Greek Hellenistic (2nd century B.C.) to me, and Professor Carbon Fourteen says they're from around 175 B.C. Originally, the horses pulled a chariot *Ben-Hur* style. These bronze statues were not hammered and bent into shape by metalsmiths, but were cast from clay molds by using the lost-wax technique. The bronze is high quality, with 97 percent copper. Originally gilded, they still have some

streaks of gold. Long gone are the ruby pupils that gave the horses the original case of "red eye."

Megalomaniacs through the ages have coveted these horses not only for their artistic value, but because they symbolize Apollo, the Greco-Roman god of the sun...and of secular power. The doge spoke to his people standing between the horses when they graced the balcony atop the church's facade (where the copies—which you'll see next—stand today).

Their expressive faces seem to say, "Oh boy, Wilbur, have we done some travelin'." Legend says they were made in the time of Alexander the Great, then taken by Nero to Rome. Constantine took them to his new capital in Constantinople to adorn the chariot racecourse. The Venetians then stole them from their fellow Christians during the looting of noble Constantinople and brought them to St. Mark's.

What goes around comes around, and Napoleon came around and took the horses when he conquered Venice in 1797. They stood atop a triumphal arch in Paris until Napoleon's empire was "blown-aparte" and they were returned to their "rightful" home.

The horses were again removed from their spot, when they were attacked by their most dangerous enemy yet—modern man. The threat of oxidation from pollution sent them galloping for cover inside the church.

• *The visit ends outside on the balcony overlooking St. Mark's Square.*

The Loggia and View of St. Mark's Square

You'll be drawn repeatedly to the viewpoint of the square, but remember to look at the facade to see how cleverly all the looted architectural elements blend together. Ramble among the statues of water-bearing slaves that serve as drain spouts. The horses are modern copies (note the 1978 date on their hoofs).

Be a doge, and stand between the bronze horses overlooking St. Mark's Square. Under the gilded lion of St. Mark, in front of the four great Evangelists (who once stood atop the columns), and flanked—like Apollo—by the four glorious horses, he inspired the Venetians in the square below to great things.

Admire the mesmerizing, commanding view of the center of this city, which so long ago was Europe's only superpower for centuries, and today is just a small town with a big history that's filled with tourists.

DOGE'S PALACE TOUR

(Palazzo Ducale)

Venice is a city of beautiful facades—palaces, churches, carnival masks—that can cover darker interiors of intrigue and decay. The Doge's Palace, with its frilly pink exterior, hides the fact that the "Most Serene Republic" (as it called itself—"serene" meaning stable) was far from serene in its heyday.

The Doge's Palace housed the fascinating government of this rich and powerful empire. It also served as the home for the Venetian ruler known as the doge (DOH-zheh), or duke. For four centuries (about 1150–1550), this was the most powerful half-acre in Europe. The rest of Europe marveled at the way Venice could govern itself without a dominant king, bishop, or tyrant. The doges wanted their palace to reflect the wealth and secular values of the Republic, impressing visitors and serving as a reminder that the Venetians were Number One in Europe.

ORIENTATION

Cost: Covered by the €11 Museum Card (valid for 3 months, 1 entry per museum), which also includes admission to the clock tower, Correr Museum, and two lesser museums at the Correr (National Archaeological Museum and the Monumental Rooms of the Marciana National Library). The pricier Museum Pass costs €15.50 and includes the above museums, plus Ca' Rezzonico, the museums on the neighboring islands, and more. (For more about these passes, see "Passes for Venice," page 24.)

Hours: Daily April–Oct 9:00–19:00, Nov–March 9:00–17:00, last entry 1 hr before closing.

Getting There: The palace is next to St. Mark's Basilica, on the lagoon waterfront, and just off St. Mark's Square. Vaporetto stop: San Marco/Vallaresso.

Doge's Palace

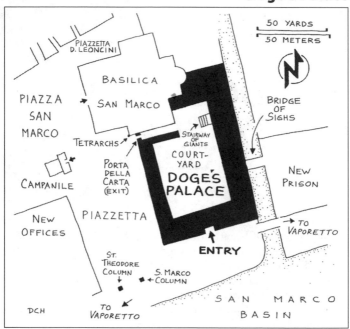

Crowd Control: To avoid the long peak-season line at the Doge's Palace, you have several options (the first is best):

    1. Buy your Museum Card at the Correr Museum (at far end of St. Mark's Square), then go directly to the turnstile of the Doge's Palace, skirting along to the right of the long line at the palace entrance. You'll need to go through the same turnstile as people buying their tickets at the palace, but you won't have to wait in line.

    2. If your visit falls between April and October, visit the palace at about 17:00, when the line disappears (but note that the museum closes at 19:00 and the last entry is 18:00).

    3. Book a guided "Secret Itineraries Tour" (see "Tours," below). The only (minor) drawback is that your palace entry fee does not include the Correr Museum.

Information: There are some English descriptions. Guidebooks are on sale in the bookshop. Tel. 041-271-5911.

Services: Some WCs are in the courtyard near the palace exit; more are halfway up the stairs to the balcony level.

Tours: The high-tech PalmPilot **audioguide tour** is informative but dry (€5.50, 90 min, need ID or credit card for deposit). Pick it up after you pass through the turnstile after the ticket counter.

The fine **"Secret Itineraries Tour,"** which follows the doge's footsteps through rooms not included in the general admission price, must be booked in advance (€12.50; in English at 9:55, 10:45 and 11:35; 75 min, arrive 20 min early to check in, no need to wait in line, just *"scusi"* your way to the information desk in the room before the ticket counter). To make the reservation for the tour, call 041-291-5911 if you're reserving for visits on the same day or the day before, or call 041-520-9070 for visits more than two days in advance. After you pick up your tickets, go to the group meeting point in the courtyard to the left just after you pass through the turnstile. If you haven't booked ahead, you could try showing up at the information desk at 9:00 to get a spot on the 9:55 tour (and pass any wait time by going up the Campanile), but since tours are limited to 25, you are most likely to get a spot by reserving in advance. The cost includes admission only to the Doge's Palace (and allows you to bypass the long line). While the tour skips the main halls inside, it finishes inside the palace, and you're welcome to visit the halls on your own (but you cannot return to visit once you leave the palace).

Length of This Tour: Allow 90 minutes.

Cuisine Art: Pricey cafeteria in Doge's Palace to the left of the bag check (behind grand staircase) accessed from the courtyard, expensive cafés on St. Mark's Square, cheaper bars/cafés off the square, and a handy canalside gelato shop on the Piazzetta (the small square with 2 big columns) across from the Doge's Palace.

Photography: Not allowed.

Starring: Tintoretto and the doges.

THE TOUR BEGINS

Exterior

"The Wedding Cake," "The Table Cloth," or "The Pink House" is also sometimes known as the Doge's Palace. The style is called Venetian Gothic—a fusion of Italian Gothic with a delicate Islamic flair. The columns originally had bases on the bottoms,

but these were covered over as the columns sank, and the square was built up over the centuries. If you compare this lacy, top-heavy structure with the massive fortress palaces of Florence, you realize the wisdom of building a city in the middle of the sea—you have no natural enemies except gravity. This unfortified palace in a city with no city wall was the doge's way of saying, "I am an elected and loved ruler. I do not fear my own people."

The palace was originally built in the 800s, but most of what we see came after 1300, as it was expanded to meet the needs of the empire. Each doge wanted to leave his mark on history with a new wing. But so much of the city's money was spent on the building that finally a law was passed levying an enormous fine on anyone who even mentioned any new building. That worked for a while, until one brave and wealthy doge proposed a new wing, paid his fine...and started building again.

• *Enter the Doge's Palace from along the waterfront. After you pass through the turnstile, ignore the signs and cross the square to stand at the foot of the grand staircase.*

The Courtyard and the Stairway of Giants (Scala dei Giganti)

Imagine yourself as a foreign dignitary on business to meet the doge. In the courtyard, you look up a grand staircase topped

with two nearly nude statues of, I think, Moses and Paul Newman (more likely, Neptune and Mars, representing Venice's prowess at sea and at war). The doge and his aides would be waiting for you at the top, between the two statues and beneath the Winged Lion. No matter who you were—king, pope, or emperor—you'd have to hoof it up. The powerful doge would descend the stairs for no one.

Many doges were crowned here, between the two statues. The doge was something like an "elected king"—which makes sense only in the "dictatorial republic" that was Venice. Technically, he was just a noble selected by other nobles to carry out their laws and decisions. Many doges tried to extend their powers and rule more as divine-right kings. Many others just put on their funny hats and accepted their role as figurehead and ceremonial ribbon-cutter. Most were geezers, elected in their seventies and committed to preserving the Venetian traditions.

The palace is attached to the church, symbolically welding together church and state. Both buildings have ugly brick behind a painted-lady veneer of marble. In this tour, we'll see the similarly harsh inner workings of an outwardly serene, polished republic.

In the courtyard, you'll see a hodgepodge of architecture

styles, as the palace was refurbished over the centuries. There are classical statues in Renaissance niches, shaded by Baroque awnings, topped by Flamboyant Gothic spires, and crusted with the Byzantine onion domes of St. Mark's Basilica.

• *Cross back to near the entrance, and follow the signs up the tourists' staircase to the first-floor balcony (loggias), where you can look back down on the courtyard (but not the backside of Paul Newman). From here on, it's hard to get lost (though I've managed). It's a one-way system, so just follow the arrows.*

Midway along the balcony, you'll find a face in the wall, the...

Mouth of Truth

This fierce-looking androgyne opens his/her mouth, ready to swallow a piece of paper, hungry for gossip. Letterboxes like this (some with lions' heads) were scattered throughout the palace. Originally, anyone who had a complaint or suspicion about anyone else could accuse him anonymously *(denontie secrete)* by simply dropping a slip of paper in the mouth. This

set the blades of justice turning inside the palace.

• *Towards Paul Newman is the entrance to the...*

Golden Staircase (Scala d'Oro)

The palace was propaganda, designed to impress visitors. This 24-karat gilded-ceiling staircase was something for them to write home about. As you ascend the stairs, look back at the floor below and marvel at its 3-D pattern.

• *Take the Golden Staircase to the first landing (Primo Piano Nobile), and turn right, which takes you up into the...*

Doge's Apartments (Appartamenti Ducale)

The dozen or so rooms on the first floor are where the doge actually lived. Wander around this once sumptuous, now sparse suite, admiring coffered wood ceilings, chandeliers, velvet-covered walls, and very little furniture, since doges were expected to bring their own. Despite his high office, the doge had to obey several rules that bound him to the city. He couldn't leave the palace unescorted, he couldn't open official mail in private, and he and his family had to leave their own home and live in the Doge's Palace.

Just off the main hall, pop up the humble stairway and look back at a Titian quickie, painted in just three days. This fresco of St. Christopher was made for a doge who believed that if you looked at St. Christopher, then you wouldn't die that day.

In the large Room 6 (the Scudo, or "Shield" Room), which is ringed with maps, work clockwise around the room to trace the eye-opening trip across Asia—from Italy to Greece (quite accurate maps) to Palestine, Arabia, and "Irac"—of local boy Marco Polo (c. 1254–1325). Finally, he arrived at the other side of the world. This last map (shown upside-down, with south on top) gives a glimpse of the Venetian worldview circa 1550. There's China, Taiwan (Formosa), and Japan (Giapan), while America is a nearby island with California and lots of Terre Incognite.

• *After browsing the dozen or so private rooms, continue up the Golden Staircase to the third floor, which was the "public" part of the palace. The first room at the top of the stairs is the...*

Square Room (Atrio Quadrato)

The ceiling painting, *Justice Presenting the Sword and Scales to Doge Girolamo Priuli* is by Tintoretto. (Stand at the top of the painting for the full 3-D effect.) It's a late-Renaissance masterpiece. So what? As you'll soon see, this palace is wallpapered with Titians, Tintorettos, and Veroneses. Many have the same theme you see here: a doge, in his ermine cape, gold-brocaded robe, and funny one-horned hat with earflaps, kneeling in the presence of saints, gods, or mythological figures.

• *Enter the next room.*

Room of the Four Doors
(Sala delle Quattro Porte)

This was the central clearinghouse for all the goings-on in the palace. Visitors presented themselves here and were directed to their destination—the courts, councils, or doge himself.

The room was designed by Andrea Palladio, the architect who did the impressive Church of San Giorgio Maggiore, across the Grand Canal from St. Mark's Square. On the intricate stucco ceiling, notice the feet of the women dangling down below the edge (above the windows), extending the illusion.

On the wall next to the door you entered is a painting by (ho-hum) Titian, showing a **doge kneeling** with great piety before a woman embodying Faith holding the Cross of Jesus. Notice old Venice in the misty distance under the cross. This is one of many paintings you'll see of doges in uncharacteristically humble poses—paid for, of course, by the doges themselves.

Paintings by Titian, Veronese, and Tintoretto

The doge had only the top Venetian painters decorate his palace. While the palace was once rich in Titians, fires in the late 1500s destroyed nearly all the work by the greatest Venetian master. As the palace was hastily reconstructed, the Titians were replaced with works by Veronese and Tintoretto. (Most of these canvases were painted in workshops, and quickly patched in to fill empty spaces.)

Veronese used the best pigments available—from precious stones, sapphires, and emeralds—and his colors have survived vividly. These Veronese paintings are by his hand and are fine examples of his genius. Tintoretto, on the other hand, didn't really have his heart in these commissions, and the pieces here were done by his workshop.

The paintings of the Doge's Palace are a study of old Venice, with fine views of the old city and its inhabitants. The extravagant women's gowns in the paintings of Veronese show off a major local industry—textiles. While the paintings are not generally of masterpiece quality, they're historically interesting. They prove that in the old days, Venice had no pigeons.

G. B. Tiepolo's well-known *Venice Receiving Neptune* (now displayed on an easel, but originally on the wall above the windows where they've put a copy; you'll get closer to the painting as you progress through the museum). The painting shows Venice as a woman—Venice is always a woman to artists—reclining in luxury, dressed in the ermine cape and pearl necklace of a doge's wife *(dogaressa)*. Crude Neptune, enthralled by the First Lady's beauty, arrives bearing a seashell bulging with gold ducats. A bored Venice points and says, "Put it over there with the other stuff."

• *Enter the small room with the big fireplace and several paintings.*

✓ Sala dell'Anticollegio

It took a big title or bribe to get in to see the doge. Once accepted for a visit, you would wait here before you entered, combing your hair, adjusting your robe, popping a breath mint, and preparing the gifts you'd brought. While you cooled your heels and warmed your hands at the elaborate fireplace, you might look at some of the paintings—among the finest in the palace, worthy of any museum in the world.

The Rape of Europa, by Paolo Veronese (on the wall opposite the fireplace), most likely shocked many small-town visitors with its risqué subject matter. Here Zeus, the king of the Greek gods,

appears in the form of a bull with a foot
fetish, seducing a beautiful earthling, while
cupids spin playfully overhead. The Venetian
Renaissance looked back to pagan Greek
and Roman art, a big change from the saints
and crucifixions of the Middle Ages. This
painting doesn't portray the abduction as a
medieval condemnation of sex and violence,
but rather as a celebration in cheery pastel
colors of the earthy, optimistic spirit of the
Renaissance.

✓ Tintoretto's ***Bacchus and Ariadne*** (to
the left of the exit door) is another colorful display of Venice's

sensual tastes. The God of Wine
seeks a threesome, offering a ring
to the mortal Ariadne, who's
being crowned with stars by
Venus, who turns slowly in zero
gravity. The ring is the center of
a spinning wheel of flesh, with
the three arms like spokes.

But wait, the doge is ready
for us. Let's go in.

• *Enter the next room and approach your imaginary doge.*

✓ Sala del Collegio

Flanked by his cabinet of six advisers—one for each Venetian
neighborhood—the doge would sit on the wood-paneled platform
at the far end to receive ambassadors, who laid their gifts at his feet
and pleaded their countries' cases. All official ceremonies, such as
the ratification of treaties, were held here.

At other times, it was the "Oval Office" where the doge and
his cabinet (the executive branch) met privately to discuss proposals to give the legislature, pull files from the cabinets (along the
right wall) regarding business with Byzantium, or rehearse a meeting with the pope. The wooden benches around the sides (where
they sat) are original. The clock on the wall is a backward-running
24-hour clock with Roman numerals and a sword for hands.

The ceiling is 24-karat gold, with paintings by Veronese.
These are not frescoes (painting on wet plaster), like in the Sistine
Chapel, but actual canvases painted in Veronese's studio and then
placed on the ceiling. Within years, Venice's humidity would have
melted frescoes like so much mascara.

The T-shaped painting of the woman with the spiderweb (on
the ceiling, opposite the big window) was the Venetian symbol of
Discussion. You can imagine the webs of truth and lies woven in

Executive and Legislative Rooms

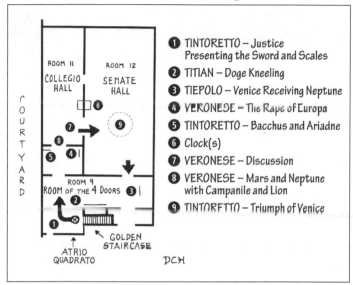

ROOM II
COLLEGIO HALL

ROOM 12
SENATE HALL

COURTYARD

ROOM 9
ROOM OF THE 4 DOORS

ATRIO QUADRATO

GOLDEN STAIRCASE

DCH

❶ TINTORETTO – Justice Presenting the Sword and Scales
❷ TITIAN – Doge Kneeling
❸ TIEPOLO – Venice Receiving Neptune
❹ VERONESE – The Rape of Europa
❺ TINTORETTO – Bacchus and Ariadne
❻ Clock(s)
❼ VERONESE – Discussion
❽ VERONESE – Mars and Neptune with Campanile and Lion
❾ TINTORETTO – Triumph of Venice

this room by the doge's nest of advisers.

✓ In *Mars and Neptune with Campanile and Lion* (the ceiling painting near the entrance), Veronese presents four symbols of the Republic's strength—military, sea trade, city, and government (plus a cherub about to be circumcised by the Campanile).

• *Enter the large Senate Room.*

Senate Chamber (Sala del Senato)

While the doge presided from the stage, senators mounted the podium (middle of the wall with windows) to address their 120 colleagues. The legislators, chaired by the doge, debated and passed laws in this room.

Venice prided itself on its self-rule (independent of popes, kings, and tyrants) with most power placed in the hands of these annually elected men. Which branch of government really ruled? All of them. It was an elaborate system of checks and balances to make sure no one rocked the boat, no one got too powerful, and the ship of state sailed smoothly ahead.

✓ Tintoretto's large *Triumph of Venice* on the ceiling (central painting, best viewed from the top) shows the city in all its glory. Lady Venice is up in heaven with the Greek gods, while barbaric lesser nations swirl up to give her gifts and tribute. Do you get the feeling the Venetian aristocracy was proud of its city?

On the wall are two large clocks, one of which has the signs of the zodiac and phases of the moon. And there's one final oddity in this room, in case you hadn't noticed it yet. In one of the wall paintings (above the entry door), there's actually a doge... not kneeling.

• *Pass again through the Room of the Four Doors, then around the corner into the large hall with a semicircular platform at the far end.*

Hall of the Council of Ten (Sala del Consiglio dei Dieci)

By the 1400s, Venice had a worldwide reputation for swift, harsh, and secret justice. The dreaded Council of Ten—10 judges, plus the doge and his six advisers—met here to dole out punishment to traitors, murderers, and "morals" violators. (Note the 17 wood panels where they presided.)

Slowly, they developed into a CIA-type unit with their own force of police officers, guards, spies, informers, and even assassins. They had their own budget and were accountable to no one, soon making them the de facto ruling body of the "Republic." It seemed no one was safe from the spying eye of the "Terrible Ten." You could be accused anonymously (by a letter dropped into a "Mouth of Truth"), swept off the streets, tried, judged, and thrown into the dark dungeons in the palace for the rest of your life without so much as a Miranda warning.

It was in this room that the Council decided who lived or died, and who was decapitated, tortured, or merely thrown in jail. The small, hard-to-find door leading off the platform (the fifth panel to the right of center) leads through secret passages to the prisons and torture chambers.

The large, central, oval ceiling painting by Veronese (a copy of the original stolen by Napoleon and still in the Louvre) shows *Jupiter Descending from Heaven to Strike Down the Vices,* redundantly informing the accused that justice in Venice was swift and harsh. To the left of that, Juno showers Lady Venice with coins, crowns, and peace.

Though the dreaded Council of Ten was eventually disbanded, today their descendants enforce the dress code at St. Mark's Basilica.

• *Pass through the next room, then up the stairs to the Armory Museum.*

Judicial Rooms

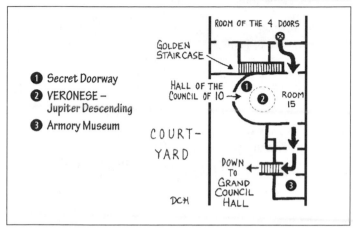

1 Secret Doorway
2 VERONESE –
Jupiter Descending
3 Armory Museum

Armory Museum ✓

The aesthetic of killing is beyond me, but I must admit I've never seen a better collection of halberds, falchions, ranseurs, targes, morions, and brigandines in my life. The weapons in these three

rooms make you realize the important role the military played in keeping the East–West trade lines open.

✓ **Room 1:** In the glass case on the right, you'll see the suit of armor worn by the great Venetian mercenary general, Gattamelata (far right, on horseback), as well as "baby's first armor" (how soon they grow up). A full suit of armor could weigh 66 pounds. Before gunpowder, crossbows (look up) were made still more lethal by turning a crank on the end to draw the bow with extra force.

✓ **Room 2:** In the thick of battle, even horses needed helmets. The hefty broadswords were brandished two-handed by the strongest and bravest soldiers who waded into enemy lines. Suspended from the ceiling is a large banner captured from the Turks at the Battle of Lepanto (1571).

✓ **Room 3:** At the far end is a very, very early (17th-century) attempt at a 20-barrel machine gun. On the walls and weapons, the "C-X" insignia means that this was the private stash of the "Council of Ten."

✓ **Room 4:** Squint out the window to see Palladio's San Giorgio Maggiore and, to the left in the distance, the tiny green dome at Venice's Lido (beach). To the right of the window, the glass case contains a tiny crossbow, some torture devices (including an effective-looking thumbscrew), the wooden "devil's box" (a clever item that could fire in four directions at once), and a nasty, two-holed chastity belt. These "iron breeches" were worn by the devoted wife of the Lord of Padua.

• *Exit the Armory Museum (enjoy a closer look at that early machine gun). Go downstairs, turn left, and pass through the long hall with a wood-beam ceiling. Now turn right and open your eyes as wide as you can to see the...*

Hall of the Grand Council (Sala del Maggiore Consiglio)

It took a room this size to contain the grandeur of the Most Serene Republic. This huge room (175 by 80 feet) could accommodate up to 2,600 people at one time. The engineering is remarkable. The ceiling is like the deck of a ship—its hull is the rooftop, creating a huge attic above that.

The doge presided from the raised dais, while the nobles—the backbone of the empire—filled the center and lined the long walls. Nobles were generally wealthy men over 25, but the title had less to do with money than with long bloodlines. In theory, the doge, the Senate, and the Council of Ten were all subordinate to the Grand Council of nobles who elected them.

On the wall over the doge's throne is Tintoretto's monster-piece, *Paradise*, the largest oil painting in the world. At 570 square feet, it could be sliced up to wallpaper an apartment with enough left over for placemats.

Christ and Mary are at the top of heaven, surrounded by 500 people—mostly Venetians. It's rush hour in heaven, and all the good Venetians made it. The painting leaves you feeling that you get to heaven not by being a good Christian, but by being a good Venetian. Tintoretto worked on this in the last years of his long life. On the day it was finished, his daughter died. He got his brush out again and painted her as saint number 501. She's dead center with the blue skirt, hands clasped, getting sucked up to heaven. (At least that's what an Italian tour guide told me.)

Veronese's *The Apotheosis of Venice* (on the ceiling at the Tintoretto end—view it from the top) is a typically unsubtle work showing Lady Venice being crowned a goddess by an angel.

Ringing the hall are portraits, in chronological order, of the first 76 doges. The one at the far end that's blacked out is the notorious **Doge Marin Falier,** who opposed the will of the

Hall of the Grand Council

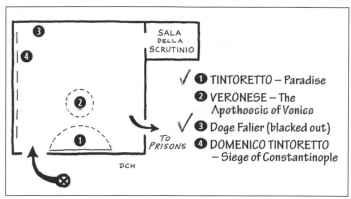

✓ **1** TINTORETTO – Paradise

2 VERONESE – The Apotheosis of Venice

✓ **3** Doge Falier (blacked out)

4 DOMENICO TINTORETTO – Siege of Constantinople

✓ Grand Council in 1355. He was tried for treason, beheaded, and airbrushed from history.

Along the entire wall to the right of Paradise, **battle scenes** (by Tintoretto's son, Domenico) show Venice's greatest military

(if not moral) victory, the conquest of the fellow-Christian city of Constantinople during the Fourth Crusade (1204). The mighty walls of Constantinople repelled every attack for nearly a thousand years. But the sneaky Venetians (in the fifth painting) circled around back and attacked where the walls rose straight up from the water's edge. Skillful Venetian oarsmen cozied their galleys right up to the dock, allowing soldiers to scoot along crossbeams attached to the masts, to the top of the city walls. In the foreground, an archer cranks up his crossbow. The gates are opened, the Byzantine emperor parades out to surrender, and tiny Doge Dandolo says, "Let's go in and steal some bronze horses."

But soon Venice would begin its long slide into historical oblivion. One by one, the Turks gobbled up Venice's trading outposts. In the West, the rest of Europe ganged up on Venice to reduce her power. By 1500, Portugal had broken Venice's East–West trade monopoly by finding a sea route to the East around the southern tip of Africa. To top it off, Venice suffered its greatest moral—if not military—victory in the draining Battle of Lepanto, 1571 (depicted in paintings in the adjoining Sala dello Scrutinio). Over the centuries, Venice remained a glorious city, but not the world power she once was. Finally, in 1797, the French general

Napoleon marched into town shouting *"Liberté, Egalité, Fraternité."* The Most Serene Republic was finally conquered, and the last doge was deposed in the name of modern democracy.

Out the windows (if they're open) is a fine view of the domes of the basilica, the palace courtyard below, and Paul Newman.

A newly elected doge was presented to the people of Venice from the balcony of the nearby Sala dello Scrutinio room that overlooks the Piazzetta. A noble would announce, "Here is your doge, if it pleases you." That was fine, until one time when the people weren't pleased. From then on they just said, "Here is your doge."

• *Consider reading about the prisons here in the Grand Council Hall, where there are more benches and fewer rats.*

Prisons

The palace had its own dungeons. In the privacy of his own home,

a doge could oversee the sentencing, torturing, and jailing of political opponents. The most notorious cells were "the Wells" in the basement, so-called because they were deep, wet, and cramped.

By the 1500s, the Wells were full of political prisoners. New prisons were built across the canal to the east of the palace and connected with a covered bridge.

• *Exit the Grand Hall (squeezing through the door to the left of Tintoretto's monsterpiece) and pass through a series of rooms and once-secret passages, following signs for* Ponte dei Sospiri/Prigioni. *Room 31 contains four fascinating paintings by Hieronymus Bosch (once hung in the Chamber of the Council of Ten), showing sinners tortured in hell by genetic mutants and Wizard of Oz monkeys. Then cross the covered Bridge of Sighs over the canal to the prisons. At the fork in the route, descend the stairs rather than continuing right into a cell, or you'll miss the basement altogether and end up at the bookshop at the end of the palace visit.*

Medieval justice was harsh. The cells consisted of cold stone with heavily barred windows, a wooden plank for a bed, a shelf, and a bucket. (My question: What did they put on the shelf?) You can feel the cold dampness.

Circle the cells. Notice the carvings made by prisoners—from olden days up until 1930—on some of the stone windowsills of the cells, especially in the far corner of the building.

The Bridge of Sighs

According to romantic legend, criminals were tried and sentenced in the palace, then marched across the canal here to the dark prisons. On this bridge, they got their one last look at Venice. They gazed out at the sky, the water, and the beautiful buildings.

• *Cross back over the Bridge of Sighs, pausing to look through the marble-trellised windows at all of the tourists and the heavenly Church of San Giorgio Maggiore. Heave one last sigh and leave the palace.*

CORRER
MUSEUM
TOUR

(Museo Civico Correr)

A doge's hat, gleaming statues by Canova, and paintings by the illustrious Bellini family—for some people, that's a major museum; for others, it's a historical bore. But the Correr Museum has one more thing to offer, and that's a quiet refuge—a place to rise above St. Mark's Square when the piazza is too hot, too rainy, or too overrun with tourists. Those who enter are rewarded with an easy-to-manage overview of Venice's art and history.

ORIENTATION

Cost: Covered by the €11 Museum Card (valid for 3 months, 1 entry per museum), which includes two lesser museums within the Correr (National Archaeological Museum and the Monumental Rooms of the Marciana National Library), the clock tower, and the Doge's Palace. Avoid ticket lines at the crowded Doge's Palace by buying your Museum Card at the Correr Museum. For details on the Museum Card and pricier Museum Pass, see page 24.

Hours: Daily April–Oct 9:00–19:00, Nov–March 9:00–17:00, last entry 70 minutes before closing.

Getting There: The entrance is on St. Mark's Square in Napoleon's Wing—the building at the far end of the square, opposite the basilica. Climb the staircase to the first-floor ticket office and bookstore.

Information: English descriptions are provided throughout. Tel. 041-240-5211.

Bag Check: Mandatory, free, and to your left; several doors down, after you pass the ticket counter.

Length of This Tour: Allow one hour.

Cuisine Art: The museum café has tables with a fine view of St. Mark's Square.

Starring: Canova statues, Venetian historical artifacts, three Bellinis, and a Carpaccio.

THE TOUR BEGINS

The Correr Museum gives you admission and access to three connected museums— the Correr proper (which we'll see), the National Archaeological Museum, and the Marciana Library.

The Correr itself is on three long, skinny floors that parallel St. Mark's Square. This tour covers the first two floors: The first floor contains Canova statues and Venetian history; the second floor displays a chronological overview of Venetian paintings. The third floor, which presents the history of Italy's *Risorgimento* (national unification), might still be undergoing renovation (ask at the ticket booth).

FIRST FLOOR

• *Buy your ticket, enter the long, skinny Room 3 and turn right. At the far end of the hall is a statue of the mythological hero, Paris. Along the way, admire the views out the windows of the Piazza.*

Room 3

Canova—*Paris*

The guy with black measles is not a marble statue of Paris; it's a plaster of Paris, a life-size model that Venice's greatest sculptor, Antonio Canova, used in carving the real one in stone. The dots are sculptor's "points," to tell the sculptor how far into the block he should chisel to establish the figure's rough outline.

Nearby, find Canova's pyramid-shaped model of the **Tomb of Maria Christina of Austria (Monumento a Tiziano).** This was Canova's design (based on the pyramid of Gaius Cestius in Rome) for a tomb he intended for the painter Titian. The design was not used for Titian, but instead for a tomb for an Austrian princess in Vienna, as well as for Canova's own memorial in the Frari Church (see page 140).

Room 4

Canova—*Daedalus and Icarus (Dedalo e Icaro, 1778–1779)*

Serious Daedalus straps wings, which he's just invented, onto his son's shoulders. The boy is thrilled with the new toy, not knowing what we know—that they will soon melt in the sun and plunge

Antonio Canova
(1757–1822)

Son of a Venetian stonemason, Canova grew up with a chisel in his hand in a studio along the Grand Canal, precociously mastering the sentimental, elegant Rococo style of the late 1700s. At 23, he went to Rome and beyond, studying ancient statues at then-recently discovered Pompeii. These new archaeological finds inspired a new Renaissance-style revival of the classical style. Canova's pure, understated elegance and "neo"-classical style soon became the rage all over Europe.

Called to Paris, Canova became Napoleon's court sculptor and carved perhaps his best-known work: Napoleon's sister as Venus, reclining on a couch (now in the Borghese Gallery, Rome). Canova combined Rococo sentiment and elegance with the cool, minimal lines of classicism.

him to his death. Daedalus' middle-aged, sagging skin contrasts with Icarus' supple form. Canova, a stonemason's son, displays the tools of the family trade on the base.

Antonio Canova was only 20 when Venice's Procurator commissioned this work from the hometown prodigy. It was so realistic that it caused a stir—skeptics accused Canova of not really sculpting it, but making it from plaster casts of live humans.

Room 5

Canova—*Orpheus and Eurydice*
(*Orfeo*, 1775–1776; *Euridice*, 1775)

Orpheus is leading his beloved back from Hell when she is tugged from behind by the cloudy darkness. She calls for help. Orpheus looks back, smacks his forehead in horror...but he can do nothing to help, and has to hurry on. In this youthful work, Canova already shows elements of his later style: high-polished, slender, beautiful figures; an ensemble piece, with more than one figure; open space between the figures that's almost as compelling as the figures themselves; and a statue group that's interesting from many angles.

Correr Museum—First Floor

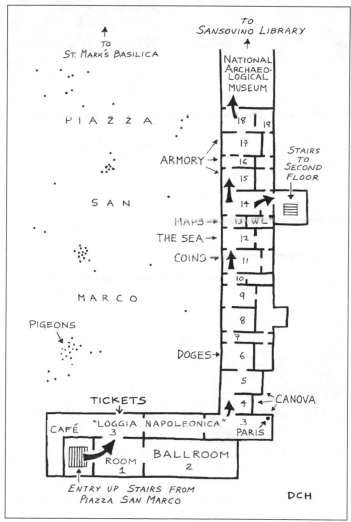

TO
SANSOVINO LIBRARY

↑
TO
ST. MARK'S BASILICA

NATIONAL
ARCHAEO-
LOGICAL
MUSEUM

P I A Z Z A

18 | 19

17

ARMORY → 16

STAIRS
TO
SECOND
FLOOR

15

14

S A N

MAPS → 13 | WC

THE SEA → 12

COINS → 11

10

9

M A R C O

8

7

PIGEONS

DOGES → 6

5

TICKETS

4 ← CANOVA

CAFÉ

"LOGGIA NAPOLEONICA"
3

3
PARIS

ROOM
1

BALLROOM
2

ENTRY UP STAIRS FROM
PIAZZA SAN MARCO

DCH

Carved by a teenage Canova, this piece (which may be in the nearby ballroom) captures the Rococo spirit of Venice in the late 1700s—elegant and beautiful, but tinged with bittersweet loss. Even Canova's later works—which were more sober, minimalist, and emotionally restrained—always retained the elegance and romantic sentiment of the last days of the Venetian Republic.

Canova— *Amor and Psyche*

Though not a great painting, this is Canova's version of a famous

work he set in stone (now in the
Louvre). The two lovers spiral
around each other in the never-
ending circle of desire. The two
bodies and Cupid's two wings
form an X. But enough X's and
O's—the center of the composition is the empty space that separates their hungry lips.

Other Canovas
The other large statues in the Canova rooms are either lesser works
or more plaster ("gesso") studies for works later executed in marble.
You'll also see small clay models, where Canova worked out ideas
before chiseling into an expensive block of marble.
• *Enter the world of Venice's doges. On an easel in Room 6, find a doge
portrait...*

Room 6: The Doge
Lazzaro Bastiani— *Portrait of Doge Francesco Foscari*
Doge Foscari, dressed in the traditional brocaded robe and cap

with cloth earflaps, introduces us to
the powerful, regal world of these
"elected princes," who served as the
ceremonial symbol of the glorious
Republic.
   Foscari (1373–1457, buried in
the Frari Church) inherited Venice
at its historical peak as a prosperous
sea-trading empire with peaceful
ties to eastern Turks and mainland
Europeans. He has a serene look of
total confidence...that would slowly
melt as he led Venice on a 31-year
war of expansion that devastated northern Italy, embroiled Venice
in messy European politics, and eventually drained the city's cof-
fers. Meanwhile, the Turks captured Constantinople. By the time
the Venetian Senate "impeached" Foscari, forcing his resignation,
Venice was sapped, soon to be surpassed by the new sea-trading
powers of Spain and Portugal.
   In the glass case, find doge memorabilia, including the funny
doge cap with a single horn at the back, often worn over a cloth
cap with earflaps.
• *High on the wall opposite the room's entrance, find the large painting
by...*

Andrea Michieli—*Arrival of Dogess Grimani (Lo Sbarco a San Marco della Dogaressa Morosina Grimani)*

Although doges were men, several wives were crowned with ceremonial titles. This painting shows coronation ceremonies (1597) along the water by the Piazzetta. The lagoon is jammed with boats. Notice the Doge's Palace on the right, the Marciana Library on the left (designed by Jacopo Sansovino), and the Campanile and clock tower in the distance. The dogess (left of center, in yellow, wearing her doge cap tilted back) arrives to receive the front-door key to the Doge's Palace.

The doge's private boat, the *Bucintoro* (docked at lower left, with red roof), has brought the First Lady and her entourage of red-robed officials, court dwarves, musicians, dancers, and ladies in formal wear. She walks toward the World Theater (on the right, in the water), a floating pavilion used for public ceremonies.

• *Find more doge memorabilia in Room 7. Along the walls of Room 7 are two depictions of big parades.*

Room 7

Processions of the Doge in St. Mark's Square (a woodcut by Matteo Pagan, and a painting by Cesare Vecellio)

The woodcut shows the doge and his court parading around St. Mark's Square in the kind of traditional festivities that Venetians

enjoy even today. At the head of the parade (to the right) come the flag bearers and the trumpet players sounding the fanfare. Next are the bigwigs, the archbishop, the bearer of the doge cap, the doge's chair, and finally *Il Serenissimo* himself, under an umbrella. The ladies look on from the windows above.

Some doges were powerful dictators, but in general their power was severely restricted by the Venetian constitution and powerful senators. Many doges were simply ceremonial figureheads, expected to show up in their funny hats for ribbon-cutting ceremonies and state funerals. Doges even needed permission to leave the city.

In the painting, locate the very same windows of the room you're standing in (at far right of the painting). The square looks much like it does today (sans pigeons).

• *The Correr Museum once housed offices, which you'll see in...*

Rooms 8–10: Government Offices

Some of the rich furnishings on display in these rooms—rare books in walnut bookcases, a Murano chandelier, wood-beamed ceiling, and paintings—are reminders that this wing once housed the administrative offices of a wealthy, sophisticated, trade-oriented Republic.

In Room 9, a glass case holds a *manino*. Not a doge backscratcher, the *manino* is a ceremonial hand-on-a-stick that counted votes in doge elections. The process was as baffling as America's Electoral College: 30 nobles were chosen by casting lots. Then 21 of the 30 were eliminated by lots. The remaining nine elected 40 nobles, whose number was whittled down to 25 by lots...and so on through several more steps, until finally, 41 electors—chosen by their peers and by chance—selected the next doge.

• *Move to the next room to view Venetian coins. The collection runs chronologically clockwise around the room.*

Room 11: Coins

The Venetian ducat weighed a bit more than a U.S. penny but was mostly gold. (By decree, 99 percent pure gold, weighing 3.5 grams.) First minted around 1280 (find Giovanni Dandolo's *zecchino,* or "sequin," in the first glass case to the right of the door that leads into the next room), it became the strongest currency in all Europe for nearly 700 years, eventually replacing the Florentine florin. In Renaissance times, 100 ducats would be an average, middle-class salary for a year. The most common design shows Christ on the "heads" side, standing in an oval of stars. "Tails" features the current doge kneeling before St. Mark, with the inscription "sacred money of Venice."

Also in Room 11, find **Tintoretto's painting** of three red-robed treasury officials who handled ducats in these offices. The richness of their fur-lined robes suggests the almost religious devotion that officials were expected to have as caretakers of the "sacred money of Venice."

Room 12: Venice and the Sea

Venice's wealth came from its sea trade. Raw materials from Europe were exchanged for luxury goods from eastern lands controlled by Muslim Turks and Byzantine Christians.

Models of Galleys (Modello di Galera)

These fast oar- and wind-powered warships rode shotgun for Venice's commercial fleets plying the Mediterranean. With up to 150 men (four per oar, some prisoners, mostly proud professionals) and three horizontal sails, they could cruise from here to

Constantinople in about a month. In battle, they specialized in turning on a dime to aim cannons, or in quickly building up speed to ram and board other ships with their formidable prows. Also displayed are large lanterns from a galley's stern.

• *Find two similar paintings depicting...*

The Battle of Lepanto (*Battaglia di Lepanto,* 1571)

The two paintings capture the confusion of a famous battle fought in 1571 between Muslim Turks and a coalition of Christians off the coast of Greece. This battle ended Turkish dominance at sea. Sort it out by their flags. The turbaned Turks fought under the

crescent moon. On the Christian side, Venetians had the winged lion, the pope's troops flew the cross, and Spain was marked with the Hapsburg eagle.

The fighting was fierce and hand-to-hand as they boarded each other's ships and cannons blasted away point-blank. Miguel de Cervantes lost his hand and had

to pen *Don Quixote* one-handed.

The Christians won, sinking 113 Turkish ships and killing up to 30,000. It was a major psychological victory, as it finally put to rest the Muslim threat to Europe.

But for Venice, it marked the end of an era. The city lost 4,000 men and many ships, and never fully recovered its trading empire in Turkish lands. Moreover, Spain's cannon-laden sailing ships proved to be masters of the waves, making it a true seagoing power. Venice's shallow-hulled galleys, so swift in the placid Mediterranean, were no match on the high seas.

Room 13: The Arsenale

A painting by Antonio di Natale shows a bird's-eye view of the shipbuilding factory located near the tail of Venice. This rectangular, artificial harbor was surrounded by workshops where ships could be mass-produced as though on a modern assembly line (but it was the workers who moved). If needed, they could crank out a galley a day. The Arsenale's entrance (lower left of painting) is still guarded today by the two lions.

Room 14: The Map Room (Venezia Forma Urbis)

Old maps show a city relatively unchanged over the centuries, hemmed in by water. Find your hotel on G.B. Arzenti's big map from circa 1600. There's the Arsenale in the fish's tail. There's Piazza San Marco with a church standing where the Correr

Museum entrance is today. The Accademia Bridge hadn't been built yet, nor had the modern train station. In the lower right is the doge's *Bucintoro.*

Rooms 15–18: Armory

You'll find weapons from medieval times to the advent of gunpowder—maces, armor, swords, Turkish pikes, rifles, cannons, shields, and a teeny-tiny pistol hidden in a book (in a glass case in Room 17).

• *Those interested in visiting the National Archaeological Museum (Greek and Roman statues) and the impressive Marciana Library can gain access to them from Room 18 (included with Correr Museum admission).*

The Library displays antique globes, manuscripts, and Roman copies of Greek statuary. The walls are richly decorated with portraits of renowned scholars and ancient philosophers, who twist and turn in their niches in classical Baroque style. Tintoretto and Veronese, among other lesser artists, worked on these. The last room at the end of the hall features tondi *(round) paintings of virtues and allegories of the liberal arts, such as mathematics, geometry, and music, and an impressive trompe l'oeil ceiling (free guided tours of the library Sat–Sun at 10:00, 12:00, 14:00, and 15:00).*

Otherwise, to continue this tour, backtrack to Room 14 (WCs nearby), then head upstairs to the second floor, following signs to La Quadreria—Picture Gallery. *Enter Room 25.*

SECOND FLOOR

Venetian Painting

The painting highlights (the Bellinis) are located at the far end of this wing, and you have permission to hurry there. But along the way, trace the development of Venetian painting from golden Byzantine icons to Florentine-inspired 3-D to the natural beauty of Bellini and Carpaccio.

Room 25

Paolo Veneziano—
Six Saints (c. 1310–1358)

Gold-backed saints combine traits from Venice's two cultural sources: Byzantine (serene, elongated, somber, and iconic, with gold background, like the mosaics in St. Mark's) and the Gothic of mainland Europe (curvy, expressive bodies posed at a three-quarters angle, colorful robes, and individualized faces).

Room 26

Lorenzo Veneziano—*Figures and Episodes of Saints (Figure e Storia di Santi,* c. 1356–1370)

Influence from the mainland puts icons in motion, adding drama to the telling of saints' lives (in the small scenes above the three saints). St. Nicholas grabs the executioner's sword and lifts him right off the ground before he even knows what's happening.

Room 27: Ornate (Flamboyant) Gothic

Architectural fragments of Gothic buildings remind us that Venice's distinctive architecture is Italian Gothic filtered through Eastern exoticism.

Room 29.II: International Gothic

Maestro dei Cassone Jarves— Two Painted Lids of a Hope Chest (c. 1425)

As humanism spread, so did art that was not exclusively religious. These scenes depict a story from Boccaccio's bawdy *Decameron.*

Done in the so-called International Gothic style, the painted lids emphasize decorative curves—curvy filigree patterns in clothes, curvy boats, curvy sails, curvy waves, curvy horses' rumps—all enjoyed as a decorative pattern.

Room 31.I: Ferrarese Painters

Baldassare Estense— *Portrait of a Young Man (Ritratto di Gentiluomo,* c. 1442–1564)

The young man in red is not a saint, king, or pope, but an ordinary citizen painted, literally, wart and all. On the window ledge is a strongly foreshortened book. And behind the young man, the curtain opens to reveal a new world— a spacious 3-D vista courtesy of the Tuscan Renaissance.

Room 32
Jacopo de' Barbari— *Venetie MD* (1500)

How little Venice has changed in 500 years! Barbari's large, intricately detailed woodcut of the city put his contemporaries in a unique position—a mile up in the air, looking down on the rooftops. He chronicles nearly every church, alleyway, and gondola. Both the final product and the reverse-image woodcut are on display, a tribute to all of Barbari's painstaking labor.

Room 33: 15th-Century Flemish Artists
Pieter Brueghel the Younger— *Adoration (Adorazione dei Magi)*

Venetian artists were strongly influenced by the detailed, everyday landscapes of Northern masters. Lost in this snowy scene of the secular working world is baby Jesus in a stable (lower left), worshipped by the Magi. Venetians learned that landscape creates its own mood, and that humans don't have to be the center of every painting.

Room 34
Antonello da Messina— *Christ with Three Angels (Pietà con Tre Angeli,* c. 1475)

The Sicilian painter wowed Venice with this work when he visited in 1475, bringing a Renaissance style and new painting techniques. After a thousand years of standing rigidly on medieval crucifixes, Christ could finally let his body relax in a natural human posture. The scene is set in a realistic, distant landscape.

Remember this work, as I'll refer to it later.

Correr Museum—Second Floor

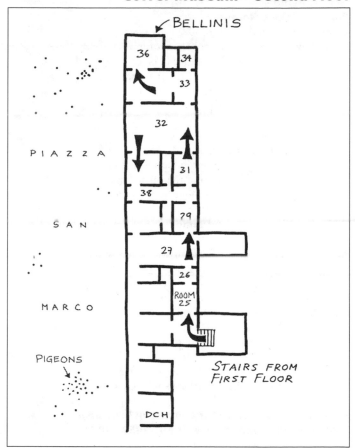

Room 36: The Bellini Family *(I Bellini)*

One family brought Venetian painting into the Renaissance—the Bellinis.

Jacopo Bellini—*Crucifixion (La Crocifissione)*

Father Jacopo (c. 1400–1470) had studied in Florence when

Donatello and Brunelleschi were pioneering 3-D naturalism.

Daughter Cecilia (not a painter) married the painter Mantegna, whose precise lines and statuesque figures influenced his brothers-in-law.

Gentile Bellini—
Portrait of Doge Mocenigo

Elder son Gentile (c. 1429–1507) took over the family business and established a reputation for documenting Venice's rulers and official ceremonies. His straightforward style and attention to detail capture the ordinary essence of this doge.

Giovanni Bellini—
Crucifixion (La Crocifissione)

Younger son Giovanni (c. 1430–1516) became the most famous Bellini, the man who pioneered new techniques and subject matter, trained Titian and Giorgione, and almost single-handedly invented the Venetian High Renaissance.

Compare this early Crucifixion (young Giovanni's earliest documented work) with his father's version. Young Giovanni weeds out all the crowded, medieval mourners, leaving only Mary and John. Behind, he paints a spacious (Mantegnesque) landscape, with a lake and mountains in the distance. Our eyes follow the winding road from Christ to the airy horizon, ascending like a soul to heaven.

Giovanni Bellini— *Christ Supported by Two Angels*
(*Cristo Morto Sorreto da Due Angeli,* 1453–1455)

In another early work, Giovanni explores human anatomy, with exaggerated veins, a heaving diaphragm, and even a hint of pubic hair. Mentally compare this stiff, static work with Antonello da Messina's far more natural *Christ with Three Angels* done 20 years later to see how far Giovanni still had to go. In fact, Giovanni was greatly influenced by Antonello, appreciating the full potential of the new invention of oil-based paint. Armed with this more transparent paint, he could add subtler shades of color and rely less on the sharply outlined forms we see here.

Giovanni Bellini— *Madonna and Child (Madonna Frizzoni)*

Though the canvas is a bit wrinkled, it reminds us of the subject Giovanni would paint again and again—lovely, forever-young Mary (often shown from the waist up) holding rosy-cheeked baby Jesus. He portrayed their holiness with a natural-looking, pastel-colored, soft-focus beauty.

Room 38

Vittore Carpaccio— *Two Venetian Ladies*
(a.k.a. *The Courtesans*, c. 1500–1510)

Two well-dressed Venetians look totally bored, despite being surrounded by a wealth of exotic pets and amusements. One lady absentmindedly plays with a dog, while the other stares into space. Romantics imagined them to be kept ladies awaiting lovers, but the recent discovery of the once-missing companion painting tells us they're waiting for their menfolk to return from hunting.

The colorful details and love of luxury are elements that would dominate the Venetian High Renaissance. Fascinating stuff, but my eyes—like theirs—are starting to glaze...

ACCADEMIA TOUR

(Galleria dell' Accademia)

The Accademia (ack-ah-DAY-mee-ah) is the greatest museum anywhere for Venetian Renaissance art, and a good overview of painters whose works you'll see all over town. Venetian art is underrated and, I think, misunderstood. It's nowhere near as famous today as the work of the florescent Florentines, but—with historical slices of Venice, ravishing nudes, and very human Madonnas—it's livelier, more colorful, and simply more fun.

ORIENTATION

Cost: €7.50.

Hours: Mon 8:15–14:00, Tue–Sun 8:15–19:15, last entry 45 min before closing (shorter hours in winter). Visit early or late to miss crowds, or call 041-520-0345 to reserve tickets in advance.

Getting There: The museum faces the Grand Canal, just over the Accademia Bridge (15-min walk from St. Mark's Square—follow signs to *Accademia*). Vaporetto stop: Accademia.

While you're in the Accademia neighborhood, consider visiting the Ca' Rezzonico, a five-minute walk west (✪ see tour on page 142); the Peggy Guggenheim Collection's excellent display of modern art, a five-minute walk east along the Grand Canal (✪ see tour on page 153); and the historic La Salute Church, just beyond the Guggenheim (✪ see tour on page 166).

Information: Some rooms have sheets of information in English. The bookshop sells guidebooks for €8.20. Tel. 041-522-2247.

Tours: An audioguide tour costs €4 (€6 for double set or €6 for PalmPilot). You can't fast-forward through the dull parts.

Length of This Tour: Allow one hour.

Accademia

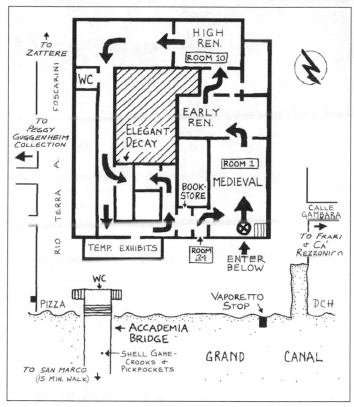

Cuisine Art: Bar Accademia Foscarini is a simple pizzeria at the base of the Accademia Bridge.

Photography: Not allowed.

Starring: Titian, Veronese, Giorgione, Bellini, and Tintoretto.

THE TOUR BEGINS

Venice—Swimming In Luxury

The Venetian love of luxury shines through in Venetian painting. We'll see grand canvases of colorful, spacious settings peopled with happy Venetians in luxurious clothes having a great time. The museum proceeds chronologically from medieval days to the 1700s. But before we start at the medieval beginning, let's sneak a peek at a work by the greatest Venetian Renaissance master, Titian.

• *Buy your ticket, check your bag, and head upstairs to a large hall filled with gold-leaf altarpieces. Immediately past the turnstile, turn left, enter the small Room 24, and take a seat.*

Titian (Tiziano Vecellio)—*Presentation of the Virgin*

A colorful crowd gathers at the foot of a stone staircase. A dog eats a bagel, a mother handles a squirming baby, an old lady sells eggs, and people lean out the windows. Suddenly the crowd turns and points at something. Your eye follows up the stairs to a larger-than-life high priest in a jeweled robe.

But wait! What's that along the way? In a pale blue dress that sets her apart from all the other colored robes, dwarfed by the enormous staircase and columns, the tiny, shiny figure of the child Mary almost floats up to the astonished priest. She's unnaturally small, easily overlooked at first glance. When we finally notice her, we realize all the more how delicate she is amid the bustling crowd, hard stone, and epic grandeur. Venetians love this painting and call it, appropriately enough, the "Little Mary."

The painting is a parade of colors. Titian (TEESH-un) leads your eyes from the massive buildings to the deep blue sky and mountains in the background to the bright red robe of the man in the crowd to glowing Little Mary. Titian painted the work especially for this room, fitting neatly around the door on the right. The door on the left was added later, cutting into Titian's masterpiece.

This work is typical of Venetian Renaissance art. Here and throughout this museum, you will find: (1) bright, rich color, (2) big canvases, (3) Renaissance architectural backgrounds, (4) slice-of-life scenes of Venice, and (5) 3-D realism. It's a religious scene, yes, but really just an excuse to display secular splendor—Renaissance architecture, colorful robes, and human details.

Now that we've gotten a taste of Renaissance Venice at its peak, let's backtrack and see some of Titian's predecessors.

• *Return to Room 1, stopping at a painting (near the turnstile) of Mary and baby Jesus.*

Medieval Art—Pre-3-D

Paolo Veneziano—*Madonna and Child with Two Donors* (*Madonna col Bambino e Due Committenti*)

Mary sits in heaven. The child Jesus is a baby in a bubble, a symbol of his "aura" of holiness.

Accademia—Medieval Art

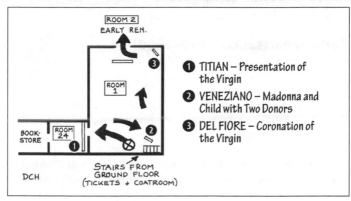

ROOM 2
EARLY REN.

ROOM 1

BOOK-STORE ROOM 24

STAIRS FROM GROUND FLOOR (TICKETS + COATROOM)

DCH

❶ TITIAN – *Presentation of the Virgin*

❷ VENEZIANO – *Madonna and Child with Two Donors*

❸ DEL FIORE – *Coronation of the Virgin*

Notice how two-dimensional and unrealistic this painting is. The size of the figures reflects their religious importance—Mary is huge, being both the mother of Christ as well as "Holy Mother

Church." Jesus is next, then the two angels who crown Mary. Finally, in the corner, are two mere mortals kneeling in devotion. The golden haloes let us know who is holy. Medieval Venetians, with their close ties to the East, borrowed techniques such as gold-leafing, frontal poses, and "iconic"
faces from the religious icons of Byzantium (modern Istanbul).

Most of the paintings in Room 1 are altarpieces, many of them of the Virgin Mary being crowned in triumph. Very impressive. But it took Renaissance artists to remove Mary from her golden never-never land, clothe her in human flesh, and bring her down to the real world we inhabit.

• *In the far right corner of the room, you'll find...*

Jacobello del Fiore—*Coronation of the Virgin (Incoronazione della Vergine)*

This swarming beehive of saints and angels is an attempt to cram as much religious information as possible into one space. The architectural setting is a clumsy try at three-dimensionality (the railings of the wedding-cake structure are literally glued on). The color-coordinated saints are simply stacked one on top of the other,

rather than receding into the distance as they would in real life.
• *Enter Room 2 at the far end of this hall.*

Early Renaissance (1450–1500)

Only a few decades later, artists rediscovered the natural world and ways to capture it on canvas. With this Renaissance, or "rebirth" of the arts and attitudes of ancient Greece and Rome, painters took a giant leap forward. They weeded out the jumble of symbols, fleshed out cardboard characters into real people, and placed them in spacious 3-D settings.

Giovanni Bellini—*Sacred Conversation (Pala di San Giobbe)*

Mary and the baby Jesus meet with saints beneath an arched half dome. A trio of musician angels jam at her feet. In its original church setting, the painting's pillars and arches matched the real ones in the church (there may be a photo reconstruction nearby), as though Bellini had blown a hole in the wall and built another chapel, allowing us mortals to mingle with holies.

Giovanni Bellini (bell-EE-nee) takes only a few figures, places them in this spacious architectural setting, and balances them half on one side of Mary and half on the other. Left to right, you'll find St. Francis (medieval founder of an order of friars), John the Baptist, Job, St. Dominic (founder of another order of monks), St. Sebastian, and St. Louis.

The painting has a series of descending arches. At the top is a Roman arch. Hanging below that is a triangular canopy. Then comes a pyramid-shaped "arch" formed by the figures themselves, with Mary's head at the peak, echoed below by the pose of the three musicians. Subconsciously, this creates a mood of serenity, order, and balance, not the hubbub of the *Coronation*. Look at St. Sebastian—even arrows can't disturb his serenity.

In Bellini's long career, he painted many altarpieces in the *Sacra Conversazione* formula: Mary and Child surrounded by saints "conversing" informally about holy matters, while listening to some tunes. The formula, developed largely by Fra Angelico (1400–1455), became a common Renaissance theme—compare this painting with other *Sacras* by Bellini in the Frari Church (on page 138) and the Church of San Zaccaria (on page 199).
• *Climb the small staircase, and pass through Room 3 and into the small Room 4.*

Accademia—Early Renaissance

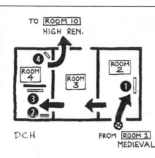

TO ROOM 10
HIGH REN.

ROOM 4
ROOM 2
ROOM 3

3
1

DCH

FROM ROOM 1
MEDIEVAL

❶ GIOVANNI BELLINI –
Sacred Conversation

❷ MANTEGNA – St. George

❸ GIO. BELLINI – Madonna and Child
between St. Catherine and
Mary Magdalene

❹ GIORGIONE – The Tempest

Andrea Mantegna—*St. George (San Giorgio)*

This Christian dragon slayer is essentially a Greek nude sculpture with armor painted on. He rests his weight on one leg *(contrapposto)*, the same as a classical sculpture, Michelangelo's *David,* or

an Italian guy on the street corner. The doorway he stands in resembles a niche designed for a classical statue.

Mantegna (mahn-TAYN-yah) was trained in the Tuscan tradition. There, painters were like sculptors, "carving" out figures (like this) with sharp outlines, filling them in with color, and setting them in distant backdrops like the winding road behind George. But when Mantegna married Giovanni Bellini's sister, he brought Florentine realism and draftsmanship to his in-laws.

St. George radiates Renaissance optimism—he's alert but relaxed, at rest but ready to spring into action, humble but confident. With the broken lance in his hand and the dragon at his feet, George is the strong Renaissance Man slaying the medieval dragon of superstition and oppression.

• *Find three women and a baby on a black background.*

Giovanni Bellini— *Madonna and Child between St. Catherine and Mary Magdalene*

In contrast to Mantegna's sharp-focus 3-D, this painting consists of just three heads on a flat plane with a black velvet backdrop. Their features are soft, hazy, and atmospheric, glowing out of the darkness as though lit by soft candlelight. It's not sculptural line that's important here, but color—warm, golden, glowing flesh tones. The faces emerge from the canvas like cameos.

Bellini painted dozens of Madonna and Childs in his day. (Others are nearby.) This Virgin Mary's pretty, but she's upstaged by the sheer idealized beauty of Mary Magdalene (on the right). Mary Magdalene's hair is down like the prostitute that legend says she was, yet she has a childlike face, thoughtful and repentant. This is the perfect image of the innocent woman who sinned by loving too much.

Bellini was the teacher of two more Venetian greats, Titian and Giorgione, schooling them in the new medium of oil painting. Mantegna painted *St. George* using tempera paint (pigments dissolved in egg yolk), while Bellini pioneered oils (pigments in vegetable oil)—a more versatile medium. Applying layer upon transparent layer, Bellini made creamy complexions with soft outlines, bathed in an even light. His gift to the Venetian Renaissance was the "haze" he put over his scenes, giving them an idealized, glowing, serene—and much copied—atmosphere. (You can see more of Bellini's work at the Correr Museum, page 109; Frari Church, page 138; and the Church of San Zaccaria, page 199.)

• *Around the partition, you'll find...*

Giorgione—*The Tempest*

It's the calm before the storm. The atmosphere is heavy—luminous but ominous. There's a sense of mystery. Why is the woman nursing her baby in the middle of the countryside? And the soldier—is he ogling her or protecting her? Will lightning strike? Do they know that the serenity of this beautiful landscape is about to be shattered by an approaching storm?

The mystery is heightened by contrasting elements. The armed soldier contrasts with the naked lady with her baby. The austere, ruined columns contrast with the lusciousness of Nature. And, most important, the stillness of the foreground scene is in direct opposition to the threatening storm in the background. The landscape itself is the main subject, creating a mood, regardless of what the painting is "about."

Giorgione (jor-JONE-ee) was as mysterious as his few paintings, yet he left a lasting impression. A student of Bellini, he learned to use haziness to create a melancholy mood of beauty. But nothing beautiful lasts. Flowers fade, Mary Magdalenes grow old, Giorgione died at 33, and, in *The Tempest*, the fleeting stillness is about to be shattered by the slash of lightning—the true center of the composition.

• *Exit and browse through several rooms. Check out the bookstore (there's another one later), then continue up the five steps to the large Room 10.*

Venetian High Renaissance (1500–1600)— Titian, Veronese, and Tintoretto

Paolo Veronese—*Feast of the House of Levi*

Parrrrty!! Stand about 10 yards away from this enormous canvas, to where it just fills your field of vision...and hey, you're invited. Venice loves the good life, and the celebration is in full swing. You're in a huge room with a great view of Venice. Everyone's dressed to kill in colorful silk and velvet robes. Conversation roars and the servants bring on the food and drink.

This captures the Venetian attitude (more love, less attitude) as well as the style of Venetian Renaissance painting. Remember: (1) bright colors, (2) big canvases, (3) Renaissance architectural settings, (4) scenes of Venetian life, and (5) 3-D realism. Painters had mastered realism and now gloried in it.

The *Feast of the House of Levi* is, believe it or not, a religious work painted for a convent. The original title was *The Last Supper.* In the center of all the wild goings-on, there's Jesus, flanked by his disciples, sharing a final meal before his crucifixion.

This festive feast captures the optimistic spirit of Renaissance Venice. Life was a good thing and beauty was to be enjoyed. Renaissance men and women saw the divine in the beauties of Nature and glorified God by glorifying man.

Uh-uh, said the Church. In its eyes, the new humanism was the same as the old hedonism. The false spring of the Renaissance froze quickly after the Reformation, when half of Europe left the Catholic Church and became Protestant.

Veronese (vayr-oh-NAY-zay) was hauled before the Inquisition. What did he mean by painting such a bawdy Last Supper? With dwarf jesters? And apostles picking their teeth (between the columns, left of center)? And dogs and cats? And a black man, God forbid? And worst of all, some German soldiers—maybe even Protestants!—at the far right!

Veronese argued that it was just artistic license, so they asked to see his—it had expired. But the solution was simple. Rather than change the painting, just fine-tune the title. *Sì, no problema.* Veronese got out his brush, and *The Last Supper* became the *Feast of the House of Levi,* written in Latin on the railing to the left: *"FECIT D. COVI..."*

Titian (Tiziano Vecellio)—*Pietà*

Jesus has just been executed, and his followers grieve over his body before burying it. Titian painted this to hang over his own tomb.

Titian was the most famous painter of his day—perhaps even more famous than Michelangelo. He excelled in every subject: portraits of dukes, kings, and popes; racy nudes for their bedrooms; solemn altarpieces for churches; and pagan scenes from Greek mythology. He was cultured and witty, a fine musician and businessman—an all-around Renaissance kind of guy.

Titian was old when he painted this. He had seen the rise and decline of the Renaissance and had experienced much sadness in his own life. Unlike Titian's colorful and exuberant "Little Mary," done at the height of the Renaissance, this canvas is dark, the mood more somber.

Jesus is framed by a Renaissance arch like Bellini's *Sacred Conversation,* but here the massive stones overpower the figures, making them look puny and helpless. The lion statues are downright scary. Instead of the clear realism of Renaissance paintings, Titian uses rough, messy brush strokes, a technique that would be picked up by the Impressionists three centuries later. Titian adds a dramatic compositional element—starting with the lion at lower right, a line of motion sweeps up diagonally along the figures, culminating in the grief-stricken Mary Magdalene, who turns away, flinging her arm and howling out loud.

Finally, the kneeling figure of old, bald Nicodemus is a self-portrait of the aging Titian, tending to the corpse of Jesus, who symbolizes the once powerful, now dead Renaissance Man. In the lower right, a painting-within-the-painting shows Titian and his son kneeling, asking the Virgin to spare them from the plague of 1576. Unfortunately, Titian's son died from it, and a heartbroken Titian died shortly after.

Accademia—High Renaissance

ROOM 10
ROOM 11
DCH
FROM EARLY REN.

❶ VERONESE – Feast of the House of Levi

❷ TITIAN – Pietà

❸ TINTORETTO – The Transporting of St. Mark's Body

(To see more Titians, visit the Frari Church, which houses the painter's tomb, on page 139, and the Doge's Palace, on page 91.)

• *On the opposite wall, find...*

Tintoretto (Jacopo Robusti)—*The Transporting of St. Mark's Body (Trafugamento del Corpo di San Marco)*

The event that put Venice on the map is frozen at its most dramatic moment. Muslim fundamentalists in Alexandria are about to burn Mark's body (there's the smoke from the fire in the center), when suddenly a hurricane appears miraculously, sending them running

for cover. (See the wisps of baby-angel faces in the storm, blowing on the infidels? Look hard, on the left-hand side.) Meanwhile, the Venetian merchants whisk the body away.

Tintoretto makes us part of the action. The square tiles in the courtyard run straight away from us, an extension of our reality, as though we could step right into the scene—or the merchants could carry Mark into ours.

Tintoretto would have made a great black-velvet painter. His colors burn with a metallic sheen, and he does everything possible to make his subject popular with common people.

In fact, Tintoretto was a common man himself, self-taught, who apprenticed only briefly with Titian before striking out on his own. He sold paintings in the marketplace in his youth and insisted on living in the poor part of town even after he became famous.

Tintorettos abound here, in the next room, and throughout Venice. Look for these characteristics, some of which became standard features of Mannerist and Baroque art that followed the Renaissance: (1) heightened drama, violent scenes, strong emotions; (2) elongated bodies in twisting poses; (3) strong contrasts between dark and light; (4) bright colors; and (5) diagonal compositions.

(Tintoretto fans will want to visit the Scuola San Rocco, Tintoretto's "Sistine Chapel"; see page 125.)

• *Spend some time in this room, the peak of the Venetian Renaissance and the climax of the museum. After browsing, enter Room 11 and find a large round painting. Stand underneath it for the full effect.*

Elegant Decay (1600–1800)

G. B. Tiepolo—*Discovery of the True Cross*
(La Scoperta della Vera Croce)

Tiepolo blasts open a sunroof and we look up into heaven. We (the viewers) stand in the hole where they've just dug up Christ's cross and look up dresses and nostrils as saints and angels cavort overhead.

Tiepolo was the last of the great colorful, theatrical Venetian painters. He took the colors, the grand settings, and the dramatic angles of previous Venetian masters and plastered them on the ceilings of Europe's Baroque palaces, such as the Royal Palace in Madrid, Spain; the Residenz in Würzburg, Germany; and the Ca' Rezzonico in Venice (✪ see Ca' Rezzonico Tour on page 142). This one is from a church ceiling.

Tiepolo's strongly "foreshortened" figures are masterpieces of technical skill, making us feel like the heavenly vision is taking place right overhead. Think back on those clumsy attempts at three-dimensionality we saw in the medieval room, and realize how far painting has come. The fresco fragments hanging around the corners of Room 11 were salvaged from a church bombed in World War I.

• *Works of the later Venetians are in rooms branching off the long corridor to your left. As you walk down the corridor, the first right leads to the WC. The first left is Room 17.*

Canaletto and Guardi: Views of Venice

By the 1700s, Venice had retired as a world power and become Europe's number-one tourist attraction. Wealthy offspring of the nobility traveled here to soak up its art and culture. They wanted souvenirs, and what better memento than a picture of the city itself?

Guardi and Canaletto painted "postcards" for visitors who lost their heart to the romance of Venice. The city produced less art...as it became art itself. Here are some familiar views of a city that has aged gracefully.

Accademia—Elegant Decay

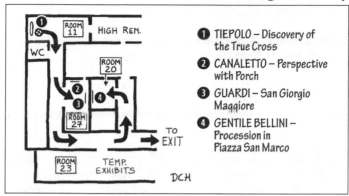

❶ TIEPOLO – Discovery of the True Cross

❷ CANALETTO – Perspective with Porch

❸ GUARDI – San Giorgio Maggiore

❹ GENTILE BELLINI – Procession in Piazza San Marco

Canaletto (Giovanni Antonio Canal, called Canaletto)— *Perspective with Porch (Prospettiva con Portico)*

Canaletto gives us a sharp-focus, wide-lens, camera's-eye perspective on the city. Although this view of a porch looks totally realistic, Canaletto has compressed the whole scene to allow us to see more than the human eye could realistically take in. We see the porch as though we were standing underneath it, yet we also see the whole porch at one glance. The pavement blocks, the lines of columns, and the slanting roof direct our eye to the far end, which looks very far away indeed. Canaletto even paints a coat of arms (at right) at a very odd angle, showing off his mastery of 3-D perspective.

Francesco Guardi—*San Giorgio Maggiore (Il Bacino di San Marco con San Giorgio Maggiore e Giudecca)*

Unlike Canaletto, with his sharp-focus detail, Guardi sweetens Venice up with a haze of messy brushwork. In this familiar view across the water from St. Mark's Square, he builds a boatman with

a few sloppy smudges of paint. Guardi catches the play of light at twilight, the shadows on the buildings, the green of the water and sky, the pink light off the distant buildings, the Venice that exists in the hearts of lovers—an Impressionist work a century ahead of its time.

• *Follow the corridor, turn left at the end, then take another left, and then left again. Are you in Room 20?*

Gentile Bellini—*Procession in Piazza San Marco* *(Processione in Piazza San Marco)*

A fitting end to our tour is a look back at Venice in its heyday. This wide-angle view by Giovanni's big brother—more than any human eye could take in at once—reminds us how little Venice has changed over the centuries.  There is St. Mark's gleaming gold with mosaics, the four bronze horses, the three flagpoles out front, the old Campanile on the right, and the Doge's Palace. There's the guy selling 10 postcards for a dollar. (But there's no clock tower with the two bronze Moors yet, the pavement's different, the church is covered with gold, and there are no café orchestras playing "New York, New York.") Every detail is in perfect focus regardless of its distance from us, presented for our inspection. Take some time to linger over this and the other views of old Venice in this room. Then get outta here and enjoy the real thing.

• *To exit, backtrack to the main corridor and turn left past the bookstore. There are often temporary exhibits in the large former chapel branching off the corridor. Say ciao to Titian's "Little Mary" on the way out.*

SCUOLA SAN ROCCO TOUR

(Scuola Grande di San Rocco)

The 50-plus paintings in the Scuola Grande di San Rocco—often called "Tintoretto's Sistine Chapel"—present one man's very personal vision of Christian history. Tintoretto (1518–1594) spent the last 20 years of his life working virtually for free, driven by the spirit of charity that the Scuola, a Christian organization, promoted. For Tintoretto fans, this is the ultimate. But even for the art-weary, his large, colorful canvases, framed in gold on the walls and ceilings of a grand upper hall, are an impressive sight.

ORIENTATION

Cost: €5.50, includes fine audioguide. (If you see an evening concert here, you can enjoy the art as a bonus; see page 248.)

Hours: Daily April–Oct 9:00–17:30, Nov–March 10:00–16:00, last entry 30 minutes before closing.

Getting There: It's next to the Frari Church (❏ see Frari Church Tour on page 135). Vaporetto: San Tomà. To walk here from the Rialto Bridge, take my recommended Rialto to Frari Church Walk, page 191.

Information: Tel. 041-523-4864. WCs are located straight ahead from the entry door; get the key from the ticket clerk.

Comfort Tip: Use the mirrors scattered about the museum (some are set in rolling tables, others are handheld), because much of this art is on the ceiling and a pain in the neck.

Length of This Tour: Allow one hour.

Starring: Tintoretto, Tintoretto, and Tintoretto.

THE TOUR BEGINS

The art of the Scuola is contained in three rooms—the Ground Floor Hall (where you enter) and two rooms upstairs. We'll start upstairs, seeing the art roughly in the order that Tintoretto painted it:

1. Albergo Hall (a small room on the upper floor), with Passion scenes.
2. Great Upper Floor Hall, with the biggest canvases.
3. Ground Floor Hall, with the life of Mary.

• *Enter on the ground floor. When you buy your ticket, you find yourself in the Ground Floor Hall, which is lined with big, colorful Tintoretto canvases. Before heading upstairs, begin in the left corner with...*

The Annunciation

An angel swoops through the doorway, dragging a trail of naked baby angels with him, to tell a startled Mary she'll give birth to Jesus.

This canvas illustrates many of Tintoretto's typical characteristics:

- **The miraculous and the everyday mingle side by side.** Glorious angels are in a broken-down house with stacks of lumber and a frayed chair.
- **Bright light and dark shadows.** A bright light strikes the brick column, highlighting Mary's face and the angel's shoulder, but casting dark shadows across the room.

- **Strong 3-D sucks you into the scene.** Tintoretto literally tears down Mary's wall to let us in. The floor tiles recede sharply into the distance, making Mary's room an extension of our real space.
- **Colors that are bright, almost harsh,** with a metallic "black-velvet" sheen, especially when contrasted with the soft-focus haze of Bellini, Giorgione, Veronese, and (sometimes) Titian.
- **Twisting, muscular poses.** The angel turns one way, Mary turns the other, and the baby angels turn every which way.
- **Diagonal composition.** Shadows run diagonally on the floor as Mary leans back diagonally.
- **Rough brushwork.** The sketchy pattern on Mary's ceiling contrasts with the precise photo-realism of the brick column. And finally, *The Annunciation* exemplifies the general theme

Scuola San Rocco

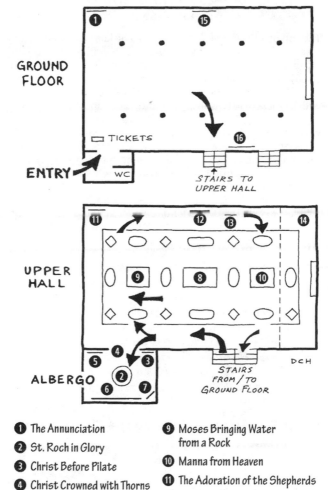

1. The Annunciation
2. St. Roch in Glory
3. Christ Before Pilate
4. Christ Crowned with Thorns
5. The Way to Calvary
6. The Crucifixion
7. Three Apples
8. Moses and the Brass Serpent
9. Moses Bringing Water from a Rock
10. Manna from Heaven
11. The Adoration of the Shepherds
12. The Resurrection
13. Tintoretto's Carved Face
14. The Last Supper
15. The Flight into Egypt
16. The Circumcision

Jacopo Tintoretto
(1518–1594)

The son of a silk dyer ("Tintoretto" is a nickname meaning "little dyer"), Tintoretto applied a blue-collar work ethic to painting, becoming one of the most prolific artists ever. He trained briefly under Titian, but their egos clashed. He was influenced more by Michelangelo's recently completed *Last Judgment,* with its muscular, twisting, hovering nudes and epic scale.

By age 30, Tintoretto was famous, astounding Venice with the innovative *St. Mark Freeing the Slave* (now in the Accademia). He married, had eight children (three of whom became his assistants), and dedicated himself to work and family, shunning publicity and living his whole life in his old Venice neighborhood.

The last 20 years of his life were spent decorating the Scuola San Rocco. It was a labor of love, showing his religious faith, his compassion for the poor, and his artistic passion.

of the San Rocco paintings—God intervenes miraculously into our everyday lives in order to save us.

• *We'll return to the ground floor later, but let's start where Tintoretto did. Climb the staircase (admire the plague scenes that are not by Tintoretto) and enter the impressive Great Hall.*

The Albergo Hall is a small room in the left corner of the Great Hall. On the ceiling of the Albergo Hall is an oval painting of St. Roch, best viewed from the doorway.

Albergo Room (Sala d'Albergo)—Christ's Passion

St. Roch in Glory (1564)

Start at the feet of St. Roch (San Rocco), a French med student in the 1300s who dedicated his short life to treating plague victims. The Scuola of San Rocco was a kind of Venetian "Elks Club" whose favorite charity was poor plague victims.

This is the first of Tintoretto's 50-plus paintings in the Scuola. It's also the one that got him the job, beating entries by Veronese and others.

Tintoretto amazed the judges by showing the saint from beneath, as though he hovered above in a circle of glory. This Venetian taste for dramatic angles and illusion would later become standard in Baroque ceilings. Tintoretto trained by dangling wax models from the ceiling and lighting them from odd angles.

• *On the walls are scenes of Christ's trial, torture, and execution. Work counterclockwise around the room, starting by the door with...*

Christ Before Pilate (Ecce Homo)

Jesus has been arrested and brought before the Roman authorities in a cavernous hall. Although he says nothing in his own defense, he stands head and shoulders above the crowd, literally "rising above" the slanders. Tintoretto shines a bright light on his white robe, making Christ radiate innocence.

At Christ's feet, an old, bearded man in white stoops over to record the events on paper—it's Tintoretto himself.

Christ Crowned with Thorns

Jesus was beaten, whipped, then mocked by the soldiers who dressed him as a king "crowned" with thorns. Seeing the bloodstains on the cloth must have touched the hearts of Scuola members, generating compassion for those who suffer.

The Way to Calvary

Silhouetted against a stormy sky, Jesus and two other prisoners trudge up a steep hill, carrying their own crosses to the execution site. The cycle culminates with...

The Crucifixion

The crucified Christ is the calm center of this huge and chaotic scene that fills the wall. Workers struggle to hoist crosses, mourners swoon, riffraff gamble for Christ's clothes, and soldiers mill about aimlessly. Scarcely anyone pays any attention to the Son of God...except us, because Tintoretto directs our eye there.

All the lines of sight point to Christ at the center: the ladder on the ground, the cross being raised, the cross still on the ground, the horses on the right, and the hillsides that slope in. In a trick of multiple perspectives, the cross being raised seems to suck us in toward the center, while the cross still on the ground seems to cause the figures to be sucked toward us.

Above the chaos stands Christ, high above the horizon, higher than everyone, glowing against the dark sky. Tintoretto lets us appreciate the quiet irony lost on the frenetic participants—that this minor criminal suffering such apparent degradation is, in fact, triumphant.

• *Displayed on an easel to the left of and beneath* The Crucifixion *is a small fragment of...*

Three Apples

This fragment, from the frieze around the upper reaches of the Albergo Hall, was discovered folded under the frieze in 1905.

Because it was never exposed to light, it still retains Tintoretto's original bright colors. All of his paintings are darker today, despite cleaning, due to the irretrievable chemical alteration of the pigments.

• *Now step back out into the Great Upper Hall...*

Great Upper Hall—Old Testament and New Testament

Thirty-four enormous oil canvases, set into gold frames on the ceiling and along the walls of this impressive room, tell biblical history from Adam and Eve to the Ascension of Christ. Tintoretto's storytelling style is straightforward, and anyone with knowledge of the Bible can quickly get the gist. Tintoretto's success in the Albergo Hall won him the job of the enormous Great Upper Hall.

Understanding What You're Standing Under

The ceiling has Old Testament scenes; the walls have New Testament scenes. The three large rectangles on the ceiling are stories of Moses.

Beyond that, it's difficult to say what overall program Tintoretto had in mind. It's not chronological. There's no consistent symbolism. Theologically, a few panels seem to belong together, matching, say, the *Fall of Man* with Christ's redemption. And some clusters of panels have similar motifs, such as water (at the Albergo end of the hall), plagues and death (middle of the hall), and nourishment (altar end).

But ultimately, Tintoretto's vision is a very personal one, open to many interpretations. The art was inspired by the charitable spirit of the Scuola—just as God has helped those who suffer, so should we.

• *Start with the large, central rectangle on the ceiling. View it from the top (the Albergo end), not directly underneath.*

Moses and the Brass Serpent

The tangle of half-naked bodies (at the bottom of the painting) represents the children of Israel, wrestling with poisonous snakes and writhing in pain. At the top of the pile, a young woman gestures

toward Moses (in pink), who points to a pole carrying a brass serpent sent by God. Those who looked at the statue were miraculously healed. His work all done, God (above in the clouds) high-fives an angel.

This was the first of the Great Hall panels that Tintoretto painted in response to a terrible plague that hit Venice in 1576. One in four died. Four hundred a day were buried. (They say that Tintoretto's colleague, Titian, died of heartbreak

soon after his son died of the plague.) Like today's Red Cross, the Scuola sprang into action, raising funds, sending doctors, and giving beds to the sick and aid to their families. Tintoretto saw the dead and dying firsthand. While capturing their suffering, he gave a ray of hope that help is on the way: Turn to the cross, and be saved by your faith.

There are dozens of figures in the painting, shown from every conceivable angle. Tintoretto was well aware of where it would hang and how it would be viewed. Walk around beneath it, and see the different angles come alive. The painting becomes a movie, and the children of Israel writhe like snakes.

• *The rectangular panel at the Albergo end of the hall is...*

Moses Bringing Water from a Rock

Moses (in pink, in the center) hits a rock in the desert with his staff, and it miraculously spouts water, which the thirsty Israelites catch in jars. The water spurts like a ray of light. Moses is a strong, calm center to a spinning wheel of activity.

Tintoretto worked fast, and if nothing else, his art is exuberant. He'd trained in fresco painting, where you have to finish before the plaster dries. With these paintings, he sketched an outline right onto the canvas, then improvised details as he went.

The sheer magnitude of the San Rocco project is staggering. This canvas alone is 300 square feet—like painting a bathroom with an artist's tiny brush. The whole project, counting the Albergo Hall, Great Upper Hall, and the Ground Floor Hall together, totals some 8,500 square feet—more than enough to cover a typical house, inside and out. (The Sistine Chapel ceiling, by comparison, is 5,700 square feet.)

• *The rectangular panel at the altar end of the hall is...*

Manna from Heaven

It's snowing bread, as God feeds the hungry Israelites with a miraculous storm. They stretch a blanket to catch it, and gather it up in baskets. Up in the center of the dark cloud is a radiant, almost transparent God painted with sketchy brush strokes that suggest he's an unseen presence.

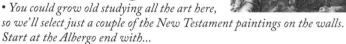

Tintoretto tells these Bible stories with a literalness that was very popular with the poor, uneducated sick who sought help from the Scuola. He was the Spielberg of his day, with the technical know-how to bring imagination to life, to make the miraculous tangible.

• *You could grow old studying all the art here, so we'll select just a couple of the New Testament paintings on the walls. Start at the Albergo end with...*

The Adoration of the Shepherds

Christ's glorious life begins in a straw-filled stable with cows, chickens, and peasants who pass plates of food up to the new parents. It's night, with just a few details lit by phosphorescent moonlight: the kneeling shepherd's forehead and leggings, the serving girl's shoulders, the faces of Mary and Joseph...and little baby Jesus, a smudge of light.

Notice the different points of view. Tintoretto clearly has placed us on the lower floor, about eye level with the cow, and looking up through the roof beams at the night sky. But we also see Mary and Joseph in the loft above as though they were at eye level. By using multiple perspectives (and ignoring the laws of physics), Tintoretto could portray every detail at its perfect angle.

• *In the middle of the long wall, find...*

The Resurrection

Angels lift the sepulchre lid, and Jesus springs forth in a blaze of light. The contrast between dark and light is extreme, with great dramatic effect.

• *On your way to* The Last Supper, *look on the wall for a wood carving of Tintoretto (third statue from altar, directly opposite entry staircase). The artist's craggy, wrinkled face squints out from under a black cap and behind a scraggly beard.*

The Last Supper

A dog, a beggar, and a serving girl dominate the foreground of Christ's final Passover meal with his followers. More servants work in the background. The disciples themselves are dining in the dark, some with their backs to us, with only a few stray highlights to show us what's going on. Tintoretto emphasizes the human, everyday element of that gathering, in contrast to, say, Leonardo da Vinci's statelier version. And he sets the scene at a diagonal for dramatic effect.

The table stretches across a tiled floor, a commonly used device to create 3-D space. But Tintoretto makes the more distant tiles unnaturally small to exaggerate the distance. Similarly, the table and the people get proportionally smaller and lower until, at the far end of the table, tiny Jesus (with glowing head) is only half the size of the disciple at the near end.

Theatrically, Tintoretto leaves it to us to piece together the familiar narrative. The disciples are asking each other, "Is it I that will betray the Lord?" Jesus, meanwhile, unconcerned, hands out Communion bread.

• *Browse the Great Upper Hall and notice the various easel paintings by other artists. Contrast Titian's placid, evenly lit, aristocratic* Annunciation *with the blue-collar Tintoretto version downstairs. After you've gotten your fill of the Great Upper Hall, head back downstairs for Tintoretto's last works.*

Ground Floor Hall—The Life of Mary

The Flight into Egypt

There's Mary, Joseph, and the baby, but they're dwarfed by palm trees. Tintoretto, in his old age, returned to composing a Venetian specialty—landscapes—after years as champion of the Michelangelesque style of painting beefy, twisting nudes. The leafy greenery, the still water, the supernatural sunset, and the hut whose inhabitants  go about their work, tell us better than any human action that the holy family has found a safe haven.

The Circumcision

This painting, bringing the circumcision of the baby Jesus into sharp focus, is the final canvas that Tintoretto did for the Scuola.

He collaborated on this work with his son Domenico, who carried on the family business.

In his long and prolific career, Tintoretto saw fame and many high-paying jobs. But at the Scuola, the commission became an obsession. It stands as one man's very personal contribution to the poor, to the Christian faith, and to art.

FRARI CHURCH TOUR

(Chiesa dei Frari)

With so much great art "in situ" (right where it was designed to be seen—rather than hanging in museums), this church offers for many travelers the best art-appreciation experience in Venice. And it's about the only Gothic church you'll tour. Since Venice's spongy ground could never support a real stone Gothic church (like you'd find in France), the Frari Church is made of light and flexible wood with plaster.

The spirit of St. Francis of Assisi warms both the church of his "brothers" *(frari)* and the art that decorates it. The Franciscan love of Nature and Man later inspired Renaissance painters to capture the beauty of the physical world and human emotions, showing worshippers the glory of God in human terms.

ORIENTATION

Cost: €2.50, covered by Chorus Pass (see page 24).

Hours: Mon–Sat 10:00–17:00, Sun 13:00–17:00 (closed Sun in Aug), last entry 15 min before closing, no visits during services.

Getting There: It's on the Campo dei Frari, near the San Tomà vaporetto and *traghetto* stops.

Tips: If you're walking to Frari Church from the Rialto Bridge, take my recommended Rialto to Frari Church Walk (✪ see page 191). For efficient sightseeing, combine your visit with the Scuola San Rocco (✪ see tour on page 125), located behind the Frari Church. The Ca' Rezzonico (✪ see tour on page 142) is a seven-minute walk away (from the back end of Frari Church, go through alleyway Sotoportego S. Rocco, turn left at the first "T" intersection, then right. The rest is easy. Along the way, you'll pass by the university).

Information: Audioguides are available (€1.60/person, €2.60/ double set). The church often hosts evening concerts (€15, tickets sold at the church; for concert details, look for fliers, call 041-272-8611, or check www.basilicadeifrari.it). Church info tel. 041-272-86118.

Length of This Tour: Allow one hour.

Dress Code: Modest dress recommended.

Starring: Titian, Giovanni Bellini, and Donatello.

THE TOUR BEGINS

• *Enter the church and look down the nave toward the altar.*

❶ Church Interior and Choir (1250–1443)

The simple, spacious (110-yard-long), well-lit Gothic church—with rough wood crossbeams and a red-and-white color scheme—is truly a remarkable sight in a city otherwise crammed with exotic froufrou.

The wooden choir area in the center of the nave allowed friars to hold smaller, more intimate services. As worshippers enter the church and look down the long nave to the altar, the sight that greets them—framed by the arch of the choir entrance—is Titian's altarpiece.

Walk prayerfully toward the Titian, stopping in the finely carved 1480s choir. Notice the fine inlay above the chairs, showing the Renaissance enthusiasm for Florentine-style 3-D. Surviving choirs such as this are rare. In response to Luther's mandate, Counter-Reformation churches discarded the idea of the altar in order to get priests closer to their flocks.

• *Approach Titian's heavenly vision.*

❷ Titian—*The Assumption of Mary* (1518)

Glowing red and gold like a stained-glass window, this altarpiece sets the tone of exuberant beauty found in the oth-  erwise sparse church. Mary, at the end of her life (though looking 17), was miraculously "assumed" into heaven. As cherubs lift her up to meet a Jupiter-like God, the stunned apostles on earth reach up to touch the floating bubble of light.

Unveiled in 1518, the work also stunned a Venice used to simpler, more subdued church art. The sheer size (22 feet tall inside its origi- nal marble frame), the vertical format, the rich colors, twisting poses, and the mix of saccharine angels with blue-collar apostles were unheard of.

In a burst of youthful innovation, Titian

Frari Church

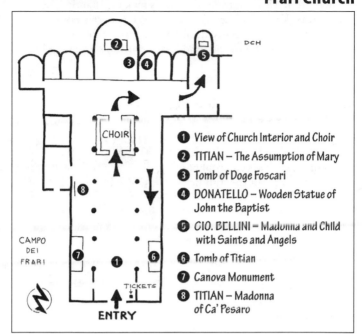

DCH

CHOIR

❶ View of Church Interior and Choir

❷ TITIAN – The Assumption of Mary

❸ Tomb of Doge Foscari

❹ DONATELLO – Wooden Statue of John the Baptist

❺ GIO. BELLINI – Madonna and Child with Saints and Angels

❻ Tomb of Titian

❼ Canova Monument

❽ TITIAN – Madonna of Ca' Pesaro

CAMPO DEI FRARI

TICKETS

ENTRY

(1488–1576) rewrote the formula for church art, hinting at changes to come with the Mannerist and Baroque styles. His complex composition overlaps a circle (Mary's bubble) and a triangle (draw a line from the apostle reaching up to Mary's face and down the other side) on three horizontal levels (God in heaven, Man on earth, Mary in between). Together, these elements draw our eyes from the swirl of arms and legs to the painting's focus—the radiant face of the once dying, now triumphant Mary.

• *Also in the apse (behind the main altar) are marble tombs lining the walls. On the wall to the right of the altar is the...*

❸ Tomb of Doge Foscari

In contrast to the poverty of the Franciscans, this heavy, ornate tomb marks the peak of Venice's worldly power. Doge Francesco Foscari (1373–1457) assumed control of Venice's powerful seafaring empire and then tried to expand it farther onto the mainland, battling Milan in a 31-year war of attrition that swept through northern Italy. Meanwhile, on the unprotected eastern front, the Turks took Constantinople (1453) and scuttled Venice's trade. Venice's long slide into historical oblivion had begun. Financially drained city fathers forced Foscari to resign, turn in his funny hat, and hand over the keys to the Doge's Palace.

• *In the first chapel to the right of the altar, you'll find...*

❹ Donatello—Wooden Statue of John the Baptist

Emaciated from his breakfast of bugs 'n' honey and dressed in animal skins, the cockeyed prophet of the desert freezes in the middle of his rant when he spies something in the distance. His jaw goes slack, he twists his face and raises his hand to announce the coming of... the Renaissance.

The Renaissance began in the Florence of the 1400s, where Donatello (1386–1466) created realistic statues with a full range of human emotions. This warts-and-all John the Baptist contrasts greatly with, say, Titian's sweet Mary. Florentine art (including painting) was sculptural, strongly outlined, and harshly realistic, with muted colors. Venetian art was painterly, soft-focus, and beautiful, with bright colors.

Donatello's statue must have made Florentine expatriate "brothers" *(frari)* feel at home when they worshiped here.

• *Enter the sacristy, through the door at the far end of the right transept. You'll bump into an elaborate reliquary altar. Opposite that (near the entrance door) is a clock, intricately carved from a single piece of wood. At the far end of the room, you'll find...*

❺ Giovanni Bellini—*Madonna and Child with Saints and Angels* (1488)

Mary sits on a throne under a half dome, propping up baby Jesus (who's just learning to stand), flanked by saints and serenaded by musician angels. Giovanni Bellini (c. 1430–1516), the father of the Venetian Renaissance, painted fake columns and a dome to match the real ones in the gold frame, making the painting seem to be an extension of the room. He completes the illusion with glimpses of open sky in the background. Next, he fills the artificial niches with symmetrically posed, thoughtful saints—left to right, find Saints Nicholas, Peter, Mark, and Sean Connery (Benedict).

Bellini pioneered painting in oil (pigments dissolved in vegetable oil) rather than medieval tempera (egg yolk–based). It allowed subtler treatment of colors, made with successive layers of paint.

Bellini virtually invented the formula (later to be broken by his precocious pupil, Titian) for Venetian altarpieces. This type of "holy conversation" *(sacra conversazione)* between saints and Mary can also be seen in Venice's Accademia (page 116) and Church of San Zaccaria (page 199).

Renaissance humanism demanded Madonnas and saints that were accessible and human. Bellini delivers, but places them in a physical setting so beautiful that it creates its own mood of serene holiness. The scene is lit from the left, but no one casts a harsh shadow. Mary and the babe are enveloped in a glowing aura of reflected light from the golden dome. The beauty is in the details, from the writing in the dome to the red brocade backdrop to the swirls in the marble steps to the angels' dimpled legs.

• *Return to the nave and head toward the far end. Turn around and face the altar, and the Tomb of Titian will be in the second bay on your right.*

❻ Tomb of Titian
(Titiano Ferdinandus MDCCCLII)

The tomb celebrates both the man (see a carved statue of Titian in the center with beard and crown of laurels) and his famous paintings (depicted in relief).

Titian (1488–1576) was the greatest Venetian painter, excelling equally in inspirational altarpieces, realistic portraits, joyous mythological scenes, and erotic female nudes.

He moved to Venice as a child, studied under Giovanni Bellini, and soon established his own bold style starring teenage Madonnas (see a relief of *The Assumption* behind Titian). He became wealthy and famous, traveling Europe to paint stately portraits of kings and nobles, and colorful, sexy works for their bedrooms. But Titian always returned to his beloved Venice (see winged lion on top)...and favorite Frari Church.

In his old age, he painted dark, tragic masterpieces, including the *Pietà* (see relief in upper left) that was intended for his tomb but ended up in the Accademia (see page 120). Nearing 90, he labored to finish the *Pietà* as the plague enveloped Venice. One in four people died, including Titian's son and assistant, Orazio. Heartbroken, Titian died soon afterward of natural causes. His tomb was built three centuries later to remember and honor this great Venetian.

• *On the opposite side of the nave is the pyramid-shaped...*

❼ Canova Monument

Antonio Canova (1757–1822, see his portrait above the door) was Venice's greatest sculptor, creating gleaming, white, high-polished statues of beautiful Greek gods and goddesses in the neoclassical style. (See several of his works at the Correr Museum, page 98.)

The pyramid shape is timeless, suggesting pharaohs' tombs and the Christian Trinity. Mourners, bent over with grief, shuffle up to pay homage to the master artist. Even the winged lion is choked up.

Follow me here. Canova himself designed this pyra-
mid-shaped tomb, not for his own use, but as the tomb of an artist he greatly admired: Titian. But the Frari Church used another design for Titian's tomb, so Canova used the pyramid for an Austrian princess... in Vienna. After his death, Canova's pupils reused the design here to honor their master. In fact, Canova isn't buried here—instead, he lies in southern Italy. But inside the tomb's open door, you can (barely) see an urn, which contains his heart.

• *Head back toward the altar. Halfway up the left wall is...*

❽ Titian—*Madonna of Ca' Pesaro* (1526)

Titian's second altarpiece for the Frari Church displays all of his many skills. Following his teacher, Bellini, he puts Mary (seated) and baby (standing) on a throne, surrounded by saints having a holy conversation. And, like Bellini, he paints fake columns that echo the church's real ones.

But wait. Mary is off-center, Titian's idealized saints mingle with Venetians sporting five o'clock shadows, and the stairs run diagonally away from us. Mary sits not on a throne, but on a pedestal. Baby Jesus is restless. The precious keys of St. Peter seem to dangle unnoticed. These things upset tradi-
tional Renaissance symmetry, but they turn a group of figures into a true scene. St. Peter (center, in blue and gold, with book) looks down at Jacopo Pesaro, who kneels to thank the Virgin for his recent naval victory over the Turks (1502). A

flag-carrying lieutenant drags in a turbaned captive. Meanwhile, St. Francis talks to baby Jesus while gesturing down to more members of the Pesaro family.

Titian combines opposites: a soft-focus Madonna with photo-realist portraits, chubby winged angels with the real-life child looking out (lower right), and a Christian cross with a battle flag. In keeping with the spirit of St. Francis' humanism, Titian lets mere mortals mingle with saints. And we're right there with them.

CA' REZZONICO TOUR

Museum of 18th-Century Venice

> *"Endowed by nature with a pleasing physical appearance, a confirmed gambler, a great talker, far from modest, always running after pretty women...I was certain to be disliked. But, as I was always willing to take responsibility for my actions, I decided I had a right to do anything I pleased."*
> —from *The Memoirs of Giacomo Casanova* (1725–1798)

Venice in the 1700s was the playground for Europe's aristocrats. The Ca' Rezzonico palace, once owned by the wealthy Rezzonico family, is decorated with furniture and artwork from the period. This grand home on the Grand Canal is the best place in town to capture the luxurious, decadent spirit of Venice in the Settecento (the 1700s).

ORIENTATION

Cost: €6.50, covered by Museum Pass (see page 24).

Hours: April–Oct Wed–Mon 10:00–18:00, Nov–March Wed–Mon 10:00–17:00, closed Tue. Last entry 1 hr before closing.

Getting There: The museum is located on the west bank of the Grand Canal, right where the canal makes its hairpin turn. It's a 10-minute walk northwest from the Accademia or a 20-minute walk southwest from the Rialto Bridge (en route, you could visit the Frari Church and the neighboring Scuola San Rocco). Or you can use vaporetto #1 and get off at the Ca' Rezzonico stop (between Rialto and Accademia). Another way to arrive is by taking a quick *traghetto* ride across the Grand Canal from San Samuele (near entrance to Palazzo Grassi).

Information: The Ca' Rezzonico (ret-ZON-ee-koh) is also known as the Museo del Settecento Veneziano. Audioguides cost €4 per person (€6/double set) and last 90 minutes. On the ground floor, there are a free, mandatory baggage check, a bookstore, and WCs. Tel. 041-241-0100.

Length of This Tour: Allow 90 minutes.

Cuisine Art: The museum's café has a few scenic tables facing the Grand Canal.

Photography: Not allowed.

Starring: A beautiful palace with 18th-century furnishings and paintings by G. B. Tiepolo, Canaletto, and Guardi.

THE TOUR BEGINS

Our Ca' Rezzonico tour covers two floors. The first floor has rooms decorated with period furniture and ceiling frescoes by G. B. Tiepolo. The second floor displays paintings by Canaletto, Guardi, G. D. Tiepolo, Longhi, and others. (The third floor painting gallery—which we won't visit—shows lots of flesh in lots of rooms.)

First, step onto the dock on the Grand Canal and admire Ca' Rezzonico's heavy stone facade. This dock was, of course, the main entrance back in the 1700s. Next, admire the 1700s-era covered gondola in the courtyard. Picture this arriving at the Ca's dock for a party during Carnevale. A charcoal heater inside kept the masked and caped passengers warm, as they sipped Prosecco and chatted in French, enjoying their winter holiday away from home....

FIRST FLOOR

• Buy tickets on the ground floor, then ascend the grand staircase to the first floor, entering the...

Ballroom

A great place for a wedding reception. At 5,600 square feet, it's the biggest private venue in the city. Stand in the center, and the room gets even bigger, with a ceiling painting that opens up to the heavens and painted, trompe l'oeil (optical illusion) columns and arches that open onto fake alcoves.

Imagine dancing under candlelit chandeliers to Vivaldi's *Four Seasons.*

Servants glide by with drinks and finger foods. The gentlemen wear powdered wigs, silk shirts with lacy sleeves, tight velvet coats and breeches, striped stockings, and shoes with big buckles. They carry snuffboxes with dirty pictures inside the lids. The ladies powder their hair, pile it high, and weave stuff in—pictures of their children or locks of a lover's hair. And everyone carries a mask on a stick to change identity in a second.

The chandeliers of gold-covered wood are original. But most of the furniture we'll see, while it is from the 1700s, is not from the Rezzonico family collection.

• *Promenade across squeaky floors into the next room.*

Room II: Nuptial Allegory Room

In fact, there *was* a wedding here—see the happy couple on the ceiling, arriving in a chariot pulled by four white horses and serenaded by angels, cupids, and Virtues. In 1757, Ludovico Rezzonico exchanged vows with Faustina Savorgnan in this room, under the bellies of the horses painted for the occasion by Giovanni Battista ("John the Baptist") Tiepolo. Tiepolo (1696–1770), the best-known decorator of Europe's palaces, was at the height of his fame and technique. He knocked this off in 12 days. His bright colors, mastery of painting figures from every possible angle, wide knowledge of classical literary subjects, and sheer, unbridled imagination made his frescoes blend seamlessly with ornate Baroque and Rococo furniture.

The Rezzonicos were a family of nouveaux riches who bought their way into the exclusive club of Venetian patrician families. The *Portrait of Clement XIII* (on easel), pink-cheeked and well-fed, shows the most famous Rezzonico. As pope (elected 1758), Clement spent his reign defending the Jesuit society from anti-Catholic European nobles. A prayer kneeler (in the tiny adjoining chapel) looks heavily used, dating from the sin-and-repent, sin-and-repent era of Settecento Venice.

Room III: Pastel Room

Europe's most celebrated painter of portraits in pastels was a Venetian, Rosalba Carriera (1675–1757). Wealthy French and English tourists on holiday wanted a souvenir of Venice, and Carriera obliged, with miniature portraits on ivory rather than the traditional vellum (soft animal skin).

Ca' Rezzonico—First Floor

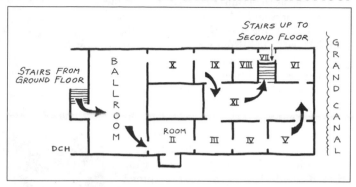

She progressed to portraits in pastel, a medium that caught the luminous, pale-skin, white-haired, heavy-makeup look that was considered so desirable. Still, her *Portrait (Ritratto) of Sister Maria Caterina* has a warts-and-all realism that doesn't hide the nun's heavy eyebrows, long nose, and forehead vein—only intensifying the spirituality she radiates.

At age 45, Carriera was invited by tourists whom she'd befriended to visit them in Paris. There, she became the toast of the town. Returning triumphantly to Venice, she settled into her home on the Grand Canal and painted until her eyesight failed.

Also in the room is the portrait of Cecilia Guardi Tiepolo: wife of famous painter Giovanni Battista Tiepolo, sister of famous painter Francesco Guardi, and mother of not-very-famous painter Lorenzo Tiepolo, who painted this when he was 21.

Room IV: Tapestry Room

Tapestries, furniture, a mirror, the original patterned floor, and a door with Asian themes that shows an opium smoker on his own little island paradise (lower panel) give a sense of the Rococo luxury of the wealthy. In a century dominated by the French court at Versailles, Venice was one of the few cities that could hold its own. The furniture ensemble of gilded wood chairs, tables, and chests hints at the Louis XIV style, but the pieces were made in a Venetian workshop.

Despite Venice's mask of gaiety, in the 1700s it was a poor, politically bankrupt, dirty city. Garbage floated in the canals, the streets were either unpaved or slippery with slime, and tourists could hardly stand visiting St. Mark's Basilica or the Doge's Palace because of the stench of mildew. But its reputation for decay and sleaze was actually romanticized into a metaphor for adventures into shady morality. With licensed casinos and a reputed "20,000 courtesans" (prostitutes), it was a fun city for foreigners freed from hometown blinders.

Room V: Throne Room

"Nowhere in Europe are there so many and such splendid fêtes, ceremonies, and public entertainments of all kinds as there are in Venice," wrote a visitor from France. As you check out the view of the Grand Canal, imagine once again that you're attending a

party here. You could watch the *Forze d'Ercole* (Force of Hercules) acrobats, who stood in boats and kept building a human pyramid—of up to 50 bodies—until they tumbled laughing into the Grand Canal. At midnight, the hosts would dim the mirrored candleholders on the walls, so you could look out on a fireworks display over the water.

Carnevale, Venice's prime party time, stretched from the day after Christmas to Lent. Everyone wore masks. Frenchmen, dressed as turbaned Turks, mingled with Turkish traders dressed as harlequins. Fake Barbary pirates fought playfully with skin-blackened "Moors." And long-nosed Pulcinella clowns were everywhere, reveling in the time when all social classes partied as one because "the mask levels all distinctions." (For information on this year's Carnevale celebration, see page 324).

The **ceiling fresco,** again by Giovanni Battista Tiepolo, certainly trompes my oeil. (It's best viewed from the center.) Tiepolo opens the room's sunroof, allowing angels to descend to earth to pick up the Rezzonico clan's patriarch. The old, bald, bearded fellow is crowned with laurels and begins to rise on a cloud up to the translucent temple of glory. The angels hold Venice's Golden

18th-Century Venetians

Canaletto (Giovanni Antonio Canal): Painter of
   Venice views
Antonio Canova: Neoclassical sculptor
Giacomo Casanova: Gambler, womanizer, revolutionary
Carlo Goldoni: Playwright of realistic comedies
Francesco Guardi: Painter of romantic Enlightened ideas
Giovanni Battista Tiepolo: Painter of Rococo ceilings
Giovanni Domenico Tiepolo: Painter son of
   famous Tiepolo
Antonio Vivaldi: Composer of *Four Seasons*

Book, where the names of the city's nobles were listed. In 1687, the Rezzonico family bought their way into the exclusive club. Tiepolo captures the moment just as the gang is exiting out the "hole" in the ceiling. The leg of the lady in blue hangs over the "edge" of the fake oval. Tiepolo creates a zero-gravity universe that must have astounded visitors. Walk in circles under the fresco, and watch the bugling angel spin.

• *Pass through the large next room and into...*

Room VI: Tiepolo Room

The ceiling painting by G. B. Tiepolo depicts Nobility and Virtue as a kind of bare-breasted Xena and Gabriela defeating Treachery, who tumbles down. The painting—which is on canvas, not a fresco like the others—was moved here from another palazzo.

Portraits around the room are by Tiepolo and his sons, Lorenzo and Giovanni Domenico. The paintings

are sober and down-to-earth, demonstrating the artistic range of this exceptional family. Giovanni Battista ("G. B.") was known for his flamboyance, but he passed to his sons his penchant for painting wrinkled, wizened old men in the Rembrandt style. In later years, G. B. had the pleasure of traveling with his sons to distant capitals, meeting royalty, and working on palace ceilings. Giovanni Domenico ("G. D.") contributed some of the minor figures in the Ca' Rezzonico ceilings and went on to carve his own niche. (We'll see his work upstairs.)

Giacomo Casanova
(1725–1798)

"I began to lead a life of complete freedom, caring for nothing except what pleased me."
—from *The Memoirs of Giacomo Casanova*

Casanova, a real person who wrote an exaggerated autobiography, typifies the Venice that so entranced the rest of Europe. In his life, he adopted many personae, worked in a number of professions, and always took the adventurous path.

Casanova was born just across the Grand Canal from the Ca' Rezzonico. The son of an actor, Casanova trained to be a priest, but was expelled for seducing nuns. To Venetians, he was first known as a fiery violinist at fancy parties in palaces such as the Ca' Rezzonico. He would later serve time in the Doge's Palace prison, accused of being a "magician."

As a professional gambler and charmer, he roamed Europe's capitals seducing noblewomen, dueling with fellow men of honor, and impressing nobles with his knowledge of Greek literature, religion, politics, and the female sex. His memoirs, published after his death, cemented his reputation as a genial but cunning rake, rogue, and rapscallion.

This room was the Rezzonicos' game room, and you can see a card table in the center. The big walnut cabinet along the wall is one of the few original pieces of furniture from the Rezzonicos' collection.

Room VII: Passage
This narrow corridor displays vessels for serving three foreign stimulants that became popular beverages in the 1700s—coffee, tea, and hot chocolate.

Room VIII: Library
Ca' Rezzonico was the home of the English poet Robert Browning (1812–1889) in his later years. Imagine him here in this study, in a melancholy mood after a long winter, reading a book and thinking of words from a poem of his: "Oh to be in England, now that April's there...."

Room IX: Lazzarini Room
The big, colorful paintings are by Gregorio Lazzarini (1655–1730), Tiepolo's teacher. Tiepolo took Lazzarini's color,

motion, and twisted poses and suspended them overhead.

Room X: Brustolon Room

Andrea Brustolon (1662–1732) carved Baroque fantasies into the custom-made tables, chairs, and vase-stands that he crafted in his Venice workshop. In black ebony, reddish boxwood, and brown walnut, they overwhelm with the sheer number of figures, yet each carving is a gem worth admiring. The big vase-stand is a harmony of different colors: a white vase supported by ebony slaves in chains and a brown boxwood Hercules. The slaves' chains are carved from a single piece of wood—an impressive artistic feat with a racist sentiment.

The room's flowery Murano glass chandelier—of pastel pinks, blues and turquoise—is original.

• *Backtrack to Room IX, then turn right into the large, sparsely decorated room called the...*

Room XI: Portego

That funny little cabin in the room is a sedan chair, a servant-powered taxi for Venice's nobles. Four strong-shouldered men ran poles through the iron brackets on either side, then carried it on their shoulders, while the rich rode in red-velvet luxury above the slimy streets.

• *The staircase to the second floor is here in Room XI in the middle of the long wall. On the second floor, you emerge into Room XII.*

SECOND FLOOR

The first floor showed the rooms and furniture of the 1700s. The second-floor paintings depict the people who sat in those chairs.

Room XII: Painting Portego

Rich tourists wanting to remember their stay in Venice sought out

Canaletto (1697–1768) for a "postcard" view. The *Grand Canal from Palazzo Balbi to Rialto* (by Giovanni Antonio Canal, called il Canaletto) captures the view you'd see from the palazzo two doors down. With photographic clarity, Canaletto depicts buildings, boats, and shadows on the water, leading the eye to the tiny, half-hidden Rialto Bridge on the distant horizon.

The *View of Rio dei Mendicante* chronicles every chimney, every open shutter, every pair of underwear hanging out to dry.

Canaletto was a young theater-set

painter working on Scarlatti operas in Rome when he decided his true calling was painting reality, not Baroque fantasy. He moved home to Venice, set up his easel outside, and painted scenes like these two, directly from nature. It was considered a very odd thing to do in his day.

Despite the seeming photorealism and crystal clarity, these wide-angle views are more than any human eye could take in without turning side to side. Canaletto, who meticulously studied the mathematics of perspective, was not above tweaking those rules to compress more of Venice into the frame. In the *Grand Canal from Palazzo Balbi to Rialto,* notice there are shadows along both sides of the canal—physically impossible, but more picturesque. His paintings still have a theater set look to them, but here, the Venice backdrop is the star.

To meet the demand for postcard scenes of Venice, Canaletto resorted in later years to painting from engravings or following formulas. But these two early works reflect his pure vision to paint accurately the city he loved.

• *From here, we'll move roughly clockwise around the second floor. Head for the door behind your right shoulder. Room XIII is actually a maze of several rooms displaying...*

Room XIII: Giovanni Domenico Tiepolo's Frescoes from the Villa in Zianigo

The son of G. B. Tiepolo decorated the family villa with frescoes

for his own enjoyment. They're far more down-to-earth than G. B.'s high-flying fantasies. **New World** features butts, as ordinary folk crowd around a building with a peepshow window. The only faces we see are the two men in profile—G. D. Tiepolo (far right, with eyeglass) and his father, G. B. Tiepolo (arms folded)—and baby brother Lorenzo (center). The **Pulcinella Room** (far right corner) has several scenes (including one overhead) of the hook-nosed, white-clothed, hunchbacked clown who, at Carnevale time, represented the lovable country bumpkin. But here, he and his similarly dressed companions seem tired, lecherous, and stupid. The decadent

Ca' Rezzonico—Second Floor

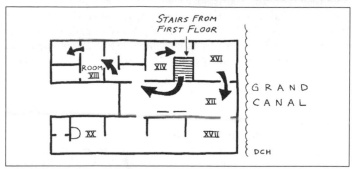

gaiety of Settecento Venice was at odds with the *Liberté, Egalité,* and *Fraternité* erupting in France.

• *Traveling through the maze of Room XIII, wind your way into a room with a harpsichord, cleverly named the...*

Room XIV: Harpsichord Room

The 1700s saw the development of new keyboard instruments that would culminate by century's end in the modern piano. This particular specimen has strings that are not hammered (like a piano) but plucked (like a mechanical guitar). The spacing of "white" keys and "black" keys is chromatic like a modern piano. This newly invented "tempered" scale of evenly spaced notes let you play in all keys without retuning.

Room XVI: Parlor Room

Francesco Guardi (1712–1793), like Canaletto, supplied foreigners with scenes of Venice. But Guardi uses rougher brushwork that casts a romantic haze over the decaying city.

The Parlor (Il Parlatorio delle Monache di S. Zaccaria) is an interior landscape featuring visiting day at a convent school. The

girls, secluded behind grills, chat and have tea with family members, friends, ladies with their pets, and potential suitors. Convents were like finishing schools for aristocratic girls, where they got an education and learned manners before reentering the world. Note the puppet show (starring spouse-abusing Pulcinella).

Guardi's *Il Ridotto di Palazzo Dandolo* shows party-goers in masks at a Venetian palace licensed for gambling. Casanova and others claimed that these casino houses had back rooms for the private use of patrons and courtesans.

The men wear the traditional *bautta*—a three-piece outfit consisting of a face mask, three-cornered hat, and cowl. This get-up was actually required by law in certain seedy establishments—to ensure that every sinner was equally anonymous. The women wear Lone Ranger masks, and parade a hint of cleavage to potential customers.

• *Continuing along, you'll pass back through the Painting Portego and into...*

Room XVII: Longhi Room

There is no better look at 1700s Venice than these genre scenes by Pietro Longhi (1702–1785), depicting everyday life among the upper classes. See ladies and gentlemen going to the hairdresser or to the dentist, dressed in

the finery that was standard in every public situation.

Contrast these straightforward scenes with G. B. Tiepolo's sumptuous ceiling painting of nude gods and goddesses. The Rococo fantasy world of aristocrats was slipping increasingly into the more prosaic era of the bourgeoisie.

• *Pass through several rooms to the far corner.*

Room XX: The Alcove

Casanova daydreamed of fancy boudoirs like this one, complete with a large bed (topped with a Carriera Madonna), a walnut dresser, neoclassical wallpaper, and silver toiletries. Even the presence of the baby cradle would not have dimmed his ardor.

PEGGY GUGGENHEIM COLLECTION TOUR

Peggy Guggenheim (1898–1979)—an American-born heiress to the Guggenheim fortune, and niece of Solomon Guggenheim (who built New York's modern art museum of the same name)—made her mark as a friend, lover, and patron of modern artists.

As a gallery owner, she introduced Europe's avant-garde to a skeptical America. As a collector, she gave instant status to modern art that was too radical for serious museums. As a patron, she fed starving artists such as Jackson Pollock. And as a person, she lived larger than life, unconventional and original, with a succession of lovers that enhanced her reputation as a female Casanova.

In 1948, Peggy "retired" to Venice, moving into a small, unfinished palazzo on the Grand Canal. Today it's a museum, decorated much as it was during her lifetime, with one of the best collections anywhere of 20th-century art. It's the only museum I can think of where the owner is buried in the garden.

ORIENTATION

Cost: €10.

Hours: Wed–Mon 10:00–18:00, closed Tue, last entry 15 min before closing. On Saturdays in June and July, the museum is open until 22:00, when it hosts concerts of contemporary music in the garden (starting around 20:30, free with price of admission); ask at the ticket counter or visit the Web site (below) for schedule.

Getting There: The museum, overlooking the Grand Canal, is at Dorsoduro 704, a five-minute walk from the Accademia Bridge (vaporetto: Accademia) or from La Salute Church (vaporetto: Salute).

Information: The museum shop sells guidebooks (€18). Tel. 041-240-5411, www.guggenheim-venice.it.

Tours: Audioguide tours cost €5. You can book a guided 60- to 90-minute tour (€60) by calling the museum. Art interns guarding the works are happy to tell you about particular pieces if you ask.

Length of This Tour: Allow one hour.

Baggage Check: Free and required.

Cuisine Art: Pricey café on site.

Photography: Allowed only in garden and terrace.

Starring: Picasso, Kandinsky, Mondrian, Dalí, Pollock...and everyone else who made a mark on modern art.

THE TOUR BEGINS

After passing through a garden courtyard sprinkled with statues, you enter the palazzo. There's a wing to the left and a wing to the right, plus a modern annex. The collection is (very) roughly chronological, starting to the left with Cubism and ending to the right with young, postwar artists.

The collection is strongest on Abstract, Surrealist, and Abstract-Surrealist art. The placement of the paintings can change, so use this chapter as an overview, not a painting-by-painting tour.

• *Walk through Peggy's collection...and through her life, which is mirrored in the art on the walls. From the sculpture garden, you walk into the...*

Entrance Hall: Meet Peggy Guggenheim

Picture Peggy Guggenheim greeting guests here—standing under the **trembling-leaf mobile by Alexander Calder,** surrounded by her yapping dogs and wearing her Calder-designed earrings, Mondrian-print dress, and "Catwoman" sunglasses.

During the 1950s and 1960s, this old palazzo on the Grand Canal was a mecca for "Moderns," from composer Igor Stravinsky to actor Marlon Brando, from painter Mark Rothko to writer Truman Capote, from choreographer George Balanchine to Beatle John Lennon and performance artist Yoko Ono. They came to sip cocktails, tour the great art, talk about ideas, and meet the woman who had become a living legend.

Pablo Picasso—*On the Beach* (1937)

Curious, balloon-animal women play with a sailboat while their friend across the water looks on. Of all Peggy's many paintings, this was her favorite.

By the time Peggy Guggenheim first became serious about modern art (about the time this was painted), Pablo Picasso—the most famous and versatile modern artist—had already been through his Blue, Rose, Fauve, Cubist, Synthetic Cubist, Classical, Abstract, and Surrealist phases, finally arriving at a synthesis of these styles. Peggy had some catching up to do.

• *Enter the first room to the left, and you'll see a dining-room table in the center.*

1900–1920: Cubists in the Dining Room

Peggy's dining-room table reminds us that this museum was, indeed, Peggy's home for the last 30 years of her life. (See the small black-and-white photo of Peggy in this room.) Most of the furniture is now gone, but the walls are decorated much as they were when she lived here, with paintings and statues by her friends, colleagues, and mentors. Here, she entertained countless artists and celebrities (more name-dropping), from actor Paul Newman to poet Allen Ginsberg, from sculptor Henry Moore to playwright Tennessee Williams, from James Bond creator Ian Fleming to glass sculptor Dale Chihuly.

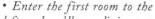

The art in the Dining Room dates from Peggy's childhood, when she was raised in the lap of luxury in New York, oblivious to the artistic upheavals going on in Europe.

In 1912, the *Titanic* went down, taking Peggy's playboy tycoon father with it...and leaving his 14-year-old daughter with a small but comfortable trust fund and a man-sized hole in her life.

Approaching adulthood, Peggy rejected her traditional American upbringing, hanging out at a radical bookstore, getting a nose job (a botched operation, leaving her with a rather bulbous schnozz)...and planning a trip to Europe.

In 1920, 21-year-old Peggy arrived in Paris, where a revolution in art was taking place.

• *Find the following art in the Dining Room.*

Pablo Picasso—*The Poet* (1911)

Picasso, a Spaniard living in Paris, shattered the Old World into brown shards ("cubes") and reassembled it in Cubist style. It's a vaguely recognizable portrait of a man from the waist up—tapering to a head at the top, smoking a pipe (?), and cradling the traditional lyre of a poet. While the newfangled motion-picture

Peggy Guggenheim Collection

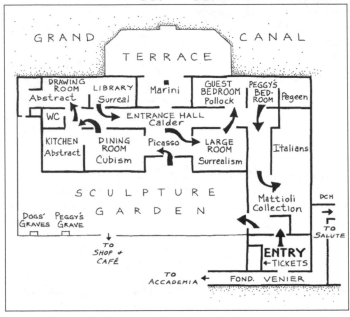

camera could capture a moving image, Picasso suggests motion with a collage of stills.

Marcel Duchamp—*Nude (Study), Sad Young Man on a Train* (1911–1912)

In a self-portrait, Duchamp poses gracefully with a cane, but the moving train jiggles the image into a blur of brown. Duchamp, who is perhaps best known for his outrageous urinal-as-statue and his moustache-on-the-*Mona Lisa*, would later become Peggy's friend and mentor in modernism, steering her to buy these early-modern "classics."

Umberto Boccioni—*Dynamism of a Speeding Horse + Houses* (assemblage, 1915)

This statue captures the blurred motion of the modern world—accelerated by technology, then shattered by World War I, which left nine million Europeans dead and everyone's moral compass spinning. (In fact, this statue was shattered by the destructive force of Boccioni's own kids, who scattered the cardboard "houses" while using it as a rocking horse.)

Constantin Brancusi—*Maiastra* (bronze statue, c. 1912)

For the generation born before air travel, flying was magical. This high-polished bird is the first of many by Brancusi, who dreamed of flight. But this bird just sits there. For centuries, a good sculptor was one who could capture movement in stone. Brancusi reverts to the style of "primitive" African art, where even the simplest statues radiate mojo.

• *Dip into the West Corridor to find...*

Marc Chagall—*Rain* (1911)

The rain clouds gather over a farmhouse, the wind blows the trees and people, and everyone pre-

pares for the storm. Quick, put the horse in the barn, grab an umbrella, take a leak, and round up the goats in the clouds.

Marc Chagall, a Russian living in France, found the romantic, weightless, child-like joy of topsy-turvy Paris.

• *Browse through the next few rooms.*

1920s: Abstraction in the Kitchen, "-Isms" in the Living Room

Peggy spent her twenties in the Roaring Twenties, right in the center of avant-garde craziness: Paris. For the rest of her life, Europe—not America—would be her permanent address.

In Paris, trust-funded Peggy lived the bohemian life. Post–WWI Paris was cheap and, after the bitter war years, ready to party. Days were spent drinking coffee in cafés, talking ideas with the likes of activist Emma Goldman, writer Djuna *(Nightwood)* Barnes, and photographer Man Ray. Nights were spent abusing the drug forbidden in America (alcohol), dancing to jazz music into the wee hours, and talking about Freud and s-e-x.

One night, on top of the Eiffel Tower, a dashing artist and intellectual nicknamed "The King of Bohemia" popped the question. Peggy and Laurence Vail soon married and had two children, but the partying only slowed somewhat. This thoroughly modern couple dug the wild life and the wild art it produced.

• *Head across the corridor to the Drawing Room to find...*

Wassily Kandinsky—
White Cross (1922)

I see white, I see crosses, but where's the "white cross"? Oh, there it is on the right, camouflaged among black squares.

Like a jazz musician improvising from a set scale, Kandinsky plays with new patterns of related colors and lines, creating something that's simply beautiful, even if it doesn't "mean" anything. As Kandinsky himself would say, his art was like "visual music—just open your eyes and look."

Piet Mondrian—*Composition* (1938–1939)

Like a blueprint for modernism, Mondrian's T-square style boils painting down to its basic building blocks—black lines, white canvas, and the three primary colors (red, yellow, and blue) arranged in orderly patterns. This stripped-down canvas even omits yellow and blue.

Mondrian started out painting realistic landscapes of the orderly fields in his native Holland. Increasingly, he simplified it

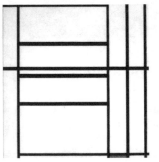

into horizontal and vertical patterns, creating rectangles of different proportions. This one has horizontal lines to the left, vertical ones to the right. The horizontals appear to dominate, until we see that they're "balanced" by the tiny patch of red.

For Mondrian, who was heavily into Eastern mysticism, "up vs. down" and "left vs. right" were metaphors for life's ever-shifting dualities—"good vs. evil," "man vs. woman," "fascism vs. communism." The canvas is a bird's-eye view of Mondrian's personal landscape.

• *Walk a few paces to the Library.*

1930s: Abstract Surrealists in the Library

In 1928, Peggy's marriage to Laurence Vail ended, and she entered into a series of romantic attachments—some loving and stable, others sexual and impersonal. Though not stunningly attractive, she was easy to be with, and she truly admired artistic men.

In 1937, she began an on-again, off-again (so to speak) sexual relationship with playwright Samuel *(Waiting for Godot)* Beckett. Beckett steered her toward modern painting and sculpture—things she'd never paid much attention to.

Abstract Art

Abstract art simplifies. A man becomes a stick figure. A squiggle is a wave. A streak of red expresses anger. Arches make you want a cheeseburger. These are universal symbols that everyone from a caveman to a banker understands. Abstract artists capture the essence of reality in a few lines and colors, even things a camera can't—emotions, abstract concepts, musical rhythms, and spiritual states of mind.

Most 20th-century paintings are a mix of the real world ("representation") and the colorful patterns of "abstract" art. Artists purposely distort camera-eye reality to make the resulting canvas more decorative.

She started hanging out with the French Surrealists, from artist Marcel Duchamp to writer André Breton to filmmaker/artist Jean *(Beauty and the Beast)* Cocteau. Duchamp, in particular, mentored her in modern art, encouraging her to use her money to collect and promote it. Nearing 40, she moved to London and launched a new career.

Yves Tanguy—*The Sun in Its Jewel Case* (1937)

In May 1938, this painting was featured at "Guggenheim Jeune," the art gallery Peggy opened in London. Tanguy's painting sums up the outrageous art that shocked a sleepy London during that first season.

Weird, phallic, tissue-and-bone protuberances cast long shadows across a moody, dream-like landscape—the landscape of the mind. (Peggy said the picture "frightened" her, but added, "I got over my fear...and now I own it.") The

figures are Abstract (unrecognizable), and the mood is Surreal, producing the style cleverly dubbed Abstract Surrealism.

Peggy was drawn to Yves Tanguy and had a short but intense affair with the married man. Tanguy, like his art, was wacky and spontaneous, occasionally shocking friends by suddenly catching and gobbling up a spider, washing it down with white wine. The Surrealists saw themselves as spokesmen for Freud's "id," the untamed part of your personality that thinks dirty thoughts when your "ego" goes to sleep.

The Guggenheim Jeune gallery exhibited many of the artists we see in this museum, including Kandinsky, Mondrian, and

Calder. Guggenheim Jeune closed a financial failure after just two years, but the outrageous art certainly created a buzz in the art world, and over the years the gallery's failure gained a rosy glow of success.

1939–1940: Peggy's Shopping Spree in Paris

Peggy moved back to Paris and rented an apartment on the Ile St. Louis. In September, Nazi Germany invaded Poland, sparking World War II. All of France waited...and waited...and waited for the inevitable Nazi attack on Paris.

Meanwhile, Peggy spent her days shopping for master-pieces. Using a list compiled by Duchamp and others, she personally visited artists in their studios—from Brancusi to Dalí to Giacometti—often negotiating directly with them. (Picasso initially turned Peggy down, thinking of her as a gauche, bargain-hunting housewife. When she entered his studio he said, "Madame, you'll find the lingerie department on the second floor.") In a few short months, she bought 37 of the paintings now in the collection, perhaps saving them from a Nazi regime that labeled such art "decadent."

In 1941, with the Nazis occupying Paris and most of Europe, Peggy fled her adopted homeland. With her stash of paintings and a new companion—Max Ernst—she sailed from Lisbon to safety in New York.

• *Pass back through the Entrance Hall—where Peggy welcomed celebrity guests, from writer Somerset Maugham to actor Rex Harrison to painter Marc Chagall—and into the east wing. The right entryway leads to a room (called the Large Room) filled with Surrealist canvases.*

1941–1945: Surrealists Invade New York

Trees become women, women become horses, and day becomes night. Balls dangle, caves melt, and things cast long shadows across film-noir landscapes—Surrealism. The world was moving fast, and Surrealists caught the jumble of images. They scattered seemingly unrelated things on the canvas, leaving us to trace the connections in a kind of connect-the-dots game without numbers.

Peggy spent the war years in America. She married the painter Max Ernst, and their house in New York City became a gathering place for exiled French Surrealists and young American artists.

In 1942, she opened a gallery/museum in New York called "Art of This Century" that featured, well, essentially the collection we see here in Venice. But patriotic, gung-ho America was not quite ready for the nonconformist, intellectual art of Europe.

Max Ernst—The Antipope (c. 1942)

The horse-headed nude in red is a portrait of Peggy—at least,

that's what she thought when she saw it. She loved the painting and insisted that Max give it to her as a wedding present, renamed *The Mystic Marriage*.

Others read more into it. Is the horse-headed warrior (at right) Ernst himself? Is he being wooed by one of his art students? Is that Peggy's daughter, Pegeen (center), watching the scene, sadly, from a distance? And is Peggy turning toward her beloved Max, subconsciously suspicious of the young student...who would (in fact) soon steal Max from her? Ernst uses his considerable painting skill to bring to light the tangle of hidden urges, desires, and fears—hidden like the grotesque animal faces in the reef they stand on.

Paul Delvaux—*The Break of Day* (1937)

Full-breasted ladies with roots cast long shadows and awaken to a mysterious dawn. If you're counting boobs, don't forget the one reflected in the nightstand mirror.

René Magritte—*Empire of Light* (1953–54)

Magritte found that, even under a sunny blue sky, suburbia has its dark side.

Salvador Dalí—*The Birth of Liquid Desires* (1931–32)

Salvador Dalí could draw exceptionally well. He painted "unreal" scenes with photographic realism, making us believe they could really happen. This creates an air of mystery—the feeling that anything can happen—that's both exciting and unsettling. His men explore the caves of the dreamworld and morph into something else before our eyes.

Personally, Peggy didn't like Dalí or his work, but she dutifully bought this canvas (through his wife, Gala) to complete her collection.

• *Across the hall is the Guest Bedroom, with a fireplace and works by Pollock.*

1945–1948, The Postwar Years: Pollock in the Guest Bedroom

Certain young American painters—from Mark Rothko to Robert Motherwell to Robert De Niro, Sr. (the actor's father)—were strongly influenced by Peggy's collection. Adopting the Abstract style of Kandinsky and Mondrian, they practiced Surrealist spontaneity to "express" their personal insights. The resulting style (duh)—Abstract Expressionism.

Jackson Pollock—*Enchanted Forest* (1947)

"Jack the Dripper" attacked America's postwar conformity with a can of paint, dripping and splashing a dense web onto the canvas. Picture Pollock in his studio, jiving to the hi-fi, bouncing off the walls, throwing paint in a moment of alcohol-fueled enlightenment.

Peggy helped make Pollock a celebrity. She bought his earliest works (which show Abstract-Surreal roots), exhibited his work at her gallery, and even paid him a monthly stipend to keep experimenting.

By the way, if you haven't yet tried the Venetian specialty *spaghetti al nero di seppia* (spaghetti with squid in its own ink), it looks something like this.

In 1946, Peggy published her memoirs, titled *Out of This Century: The Informal Memoirs of Peggy Guggenheim*. The front cover was designed by Max Ernst, the back by Pollock. Peggy herself was now a celebrity.

• *The room on the other side of the fireplace was Peggy's Room.*

1950s: Peggy in the Bedroom

As America's postwar factories turned swords into kitchen appliances, Peggy longed to return "home" to Europe. The one place that kept calling to her was Venice, ever since a visit with Laurence Vail in the 1920s. "I decided Venice would be my future home," she wrote. "I felt I would be happy alone there."

In 1947, after a grand finale exhibition by Pollock, she closed the "Art of This Century" gallery, crated up her collection, and moved to Venice. In 1948, she bought this palazzo and moved in.

This was Peggy's bedroom. She painted it turquoise. She commissioned the **silver headboard by Alexander Calder** for her canopy bed, using its silver frame to hang her collection of earrings, handmade by the likes of Calder and Tanguy. Venetian mirrors hung on the walls, along with a sentimental portrait of herself and her sister as children. Ex-husband Laurence Vail's collage-decorated bottles sat on the nightstand.

In 1951, Peggy met the last great love of her life, an easygoing, blue-collar Italian with absolutely no interest in art. She was 53, Raoul was 30, and their relationship, though rather odd, was tender and mutually satisfying. Raoul died in 1954 in a car accident, and Peggy comforted herself with her pets.

• *The tiny corner room adjoining the bedroom displays paintings by Pegeen.*

Pegeen

Peggy's daughter, named Pegeen, inherited some of Laurence Vail's artistic talent, painting childlike scenes of Venice, populated by skinny Barbie dolls with antennae.

The Guest Bedroom (where the Pollocks are) was a busy place. Pegeen and her brother, Sinbad, visited their mother, as did Peggy's ex-husbands and their new loves. Other overnight guests ranged from sculptor Alberto Giacometti (who honeymooned here) to author and cultural explorer Paul Bowles to artist Jean Arp.

• *Cross the hall and go down a few steps into the wing perpendicular to the palazzo, the Mattioli Annex.*

Italians in the Annex

You'll find a few paintings by famous Italians (**Modigliani, Boccioni**) and a lot by the postwar generation of young Italians who were strongly influenced by Peggy's collection. In 1948, Peggy showed her collection in its own pavilion at the Biennale, Venice's "world's fair of art," and it was the hit of the show. Europeans were astounded and a bit shocked, finally seeing the kind of "degenerate" art forbidden during the fascist years, plus the radical new stuff coming out of New York City.

Peggy sponsored young artists, including **Tancredi**—just one name, back when that was odd—who was given a studio in the palazzo's basement. Tancredi had a relationship with daughter Pegeen, with her mother's blessing. (Pegeen died in 1967 of an overdose of barbiturates.)

• *Return to the Entrance Hall, then go out onto the Terrace, overlooking the Grand Canal.*

Exhibitionists on the Terrace

> *"You fall in love with the city itself. There is nothing left over in your heart for anyone else."*
>
> —Peggy Guggenheim

Marino Marini's equestrian statue, *The Angel of the City* (1948), faces the Grand Canal, spreads his arms wide, and tosses his head back in sheer joy, with an eternal hard-on for the city of Venice. Every morning, Peggy must have felt a similar exhilaration as she sipped coffee with this unbelievable view.

Marini originally designed his bronze rider with a screw-off penis (which sounds dirtier than it is) that could be removed for prudish guests or by curious ones. Someone stole it for some unknown purpose, so the current organ is permanently welded on.

The palazzo—called Palazzo Venier dei Leoni—looks modern but is old. Begun in 1748, only its ground floor was built before construction was halted. Legend has it that members of the rival family across the canal in Palazzo Corner squelched the plans for the upper stories to prevent their home from being upstaged. The palazzo remained unfinished until Peggy bought it in 1948 and spruced it up. She added the annex in 1958. The **lions** *(leoni)* of the original palace still guard the waterfront entrance.

Peggy's outlandish and rather foreign presence in Venice—drinking, dressing up outrageously, and sunbathing on her rooftop for all to see—was not immediately embraced by the Venetians. But for artists in the 1950s and 1960s, Peggy's palazzo was *the* place to be, especially when the Biennale brought the jet set. Everyone from actor Alec Guinness to columnist Art Buchwald to costume designer Hedda Hopper signed her guest book. Picture Peggy and guests, decked out in evening clothes, hopping into Peggy's custom-built gondola (nicknamed *La Barchessa,* after the doge's private boat) to ride slowly down the canal for a martini and a Bellini at Harry's Bar.

• *Pass back through the Entrance Hall, then outside to the...*

Sculpture Garden

Peggy opened her impressive collection of sculpture to the Venetian public for free. It features first-rate works by all the greats, from Brancusi to Moore to Giacometti. After so much art already, you might find the trees—so rare in urban Venice—more interesting.

If, after your visit here, you still don't like modern art, think of what Peggy used to tell puzzled visitors: "Come back again in fifty years."

• *In the southwest corner of the garden (along the brick wall), find...*

Peggy's Grave and Her Dogs' Grave

"Here Lie My Beloved Babies," marks the grave of her many dogs that were her steady companions as she grew old. Note the names of some of these small, long-haired Lhasa apsos. Along with "Cappuccino" and "Baby," you'll see "Pegeen," after her daughter, and "Sir Herbert," for Herbert Read, the art critic who helped Peggy select her collection.

Peggy's ashes are buried alongside, marked with a simple plaque: "Here Rests Peggy Guggenheim 1898–1979."

Over your right shoulder, the stumpy olive tree is a gift from one of Peggy's old traveling buddies—Yoko Ono.

In the nonconformist 1960s, Peggy's once shocking art and unconventional lifestyle became more acceptable, even commonplace. By the 1970s, she was universally recognized as a major force in early modern art and was finally even honored by the Venetians with a nickname—"The Last Dogess" (L'Ultima Dogaressa). When she died in a Padua hospital in 1979, she was mourned by the art world, from sculptor Henry Moore to composer Virgil Thomson, from choreographer Jerome Robbins to writer George Plimpton, from composer John Cage to...

LA SALUTE CHURCH TOUR

(Santa Maria della Salute)

Where the Grand Canal opens up into the lagoon stands one of Venice's most distinctive landmarks, the church dedicated to Santa Maria della Salute (Our Lady of Health). The architect, Baldassare Longhena—who also did St. Mark's Square's "New" Wing and the Ca' Rezzonico—remade Venice in the Baroque style. Crown-shaped La Salute was his crowning achievement, and the last grand Venetian structure built before Venice's decline began.

ORIENTATION

Cost: Free (€1.50 for sacristy, if it's open).

Hours: Daily 9:00–12:00 & 15:00–18:00 (tel. 041-522-5558 to confirm).

Getting There: On the Grand Canal, near the point where the canal spills into the lagoon. It's a 10-minute walk from the Accademia Bridge (past the Peggy Guggenheim Collection). The Salute Vaporetto stop is at the doorstep. Or take a cheap *traghetto* from near St. Mark's Square (on the lagoon near TI and Harry's Bar). If it's November 21 (see below), you can walk directly to the church across the Grand Canal on a floating, pontoon-like bridge.

Length of This Tour: Allow 30 minutes.

Starring: Baldassare Longhena's church and works by Titian and Giordano.

THE TOUR BEGINS

Exterior

The white stone church has a steep dome that rises above a circular structure. It's crusted with Baroque scrolls, leafy Corinthian

La Salute Church

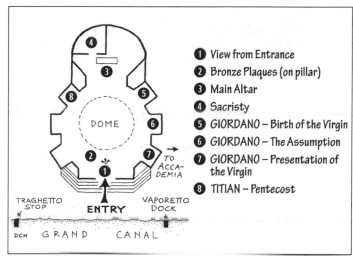

① View from Entrance
② Bronze Plaques (on pillar)
③ Main Altar
④ Sacristy
⑤ GIORDANO – Birth of the Virgin
⑥ GIORDANO – The Assumption
⑦ GIORDANO – Presentation of the Virgin
⑧ TITIAN – Pentecost

columns, and 125 statues, including the lovely ladies lounging over the central doorway. The architect conceived of the church "in the shape of a crown."

During the bitter plague of 1630, the Virgin Mary took pity on the city of Venice, miraculously allowing only one in three Venetians (46,000 souls) to die. During this terrible time,

Venetians built this church in honor of Our Lady of Health. Her statue tops the lantern, and she's dressed as an admiral, hand on a rudder, welcoming ships to the Grand Canal.

Even today, Mary's intercession is celebrated every November 21, when a floating bridge is erected across the Grand Canal, the *traghetto* driver takes a day off, and Venetians can walk from San Marco across the water and right up the seaweed-covered steps to the front door.

At age 32, architect Baldassare Longhena (1598–1682) supported the city's heaviest dome by sinking countless pilings (locals claim over a million) into the sandy soil to provide an adequate foundation. The 12 Baroque scrolls at the base function as buttresses to help support the mammoth dome.

Interior
❶ View from the Entrance

The church has a bright, healthy glow, with white stone (gray because of a fungus) illuminated by filtered light from the windows of the dome. The church is circular, surrounded by chapels. In contrast with the ornate Baroque exterior, the inside is simple, with only some Corinthian columns and two useless balcony railings up in the dome. The red, white, and yellow marble of the floor adds a cheerful note.

Longhena focuses our immediate attention on the main altar. Every other view is blocked by heavy pillars. Longhena, a master of "theatrical architecture," only reveals the side chapels one by one as we walk around and explore.

The church is an octagon surrounding a circular nave that's topped by the dome. Viewed from the center of the church, the altar and side chapels are framed by arches.

Some of the "marble" is brick covered with marble dust. The windows are the simple shape that a drop of molten glass makes, to bring in maximum light.

• Look at the pillars in the rear of the church, opposite the altar, to find the...

❷ Bronze Plaques

The church is dedicated not just to physical health but to spiritual health as well. The plaques tell us that on September 16, 1972, the future Pope John Paul I—the predecessor of John Paul II—visited here and paid homage to the Virgin of Health (six years later, he fell sick and died after only 30 days in office).

❸ Main Altar

The marble statues on the top tell the church's story: Mary and Child (center) are approached for help by a kneeling, humble Lady Venice (left). Mary takes compassion and sends an angel baby (right) to drive away Old Lady Plague.

The icon of a black, sad-eyed Madonna with a black baby (12th-century Byzantine) is not meant to be racially accurate. Here, a "black" Madonna means an otherworldly one.

• Through the door to the left of the altar is the...

❹ Sacristy

If it's open, you can see several great paintings in the sacristy. The three Titians on the ceiling were made by the artist during his "Mannerist crisis." After visiting Rome and seeing the work of Michelangelo in the Sistine Chapel, Titian left his standard, sweet, and tested style (such as the smaller painting over the Sacristy altar) and painted big, statuesque, and dramatic works in the Mannerist style.

In Tintoretto's equally dramatic *Marriage at Cana*, the 12 apostles actually portray leading Venetian artists of his day. While it costs €1.50 to get in, cheapskates can get a glimpse of the paintings for free at the entry.

• *Back in the circular nave, there are six side chapels—three to the left, three to the right. Start near the altar, on the right side (to your right as you face the altar).*

Side Chapel Paintings

Luca Giordano (1632–1705) celebrates the Virgin in three paintings with a similar composition—heaven and angels above, dark earth below.

Giordano, a prolific artist from Naples, was known as "*Luca fa presto*" (Fast Luke) for his ambidextrous painting abilities.

• *In the chapel to the right of the altar is...*

❺ Giordano—*Birth of the Virgin* (1674)

Little baby Mary in her mom's arms seems like nothing special. But God the Father looks down from above and sends the dove of the Spirit.

• *In the middle chapel...*

❻ Giordano—*The Assumption*

Mary, at the end of her life, is being taken gloriously by winged babies, up from the dark earth to the golden light of heaven. The apostles cringe in amazement. A later artist thought his statue was better and planted it right in our way.

• *In the chapel closest to the entrance...*

❼ Giordano—*Presentation of the Virgin*

Notice how the painting fits the surrounding architecture. It's great to enjoy art "in situ." The child Mary (in blue, with wispy halo) ascends a staircase that goes diagonally "into" the canvas. Giordano places us viewers at the foot of the stairs. The lady in the lower left asks her kids, "Why can't you be more like her?!"

• *From here, look directly across to the other side of the nave, to the chapel closest to the main altar. At this distance and angle, Titian's painting looks its best.*

❽ Titian (Tiziano Vecellio)—*Pentecost* (1546)

The dove of the Holy Spirit sends spiritual rays that fan out to the apostles below, giving them tongues of fire above their heads. They gyrate in amazement, each one in a different direction. Using floor tiles and ceiling panels, Titian has created the 3-D illusion of a barrel-arched chapel, with the dove coming right into the church through a fake window. But the painting was not designed for this location

and, up close, the whole fake niche looks...fake.

SAN GIORGIO MAGGIORE TOUR

This dreamy church-topped island is a five-minute vaporetto ride away from St. Mark's Square. Even if you're not interested in Palladio's influential architecture, Tintoretto's famous *Last Supper,* or even the stunning view back at the city skyline, it's worth a trip just to escape from tourist-mobbed St. Mark's Square.

ORIENTATION

Cost: Admission to the church is free.

Hours: Daily May–Sept 9:30–12:30 & 14:30–18:30, Oct–April 9:30–12:30 & 14:30–16:30, closed Sun to sightseers during Mass. The bells ring (very loudly!) at 12:00. A Gregorian Mass is sung at 8:00 Mon–Sat and at 11:00 on Sun (confirm times at a Venice TI).

Getting There: San Giorgio Maggiore is the impressive church you see across the lagoon from St. Mark's Square. Catch vaporetto #82 from the San Zaccaria Jolanda stop, just past the Bridge of Sighs, closest to the big statue. (Note: This is not the same vaporetto stop as San Marco/Vallaresso.)

Bell Tower: The tower is closed for renovation through 2006. When it's open, the elevator to the top costs €3 (runs until 30 min before church's closing time).

Length of This Tour: Allow 30 minutes.

Starring: Palladio, Tintoretto, and views of Venice.

THE TOUR BEGINS

Exterior

The facade looks like a Greek temple, a style so common today only because the architect Palladio was so influential. In fact, the

San Giorgio Maggiore

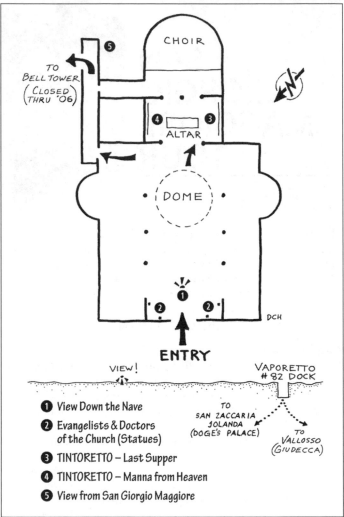

1 View Down the Nave

2 Evangelists & Doctors of the Church (Statues)

3 TINTORETTO – Last Supper

4 TINTORETTO – Manna from Heaven

5 View from San Giorgio Maggiore

facade is like two temple fronts overlapping. The four tall columns topped by a triangular pediment resemble a Greek porch, marking the entryway to the tall, central nave. This is superimposed over the facade of the lower side aisles. Behind the facade rises a dome topped with a statue of St. George (the Christian slayer of medieval dragons) holding a flag. The whole complex is completed by the bell tower, which echoes St. Mark's Campanile across the water.

Andrea Palladio (1508–1580) influenced centuries of architects in England and America with his revival of Greco-Roman styles.

His churches, palaces, and villas were popularized by a famous treatise he wrote on architecture.
• *Walk into the interior of the church...*

❶ View Down the Nave

The interior matches the outer facade, with a high nave flanked by lower side aisles. The walls are white; the windows have clear, rather than stained, glass; and the well-lit church has a clarity and mathematical perfection that exudes the classical world.

• *Above the entrance door are eight statues...*

❷ Evangelists and Doctors of the Church

The four Evangelists in the upper niches and four Doctors of the Church below are all as pure white as the rest of the church. But the Evangelists are white stucco, the Doctors are whitewashed wood... and the rest of the church is a mix of white Istrian stone (the columns) with white-painted cheaper materials (the pilasters).

In the transepts are works by Giovanni Domenico Tiepolo, the son and assistant of his more famous father.

Main Altar and Tintoretto

The altar is topped with a bronze globe of the world. The monks who once lived on this island congregated in the choir area behind the main altar.
• *On the wall to the right of the altar is...*

❸ Tintoretto—*Last Supper*

This is the last of several versions of the *Last Supper* by Tintoretto (1518–1594) that decorate Venice, each one different and inventive. Here, the table stretches diagonally away from us on a tiled floor, with such a convincing 3-D effect that the tiny diners at the far end look a mile away. The scene is crowded—servants and cats

mingle with wispy, unseen angels. A blazing lamp radiating supernatural light illuminates the otherwise dark interior. Dark shadows are cast on the table. In the foreground, a lady offers a man a breath mint.

Tintoretto's jumble of the spiritual with the mundane proclaims his common theme that God works miraculously with us on an every-day level. Almost lost in the hubbub is Jesus (middle of the table, in red and blue), serving the bread and wine.

• *On the wall to the left of the altar is...*

❹ Tintoretto—*Manna from Heaven*

This shows the sunny morning after the storm when God rained bread down on the hungry Israelites. They luxuriate on the ground, gathering the heavenly meal in baskets, basking in the glow of the miracle.

• *If the bell tower happens to be open, you'll find the lift to the top in the far left corner of the church. In 2006, the tower will probably be closed, but you can still head back outside and enjoy the...*

❺ View from San Giorgio Maggiore

Enjoy identifying these Venice landmarks from the island (or from your vaporetto on the way back to St. Mark's Square).

Face **north** (toward the city). This is the famous view of Venice's skyline, with St. Mark's Campanile dominating. If the bell tower is open and you're up there, you'll see more details: The big, long, brick church farther inland is Santi Giovanni e Paolo. Farther to the right (east) is the artificial bay of the Arsenale, the former ship factory, which was capable of producing a ship a day, or 100

in three months. Farther still is the green parkland where the Biennale International Art Exhibition is held (next in the summer of 2007; see page 324). North of Venice, in the hazy distance, you may catch a glimpse of several islands: tiny San Michele (with cypress trees and cemetery), Murano (the next-closest), Burano (leaning bell tower), and Torcello (see page 176).

The closest island to the **east** is where visiting merchants were required to spend 40 (*quaranta*) days in quarantine before setting foot on the main island, to prevent the arrival of diseases. The next island after that (with the onion-dome bell tower) was given to religious Armenians and still houses a dozen friars.

Farther east is the looong, narrow Lido island—six miles long and only a half mile (almost 9 football fields) wide. The green dome on the island marks the Lido's main town, home to modern hotels, casinos, and beaches. Cars are allowed, which is why car ferries shuttle between Lido and the mainland.

View from San Giorgio Maggiore

AIRPORT

LAGOON

TORCELLO

BURANO

MESTRE

CAUSEWAY

SAN
MICHELE

MURANO

N

TRONCHETTO

RIALTO

SAN GIOVANNI

GRAND
CANAL

SAN
MARCO

ARSENALE

SALUTE

G I U D E C C A

BIENNALE
PARK

REDENTORE

SAN
GIORGIO

NOT TO SCALE— SAN GIORGIO TO:
  TORCELLO = 6 MILES
  MESTRE = 5 MILES
  LIDO = 2 MILES

LIDO

DCH

The Lido serves as a natural breakwater against the wind and waves of the Adriatic, helping create the placid waters of the Venetian lagoon. At the right (south) end of the island is the narrow opening to the Adriatic. This is where underwater flood barriers are proposed to be built—the 10-year, $3.5 billion "Moses Project"—to stop the wind and waves from the southeast that cause the *acqua alta* flooding. These hinged barriers will raise up to block high tides threatening the lagoon's serenity.

Once a year, the mayor of Venice sails here to celebrate the ritual marriage of Venice and the sea—the same ritual performed centuries ago by the doges in their gold-leaf boat.

Stretching to the **west** is the island of Giudecca, which is oh-so-close to the Isle of San Giorgio Maggiore but must be reached by a short swim or vaporetto #82. On Giudecca is Palladio's other masterpiece in Venice, the domed Redentore Church. To the right, across the water on the point at the opening of the Grand Canal, sits the golden globe of the old Customs House and the nearby dome of La Salute Church. Beyond that, through the smog, are the burning smokestacks and cranes of lovely Mestre on the mainland.

VENICE'S LAGOON TOUR

Cimitero, Murano, Burano, and Torcello

Several interesting islands (including San Giorgio Maggiore, see previous chapter), hide out in Venice's lagoon, a calm section of the Adriatic protected from wind and waves by the natural breakwater of the Lido. The marshy ecosystem—a mix of fresh water and silt from the mainland's rivers, plus the shifting tides of the Adriatic—result in a maze of sandbars. The lagoon is big (212 square miles) and shallow; the average depth is just two feet. The shallow water and treacherous sandbars made the Isle of Venice safe from attack by land or sea. It's the only medieval city that never needed a city wall.

Cradled by the lagoon are three islands easily laced together in a side trip, a nice escape from the hubbub of Venice. Murano is known for glass, Burano for lace, and tranquil Torcello for its church.

ORIENTATION

Cost: Transportation to and between the islands can be free (if you sit through a sales pitch), or it can cost €8.50, €10.50, or €20, depending on how and where you go (see "Getting There," below).

The €15.50 Museum Pass covers the Glass and Lace museums as well as many other Venice sights. (For more on the pass, see "Passes for Venice" on page 24.) Separately, the Glass and Lace museums each cost €4. Torcello's church and other sights are €2 each or are covered by a €6 combo-ticket.

Closed Days: Murano's Glass Museum is closed Wed, Burano's Lace Museum is closed Tue, and Torcello's museum is closed Mon (though the island's other sights are open).

Getting There: The islands are reached easily, cheaply, and slowly by **vaporetto**. (All boats, even speedboats, must obey strict

Venice's Lagoon

speed limits designed to reduce the wakes that boats throw.)
Pick up a free map of the islands from any TI. Depart from the
San Zaccaria Jolanda dock, past the Bridge of Sighs and near
the big statue. Line #12 connects all three islands, or take #41
to Murano (get off at Murano Colonna), and then #12 to the
other islands. If you plan to visit even two of these islands, get
a 24-hour €10.50 vaporetto pass or a 12-hour €8.50 "Laguna
Tour" pass for convenience.

Speedboat tours of these three lagoon destinations take
three to five hours, and leave twice a day from the dock past
the Doge's Palace near the shuttle dock. Look for the signs
and booth (€20, April–Oct usually at 9:30 and 14:30; Nov–
March 14:30 only, tel. 041-523-8835). The tours are speedy
indeed—live guides race through the commentary in up to
five languages, stopping for roughly 40 minutes at each island
(for glassblowing and lacemaking demonstrations followed by
sales pitches).

Many tourists are almost kidnapped from St. Mark's
Square by sales reps who bundle people onto a **free speedboat**

shuttle to Murano island, with no obligation other than to check out their factory/salesroom. It's a free and handy way to get to Murano. You must watch the 20-minute glassmaking show (and sales pitch), but then you're free to escape and see the rest of the island.

Length of This Tour: Allow five hours to see all three islands.

Starring: World-famous Venetian glass and lace, and the mosaics of the oldest Venetian church.

THE TOUR BEGINS

Cimitero

Most *vaporetti* connecting Venice and Murano stop at the cemetery island. Consider a quick stopover, since boats come every few minutes. Provided you are continuing on, rather than returning to the Venice mainland, you can hop off and back on using the same ticket. If you enjoy wandering through old cemeteries, Venice's is among the best—take some time for a quick look.

The island, which also holds a Renaissance church, is dedicated to St. Michael. The island became the city's cemetery in 1806, when Napoleon decreed that the graves in the city were unhygienic. Bodies were removed from the town to this island, and since then, locals have been buried here. Foreign Romantics and artists who made Venice their adopted hometown (including the Russian-born composer Igor Stravinsky and the American-born poet Ezra Pound) also chose this spot as their final resting place.

Murano

Approaching the island of Murano, you'll see its striped **lighthouse** *(faro)*. In centuries past, the *faro* guided boats from the open sea into town.

Murano is famous for its **glass factories**. A 1292 law restricted glass production (and its dangerous furnaces) to the isle of Murano to prevent fires on the main island...and to protect the secrets of Venetian glassmaking. Originally, they made mosaic tiles. They then branched out, producing the ornate vases, beaded necklaces, glass sculptures, and wine decanters you'll see here today.

Upon arrival, wander up Via Fondamenta Vetrai (along the canal of the glassmakers), and check out the various factories *(fabricca* or *fornace)*, each offering a free 20-minute glassblowing demonstration of an artisan in action firing up something in a furnace, followed by an almost comically high-pressure sales pitch. (The spiel is brief, and there's absolutely no obligation to buy anything.)

Continue up Via Fondamenta Vetrai. The many 19th-century factories give the city a brick, Industrial Age look and feel. For

Boating in Venice

Italian law stipulates that a luxury tax is levied on all boats—except in Venice, where they're considered a necessity. Locals go everywhere by boat. Calling a taxi? A boat comes. Going to the hospital to have a baby? Just hop the vaporetto. Garbage day? You put your bag on the canal edge and a garbage boat mashes it and takes it away.

Many locals own a boat, though it's not always practical for everyday activities. If you want to cruise to the grocery store, you first have to check the tide table to make sure your boat can fit beneath certain bridges. And parking is always a huge problem everywhere—either you know a friend nearby with a grandfathered parking space or your partner has to "circle the block" while you shop.

Locals rely more on the public *vaporetti* and *traghetti*. While tourists pay plenty for these boats, locals ride cheap and easy. An all-year pass costs €253 (less than €1/day).

Gondolas are strictly for tourists these days, but in earlier times these flat-bottomed boats were the only way to negotiate the tricky, shallow lagoon. The oarsman had to stand up in the back of the boat to see oncoming sandbars. Today, boats ply confidently between the shifting sand banks of the lagoon, thanks to thoroughfares defined by modern pilings.

While many Venetians own a car for driving on the isle of Lido or the mainland, they admit, "We're not very much beloved on the road."

lunch, consider **Trattoria Busa alla Torre**, located at the end of the canal under a cute little tower (which was built as a fire lookout); it has pleasant seating on the square. At the Grand Canal of Murano, cross the big, green, metal bridge and head right for the Glass Museum (following signs for *Museo Vetrario*).

The **Glass Museum** displays the very best of 700 years of Venetian glassmaking, as well as exhibits on ancient and modern glass art. While the display is pretty old-school musty, it's well-described in English (€4, covered by €15.50 Museum Pass, April–Oct Thu–Tue 10:00–17:00, Nov–March Thu–Tue 10:00–16:00, closed Wed, last entry 30 min before closing, tel. 041 739 586).

Art-lovers might like the **Church of San Pietro Martire** at the far (north) end of the main drag, featuring a Giovanni Bellini (*Virgin Enthroned with Mark and a Kneeling Doge*, with rich reds, blues, greens, and gold), a Tintoretto *(Baptism of Jesus)*, and a Veronese.

But be sure to see more than glass while on Murano. Get off the beaten path by taking the backstreets behind the Duomo on Calle di Conterie for a look at village Venezia. In this old shell there's a new vibrancy, as high prices of real estate and apartments in Venice drive locals to outlying islands such as these. Murano is a workaday community of 6,000 residents. It has real neighborhoods, with moms shopping at markets, schools filled with noisy children, and benches warmed by Venetian old-timers. They give Murano a "Venice without the tourism" charm.

When you're ready to go, head to the Faro vaporetto stop and take the #12 to either Burano or the #41 back to San Zaccaria.

Burano

Famous for its lace, Burano is a sleepy island with a sleepy community (pop. 2,700)—village Venice without the glitz. Its colorfully painted homes look like Venice before the plaster peeled off. Each adjoining townhouse is painted its own color. While Venice is a showy city of merchants, Burano is a humble town of fishermen. At night it's almost entirely tourist-free. Laundry hangs over alleyways, and sunshades (typical of the area) cover the doors of residents' homes. The church's bell tower leans at an 85-degree angle... the same as Pisa's.

This town's history is ancient, explained in part by its name. "Burano" comes from the local word for "breeze"—and a breeze meant survival on the lagoon. It kept away the malaria-carrying mosquitoes that made other places (like Torcello) less habitable.

The island can be covered in a five-minute walk. From the vaporetto dock, follow the crowds into the center. Turn left at the canal. A bridge leads to the piazza, and beyond that—on the far side of the little island—is Burano's famous leaning church **bell tower**. The church has a fine and newly restored Tiepolo painting about the Crucifixion.

The main drag from the vaporetto stop into town is packed with tourists and lined with shops, some of which sell Burano's locally produced white wine. Simply wander to the far side of

the island, and the mood shifts. Explore to the right of the leaning tower for a peaceful yet intensely pastel, small-town lagoon world. Benches lining a little promenade at the water's edge make another pretty picnic spot.

Most tourists visit Burano for its lace, and they're not disappointed.

Burano

TO TORCELLO

MAZZORBO

VAPORETTO STOP

100 YARDS
100 METERS

TO MURANO

SAN MAURO

MARCELLO

LACE MUSEUM

❷

❶

PITONA

VIA GALUPPI

VIGNA

POST

N

LAGOON

FISH

PARK

PIAZZA GALUPPI

S. MARTINO CHURCH & LEANING BELL TOWER

❶ Merletti d'Arte dalla Lidia Lace Shop & Museum

❷ Ristorante al Vecio Pipa

DCH

Of the many shops, **Merletti d'Arte dalla Lidia** has a fine private museum. Ask for a magnifying glass to marvel at the intricate knots, and be sure to go upstairs (daily until 19:30, just off the big square opposite the leaning tower at Via Galuppi 215, tel. 041-730-052).

Lace fans enjoy the **Lace Museum** (Museo del Merletto di Burano, €4, covered by €15.50 Museum Pass, April–Oct Wed–Mon 10:00–17:00, Nov–March Wed–Mon 10:00–16:00, closed Tue, tel. 041-730-034).

You'll find plenty of touristy eateries on Burano, all enthusiastic about their fish. The **Ristorante al Vecio Pipa** serves lovingly prepared local specialties at affordable prices, with both indoor and outdoor seating (€10 pastas, great fish splurges, daily 12:00–15:00—lunch only, on the main drag near the vaporetto dock at San Sauro 397, tel. 041-730-045, Carlo).

For a picnic, the park next to Burano's only vaporetto dock is hard to beat.

On Burano, there's only one dock with boats to and from the Venice mainland. From that dock, a shuttle boat runs back and forth to and from Torcello, located just a few minutes away. Shuttle boats leave twice an hour; check the times upon arrival.

Torcello

This is the birthplace of Venice, where the first mainland refugees settled, escaping the barbarian hordes. Yet today, it's the least-developed island (pop. 20), showing off the marshy, shrub-covered ecosystem of the lagoon. There's little for the tourist to see except the church (a 10-min walk from the dock), which claims to be the oldest in Venice and has impressive mosaics.

From the vaporetto dock, walk through a salty landscape and think of the original inhabitants. Romanized farmers came here, escaping the Germanic barbarians streaming through the mainland. By the 11th century, the teeny island had 11 churches. But one look around tells you that this place was inhospitable—the farming was poor, there was no fresh water, and mosquitoes and malaria were a big problem. Even though they diverted the flow of mainland rivers, the lagoon silted up around them anyway, and the island was slowly abandoned.

Approaching the church, you'll pass by the remote yet fancy Locanda Cipriani Hotel next door, with its five rooms, which has hosted Thomas Mann, Queen Elizabeth II, and Princess Diana.

The **church complex** consists of the church itself, the bell tower (behind the church, climb a ramped stairway for great lagoon views), a sacristy, and a small museum (facing the church, in two separate buildings) that displays Roman sculpture and medieval sculpture and manuscripts. A €6 combo-ticket gets you into all the sights, or pay €2 for each (most open daily 10:30–17:30, museum closed Mon, tel. 041-730-761). There's a pay WC between the museum's two buildings.

The ruins in front of the church used to be a baptistery from the sixth century, the days when you couldn't enter a church until you were baptized.

Inside the **church**, the brick walls and wood-beam ceiling are classic Venetian building materials—that is, flexible—to accommodate the ever-shifting sands. The altar has the relics of St. Heliodorus (d. 390), a local-born Bishop who was the travel partner of the famed St. Jerome on a trip to the Holy Land. The columns of the rood screen (separating the altar area from the congregation) were obviously scavenged from elsewhere—note the variety of different capitals. You can see a bit of the church's original black-and-white mosaic floor (7th century) under a small glassed-over section on the right side of the nave. In the 12th century, flooding forced them to rebuild eight inches higher. The apse mosaic (over the altar) shows Mary and baby Jesus above, and the 12 apostles below.

The mosaic on the back wall is famous. Six horizontal bands depict the Last Judgment (and other scenes). From top to bottom, see:

1. The Crucifixion.

2. A striding Christ pulling a soul out from Limbo while stepping on a devil.

3. Christ, in an almond-shaped bubble, as the Creator, flanked by souls in Paradise. From the bottom of the bubble pours a river of fire, which runs down the wall to Hell.

4. Angels preparing the Throne of Judgment—empty except for a book.

5 and 6. Archangel Michael (over the door) weighing souls in a scale, while mischievous devils try to tip the scales in their favor. On the right are the fires of hell, where sinners—many of them turbaned Muslims—are tormented by black-skinned demons. A crude display of the seven deadly sins on the lower right: pride (crowned heads in flames), lust (bodies in flames), gluttony (guys eating even their hands), envy (skulls with worms eating out their coveting eyes), greed (fancy earrings), laziness (useless hands and cut-off feet), and anger.

Avoid the eighth deadly sin—missing your vaporetto—by allowing at least 10 minutes to get from the church back to the boat dock.

ST. MARK'S TO RIALTO WALK

Two rights and a left (simple!) can get you from St. Mark's Square to the Rialto Bridge via a completely different route from the one most tourists take. Along the way, take in some lesser sights in the area west of St. Mark's Square, including an often-photographed but rarely found architectural gem, the spiral staircase of Scala Contarini del Bovolo.

ORIENTATION

Church of San Moisè: Free. Open daily 15:30–18:30 (may also be accessible at other times through door along left side of church).

Scala Contarini del Bovolo: €3.50 to enter and climb it (daily 10:00–18:00, Nov–March open Sat–Sun only), but it's viewable for free any time from the outside.

The Route

The route takes about 30 minutes.

- From the waterfront at St. Mark's Square, head 100 yards west along the water, jogging inland at Harry's Bar, then continuing west on Calle Larga XXII Marzo.
- Turn right on Calle del Sartor da Veste; head north 200 yards.
- Turn right at the T intersection on Calle de la Mandola; head east 100 yards.
- Turn left on Calle del Forno and work your way north to the Grand Canal.

There are actually three easy routes from St. Mark's Square to Rialto: (1) along the crowded Mercerie (follow the tourists underneath the clock tower), (2) a straight shot on Calle dei Fabbri (exit

St. Mark's to Rialto Walk

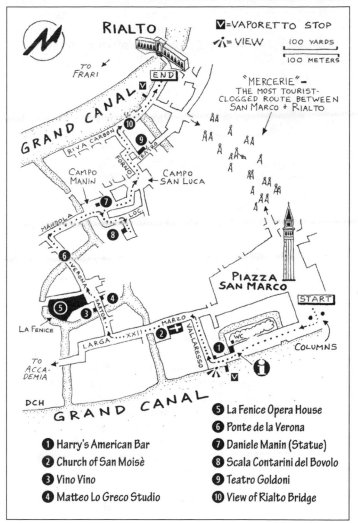

Ⅴ=VAPORETTO STOP
⋏= VIEW

"MERCERIE" –
THE MOST TOURIST-
CLOGGED ROUTE BETWEEN
SAN MARCO & RIALTO

RIALTO

TO FRARI

GRAND CANAL

END

RIVA CARBON

FORNO

TEATRO

CAMPO MANIN

CAMPO SAN LUCA

MANDOLA

LOC

VERONA

SARTOR

LA FENICE

LARGA · XXII · MARZO

VALLARESSO

PIAZZA SAN MARCO

START

WC

COLUMNS

TO ACCADEMIA

DCH

GRAND CANAL

❶ Harry's American Bar
❷ Church of San Moisè
❸ Vino Vino
❹ Matteo Lo Greco Studio
❺ La Fenice Opera House
❻ Ponte de la Verona
❼ Daniele Manin (Statue)
❽ Scala Contarini del Bovolo
❾ Teatro Goldoni
❿ View of Rialto Bridge

St. Mark's Square next to the Quadri Café), and (3) the slightly longer route in this chapter.

THE WALK BEGINS

Start at St. Mark's Square

• *From the square, walk to the waterfront and turn right, continuing along the water until you must turn right again at Harry's Bar and the San Marco/Vallaresso vaporetto stop.*

Along the waterfront, you'll see the various boats that ply Venice's waters. The gondolas here are often more expensive than elsewhere. Water taxis, in classic wooden motorboats, are pricey (about €50 from here to the train station), but a classy splurge if you can split the fare with others. Hotel shuttle boats bring guests here from distant, $700-dollar-a-night hotels. Huge, building-sized cruise boats kiss right up to the quay to disgorge day-trippers. The vaporetto stop up ahead is next to a *traghetto* that ferries locals across to La Salute Church.

The Royal Gardens (Giardinetti Reali) offer some precious greenery in a city built of stone on mud. There are WCs, a TI in the nearby pavilion, and public pay phones where you can call home just to tell everyone where you are right now. From the top of the little bridge at the TI, look across the mouth of the Grand Canal to view the big dome of La Salute Church, and the guy balancing a bronze ball on one foot—the old Customs House.

• *Twelve steps down and 20 yards ahead, on the right, is Harry's Bar...*

❶ Harry's American Bar

Hemingway put this bar on the map by making it his hangout in the late 1940s. If Dennis Hopper or Henry Winkler are in town (I've seen both), this is where they'll be. If they're not, you'll see plenty of dressed-up Americans looking around for celebrities who rarely show. The food is expensive, but if you wear something a bit fancy (or artsy bohemian), you can pull up a stool at the tiny bar by the entrance and enjoy a decent martini or a Bellini (Prosecco and peach juice)—which was invented right here.

• *Head inland on Calle Vallaresso, one of Venice's most exclusive streets, past fancy boutiques like Pucci, Gucci, Sisley, and Bruno Magli. At the T intersection, turn left and head west on (what becomes) Calle Larga XXII Marzo. You'll pass American Express, then continue to the first bridge and a square dominated by the ornate facade of the...*

❷ Church of San Moisè

While this is one of Venice's oldest churches, dating from the 10th century (note the old tower on the right), its busy facade is only Baroque (17th century). This was an age when big shots funded such facades and expected to see their faces featured (see the bust in the center). Moses *(Moisè)* caps the facade.

The ugly modern building on the right marks the former Venice headquarters of the Nazis during World War II. Its fascist facade still gives locals the Mussolini-creeps. Now a five-star hotel, it's one of the few modern buildings in town.

• *Continue over the bridge, then go west halfway to the end of the street and turn right on tiny Calle del Sartor da Veste. (If you pass the La Caravella restaurant, you've overshot the turn.) Head north on Calle Sartor da Veste 75 yards, crossing a bridge, where on the left you'll find...*

❸ Vino Vino

Here you can taste wines and enjoy a reasonably priced meal in a casual setting (Wed–Mon 10:30–24:00, closed Tue, at Calle Sartor da Veste 2007a).

• *A few doors farther ahead, on the right, is...*

❹ Matteo Lo Greco Studio

This sculptor makes plump people in bronze, celebrating life with lighter-than-air joy (Calle Sartor da Veste 1998).

• *Just ahead (on the left) is...*

❺ Gran Teatro alla Fenice (La Fenice)

Venice's famed opera house, built in 1792, was reduced to a hollowed-out shell by a disastrous fire in 1996. After a vigorous restoration campaign, "The Phoenix"—true to its name—has risen again from the ashes. La Fenice resumed opera productions in

2004, opening with *La Traviata.*

Venice is one of the cradles of the art form known as opera. An opera is a sung play and a multimedia event, blending music, words, story, costume, and set design. Some of the great operas were first performed here in this luxurious setting. Verdi's *Rigoletto* (1851) and *La Traviata* (1853) were

actually commissioned by La Fenice. Mozart's librettist was a Venetian who drew inspiration from the city's libertine ways and joie de vivre. In recent years, La Fenice's musical reputation was overshadowed by its reputation as a place for the wealthy to parade in furs and jewels.

The small square nearby, Campo San Fantin, has several nice cafés that cater to theater patrons.

• *Continue north along the same street (though its name is now Calle de La Verona), to a small bridge over a quiet canal.*

❻ Ponte de la Verona

Straddle a bridge over a canal with reflections that can make you wonder which end is up. Looking up, see bridges of stone propping up leaning buildings, and there's a view of the "Leaning Tower" of Santo Stefano.

People actually live in Venice. See their rooftop gardens, their laundry, the electricity lines snaking into their apartments, and the rusted iron bars and bolts that hold their crumbling homes together. On one building, find centuries-old art—a bearded face and a relief panel of an eagle with its prey. While many Venetians own (and love) their own boat, parking a boat is a huge problem. Getting a spot is tough, and when you finally find one, it's very expensive and rarely near your apartment. For more on boating in Venice, see the sidebar on page 179.

• *Continue north. At the T intersection, turn right on Calle de la Mandola. You'll cross over a bridge into a spacious square dominated by a statue and an out-of-place modern building.*

❼ Campo Manin

The centerpiece of the square is a statue of Daniele Manin (1804–1857), Venice's fiery leader in the battle for freedom from Austria and eventually a united Italy (the Risorgimento). The statue faces the red house that he lived in. Chafing under Austrian rule, the Venetians rose up. The Austrians laid siege to the city (1849) and bombed it into surrender. Manin was banished and spent his final years in Paris, still proudly drumming up support for modern Italy.

• *The Scala Contarini del Bovolo is well sign-posted a block south of here. Facing the Manin statue, turn right and exit the square down an alley. Follow yellow signs to the left, then right, into a courtyard with one of Venice's hidden treasures...*

❽ Scala Contarini del Bovolo

Sometimes called "Venice's Non-Leaning Tower of Pisa," the Scala is a cylindrical brick tower with five floors of spiral staircase faced with white marble banisters. Built in 1499, it was the external staircase of a palace (external stairs saved interior space for rooms). Architecture buffs admire the successful blend of Gothic, Byzantine, and Renaissance styles.

Pay €3.50 to wind your way up the "snail shell" (*bovolo* in the local dialect) 113 steps to the top, where you're rewarded with views of the sublime Venetian skyline. There are the onion domes of St. Mark's, the Campanile, the dome of La Salute, and the roofline of La Fenice. You'll also see plenty of red-tiled rooftops, underwear on clotheslines, and a curious relic of a bygone era—TV antennas.

• *Unwind and return to the Manin statue. Continue east, circling around the big, modern Cassa di Risparmio bank, into Campo San Luca. At Campo San Luca, turn left (north) on Calle del Forno. Note the 24-hour pharmacy vending machine that dispenses shower gel, Band-Aids, bug repellant, toothbrushes, toothpaste, and condoms. Heading north, glance down the street to the right at the...*

❾ Teatro Goldoni

Though this theater looks modern, it dates from the 1500s, when Venice was at the forefront of secular entertainment. Many of Carlo Goldoni's (1707–1793) groundbreaking comedies got their first performance here, and the theater was renamed in his honor. It's still a working theater (mainly Italian productions).

• *Continue north on Calle del Forno. You're very close to the Grand Canal. Keep going north, jogging to the right, then left down a teeny-tiny alleyway. Pop! You emerge on the Grand Canal, about 150 yards "downstream" from the...*

❿ Rialto Bridge

Of Venice's more than 400 bridges, only three cross the Grand Canal. Of these three bridges, the Rialto was the first.

The original Rialto Bridge, dating from 1180, was a platform supported by boats tied together. It linked the political side (Palazzo Ducale) of Venice with the economic center (Rialto). Rialto, which takes its name from *riva alto* (high bank), was one of the earliest Venetian settlements. When Venice was Europe's economic superpower, it was where bankers, brokers, and merchants conducted their daily business.

Rialto Bridge II was a 13th-century wooden drawbridge. It

was replaced in 1588 by the current structure, with its bold single arch spanning 160 feet and arcades on top designed to strengthen the stone structure. Its immense foundations stretch 650 feet on either side. Heavy buildings were then built atop the foundations to hold every-

thing in place. The Rialto remained the only bridge crossing the Grand Canal until 1854.

Reliefs of the Venetian Republic's main mascots, St. Mark and St. Theodore, crown the arch as barges and *vaporetti* run the busy waterways below and merchants vie for tourists' attention topside.

The Rialto has long been a symbol of Venice. Aristocratic inhabitants built magnificent palaces just to be near it. The poetic Lord Byron swam to it all the way from Lido Island. And thousands of marriage proposals have been sealed right here, with a kiss, as the moon floated over *La Serenissima*.

RIALTO
TO FRARI
CHURCH
WALK

The area west of the Grand Canal is less touristy—the place where "real" Venetians live. This walk is the most direct route from the Rialto Bridge to the Frari Church and Scuola San Rocco, but along the way you'll see lively produce and stinky fish markets, local pubs, squares, and churches that are at least a bit off the tourist path.

ORIENTATION

Rialto Market: The souvenir stalls are open daily; the produce market is closed on Sunday; and the fish market is closed on Sunday and Monday.

Church of San Polo: €2.50, covered by €8 Chorus Pass (see page 24). Mon–Sat 10:00–17:00, Sun 10:00–13:00, last entry 15 min before closing.

Casa Goldoni: €2.50, covered by €15.50 Museum Pass (see page 24). April–Oct Mon–Sat 10:00–17:00, Nov–March Mon–Sat 10:00–16:00, closed Sun.

Frari Church: €2.50, covered by €8 Chorus Pass, audioguides available (€1.60/person, €2.60/double set). Mon–Sat 10:00–17:00, Sun 13:00–17:00 (closed Sun in Aug), last entry 15 min before closing, no visits during services.

Scuola San Rocco: €5.50, includes audioguide. Daily April–Oct 9:00–17:30, Nov–March 10:00–16:00, last entry 30 min before closing.

The Route

- Head west from the Rialto Bridge one long block, through the colorful market. Make time to explore.
- After 100 yards, turn left and head down Ruga Vecchia San

Rialto to Frari Church Walk

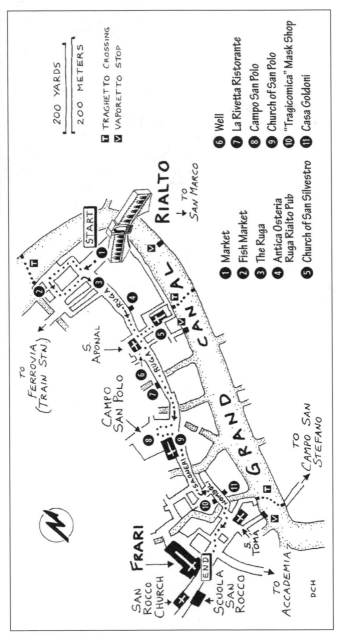

200 YARDS
200 METERS

T TRAGHETTO CROSSING
V VAPORETTO STOP

1 Market
2 Fish Market
3 The Ruga
4 Antica Osteria Ruga Rialto Pub
5 Church of San Silvestro
6 Well
7 La Rivetta Ristorante
8 Campo San Polo
9 Church of San Polo
10 "Tragicomica" Mask Shop
11 Casa Goldoni

RIALTO

↓ TO SAN MARCO

GRAND CANAL

TO FERROVIA (TRAIN STN.)

S. APONAL

RUGA

CAMPO SAN POLO

SAONERI

TOLETA

S. TOMA

TO CAMPO SAN STEFANO

TO ACCADEMIA

FRARI

SAN ROCCO CHURCH

SCUOLA SAN ROCCO

START

END

DCH

Giovanni. Walk southwest along the Ruga (paralleling the Grand Canal) about a quarter mile to spacious Campo San Polo.

- From San Polo, continue southwest another 200 yards, then jog left, then right, where you'll soon see signs directing you to the Scuola Grande di San Rocco.

THE WALK BEGINS

❶ Market (Erberia)

The street west of the Rialto Bridge is lined with stalls selling

cheese, arugula, dripping coconut slices, glass beads, postcards, masks, leather purses, and T-shirts. Beyond that along the canal is a thriving produce market that offers a good peek at workaday Venice. The area is busy with colorful cafés, fragrant with cheese and meat shops, and slimy with a colonnaded fish market (which is closed Sun–Mon).

• *At the end of the market stalls (200 yards past Rialto Bridge), look left down the busy street, the Ruga Vecchia San Giovanni, which we'll follow in a moment. But first, jog to the right and follow your nose to the...*

❷ Fish Market

The open-air stalls have the catch of the day—Venice's culinary specialty. Find eels, scallops, and crustaceans with five-inch antennae. This is the Venice that has existed for centuries: Workers toss boxes of fish from delivery boats while shoppers step from the *traghetto* (gondola shuttle) into the action.

• *Return to the Ruga Vecchia San Giovanni and head southwest, roughly paralleling the Grand Canal.*

❸ The Street Called the "Ruga"

The busy street is lined with shops that get increasingly less touristy. You'll see fewer trinkets and more clothes, bread, shoes, watches, shampoo, and underwear.

• *About 100 yards along the Ruga—10 yards past a Chinese restaurant—is a pub on the left-hand side.*

❹ Antica Osteria Ruga Rialto Pub

With a wine barrel out front, paintings of old Venice on the walls, and outdoor tables, this bar/café is one of several pubs in the area that cater to tourists by day and locals by night. Even teetotaling Venetians hang out in pubs, grabbing a sandwich while on their feet, nibbling finger-food appetizers *(cicchetti),* or ordering a small tumbler of cheap wine (an *ombra)* for friends.

• *A block or so farther along the Ruga, a detour to the left on Rio Tera S. Silvestro leads to a big, white church.*

❺ Church of San Silvestro

True Tintoretto gourmets on their way to the Scuola may want a Tintoretto appetizer. His *Baptism of Christ* (1st chapel on right) shows a twisted, unbalanced John the Baptist as Jesus gingerly tests the waters of the Jordan River.

• *Continue southwest along the Ruga to Campo S. Aponal, with a...*

❻ Well

Wells like this were the center of village Venice, back before 1886, when drinking water was piped in from the mainland. The well (now capped) sits in a square that slopes into drains that caught rainwater, which filtered down through sand into a cistern (roughly the size of the white outline in the paving stones). For more information on wells, see page 44.

• *Continue southwest along Calle di Mezo, past the recommended...*

❼ La Rivetta Ristorante

If you're ready to eat, consider a canalside meal at La Rivetta Ristorante for their inexpensive Venetian specialties, such as *spaghetti al nero di seppie* (spaghetti in squid ink) or *fegato alla Veneziana* (calf liver and onions; open daily, San Polo 1479). Or, even better, have a pizza on the nearby Campo San Polo (see page 231).

• *Beyond the restaurant, follow signs to* Ferrovia. *Calle di Mezo opens up into...*

❽ Campo San Polo

One of the largest squares in Venice, Campo San Polo is shaped like an amphitheater, with its church tucked away in the corner (just ahead of you). The amphitheater shape comes from when there was a curved canal at the foot of the buildings. Today the canal is a *rio terra*—a street made of landfill. There are a few rare trees and rare benches with grateful locals sitting on them. In the summer, bleachers and a screen are erected for open-air movies, a true *Cinema Paradiso* experience.

• *On the square is the...*

❾ Church of San Polo (S. Paolo Apostolo)

The church is one of the oldest in Venice, from the ninth century (€2.50 entry fee). The wooden boat-shaped ceiling recalls the earliest basilicas built after Rome's fall.

Tintoretto's *Last Supper* (*Ultima Cena*, 1568–1569; immediately to left of entrance) is a different take on the scene than you'll see at Scuola San Rocco. The table is set on diagonal floor tiles. Only Christ is facing us—the others twist and turn, their body language following the left-to-right flow of the table and floor tiles...until the eye settles on brooding Judas on the right. (As Tintoretto and theater directors know, characters going "against the flow" attract our attention.)

G. B. Tiepolo's *Virgin Appearing to St. John of Nepomuk* (1754; opposite entry door, on the second altar on the left, as you face the main altar) was designed for this location by the master of 3-D perspective. He foreshortens the figures, knowing we're on church level looking up at it.

Turn 90 degrees to the right and compare Tiepolo with the work of the man he most admired, Paolo Veronese. In **Veronese's** *Betrothal of the Virgin, with Angels* (c. 1580; left corner, as you face the main altar), God the Father rides above it all, but at an odd perspective—he's looking "down" at Mary and Joseph, while we are looking "across" at him.

• *In an adjoining room at the back of the church, find the cycle of paintings by G. D. Tiepolo.*

G. D. Tiepolo, the son of the more famous G. B. Tiepolo, has a more sober, down-to-earth style. In his **Stations of the Cross** (*Via Crucis*, 1747–1749), we follow Christ's last excruciating days (moving around the room clockwise from the entrance), from his death sentence to torture to crucifixion to removal of his body from the cross. The scenes are evenly lit in the glow of a luminous gray-sky background. We catch hints of the elder Tiepolo in the bright colored robes, but these scenes are more understated...and ultimately more moving.

• *From the Church of San Polo, continue southwest about 200 yards (still following signs to* Ferrovia*). Jog left when you have to, then right when you have to, onto Calle dei Nomboli. On the right, just before a small bridge, you'll see the...*

❿ "Tragicomica" Mask Shop

One of Venice's best mask stores (daily 10:00–19:00, tel. 041-721-102), it's also a workshop that lets you see mask-making in action.

Venice's masks date from the celebration of Carnevale (the local pre-Lent, Mardi Gras–like blowout). Many masks are patterned after standard characters of the theater style known as Commedia dell'Arte: the famous trickster Harlequin, the beautiful and cunning Columbina, the country bumpkin Pulcinella (who later evolved into the wife-beating "Punch" of marionette shows), and the solemn, long-nosed Doctor *(dottore)*.

• *Across the narrow street from the mask shop is...*

⓫ Casa Goldoni

Those with a hearty passion for theater (or with a Museum Pass, allowing free admission) will want to tour this small, sparse, Italian-language-only museum. The playwright Carlo Goldoni (1707–1793) was born in this building, and it's now a museum to his life in theater.

• *Continue along, cross the bridge, and veer right. You'll see purple signs directing you to* Scuola Grande di San Rocco. *Follow these until you bump into the back end of the Frari Church (❂ see tour on page 135), with the Scuola San Rocco next door (❂ see tour on page 125).*

ST. MARK'S TO SAN ZACCARIA WALK

San Zaccaria, one of the oldest churches in Venice, with a Bellini altarpiece and a submerged crypt (the oldest place in Venice?), is just a few minutes on foot from St. Mark's Square. Along the way, there's a great view of the Bridge of Sighs.

ORIENTATION

Church of San Zaccaria: Free, Mon–Sat 10:00–12:00 & 16:00–18:00, Sun 16:00–18:00 only. Admission to the crypt costs €1. A €0.50 coin buys a light for Bellini's altarpiece.

The Route

You can make a square circuit from St. Mark's Square to the Church of San Zaccaria to the waterfront, and back to St. Mark's Square. Along the way you'll pass a variety of lace and mask shops.

- From St. Mark's Square, walk behind St. Mark's Basilica to the Church of San Zaccaria.
- Turn right at San Zaccaria and walk a block to the waterfront.
- Turn right and walk along the Riva, returning to St. Mark's Square.

THE WALK BEGINS

❶ Start at St. Mark's—Piazzetta dei Leoncini

Facing St. Mark's Basilica, start in the small square to the left of the church (the Piazzetta dei Leoncini), with the 18th-century stone lions that kids love to sit on. The white building at the east end of the square houses the offices of Venice's "patriarch," the

St. Mark's to San Zaccaria Walk

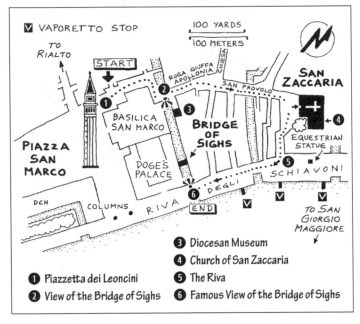

3 Diocesan Museum
4 Church of San Zaccaria
5 The Riva
6 Famous View of the Bridge of Sighs

1 Piazzetta dei Leoncini
2 View of the Bridge of Sighs

special title given to the local bishop (see the yellow Vatican flag). In the 1950s, this is where the future Pope John XXIII presided as Venice's patriarch and cardinal. The popular, warm-hearted bishop went on to become the "Sixties pope," who oversaw major reforms in the Catholic Church.

• *Head east along Calle de la Canonica, circling behind the church. You'll reach a bridge with a...*

❷ View of the Bridge of Sighs

This lesser-known view of the Bridge of Sighs also lets you see the white facade of the Church of San Giorgio Maggiore in the distance, framed by the arch of the Bridge of Sighs.

• *Continuing east, cross the bridge. Immediately on the other side, to the right, is the low-profile...*

❸ Diocesan Museum (Museo Diocesano)

Shock the museum attendant by actually visiting what may be the city's least-visited museum (free, but may be renovated and charge admission in 2006; Mon–Sat 10:00–12:30, closed Sun). You first enter a tiny, quiet, cloistered courtyard from the 1100s—unique in Venice. Go upstairs to the museum, which shows off art from local churches and a bit of plunder that never found a place in local facades.

• *Continuing east, you'll cross another bridge with a view of a "Modern Bridge of Sighs," which connects two wings of the exclusive Danieli Hotel. Continue east another 50 yards, through the former gate of a cloistered Benedictine convent, until you run into the...*

❹ Church of San Zaccaria

Back in the ninth century, when Venice was just a collection of wooden houses and before there was a St. Mark's Basilica, a

stone church and convent stood here. This is where the doges worshipped, public spectacles occurred, and sacred relics were kept. Today's structure dates mostly from the 15th century.

The tall facade by Mauro Codussi (who also did the clock tower in St. Mark's Square) is early Renaissance. The "vertical" effect produced by the four support pillars that rise up to an arched crown is tempered by the horizontal, many-layered stories and curved shoulders.

In the northwest corner of Campo San Zaccaria (near where you entered) is a plaque from 1620 listing all the things that were prohibited "in this square" *(in questo campo)*, including games, obscenities, dishonesty, and robbery, all "under grave penalty" *(sotto gravis pene)*.

• *Enter the church. The second chapel on the right holds the...*

Body of Zechariah (S. Zaccaria, Patris S. Jo: Baptista)

Of the two bodies in the chapel, the upper one in the glass case

(supported by stone angels) is the reputed body of Zechariah, the father of John the Baptist. Back when mortal remains were venerated and thought to bring miracles to the faithful, Venice was proud to own the bones of St. Zechariah ("San Zaccaria").

• *The church is virtually wallpapered with art. On the opposite side of the nave (2nd chapel on the left), you'll find...*

Giovanni Bellini's *Madonna and Child with Saints* (*Sacra Conversazione*, 1505)

Mary and the baby, under a pavilion, are surrounded by various saints engaged in a so-called "holy conversation," which in this painting is more like a quiet meditation. The saints' mood is melancholy, with lidded eyes and downturned faces. A violinist angel plays a sad solo at Mary's feet.

This is one of the last of Bellini's paintings in the *sacra conversazione* formula (see his others in the Accademia and Frari Church). The life-size saints stand in an imaginary extension of the church—the pavilion's columns match the real church columns. We see a glimpse of trees and a cloudy sky beyond. He establishes a 3-D effect using floor tiles. The four saints pose symmetrically, and there's a harmony of big blocks of rich-colored robes—blue, green, red, white, and yellow. A cool white light envelops the whole scene, casting no dark shadows.

The 75-year-old Bellini was innovative and productive until the end of his long life. The German artist Albrecht Dürer said of him: "He is very old, and still he is the best painter of them all."

• *On the right-hand side of the nave is the entrance (€1 entry fee) to...*

The Crypt

Before you descend into the crypt, the first room (Chapel of the Choir) contains **Tintoretto's *Birth of John the Baptist*** (on the altar). Mother Elizabeth lies in bed in the background, while nurses hold and coo over little John. The father, Zechariah—the star of this church—is on the far right, witnessing the heavens open up.

The five **gold chairs** were once seats for doges. Every Easter, the current doge would walk from St. Mark's Square to this religious center and thank the nuns of San Zaccaria for giving the land that would become Piazza San Marco. In the small next room, with religious objects, there's an engraving of the doge parading into Campo San Zaccaria.

The Chapel of Gold (to the left of the room with the religious objects) is dominated by an impressive 15th-century prickly-gold altarpiece by Vivarini. Look down  through glass in the floor to see the 12th-century mosaic floor from the original church. In fact, these rooms were parts of the earlier churches.

Finally, go downstairs into the **crypt**—the foundation of a church built in the 10th century. The crypt is low and the water table high, so the room is often flooded. It's a weird experience, calling up echoes of the Dark Ages.

• *Emerge from the Church of San Zaccaria into the small* campo *in front, and turn left (south). Exit the* campo *past the pink ex-convent (now the Carabinieri station), and pop out at the waterfront.*

❺ The Riva

The waterfront promenade known as the "Riva" gives a great view of the Church of San Giorgio Maggiore. (To get there, catch vaporetto #82—to your left, not in front of you—from the nearby San Zaccaria Jolanda stop; ✪ see San Giorgio Maggiore Tour, page 166.) The big equestrian statue is of Victor Emmanuel II, who helped lead Italy to unification and who became the country's first king in 1861. Beyond that (over the bridge) is the four-columned

La Pietà Church, where Antonio Vivaldi once directed the music. A bit beyond that (not visible from here) is the Arsenale.

The Riva is lined with many of Venice's most famous luxury hotels. For a peek at the most famous and luxurious, turn right, cross over one bridge, and nip into the Danieli Hotel. Tuck in your shirt, stand tall and aristocratic, and (with all the confidence of a guest) be swept by the revolving door into the sumptuous interior of what was the Gothic Palazzo Dandolo. Since 1820, this has been Venice's most exclusive hotel. Exquisite as all this is, it still gets flooded routinely in the winter.

• *Facing the water, turn right and head west toward St. Mark's Square. The commotion atop a little bridge marks...*

❻ The Famous View of the Bridge of Sighs

From this bridge (according to romantic legend), prisoners took one last look at Venice before entering the dark and dank prisons. And

sighed. While that rogue Casanova wrote of the bridge in his memoirs, he was actually imprisoned in the Doges' Palace (high up on your left). Lord Byron picked up on the legend in the early 1800s and gave it the famous nickname, and this sad bridge became a big stop on the Grand Tour. While the bridge is a human traffic jam of gawking tourists and clever pickpockets during the day, it's breathtakingly romantic in the lonely late-night hours.

From here, you can take one last look at the lagoon before returning to the crowded and sweaty St. Mark's Square...and sigh.

SLEEPING

For hassle-free efficiency and the sheer magic of being close to the action, I favor hotels that are handy to sightseeing activities. I've listed rooms in three neighborhoods: the Rialto action, St. Mark's bustle, and the quiet Dorsoduro area behind the Accademia art museum. Hotel Web sites are particularly valuable in Venice, because they often come with a map.

I list accommodations that are clean, small, central, relatively quiet at night, traditional, inexpensive, friendly, and come with firm beds. I also prefer those not listed in other guidebooks. (In Venice, a hotel with six out of these nine characteristics is a keeper.)

It's possible to visit Venice without booking ahead, but given the high stakes and the quality of the gems I've listed here, I'd recommend making reservations (see "Making Reservations," below). Reserve a room as soon as you know when you'll be in town. Book direct, not through any tourist information room-finding service (they can't give opinions on quality). If everything's full, don't despair. Call a day or two in advance and fill in a cancellation.

TYPES OF ACCOMMODATIONS

Hotels

My listings range in price from €21 bunks to plush €240 doubles with Grand Canal views. Double rooms run as low as about €90 (very simple), with most clustered around €140 to €170 (with private bathrooms). Three or four people economize by sharing larger rooms. Solo travelers find that the cost of a *camera singola* (single room) is often only 25 percent less than a *camera doppia* (double room). Most listed hotels have rooms for anywhere from one to five people. If there's room for an extra cot, they'll cram it in for you.

Double beds are called *matrimoniale,* even though hotels aren't interested in your marital status. Twins are *due letti singoli*. Even if a single or triple room isn't listed, ask—they can accommodate you.

Many hotel rooms have a TV and phone. Rooms in fancier hotels usually come with a small safe; a stocked mini-fridge called a *frigo bar* (FREE-goh bar) where you pay for what you use; and air-conditioning (sometimes with an extra per-day charge). The government stipulates that air-conditioning can only be used mid-May through September, unless conditions are extreme. The same goes for heat from October through April.

If you arrive on an overnight train, your room might not be ready. Drop your bag at the hotel and dive right into Venice.

When you check in, the receptionist will normally ask for your passport and keep it for a couple of hours. Italian hotels are legally required to register each guest with the local police. Relax. Americans are notorious for making this chore more difficult than it needs to be.

Rooms are safe. Still, zip cameras and keep money out of sight. More pillows and blankets are usually in the closet or available on request. In Italy, towels and linens aren't always replaced every day. Hang your towel up to dry.

Your hotelier, a good source of advice, can direct you to the nearest launderette and Internet café.

Apartment Rentals

Those staying three nights or longer can book an apartment with **Venice Rentals**. This can make sense for families who want a bit more space and a kitchen. Doubles start at €90 per night; a bigger place for a family of five rents for around €200. Denise (a Bostonian) or her Venetian husband, Maurizio, meet you at the boat dock and get you oriented. For details, see www.venicerentals.com.

PRACTICALITIES

Pricing and Discounts

The major advantages of this book are its extensive listing of good-value hotels and the special prices promised to my readers (often much below the "rack rates"—the highest rates a hotel charges).

Venetian hoteliers are hard to pin down. They're experts at perfect price discrimination: They list a huge range of rates for the same room (e.g., €90–160) and refuse to give a firm price, enabling them to judge the demand and charge accordingly. Once they know what the market will bear, they max it out. Also, hotels are being squeezed by the very popular online booking services (which take about a 20 percent commission). Between wanting to keep their gouging options open for high-season weekends and trying to recover these online commissions, hoteliers set their rack rates sky-high.

Sleep Code

(€1 = about $1.20)

To help you easily sort through these listings, I've divided the rooms into three categories based on the price for a standard double room with bath:

> $$$ **Higher Priced**—Most rooms €180 or more.
>
> $$ **Moderately Priced**—Most rooms between €130–180.
>
> $ **Lower Priced**—Most rooms €130 or less.

To give maximum information in a minimum of space, I use the following code to describe the accommodations. Prices listed are per room, not per person. Unless I note otherwise, the staff speaks English and breakfast is included. You can assume a hotel takes credit cards unless you see "cash only" in the listing.

> **S** = Single room (or price for one person in a double).
>
> **D** = Double or Twin room. "Double beds" are often two twins sheeted together, and are usually big enough for nonromantic couples.
>
> **T** = Triple (generally a double bed with a single).
>
> **Q** = Quad (usually a double bed and 2 small singles).
>
> **b** = Private bathroom with toilet and shower or tub.
>
> **s** = Private shower or tub only (the toilet is down the hall).

According to this code, a couple staying at a "Db-€140" hotel would pay a total of €140 (about $170) for a double room with a private bathroom.

My listings are more likely to give a straight price. I've assured hoteliers that my readers will book direct, so they'll get 100 percent of what you pay; therefore, you'll get the fair net rate. I've listed only prices for peak season: April, May, June, September, and October. Prices will be higher during festivals, and virtually all places drop prices from November through March (except during Carnevale) and in July and August.

Booking direct (not through a Web site) is your ticket to better rates. Prices can be soft if you do any of the following: offer to pay cash, stay at least three nights, or mention this book. You can also try asking for a cheaper room or a discount, or offer to skip breakfast. To save money during a relatively slow time, consider arriving without a reservation and dropping in at the last minute.

If you book via a Web service, I wash my hands of your problems. Help me enforce honest business practices by reporting any hotel charging more than the listed rates in 2006 to those who book direct. E-mail me at rick@ricksteves.com. Thanks.

Country Code

If you're phoning Italy, you'll need to know its country code: 39. To call Italy from the U.S.A. or Canada, dial 011-39—followed by the 10-digit local number (in Venice that starts with 041). If calling Italy from another European country, dial 00-39—then the entire local number. To call a Venice hotel from anywhere in Italy (including Venice), simply dial the local 10-digit number.

Making Reservations

To reserve from home, e-mail or fax your request. It's also easy to reserve by phone. (For detailed instructions on making calls, see "Telephones" in this book's introduction.) Most hotels listed are accustomed to English-only speakers. E-mail's a steal, fax costs are reasonable, and simple English is usually fine. For your e-mail, try the form at www.ricksteves.com/reservation; to fax, use the handy form in the appendix. If you don't get an answer to your fax request, consider that a "no." (Many little places get 20 faxes a day after they're full and can't afford to respond.)

A two-night stay in August would be "2 nights, 16/8/06 to 18/8/06" (Europeans write the date day/month/year, and hotel jargon uses your day of departure). You'll often receive a response back requesting one night's deposit.

Your credit-card number will usually be accepted as the deposit. Be sure to fax your card number (rather than e-mailing it) to keep it private, safer, and out of cyberspace. You can pay with your card or cash when you arrive; if you don't show up, your card will be billed for one night. Hotels with stringent cancellation policies will inform you of the conditions when they confirm your reservations.

Always reconfirm your reservations a day or two in advance by phone, and let your hotel know your estimated time of arrival, especially if it will be after 16:00. Don't needlessly reconfirm rooms through the tourist office; they'll take a commission. Honor your reservations, or cancel them by phone or e-mail. Long distance is cheap from public phone booths.

ACCOMMODATIONS IN VENICE

Hotels in Venice can be tricky to locate. Follow my directions closely, and visit your hotel's Web site before you leave to see if they have a map. (If they do, print it out.) Remember that Venice has six

St. Mark's Square Area Hotels

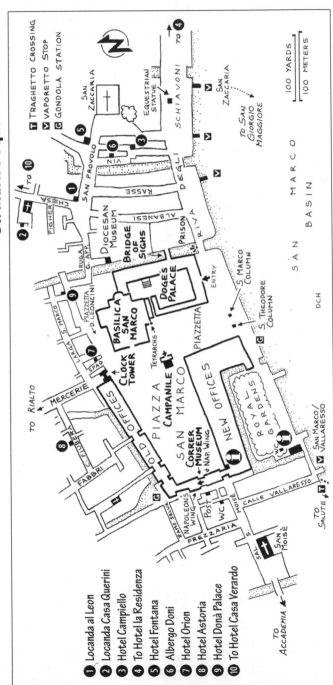

1 Locanda al Leon
2 Locanda Casa Querini
3 Hotel Campiello
4 To Hotel la Residenza
5 Hotel Fontana
6 Albergo Doni
7 Hotel Orion
8 Hotel Astoria
9 Hotel Donà Palace
10 To Hotel Casa Verardo

districts: San Marco, Castello, Cannaregio, San Polo, Santa Croce, and Dorsoduro. Each district has about 6,000 address numbers.

Near St. Mark's Square

East of St. Mark's Square

Located near the Bridge of Sighs, just off the Riva degli Schiavoni waterfront promenade, these places rub drainpipes with Venice's most palatial five-star hotels. The first, while a bit pricey because of its location, is professional and comfortable. Ride the vaporetto to San Zaccaria (#51 from train station, #82 from Tronchetto parking lot).

✗ **$$$ Hotel Campiello,** lacy and bright, was once part of a 19th-century convent. Ideally located 50 yards off the waterfront, its 16 rooms offer a tranquil, friendly refuge for travelers who appreciate affordable elegance (Sb-€120, Db-€190, 10 percent discount with cash, strict cancellation penalties enforced, air-con, elevator; from the waterfront street—Riva degli Schiavoni—take Calle del Vin, between Hotel Danieli and Hotel Savoia e Jolanda, to #4647, Castello; tel. 041-520-5764, fax 041-520-5798, www.hcampiello .it, campiello@hcampiello.it; family-run for 4 generations: sisters Monica and Nicoletta, and Thomas).

✗ **$$ Locanda al Leon** has 14 renovated, 18th-century Venice-style rooms just off Campo S.S. Filippo e Giacomo (Db-€140, bigger Db-€165, these prices with cash and this book in 2006, Campo S.S. Filippo e Giacomo 4270, Castello, tel. 041-277-0393, fax 041-521-0348, www.hotelalleon.com, leon@hotelalleon.com, Juliano and Marcella). From the San Zaccaria vaporetto stop, take Calle delle Rasse (left of pink Hotel Danieli) to Salizada S. Provolo; turn left, then right to get to Campo S.S. Filippo e Giacomo. The hotel is on Calle dei Albanesi.

✗ **$$ Hotel Fontana** is a two-star, family-run place with 14 rooms and lots of stairs on a touristy square two bridges behind St. Mark's Square (Sb-€110, Db-€155, family rooms, air-con, 10 percent discount with cash, quieter rooms on garden side, 2 rooms have terraces, Campo San Provolo 4701, Castello; tel. 041-522-0579, fax 041-523-1040, www.hotelfontana.it, info@hotelfontana .it, Diego and Gabriele). Take vaporetto #1 or #51 to San Zaccaria, find Calle delle Rasse to the left of Hotel Danieli—take it, turn right at the end, and continue to the first square.

✗ **$$ Hotel la Residenza** is a grand old palace facing a peaceful square. Its 15 great rooms ring a huge, luxurious lounge. Relaxing in the lounge, you'll really feel like you're in the Doge's Palace after hours. This is a great value for romantics (Sb-€95, Db-€150, air-con, Castello 3608, tel. 041-528-5315, fax 041-523-8859, www .veniceLaresidenza.com, info@veniceLaresidenza.com). From the Bridge of Sighs, walk east along Riva degli Schiavoni, cross three bridges, and take the first left up Calle del Dose to Campo Bandiera e Moro.

$ Locanda Casa Querini rents 11 plush rooms on a quiet square tucked away behind St. Mark's. You can enjoy your breakfast sitting right on the square (Db-€130 with cash and this book through 2006, €5 more for view rooms, air-con, halfway between San Zaccaria vaporetto stop and Campo Santa Maria Formosa at Campo San Giovanni in Oleo 4388, Castello, tel. 041-241-1294, fax 041-241-4231, www.locandaquerini.com, casaquerini@hotmail .com, Patricia and Silvia). Take the street to the right of the Bridge of Sighs to Campo S.S. Fillipo e Giacomo, continue on Calle Rimpeto la Sacrestia, take the second left, and curl around to the left into the little square.

$ Albergo Doni is dark, hardwood, clean, and quiet—a bit of a time-warp—with 13 dim but classy rooms run by a likable smart aleck named Gina (D-€90, Db-€115, T-€120, Tb-€155, ceiling fans, reserve with credit card but pay in cash, Castello 4656, tel. & fax 041-522-4267, www.albergodoni.it, albergodoni@libero.it; Gina, Nicolò, and Tessa). From the San Zaccaria vaporetto stop, cross one bridge to the right, take the first left past the Hotel Danieli, then turn left at the little square named Fondamenta del Vin.

North of St. Mark's Square

X **$$ Hotel Orion** has 18 neat-as-a-pin, relaxing, and spacious rooms. Just off St. Mark's Square, it's a tranquil haven from the bustling streets (Db-€165 with this book in 2006, 5 percent discount with cash, air-con; from St. Mark's Square walk to the left of the facade, and then turn left on Spadari, hotel is just before timbered overpass, Spadaria 700a, San Marco 30100; tel. 041-522-3053, fax 041-523-8866, www.hotelorion.it, info@hotelorion.it, Stefano).

$ Hotel Astoria has 24 simple, tidy rooms tucked away a few blocks off St. Mark's Square (Db-€120 promised with this book in 2006, 2 blocks from San Zulian Church at Calle Fiubera 951, San Marco; from Rialto vaporetto #1 dock, go straight inland on Calle Bembo—which becomes Calle dei Fabbri—and turn left on Calle Fiubera; tel. 041-522-5381, fax 041-528-8981, www.hotelastoriavenezia .it, info@hotelastoriavenezia.it, Giorgia).

Near the Rialto Bridge
Vaporetto #82 quickly connects the Rialto with both the train station and the Tronchetto parking lot.

West of the Rialto Bridge
$$$ Locanda Sturion, with 11 rooms, air-conditioning, and all the modern comforts, is pricey because it overlooks the Grand

Rialto Area Hotels

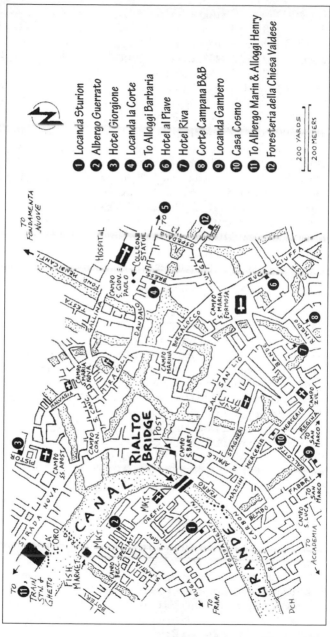

1. Locanda Sturion
2. Albergo Guerrato
3. Hotel Giorgione
4. Locanda la Corte
5. To Alloggi Barbaria
6. Hotel al Piave
7. Hotel Riva
8. Corte Campana B&B
9. Locanda Gambero
10. Casa Cosmo
11. To Albergo Marin & Alloggi Henry
12. Foresteria della Chiesa Valdese

Canal (Db-€240, canal-view rooms cost €50 extra, 10 percent discount with cash, family deals, piles of stairs, 100 yards from Rialto Bridge, opposite vaporetto dock, Calle del Sturion 679, San Polo, tel. 041-523-6243, fax 041-522-8378, www.locandasturion .com, info@locandasturion.com).

$ Albergo Guerrato, above a handy and colorful produce market two minutes from the Rialto action, is run by friendly, creative, and hardworking Roberto and Piero. Giorgio takes the night shift. Their 800-year-old building—with 24 spacious, air-conditioned rooms—is simple, airy, and wonderfully characteristic (D-€90, Db-€115, top-floor "Guerratino" rooms go for Db-€135, Tb-€145, Qb-€170, prices promised through 2006 with this book and cash, a further 15 percent discount Nov–Feb and Aug, Calle drio la Scimia 240a, San Polo, tel. 041-522-7131 or 041-528-5927, fax 041-241-1408, www.pensioneguerrato.it, hguerrat@tin.it). Walk over the Rialto Brige away from St. Mark's Square, go straight about three blocks, turn right on Calle drio la Scimia (not simply Scimia, the block before) and you'll see the hotel sign. My tour groups book this place for 40 nights each year. Sorry. They rent family apartments in the old center (great for groups of 4–8) for around €55 per person.

East of the Rialto Bridge

$$ Locanda la Corte, a three-star hotel, is perfumed with elegance. Its 18 attractive, high-ceilinged, wood-beamed rooms—done in pastels—circle a small, quiet courtyard (Sb-€120, standard Db-€150, superior Db-€170, 10 percent discount with cash, suites available, air-con, Castello 6317, tel. 041-241-1300, fax 041-241-5982, www .locandalacorte.it, info@locandalacorte.it, Marco and Raffaela). Take vaporetto #52 from the train station to Fondamente Nove, exit the boat to your left, follow the waterfront, and turn right after the second bridge to get to S.S. Giovanni e Paolo square. Facing the Rosa Salva bar, take the street to the left (Calle Bressana); the hotel is a short block away at #6317 before the bridge.

$ Alloggi Barbaria rents six quiet, spacious, Ikea-style rooms with the basic comforts. Beyond Campo S.S. Giovanni e Paolo, it's a long walk from the action but a good value (Db-€100 with this book in 2006, extra bed-€30, family deals, air-con, tel. 041-522-2750, fax 041-277-5540, www.alloggibarbaria.it, info@alloggibarbaria.it, Giorgio and Fausto). Take vaporetto #52 to Ospedale stop, turn left as you get off the boat, then right down Calle de le Capucine to #6573 (Castello).

Southeast of the Rialto Bridge

$$$ Locanda Gambero, with 31 pricey rooms, is a comfortable and very central three-star hotel (Sb-€130, Db-€230, Tb-€260, 10 percent discount with cash, air-con, Internet in lobby; from

Rialto vaporetto dock walk away from the Rialto Bridge, cross one bridge, and take first left down skinny Calle Bembo/Calle dei Fabbri; or from St. Mark's Square go through Sotoportego dei Dai, then down Calle dei Fabbri; Calle dei Fabbri 4687, San Marco, tel. 041-522-4384, fax 041-520-0431, www.locandaalgambero .com, hotelgambero@tin.it, Sandro). Gambero runs the pleasant, Art Deco–style La Bistrot on the corner, which serves old-time Venetian cuisine.

$$ Hotel al Piave, with 27 fine air-conditioned rooms above a bright and classy lobby, is fresh, modern, and comfortable. You'll enjoy the neighborhood and always get a cheery welcome (Db-€150, Tb-€190, family suites-€250 for 4 or €280 for 5, prices good through 2006 with this book, discount for cash; vaporetto #82 to San Zaccaria, find your way to Ruga Giuffa, it's at #4838/40, Castello; tel. 041-528-5174, fax 041-523-8512, www.hotelalpiave .com, info@hotelpiave.com; Mirella, Paolo, and Ilaria speak English, faithful Molly doesn't).

$ Hotel Riva, with gleaming marble hallways and bright modern rooms, is romantically situated on a canal along the gondola serenade route. You could actually dunk your breakfast rolls in the canal (but don't). Sandro might hold a corner *(angolo)* room if you ask, and there are also a few rooms overlooking the canal. Ten of the 32 rooms come with air-conditioning for the same price—request one when you reserve (Sb-€90, two D with adjacent showers-€100, Db-€120, Tb-€170, €10 extra for view, reserve with credit card but pay with cash only, Ponte dell'Angelo, tel. 041-522-7034, fax 041-528-5551). Facing St. Mark's Basilica, walk behind it on the left along Calle de la Canonica, take the first left (at blue *Pauly & C* mosaic in street), continue straight, go over the bridge (might be marked *Angelo* or *Anzolo*), and angle right to the hotel at Ponte dell'Angelo.

$ Corte Campana B&B, run by enthusiastic and helpful Riccardo, rents three quiet rooms just behind St. Mark's Square (Db-€129, Tb-€165, Qb-€200, cash only, air-con, Calle del Remedio 4410, Castello, tel. 041-523-3603, mobile 389-272-6500, www.cortecampana.com, info@cortecampana.com). Facing St. Mark's Basilica, take Calle de la Canonica (left of church); turn left before the canal on Calle dell'Anzolo. Take the second right (onto Calle del Remedio), cross the bridge, and follow signs. Ring the bell at the black gate; the door is across the courtyard on the left wall, and the B&B is up three flights of stairs.

$ Casa Cosmo is a humble little five-room place run by Davide and his parents. While it comes with minimal services and no public spaces, it's air-conditioned, extremely central, inexpensive, and quiet, with a tiny terrace (Db-€100 with this book and cash in 2006, on tiny Calle di Mezzo just off Calle delle Ballotte a block from

---

Flexible Floors

All over town, from palaces to cheap old hotels, you'll find speckled floors *(pavimento alla Veneziana)*. While they might look like cheap linoleum, these are historic—protected by the government and a pain for local landlords to maintain. As Venice was built, it needed flexible flooring to absorb the inevitable settling of the buildings. Through an expensive and laborious process, several layers of material are built up and finished with a broken marble top that is shaved and polished to what you'll see today. While patterns were sometimes designed into the flooring, it's often just a speckled hodgepodge. Keep an eye open for this. Once a year, the floor is rubbed with natural oil to maintain its flexibility. Craftspeople still give landlords fits when repairs are needed.

---

the Merceria, San Marco 4976, tel. 041-296-0710, www.casacosmo .com, info@casacosmo.com).

Near the Accademia Bridge

When you step over the Accademia Bridge, the commotion of touristy Venice is replaced by a sleepy village laced with canals. This quiet area, next to the best painting gallery in town, is a 15-minute walk from St. Mark's Square and the Rialto, or you can take the Santa Maria del Giglio or Salute *traghetto* for a shortcut to St. Mark's. The fast vaporetto #82 connects the Accademia Bridge with both the train station (15 min) and St. Mark's Square (5 min).

South of the Accademia Bridge

To reach these hotels from the train station, you can take a vaporetto to the Accademia stop (more scenic, down Grand Canal) or the Zattere stop (less scenic, around outskirts of Venice, but cheaper and faster).

$$$ Hotel Belle Arti is a good bet if you want modern freshness in the old center. With a grand entry and all the American hotel comforts, it's a big, 67-room, three-star place that sits on a former schoolyard (Sb-€120, Db-€180-215, Tb-€265, plush public areas, air-con, elevator; 100 yards behind Accademia art museum: facing museum, take left, then forced right, to Via Dorsoduro 912, Dorsoduro; tel. 041-522-6230, fax 041-528-0043, www .hotelbellearti.com, info@hotelbellearti.com).

$$$ Pensione Accademia fills the 17th-century Villa Maravege. Its 27 rooms are comfortable, elegant, and air-conditioned. You'll feel aristocratic gliding through its grand

Accademia Area Hotels

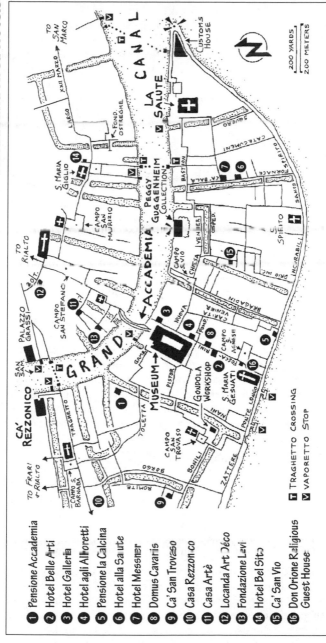

1 Pensione Accademia
2 Hotel Belle Arti
3 Hotel Galleria
4 Hotel agli Alboretti
5 Pensione la Calcina
6 Hotel alla Salute
7 Hotel Messner
8 Domus Cavanis
9 Ca' San Trovaso
10 Casa Rezzonico
11 Casa Artè
12 Locanda Art Déco
13 Fondazione Levi
14 Hotel Bel Sito
15 Ca' San Vio
16 Don Orione Religious
   Guest House

T TRAGHETTO CROSSING
V VAPORETTO STOP

public spaces and lounging in its wistful, breezy gardens (Sb-€130, standard Db-€190, bigger "superior" Db-€240, Qb-€310, 10 percent discount promised with this book in hand in 2006; facing Accademia art museum, take first right, cross first bridge, go right to Dorsoduro 1058; tel. 041-523-7846, fax 041-523-9152, www.pensioneaccademia.it, info@pensioneaccademia.it).

$$$ Hotel agli Alboretti is a cozy, family-run, 23-room place in a quiet neighborhood a block behind the Accademia art museum. With red carpeting and wood-beamed ceilings, it feels plush (Sb-€105, Db-€180, Tb-€205, Qb-€230, air-con, elevator; 100 yards from the Accademia vaporetto stop on Rio Terra a Foscarini at Accademia 884, Dorsoduro; facing Accademia art museum, go left, then forced right; tel. 041-523-0058, fax 041-521-0158, www .aglialboretti.com, info@aglialboretti.com). They run a near-gourmet restaurant that is quickly becoming a local favorite.

$$ Pensione la Calcina, the home of English writer John Ruskin in 1876, maintains a 19th-century formality. It comes with all the three-star comforts in a professional yet intimate package. Its 33 rooms are squeaky clean, with good wood furniture, hard-wood floors, and a peaceful canalside setting facing Giudecca island (Sb-€96, Sb with view-€106, Db-€148–186 depending on size of room and view, air-con, rooftop terrace, killer sundeck on canal and canalside buffet-breakfast terrace, Dorsoduro 780, at south end of Rio di San Vio, tel. 041-520-6466, fax 041-522-7045, www .lacalcina.com, la.calcina@libero.it). From the Tronchetto parking lot take vaporetto #82, or from the train station take #51 or #61, to Zattere (at vaporetto stop, exit right and walk along canal to hotel). Guests get a fine dinner at their La Piscina restaurant discounted to €22. Guests are welcome to use the terrace outside of meal times without buying anything.

$$ Casa Rezzonico is a silent getaway far from the madding crowds. Its private garden terrace has perhaps the lushest grass in Italy, and its seven spacious rooms have views of this garden and of the adjacent canal (Sb-€120, Db-€150, Tb-€180, Qb-€220, some rooms with air-con, Fondamenta Gherardini 2813, Dorsoduro, tel. 041-277-0653, fax 041-277-5435, www.casarezzonico.it, info@casarezzonico.it). Take vaporetto #1 to the Ca' Rezzonico stop, head up Calle del Traghetto, cross Campo San Barnaba to the canal, and continue forward on Fondamenta Gherardini to #2813.

$$ Hotel alla Salute, a basic retreat buried deep in Dorsoduro with 50 rooms and indifferent owners, works for those wanting a quiet Venice residence (Db-€140, cheaper if you pay in cash, facing the canal Rio delle Fornace near La Salute church, Salute 222, Dorsoduro, tel. 041-523-5404, fax 041-522-2271, www.hotelsalute .com, info@hotelsalute.com).

$$ Hotel Messner, a sprawling place popular with groups, rents 40 nondescript rooms in a peaceful canalside neighborhood near La Salute Church. While remote, it has cheap and handy *traghetto* access to St. Mark's Square (Sb-€110, Db with air-con-€140, Db without air-con in simpler annex-€115, Tb-€145, Qb-€160, peaceful garden, midway between lagoon and Grand Canal on Rio delle Fornace canal, Dorsoduro 216, tel. 041-522-7443, fax 041-522-7266, www.hotelmessner.it, messnerinfo@tin.it).

$ Hotel Galleria has nine tight, velvety rooms, most with views of the Grand Canal. Some rooms are quite narrow (S-€80, D-€110, Db-€120, big canal-view Db #8 and #10-€155, includes scant breakfast in room, fans, near Accademia art museum, and next to recommended Foscarini pizzeria, Dorsoduro 878a, tel. 041-523-2489, tel. & fax 041-520-4172, www.hotelgalleria.it, galleria @tin.it).

$ Ca' San Trovaso rents 14 classy, spacious rooms split between the main hotel and a nearby annex. The location is peaceful, on a small canal (Sb-€90, Db-€110, bigger canal-view Db-€130, Tb-€145, these prices promised with this book in 2006, breakfast in your room, fans, small roof terrace, Dorsoduro 1350/51, tel. 041-277-1146, fax 041-277-7190, www.casantrovaso.com, s.trovaso@tin .it, Mark and his son Alessandro). Take vaporetto #82 from the Tronchetto parking lot (or #51 from Piazzale Roma or the train station), get off at Zattere, exit left, turn right at tiny Calle Trevisan, cross the bridge, cross the adjacent bridge, take an immediate right, and then the first left.

$ Ca' San Vio is a tiny, new place run by the Ca' San Trovaso folks on a quiet canal with five fine air-conditioned rooms (small French bed Db-€100, bigger Db-€110, Tb-€140, breakfast in room, no public spaces, Calle delle Mende 531, Dorsoduro, tel. 041-277-1146, www.casanvio.com, Roberto and Marco).

$ Domus Cavanis, across the street from—and run by—Hotel Belle Arti (described above), is a big, practical, stark place, renting 30 quiet, simple rooms (Sb-€55, Db-€100, Tb-€135, family rooms, includes breakfast at Hotel Belle Arti, air-con, elevator, Dorsoduro 895, tel. 041-528-7374, fax 041-528-0043, info@hotelbellearti.com).

$ Don Orione Religious Guest House is a big cultural center dedicated to the work of a local man who became a saint in modern times. Filling an old monastery, it feels like a modern retreat center—clean, peaceful, and strictly run, with 50 rooms. It's beautifully located, comfortable, and a fine value (Sb-€70, Db-€115, Tb-€147, air-con, profits go to their mission work in the developing world, groups welcome, on the Giudecca Canal directly across from the Accademia Bridge facing Campo Sant'Agnese, Zattere 909a, Dorsoduro, tel. 041-522-4077, fax 041-528-6214, www.donorione -venezia.it, info@donorione-venezia.it).

North of the Accademia Bridge

$$ Hotel Bel Sito, friendly for a three-star hotel, offers comfortable yet well-worn Old World character, 38 rooms, a peaceful courtyard, and a picturesque location—facing a church on a small square between St. Mark's Square and the Accademia (Sb-€98, Db-€160 promised with this book in 2006, air-con, elevator, some rooms with canal or church views; vaporetto #1 to Santa Maria del Giglio stop, take narrow alley to square, hotel at far end to your right; Santa Maria del Giglio 2517, San Marco, tel. 041-522-3365, fax 041-520-4083, www.hotelbelsito.info, info@hotelbelsito.info).

$$ Locanda Art Déco is a charming little place. While the Art Deco theme is scant, a wrought-iron staircase leads from the inviting lobby to seven thoughtfully decorated rooms (Db-€170, 3-night minimum on weekends, 5 percent discount with cash, 2 family rooms, air-con, just north of the Accademia Bridge off Campo Santo Stefano at 2966 Calle delle Botteghe, San Marco, tel. 041-277-0558, fax 041-270-2891, www.locandaartdeco.com, info@locandaartdeco.com, Giuseppe).

$ Casa Artè has eight homey rooms with high ceilings, old-style Venetian furnishings, air-conditioning, and thoughtful touches in a red-velvet ambience (Sb-€90, Db-€130, 10 percent discount with cash, family room sleeps up to 6, just north of Accademia Bridge, 100 yards west of Campo San Stefano on Calle de Frutariol, San Marco 2900/01, tel. 041-520-0882, fax 041-277-8395, www.casaarte.info, info@casaarte.info, Gian Carlo).

$ Fondazione Levi, run by a foundation that promotes research on Venetian music, offers 18 quiet, institutional, yet comfortable and spacious rooms (Sb-€65, Db-€105, Tb-€124, Qb-€145, twin beds only, elevator, San Vidal 2893, San Marco, tel. 041-786-711, fax 041-786-766, foresterialevi@libero.it). It's 80 yards from the base of the Accademia Bridge on the St. Mark's side. From the Accademia vaporetto stop, cross the Accademia Bridge, take an immediate left, crossing the bridge Ponte Giustinian and going down Calle Giustinian directly to the Fondazione. Buzz the *Foresteria* door to the right.

Near the Train Station

I don't recommend the train station area. It's crawling with noisy, disoriented tourists with too much baggage and people whose life's calling is to scam them out of their money. It's so easy just to hop a vaporetto upon arrival and get into the Venice of your dreams. Still, some like to park their bags near the station, and these two places work well.

$ Albergo Marin and its friendly, helpful staff offer 17 good-value, immaculate, quiet rooms handy to the train station (Sb-€80, Db-€95, these are the maximum prices with this book in 2006,

5 percent discount with cash, fans on request, Campiello delle Muneghe 670b, Santa Croce, tel. 041-718-022, fax 041-721-485, www.albergomarin.it, info@albergomarin.it). From the station, cross the Grand Canal and turn immediately right. Walk along the water, take the first left (after passing the church) down Calle del Traghetto di S. Lucia, and then jog left again to Campiello delle Muneghe.

$ Alloggi Henry, a homey little family-owned hotel, has eight ramshackle rooms in a quiet neighborhood a five-minute walk from the train station (Db-€90 with this book in 2006, no breakfast, Calle Ormesini 1506e, Cannaregio, tel. 041-523-6675, fax 041-715-680, www.alloggihenry.com, info@alloggihenry.com). From the station, follow Lista di Spagna, Rio Terra San Leonardo, and Rio Terra Farsetti, then take the second left on Calle Ormesini; the hotel's at #1506.

Big, Fancy Hotels

Here are three big, plush, four-star places with greedy, sky-high rack rates (around Db-€300) that often have great discounts (as low as Db-€160) for drop-ins, off-season travelers, or online booking through their Web site. If you want a sliding-glass-door, uniformed-receptionist kind of comfort and formality in the old center, these are worth considering: **$$$ Hotel Giorgione** (big, garish, shiny, near Rialto Bridge, www.hotelgiorgione.com); **$$$ Hotel Casa Verardo** (elegant and quietly parked on a canal behind St. Mark's, more stately, www.casaverardo.it); and **$$$ Hotel Donà Palace** (sitting like Las Vegas in the touristy zone just northeast of St. Mark's, www.donapalace.it).

Cheap Dormitory Accommodations

$ Foresteria della Chiesa Valdese, warmly run by the Methodist Church, offers 33 beds in doubles and three- to 10-bed dorms, halfway between St. Mark's Square and the Rialto Bridge. This run-down but charming old place has elegant ceiling paintings (dorm bed-€22, D-€58, Db-€75, includes breakfast, sheets, and lockers; must check in and out when office is open—9:00–13:00 & 18:00–20:00, Castello 5170, tel. 041-528-6797, fax 041 241-6238, foresteriavenezia@diaconiavaldese.org). From Campo Santa Maria Formosa, walk past Bar all'Orologio to the end of Calle Lunga and cross the bridge.

$ Venice's **youth hostel,** on Giudecca Island, is crowded and inexpensive (€21 beds with sheets and breakfast in 10- to 16-bed dorms, cheaper for hostel members, office open daily 7:00–9:30 & 13:30–23:30, catch vaporetto #82 from station to Zittele, tel. 041-523-8211, can reserve online at www.hostelbooking.com). The budget cafeteria welcomes non-hostelers (nightly 16:30–21:30).

EATING

The Italians are masters at the art of fine living. That means eating...long and well. Lengthy, multicourse lunches and dinners and endless hours sitting in outdoor cafés are the norm. Americans eat on their way to an evening event and complain if the check is slow in coming. For Italians, dining is an end in itself, and only rude waiters rush you. When you want the bill, mime-scribble on your raised palm or ask for it: *"Il conto?"*

Even those of us who liked dorm food will find that the local cafés, cuisine, and wines become highlights of our Italian adventure. Trust me, this is sightseeing for your palate, and even if the rest of you is sleeping in cheap hotels, your taste buds will relish an occasional first-class splurge. You can eat well without going broke. But be careful: You're just as likely to blow a small fortune on a disappointing meal as you are to dine wonderfully for €20.

Restaurants

When restaurant-hunting, choose places filled with locals, not the place with the big neon signs boasting, "We speak English and accept credit cards." Restaurants parked on famous squares or canals generally serve tourists bad food at high prices. Locals eat better at lower-rent locales. Family-run places operate without hired help and can offer cheaper meals. *Osteria*—indicating a small, generally family-run and traditional place—is my favorite word when I'm hungry.

A full meal consists of an appetizer (antipasto, €3–6), a first course (*primo piatto*, pasta or soup, €5–10), and a second course (*secondo piatto*, expensive meat and fish dishes, €10–20). Vegetables *(contorni, verdure)* may come with the *secondo* or cost extra (€4) as a side dish. The euros can add up in a hurry. Light and budget eaters get a *primo piatto* each and share an antipasto.

Or they indulge in the local appetizers—*cicchetti*—explained below.

Note that seafood and steak may be sold by weight; if you see "100 g" or "*l'etto*" by the price on the menu, you'll pay that price per 100 grams—about a quarter pound. Similarly, "*s.q.*" means according to quantity.

Some special dishes come in large quantities meant for two people; the shorthand way of showing this on a menu is "x2" (meaning "times two").

Restaurants normally pad the bill with a cover charge (*pane e coperto*—"bread and cover charge," of around €2) and occasionally a service charge (*servizio*, 15 percent, see "Tipping," below); these charges are listed on the menu.

Tipping

Tipping is an issue only at restaurants that have waiters and waitresses. If you order your food at a counter, don't tip. (Many Italians never tip.)

If the menu states that service is included *(servizio incluso)*, there's no need to tip beyond that, but if you like to tip and you're pleased with the service, throw in €1 to €2 per person.

If service is not included, tip 5 to 10 percent by rounding up or leaving the change from your bill. Leave the tip on the table or hand it to your server. It's best to tip in cash even if you pay with your credit card. Otherwise the tip might never reach your waiter.

Pizzerias

Pizza is cheap and everywhere. Key pizza vocabulary: *capricciosa* (generally ham, mushrooms, olives, and artichokes), *funghi* (mushrooms), *marinara* (tomato sauce, oregano, garlic, no cheese), *quattro formaggi* (4 different cheeses), and *quattro stagioni* (different toppings on each of the 4 quarters, for those who can't choose just one menu item). If you ask for pepperoni on your pizza, you'll get green or red peppers, not sausage. Kids like *diavola* (the closest thing in Italy to American "pepperoni") and *margherita* (tomato and cheese) pizzas.

Bars/Cafés

Italian "bars" are not taverns but cafés. These local hangouts serve coffee, mini-pizzas, sandwiches, and drinks from the cooler. Many dish up plates of fried cheese and vegetables from under the glass counter, ready to reheat. This is my budget choice, the Italian equivalent of English pub grub.

For quick meals, bars usually have trays of cheap, ready-made sandwiches (*panini* or *tramezzini*)—some kinds are delightful grilled. (Others are lots of mayo between crustless slices of Wonder Bread.) To get food "for the road," say, "*Da portar via*" (or *canale*...

for the canal). All bars have a WC *(toilette, bagno)* in the back, and customers (and the discreet public) can use it.

Bars serve great drinks—hot, cold, sweet, or alcoholic. Chilled bottled water *(natural* or *frizzante)* is sold cheap to-go. Fresh-squeezed orange and grapefruit juice *(una spremuta)* are common.

Coffee: If you ask for *"un caffè,"* you'll get espresso. Cappuccino is served to locals before noon and to tourists at any time of day. (To an Italian, cappuccino is a breakfast drink and a travesty after anything with tomatoes.) Italians like it only warm. To get it hot, request *"Molto caldo"* (very hot) or *"Più caldo, per favore"* (hotter, please; pew KAHL-doh, pehr fah-VOH-ray).

Experiment with a few of the options...

* *caffè freddo:* sweet and iced espresso
* *cappuccino freddo:* iced cappuccino
* *caffè hag:* instant decaf (you can order decaffeinated versions of any coffee drink—just ask for it *decaffeinato)*
* *macchiato:* espresso with only a little milk
* *caffè latte:* coffee with lots of hot milk, no foam
* *caffè americano:* espresso diluted with water
* *caffè corretto:* espresso with a shot of liqueur

Beer: Beer on tap is *"alla spina."* Get it *piccola* (33 centiliters or 1.4 cups), *media* (50 cl, about a pint), or *grande* (a liter, about 2 pints).

Wine: To order a glass *(bicchiere;* bee-kee-AY-ree) of red *(rosso)* or white *(bianco)* wine say, *"Un bicchiere di vino rosso/bianco."* *Corposo* means full-bodied. House wine often comes in a quarter-liter carafe *(un quarto).* An *ombra* is the smallest glass.

Prices: You'll notice a two-tiered pricing system. Drinking a cup of coffee while standing at the bar is cheaper than drinking it at a table. If you're on a budget, don't sit without first checking out the financial consequences.

If the bar isn't busy, you'll often just order and pay when you leave. Otherwise: (1) decide what you want; (2) find out the price by checking the price list on the wall, the prices posted near the food, or by asking the barman; (3) pay the cashier; and (4) give the receipt to the barman (whose clean fingers handle no dirty euros) and tell him what you want.

Picnics

In Venice, picnicking saves lots of euros and is a great way to sample local specialties. For a colorful experience, gather your ingredients in the morning at Venice's produce market (near the Rialto Bridge); you'll probably visit several market stalls to put together a complete meal. A local *alimentari* is your one-stop corner grocery store (most will slice and stuff your sandwich for you if you buy the ingredients there).

Eating with the Seasons

Italian cooks love to serve you fresh produce and seafood at its tastiest. If you must have porcini mushrooms outside of October and November, they'll be frozen. To get the freshest veggies at a fine restaurant, request *"Il piatto di verdure della stagione, per favore"* (A plate of seasonal vegetables, please). Here are a few examples of what's fresh when:

April–May:	Squid, green beans, asparagus, artichokes, and zucchini flowers
April, May, Sept, Oct:	Black truffles
May–June:	Asparagus, zucchini, cantaloupe, and strawberries
May–Aug:	Eggplant
Oct–Nov:	Mushrooms and white truffles
Fresh year-round:	Clams, meats, and cheese

Juice-lovers can get a liter of O.J. for the price of a Coke or coffee. Look for "100% *succo*" (juice) on the label. Hang onto the half-liter mineral-water bottles (sold everywhere for about €1). Buy juice in cheap liter boxes, drink some, and store the extra in your water bottle. (I drink the tap water—*acqua del rubinetto*.)

Picnics can be adventures in high cuisine. Be daring. Try the fresh mozzarella, presto pesto, shriveled olives, marinated egg-plant or artichokes, sundried tomatoes, and any UFOs the locals are excited about. Shopkeepers are happy to sell small quantities of produce. Rather than pick your own produce, it is customary to say when you plan to eat it. If you plan to eat it today, say, *"Per oggi"* (pehr OH-jee), and let her grab the pieces that are best for you. If you suspect you're being overcharged, know the cost per kilo and watch the weighing procedure.

A typical picnic for two might be fresh rolls, 100 grams of cheese, 100 grams of meat (100 grams = about a quarter pound, called *un etto* in Italy), two tomatoes, three carrots, two apples, yogurt, and a liter box of juice. Total cost—about €10.

There's a tiny ***allmentari*** just around the corner from the Rialto market that has *salumi,* cheese, bread, and an intriguing (and spicy!) concoction of cheese, kalamata olives, sundried toma-toes, olive oil, and hot peppers. It goes great with a fresh roll. To get there from the market, walk to the end of Ruga degli Orefici, turn left onto Ruga Vecchia S. Giovanni and then right under Sotoportego do' Mori—it's just on your left.

Supermarkets: A handy supermarket is on the corner of Salizada S. Lio and Calle Mondo Nuovo, between St. Mark's and

Campo S. Maria Formosa (Mon–Sat 8:30–19:30, closed Sun). Billa supermarket is at the far west end of Dorsoduro, on the corner of Zattere al Ponte Longo and Calle della Masena (open daily, tel. 041-522-6187). Assemble your picnic, and then dine in style overlooking Giudecca Canal.

VENETIAN CUISINE

Venetian cuisine relies more heavily on fish, shellfish, risotto, and polenta than the rest of Italy. Along with the usual pizza and pasta fare, here are some typical foods you'll encounter:

Bar Snacks

Venetians often eat a snack—*cicchetti* or *panini*—while standing at a bar. (Remember, you'll usually pay more if you sit, rather than stand.)

Cicchetti: Generic name for various small finger foods served in some pubs—like appetizers or tapas, Venetian-style. Designed as a quick meal for working people, the selection and ambience are best on workdays (Mon–Sat lunch and early dinner). See "The Stand-Up Progressive Venetian Pub-Crawl Dinner," page 225.

Panini: Sandwiches made with rustic bread, filled with meat, vegetables, and cheese, served cold or toasted (you can eat in or take out).

Tramezzini: Crustless, white bread sandwiches served cold and stuffed with a variety of fillings (e.g., egg, tuna, or shrimp), mixed with a mayonnaise dressing.

Appetizers (Antipasti)

Antipasto di mare: A marinated mix of fish and shellfish served chilled.

Asiago cheese: The Veneto region's specialty, a cow's-milk cheese that's either *mezzano*—young, firm, and creamy; or *stravecchio*—aged, pungent, and granular.

Sarde in saor: Sardines marinated with onions.

Rice (Riso), Pasta, and Polenta

Risotto: Short-grain rice, simmered in broth and often flavored with fish and seafood. For example, *risotto nero* is risotto made with squid and its ink, or *risotto ai porcini* with porcini mushrooms.

Risi e bisi: Rice and peas.

Pasta e fagioli: White bean and pasta soup.

Bigoli in salsa: A long, fat, whole-wheat noodle (one of the few traditional pastas) with anchovy sauce.

Polenta: Cornmeal boiled into a mush and served soft or cut into firm slabs and grilled. Polenta is a standard accompaniment with cod *(baccalà)*, or calf liver and onions *(fegato alla veneziana)*.

Seafood *(Frutti di Mare)*

Some sea creatures found in the Adriatic are slightly different from their American cousins. Generally, Venetian fish are smaller than American salmon and trout (think sardines and anchovies). The shellfish are more exotic. The weirder the animal (eel, octopus, frog-fisher), the more local it is. Instead of a set price, seafood can be sold by weight (if you see "100 g" or *"l'etto"* by a too-good-to-be-true price on the menu, that's the cost per 100 grams—about a quarter pound).

Baccalà: Salt cod served with polenta, or chopped up and mixed with mayonnaise as a topping for *cicchetti* (appetizers).

Branzino: Sea bass, served whole (head and tail) and grilled.

Calamari: Squid, usually cut into rings and either deep-fried or marinated.

Cozze: Mussels steamed in an herb broth with tomato.

Gamberi: The generic name for shrimp. *Gamberetti* are small shrimp, and *Gamberoni* are large shrimp. (Language tip: *-etti* signifies little, and *-oni* indicates big.)

Moleche col pien: Fried soft-shell crabs.

Pesce fritto misto: Assorted deep-fried seafood (often it's calamari and prawns).

Seppia: Cuttlefish, a squid-like creature that sprays black ink when threatened. *Seppia al nero* is the squid in its own ink, often served over spaghetti.

Sogliola: Sole, served poached or oven roasted.

Vitello di mare: "Sea veal," like swordfish—firm, pink, mild, and grilled.

Vongole: Small clams steamed with fresh herbs and wine, or served as a first course, such as *spaghetti alle vongole*.

Zuppa di pesce: Seafood stew.

Dessert *(Dolci)*

Tiramisù: Spongy ladyfingers soaked in coffee and marsala, layered with mascarpone cheese and bitter chocolate. Arguably

Venetian in origin, the literal meaning of the word is "pick-me-up."

Venetian cookies: There are numerous varieties, due perhaps to Venice's position in trade (spices) and the Venetians' love of celebrations. Many treats were created for certain feast days and religious holidays. *Pinza,* a sweet made with corn, wheat flour, and raisins (and sometimes figs, almonds, and lemon) is made for Epiphany, January 6. *Fritole* are tiny doughnuts associated with Carnevale (Mardi Gras). *Bussola* rings are made for Easter. Other popular treats are *bisse* (seahorse-shaped cookies) and *croccante* (made with toasted corn and almonds, similar in texture to peanut brittle).

Wine *(Vino)* and Stronger

For information about wines from nearby Verona, see page 298.

Valpolicella: Light, dry, fruity red from the hills north of Verona. It's likely what you're drinking if you ordered the house wine *(vino della casa).*

Bardolino: Also made from Valpolicella grapes, it's a similar wine but grown near Lake Garda.

Amarone: Rich, intense red, with alcohol content at about 16 percent, made from Valpolicella grapes.

Soave: Crisp white (great with seafood) from near Verona. *Soave Classico* designates a higher quality.

Prosecco: Sparkling wine, rather neutral-tasting, making it easy to drink too much.

Bellini: A cocktail of Prosecco and white-peach puree; invented (by Hemingway) at the pricey Harry's Bar (near San Marco vaporetto stop).

Tiziano: Grape juice and Prosecco.

Grappa: Distilled *vinacce* (grape skins and stems left over from winemaking) make this powerful local firewater.

Spritz: This common, refreshing pre-dinner drink mixes white wine, soda, and ice with a liquor of your choice. Most popular with locals are *uno spritz con Campari* (bitter!) or *con Aperol* (sweeter).

Fragolino: A sweet dessert wine made from a raspberry-flavored grape.

RESTAURANTS

While touristy restaurants are the scourge of Venice, and most restaurateurs believe you can't survive in Venice without catering to tourists, there are plenty of places that are still popular with locals and respect the tourists who happen in. First trick: Walk away from triple-language menus. Second trick: Order the daily special. Third trick: For freshness, eat fish. Most seafood dishes are the local catch-of-the-day.

Near the Rialto Bridge

North of the Rialto Bridge

These restaurants are located between Campo S.S. Apostoli and Campo S.S. Giovanni e Paolo.

Trattoria da Bepi is a classy, family-run place where Mamma scours the market for just the best ingredients, and son, Loris, takes good care of the hungry clientele (€30 meals, Fri–Wed 12:00–14:30 & 19:00–22:00, closed Thu, near Rialto, half a block north of Campo Santi Apostoli on Salizada Pistor, tel. 041-528-5031).

Osteria da Alberto has excellent €20 seafood dinners and €8 pastas (Mon–Sat 12:00–15:00 & 19:00–23:00, closed Sun, midway between Campo S.S. Apostoli and Campo S.S. Giovanni e Paolo, next to Ponte de la Panada on Calle Larga Giacinto Gallina, tel. 041-523-8153, run by Graziano and Giovanni).

Cicchetti: **Osteria al Bomba** is a *cicchetti* bar with a female touch. It's unusual (clean, no toothpicks, no cursing) but actually quite good, with lots of veggies. You can stand and eat at the bar, or oversee the construction of the house *"antipasto misto di cicchetti"* plate (€15, enough for 2), and then grab a seat at the long table (daily 18:00–23:00, near Campo S.S. Apostoli, a block off Strada Nuova on Calle dell'Oca, tel. 041-520-5175). You'll find more pubs nearby, in the side streets opposite Campo Santa Sofia, across Strada Nuova.

East of the Rialto Bridge, Near Campo San Bartolomeo,

Osteria di Santa Marina, on the wonderful Campo Marina square, serves pricey, near-gourmet food that's made with only the best seasonal ingredients. The quality food and classy ambience make this a good splurge (fun menu with €14 pastas and €25 *secondi,* Sun–Mon 19:30–21:30, Tue–Sat 12:30–14:30 & 19:30–21:30, reservations smart for dinner, eat indoors or outdoors on pleasant little square, midway between Rialto and Campo Santa Maria Formosa on Campo Marina, tel. 041-528-5239).

Osteria il Milion, with bow-tied waiters and dressy, candlelit tables indoors and out, is quietly situated next to Marco Polo's home. It's touristy but tasty—traditional Italian meals are about €25 (Thu–Tue 12:00–15:00 & 18:30–23:00, closed Wed, near Rialto, head north from Campo San Bartolomeo, over one bridge, take first right off San Giovanni Grisostomo before the church, walk under the sign Corte *Prima del Milion o del forno,* it's at #5841; tel. 041-522-9302).

The Stand-Up Progressive Venetian Pub-Crawl Dinner

My favorite Venetian dinner is a pub crawl *(giro d'ombra)*—a tradition unique to Venice, where no cars means easy crawling. (*Giro*

Rialto Area Restaurants

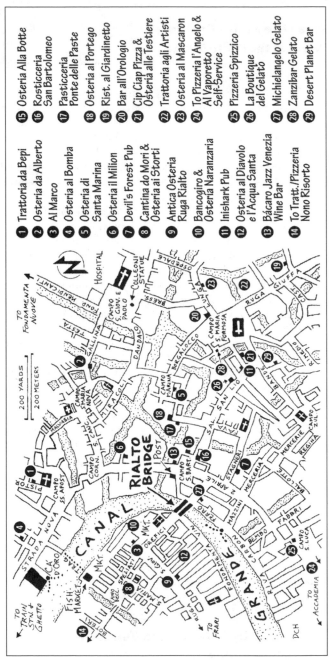

1. Trattoria da Bepi
2. Osteria da Alberto
3. Al Marco
4. Osteria al Bomba
5. Osteria di Santa Marina
6. Osteria il Milion
7. Devil's Forest Pub
8. Cantina do Mori & Osteria ai Storti
9. Antica Osteria Ruga Rialto
10. Bancogiro & Osteria Naranzaria
11. Inishark Pub
12. Osteria al Diavolo e l'Acqua Santa
13. Bácaro Jazz Venezia Wine Bar
14. To Tratt./Pizzeria Nono Risorto
15. Osteria Alla Botte
16. Rosticceria San Bartolomeo
17. Pasticceria Ponte delle Paste
18. Osteria al Portego
19. Rist. al Giardinetto
20. Bar all'Orologio
21. Cip Ciap Pizza & Osteria alle Testiere
22. Trattoria agli Artisti
23. Osteria al Mascaron
24. To Pizzeria l'Angelo & Al Vaporetto Self-Service
25. Pizzeria Spizzico
26. La Boutique del Gelato
27. Michielangelo Gelato
28. Zanzibar Gelato
29. Desert Planet Bar

means stroll, and *ombra*—slang for a glass of wine—means shade, from the old days when a portable wine bar scooted with the shadow of the Campanile bell tower across St. Mark's Square.)

Venice's residential back streets hide plenty of characteristic bars *(baccari)* with countless trays of interesting toothpick munchies *(cicchetti)* and blackboards listing the wines that are uncorked and served by the glass. This is a great way to mingle and have fun with the Venetians.

Cicchetti bars have a social stand-up zone and a cozy gaggle of tables where you can generally sit down with your *cicchetti* or order from a simple menu. In some of the more popular places, the local crowds spill happily out into the street. Food generally costs the same price whether you stand or sit.

I've listed plenty of pubs in walking order for a quick or extended crawl below. If you've crawled enough, most of these bars make a fine one-stop, sit-down dinner.

Try deep-fried mozzarella cheese, gorgonzola, calamari, artichoke hearts, and anything ugly on a toothpick. *Crostini* (small toasted bread with something on it) are popular, as are marinated seafood, olives, and prosciutto with melon. Meat and fish *(pesce; PESH-shay)* munchies can be expensive; veggies *(verdure)* are cheap, at about €3 for a meal-sized plate. In many places, there's a set price per food item (e.g., €1.50). To get a plate of assorted appetizers for €8 (or more, depending on how hungry you are), ask for: *"Un piatto classico di cicchetti misti da €8"* (oon pee-AH-toh KLAH-see-koh dee cheh-KET-tee MEE-stee da OH-toh ay-OO-roh). Bread sticks *(grissini)* are free for the asking.

Drink the house wines. A small glass of house red or white wine *(ombra rosso* or *ombra bianco)* or a small beer *(birrino)* costs about €1. The house keg wine is cheap—€1 per glass, about €4 per liter. *Vin bon,* Venetian for fine wine, may run you from €1.50 to €6 per little glass. There are usually several fine wines uncorked and available by the glass. *Corposo* means full-bodied. A good last drink is *fragolino,* the local sweet wine—*bianco* or *rosso.* It often comes with a little cookie *(biscotti)* for dipping.

Bars don't stay open very late, and the *cicchetti* selection is best early, so start your evening by 18:00. Most bars are closed on Sunday.

Cicchetterie and Light Meals West of the Rialto Bridge

All of these places are within 200 yards of each other, in the neighborhood around the Rialto market. This area is very crowded by day but nearly empty after dark.

Cantina do Mori has been famous with locals (since 1462) and savvy travelers (since 1982) as a classy place for fine wine and *francobolli* (a spicy selection of 20 tiny, mayo-soaked sandwiches nicknamed "stamps"). Choose from the featured wines. Confirm the price, or they'll rip you off (Mon–Sat 12:00–20:30, closed Sun, stand-up only, arrive early before the *cicchetti* are gone, San Polo 429, tel. 041-522-5401). From Rialto Bridge, walk 200 yards down Ruga degli Orefici, away from St. Mark's Square—then left on Ruga Vecchia S. Giovanni, then right at Sotoportego do' Mori.

Osteria ai Storti, just opened in 2005, offers lots of veggies, great prices, a homey feel, and a wonderful, fun place to congregate outdoors. Check out the photo of the market in 1909, below the bar (Mon–Sat 12:00–22:30, closed Sun, 20 yards from Cantina do Mori on Calle do Spade).

Antica Osteria Ruga Rialto, "the Ruga," is a local fixture where Marco serves great bar snacks and wine to his devoted clientele (daily 11:00–14:30 & 19:00–24:00, easy to find, just past the Chinese restaurant on Ruga Vecchia S. Giovanni 692, tel. 041-521-1243).

Osteria al Diavolo el'Acqua Santa, three blocks west of the Rialto Bridge, serves good—if pricey—pasta and makes a handy lunch stop for sightseers and gondola-riders. While they list *cicchetti* and wine by the glass on the wall, I'd come here for a light meal rather than for appetizers (Mon 12:00–15:00, Wed–Sun 12:00–15:00 & 19:00–23:00, closed Tue, hiding on a quiet street just off Rua Vecchia S. Giovanni, on Calle della Madonna, tel. 041-277-0307).

Al Marco, on Campo Cesare Battisti square, is a literal hole-in-the-wall where young locals gather to grab drinks and little snacks. The father-and-son team clearly lists the prices for wine and sandwiches (Mon–Sat 18:00–21:00, closed Sun, located on empty part of square just below courthouse).

Bancogiro (Osteria da Andrea), a simple bar behind the Rialto market, has stark yet powerfully atmospheric outdoor seating overlooking the Grand Canal. Peruse their wine list and basic menu at the bar (strong local cheeses are *a forte*), order, and grab a table—worth the reasonable cover charge (Tue–Sat 10:30–24:00, closed Mon, less than 200 yards from Rialto Bridge on Campo San Giacometto, San Polo 122, tel. 041-523-2061). Consider their €15 fish and vegetable plate.

Osteria Naranzaria, which shares a prime piece of Grand Canal real estate with Bancogiro next door, is described below, under "Romantic Canalside Settings."

Cicchetterie and Light Meals East of the Rialto Bridge, near Campo San Bartolomeo

Osteria "Alla Botte" Cicchetteria is packed with a young, local, bohemian-jazz clientele. It's good for a *cicchetti* snack with wine at the bar or for a light meal in the small back room—find the posted menus (Fri–Tue 10:00–15:00 & 17:00–23:00, closed Thu and Sun eve, 2 short blocks off Campo San Bartolomeo in the corner behind the statue—down Calle de la Bissa, notice the "day after" photo showing a debris-covered Venice after the notorious 1989 Pink Floyd open-air concert, tel. 041-520-9775).

Rosticceria San Bartolomeo is a cheap—if confusing—self-service restaurant with a likeably surly staff. Take out, grab a table, or munch at the bar (good €6–7 pasta, great fried *mozzarella al prosciutto* for €1.30, delightful fruit salad, and €1 glasses of wine, prices listed on wall behind counter, no cover or service charge, Tue–Sun 9.00–21.30, closed Mon, tel. 041-522-3569). To find this venerable budget eatery, imagine the statue on the Campo San Bartolomeo walking backwards 20 yards, turning left, and going under a passageway—now, follow him.

From Rosticceria San Bartolomeo, continue over a bridge to Campo San Lio. Here, turn left, passing Hotel Canada on your right and following Calle Carminati straight about 50 yards over another bridge. On the left is the pastry shop *(pasticceria)*, and straight ahead is Osteria Al Portego (at #6015). Both are listed below:

Pasticceria Ponte delle Paste is a feminine and pastel *salon de tè*, popular for its pastries and pre-dinner drinks. Italians love taking 15-minute breaks to sip a *spritz* aperitif with friends after a long day's work, before heading home. Ask sprightly Monica for a *spritz al bitter* (white wine, *amaro*, and soda water, €1.55; or choose from the menu on the wall) and munch some of the free goodies at the bar around 18:00 (daily 7:00–20:30, Ponte delle Paste).

Osteria al Portego is a friendly, local-style bar—one of the best in town—serving great *cicchetti* and good meals (Mon–Sat 10:30–15:00 & 18:00–22:00, closed Sun, Calle Malvasia 6015, Castello, tel. 041-522-9038). The *cicchetti* here can make a great meal, but you should also consider sitting down for an actual dinner. They have a fine menu.

On or near Campo Santa Maria Formosa

These eateries can be found on the map on page 226.

Campo Santa Maria Formosa is a classic Venetian square. For a balmy outdoor meal, have a pizza with wine on the square. Bar all'Orologio has a good setting and friendly service but mediocre "freezer" pizza (they're happy to let you split a pizza, Mon–Sat 6:00–23:00, closed Sun). To have a great pizza picnic on the square, cross the bridge behind the canalside *gelateria,* and grab a slice to go from **Cip Ciap Pizza** (Wed–Mon 9:00–21:00, closed Tue; facing *gelateria,* take bridge to the right; Calle del Mondo Novo). For a healthy snack, try the **fruit-and-vegetable stand** next to Campo Santa Maria Formosa's water fountain (Mon–Sat closes at about 19:30, closed Sun). Also on the square, the *gelateria* **Zanzibar** is perhaps too popular with tourists, but it's well-situated and the locals love it (daily 8:00–24:00, in winter 8:00–20:30).

Trattoria agli Artisti is efficient and friendly, with good food, especially the *frutti di mare*—spaghetti with seafood (Thu–Tue dinner from 18:00, closed Wed, half block off square down Ruga Giuffa, tel. 041-277-0029).

Ristorante al Giardinetto has white tablecloths, a formal but fun waitstaff, and a spacious, shady garden under a grape-vine canopy. While it used to be set up for big tour groups—and still feels it—groups no longer come here, and now the dining experience has improved (€9 pastas, €13 main courses, €2 *coperto,* closed Thu, at intersection of Ruga Giuffa and Calle Corona, tel. 041-528-5332).

Osteria alle Testiere is my most gourmet recommendation in Venice. Hugely respected, they are passionate about quality, serving up creative, artfully presented market-fresh seafood (there's no meat on the menu) and fine wine in what the chef calls a "Venetian Nouvel" style. Reservations are required for their three daily sittings: 12:30, 19:00 and 21:15. With only 22 seats, it's tight and homey yet elegant (€15 pastas, €24 *secondi,* plan on spending €50 for dinner, closed Sun–Mon, Calle del Mondo Novo, tel. 041-522-7220).

Osteria al Mascaron is where I've come for 20 years to watch Gigi and his food-loving band of ruffians dish up rustic-yet-sumptuous pastas with steamy seafood (€13) to salivating local foodies. The €15 *antipasto misto* plate and two glasses of wine make a wonderful light meal (a block past Campo Santa Maria Formosa at Calle Longa Santa Maria Formosa 5225, tel. 041-522-5995).

In Dorsoduro
Near the Accademia
For locations, see the map on page 232.

Ristorante/Pizzeria Accademia Foscarini, next to the Accademia Bridge and Galleria, offers decent €7–8 pizzas in a great canalside setting. This place is both scenic and practical—I grab a quick lunch here on each visit to Venice (Wed–Mon 9:00–21:00 in summer, until 20:00 in winter, closed Tue, Dorsoduro 878C, tel. 041-522-7281).

Enoteca Cantine del Vino Gia Schiavi is much loved for its €1 *cicchetti.* It's also a good place for a €2 glass of wine and appetizers (Mon–Sat 8:00–20:30, closed Sun, 100 yards from Accademia

Gallery on San Trovaso canal; facing Accademia, take a right and then a forced left at the canal to the 2nd bridge—S. Trovaso 992, tel. 041-523-0034). You're welcome to enjoy your wine and finger food while sitting on the bridge.

Ai Gondolieri is considered one of the best restaurants for meat—not fish—in Venice. Its sauces are heavy and prices are high, but gourmet carnivores love it (€17 pastas, €25 *secondi*, €5 cover, Wed–Mon 12:00–15:00 & 19:00–22:00, closed Tue, closed for lunch July–Aug, reservations smart, Dorsoduro 366 San Vio, behind Peggy Guggenheim Collection on west end of Rio delle Torreselle, tel. 041-528-6396).

Near Campo San Barnaba

A number of less-touristed restaurants cluster around this small square. From the Accademia, head northwest, following the curve of the Grand Canal. In five minutes, you'll spill out onto Campo San Barnaba (and the nearby Campo Santa Margherita). Follow the straight and narrow path (Calle Lunga San Barnaba) west of the square for more restaurants.

Casin dei Nobili (Pleasure Palace of Nobles) has a diverse, reasonably priced menu in a high-energy, informal, modern setting. The patio is filled with simple tables, happy tourists, and their inviting €10 daily specials (closed Mon, a half-block south of Campo San Barnaba, tel. 041-241-1841).

Ai Quattro Feri is a noisy, bustling, trattoria-style eatery, best for its catch-of-the-day seafood, especially the excellent grilled fish (€8 pastas, €12 *secondi*, closed Sun, just off the square on Calle Lunga San Barnaba 2757, tel. 041-520-6978).

Enoteca e Trattoria la Bitta, dark and woody, with a forgettable back patio, serves nicely presented, traditional Venetian food with—proudly—no fish. Their small menu is clearly focused on quality cooking (€9 pastas, €14 *secondi*, dinner only, Mon–Sat 18:30-23:00, closed Sun, cash only, next to Quattro Feri on Calle Lunga San Barnaba, tel. 041-523-0531).

Ristorante Oniga, right on Campo San Barnaba, is a wine bar/restaurant serving up Italian cuisine with a modern twist (closed Tue, tel. 041-522-4410).

On or near Campo San Polo

Antica Birraria la Corte is an everyday eatery on the very special Campo San Polo. Enjoy a pizza or simple meal on the far side of one of this great, homey, children-filled square (daily 12:00–14:30 & 19:00–22:30, on the way to Frari Church, Calle di Mezo 2168, San Polo, tel. 041-275-0570).

La Rivetta Ristorante offers a canalside setting and well-priced Venetian cuisine. Consider *spaghetti al nero di seppie*

Accademia Area Restaurants

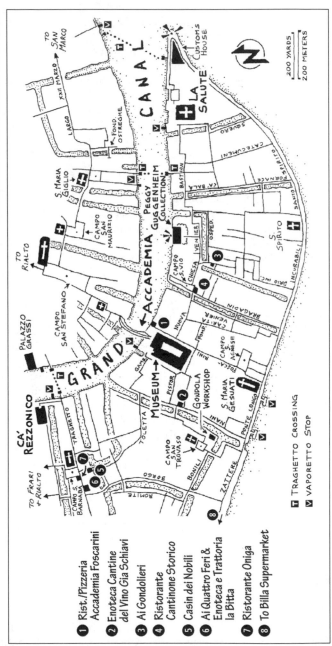

T TRAGHETTO CROSSING

V VAPORETTO STOP

1. Rist./Pizzeria Accademia Foscarini
2. Enoteca Cantine del Vino Gia Schiavi
3. Ai Gondolieri
4. Ristorante Cantinone Storico
5. Casin dei Nobili
6. Ai Quattro Feri & Enoteca e Trattoria la Bitta
7. Ristorante Oniga
8. To Billa Supermarket

(spaghetti in squid ink) or *fegato alla Veneziana* (calf liver and onions; open daily, Calle di Mezo 1479, San Polo).

Romantic Canalside Settings

Of course, if you want a canal view, it comes with lower quality or a higher price. But the memory is sometimes most important.

At **Trattoria da Giorgio ai Greci,** a few blocks behind St. Mark's, Giorgio and sons Robert and Davide serve homemade pastas and fresh seafood. While they have inside seating, you come here for the canalside dining—it's the best I've found anywhere in town. Call to reserve a canalside table (€20 tourist menu, daily

12:00–24:00, closed Mon in winter, 2 canals east of St. Mark's on Ponte dei Greci 4988, tel. 041-528-9780).

Osteria Naranzaria is one of two wonderful eateries (Bancogiro, next door, is listed on page 228) on the Grand Canal between the market and the Rialto Bridge. Somehow they've taken a stretch of unbeatable but overlooked canalfront property and filled it with trendy candlelit tables. Stefano Monti loves sushi, and since Venice was the gateway to the Orient (remember Marco Polo), he includes it on his simple menu, along with coldcuts and fine wine. Peasants can take their glasses to the steps along the canal for bar prices, but the romantic table service doesn't cost that much extra. This is the best-value Grand Canal eatery I have found (closed Mon, tel. 041-724-1035).

Ristorante Cantinone Storico sits on a peaceful canal in Dorsoduro between the Accademia Bridge and the Peggy Guggenheim Collection. It's dressy, specializes in fish and traditional Venetian dishes, has six or eight tables on the canal, and is worth the splurge (€15 pasta, €20 *secondi*, €3 cover, Mon–Sat 12:30–14:30 & 19:30–21:30, closed Sun, be wise and make reservations, on the canal Rio de S. Vio, tel. 041-523-9577).

Rialto Bridge Tourist Traps: Locals are embarrassed by the lousy food and aggressive "service" of the string of joints dominating the best romantic Grand Canal real estate in town. Still, if you want to linger over dinner with a view of the most famous bridge and the romantic song of gondoliers oaring by (and don't mind eating with other tourists), this can be enjoyable. Don't trust the waiter's recommendations for special meals. Just get a simple pizza or pasta and a drink for €12, and you'll savor the ambience without getting ripped off.

Near St. Mark's Square

For locations, see the map on page 235.

Osteria Enoteca San Marco offers beautifully presented "creative new Italian" cuisine with a mod ambience in a classic medieval shell. They proudly offer fine wine by the glass. This place is pricey, but the food is always top quality (€20 meals, Mon–Sat 12:30–23:00, closed Sun, a long block west of St. Mark's Square at Frezzeria 1610, tel. 041-528-5242, Carlo and his white-aproned army speak English).

At **Salad and Juice Bar Oasi 2000,** hardworking, English-speaking Paco serves big salads, sandwiches, and fresh-squeezed juice in a student cantina atmosphere just behind St. Mark's Basilica (Mon–Sat 8:00–19:00, closed Sun, off Calle San Provolo at Calle di Albanesi 4263, tel. 041-528-9937).

Trattoria alla Rivetta is a high-spirited hole-in-the-wall popular with gondoliers at lunch and mobbed with tourists at dinner. Even if they treat tourists as second-class eaters, pasta here for lunch is both a great meal and a great memory (just behind St. Mark's Basilica at the Ponte San Provolo bridge between Campo S.S. Filippo e Giacomo and Campo S. Provolo, tel. 041-528-7302). They also have bar munchies—see the *Prezzi al banco* price list on the wall by the bar.

Antica Sacrestia, a local institution, has à la carte choices and several different fixed-price menus: vegetarian, Venetian, tourist, seafood, fine pizza, and house specialties. I like the antipasto buffet. You can help the waiter construct your €14.50 plate with all the local goodies, including great seafood, and call it a meal (Tue–Sun 12:00–15:00 & 18:30–22:30, closed Mon, on Calle della Sacrestia 4442, 2 blocks behind St. Mark's, tel. 041-523-0749, www.anticasacrestia.com).

Trattoria da Remigio is well-known for high-quality, serious Venetian cuisine. Its indoors-only setting is a bit dressy, with a mix of tourists and locals and lots of commotion (Wed–Sun lunch from 12:30, dinner from 19:30, closed Mon–Tue, just past Rio dei Greci on a tiny square at the end of Calle Madonna, tel. 041-523-0089).

The **cafés on St. Mark's Square** offer music, inflated prices, and an unbeatable setting for a drink or light meal (for a description, see page 60).

Near the Train Station and in Cannaregio

For fast, cheap food near the station, consider **Brek,** a popular self-service cafeteria (after serving breakfast, it's open daily 11:30–22:00; with back to station, facing canal, go left on Rio Terra—it becomes Lista di Spagna in 2 short blocks, Lista di Spagna 124, tel. 041-244-0158).

St. Mark's Square Area Restaurants and Nightlife

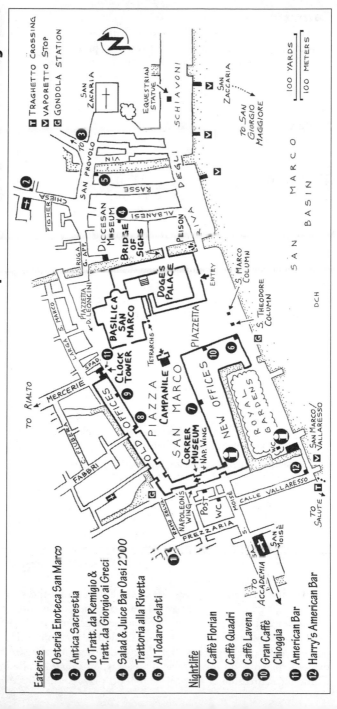

Eateries

1. Osteria Enoteca San Marco
2. Antica Sacrestia
3. To Tratt. da Remigio & Tratt. da Giorgio ai Greci
4. Salad & Juice Bar Oasi 2000
5. Trattoria alla Rivetta
6. Al Todaro Gelati

Nightlife

7. Caffè Florian
8. Caffè Quadri
9. Caffè Lavena
10. Gran Caffè Chioggia
11. American Bar
12. Harry's American Bar

Eating Elsewhere

Trattoria Pizzeria Nono Risorto is unpretentious, inexpensive, youthful, and famous for some of the best pizza in town. You'll sit in a gravelly garden, under a leafy canopy, surrounded by a young, enthusiastic waitstaff and Italian speakers enjoying huge salads, €9 pastas, and delicious €8 pizzas (€14 *secondi*, Wed–Mon 12:00–14:30 & 19:00–23:00, closed Tue; a 3-min walk from the Rialto fish market, find Campo San Cassiano and it's just over the bridge on Sotoportego de Siora Bettina; tel. 041-524-1169).

Osteria al Bacco, far beyond the crowds in a rustic Venetian setting, is worth the hike for its local cuisine (€35 for 3 courses and wine, Tue–Sun 12:00–14:00 & 19:00–22:00, closed Mon, reservations recommended, halfway between train station and the northernmost tip of Venice, Fondamenta Cappuccine, Cannaregio 3054, tel. 041-717-493).

Osteria la Zucca, on the Rio del Megio canal, is hardworking, homey, and away from the crowds. You'll get good, typical Venetian cuisine at a moderate price (€20 meals, Mon–Sat 12:30–14:30 for lunch, dinner guests usually have 2 seating choices—19:00 or 21:00, closed Sun, mostly indoors, reserve for canal windows, a few outdoor tables with one on the canal, midway between train station and Rialto Bridge at San Giacomo dell'Orio 1762, Calle Larga, Santa Croce, tel. 041-524-1570). A short block away is the square called San Giacomo dell'Orio—a breezy scene with trees, families at play, and a couple of simple trattorias offering basic food and classic, non-touristy, outdoor seating.

Cheap Meals

A key to cheap eating in Venice is **bar snacks** (see page 222), especially stand-up mini-meals in out-of-the-way bars. Order by pointing. *Panini* (sandwiches) are sold fast and cheap at bars everywhere. Basic reliable ham-and-cheese sandwiches (white bread, crusts trimmed) come toasted—simply ask for "toast"; these make a great supplement to Venice's skimpy hotel breakfasts.

For budget eating, I like small *cicchetti* bars (see page 227). For speed, value, and ambience, you can get a filling plate of local appetizers at nearly any of the bars.

Pizzerias are cheap and easy—try for a sidewalk table at a scenic location.

Pizzeria l'Angelo serves up piping-hot pizza by the slice for under €2 or whole pizzas to go. Grab a beer or a soda and find a bench in nearby Campo Manin or Campo Sant'Angelo (Tue–Sun 11:30–22:00, Mon 11:30–16:00, Calle della Mandola 3711, tel. 041-277-1126). **Al Vaporetto Self-Service,** just across the street, is bright, efficient, and forgettable (€5 pastas, €6 *secondi*, Calle della Mandola). **Spizzico** is a cheap fast-food pizza shop on Campo

San Luca. Here's a chance to compare American and Italian fast food—there's a Burger King nearby (between St. Mark's Square and the Rialto Bridge).

The **produce market** that sprawls for a few blocks just past the Rialto Bridge is a great place to assemble a picnic (best Mon–Sat 8:00–13:00, closed Sun). The adjacent fish market is wonderfully slimy. Side lanes in this area are speckled with fine little hole-in-the-wall munchie bars, bakeries, and cheese shops.

Gelato

For locations of first two places, see the map on page 226. For the last place, see the map on page 235.

La Boutique del Gelato is considered the best *gelateria* in Venice (daily 10:00–20:30, closed Dec–Jan, 2 blocks off Campo Santa Maria Formosa on corner of Salizada San Lio and Calle Paradiso, next to Hotel Bruno, at #5727—just look for the crowd).

Late-Night Gelato: At the Rialto, try **Michielangelo,** just off Campo San Bartolomeo, on the St. Mark's side of the Rialto Bridge on Salizada Pio X (daily 10:00–23:00). At St. Mark's Square, the **Al Todaro** *gelateria* opposite the Doge's Palace is open late (daily 8:00–22:00, closes at 20:00 and on Mon in winter).

VENICE WITH CHILDREN

Some of the best kid fun I've had with my family has been in Venice. The city doesn't need an amusement park...it's one big fantasy world. It's safe and like nothing else your kids have ever seen. While there's lots of pavement and few parks or playgrounds, just being there—and free to wander—can be lots of fun. Consider these tips:

- Don't overdo it. Tackle just one or two key sights each day and mix in a healthy dose of fun activities. A vaporetto ride is a great way to start your visit.
- Follow this book's crowd-beating tips. Kids dislike long lines even more than you do.
- Eat dinner early (19:00 at restaurants), and skip the romantic places. Try self-service cafeterias, out-of-the-way bars (kids are welcome), or fast-food restaurants, where kids can move around without bothering others. For pizza, kids' favorite choices are usually *margherita* (tomato and cheese) and spicy *diavola* (the closest thing on the menu to kid-friendly pepperoni). Note that *peperoni* in Italian means bell peppers, not pepperoni. Picnic lunches and dinners work well. For ready-made picnics, drop by the *rosticcerie* (delis).
- Give your kid a cheap camera. Venice turns anyone into a photographer.
- If you're traveling with a toddler, a stroller might not be worth the hassle. There's rarely a long, flat stretch of walkway in Venice, and around the city, you see parents lifting strollers up and over the city's many small canal bridges (and probably regretting it). Also, keep in mind that there are rarely any fences or walls between the sidewalk and the water, so keep kids safely in hand.
- While Venice is short on parks, its hundreds of small squares

have been kids' playground for generations. Let them run around while you enjoy a nice café coffee.

- Turn the city into a scavenger hunt. Look on buildings for a winged lion, search the shop windows for a mask with a long nose, scour the canal for a fire boat—and extra points for a (yuk) dead pigeon!

- In Venice, pick up a copy of *VivaVenice: A Guide to Exploring, Learning, and Having Fun* by Paola Zoffoli. It's full of interesting facts, and it's available at many bookstores in the city.

- Involve your children in the trip. Let them lead you through the maze of Venice's back streets. Get lost together.

SIGHTS AND ACTIVITIES

Feed the pigeons on St. Mark's Square. If you yell the birds will just ignore you, but tossing a sweater into the air kicks off a pigeon evacuation. And anyone of any age enjoys the magic of St. Mark's Square at night.

Ride the elevator to the top of the **Campanile** bell tower to enjoy the grand view, and be there as the huge bells whip into ear-shattering action at the top of each hour (open July–Sept 9:00–21:00, Oct–June until 19:00, see page 38).

Take in a **glassblowing demonstration** (just off St. Mark's Square, see page 242). Part of the **Doge's Palace** tour includes the dark, dank prison and a creative armory (see page 93).

Ride lots of **boats** (vaporetto, gondola, *traghetto*, or speedboat tours of the lagoon). Sit in the front seat of a vaporetto for the Grand Canal Cruise (see page 46) and let your child be the guide. See how many kinds of service boats you can spot during your time on the canal (UPS, police, fire, and so on).

The Rialto **fish market** is as fishy as they get (closed Sun–Mon; it's canalside, 2 blocks west of Rialto Bridge). Watch the people unload the boats at the market. You can leave by *traghetto* and cross the Grand Canal (*traghetto* dock at market).

Be choosy when taking kids to museums. The venerable and fascinating (to adults) Accademia will probably bore children, but they'll have a good time creeping through the Church of San Zaccaria's spooky **crypt**. But don't skip art entirely. Kids like holding mirrors to see the ceiling paintings at the **Scuola Grande di San Rocco**. The **Peggy Guggenheim Collection** has colorful modern art—by Picasso and others—that interests kids.

A **children's park** is near the train station (facing the canal with your back to station, walk down the stairs and a block left past the shops to a small opening in wall on left—you'll see the playground inside). The bigger **Public Gardens** (Giardini Pubblici) have swings and playground equipment (on the far end of town—in Venice's "fishtail," near Giardini vaporetto stop). The **Lido** (beach) might sound intriguing, but it's filled with cars and offers only congested, dirty beaches.

If your kids are likely to enjoy a **soccer game,** consider a trip to the stadium located in the Sant'Elena district. Venice's team is currently in the second division (the equivalent of our minor league), but even though their team hasn't won a league championship since World War II, the fans are passionate nevertheless. Matches take place on Sundays from August to June (ask at the TI). Buy a scarf with the team colors—black, orange, and green—and join the fun. Goal!

Make a point to include some **Venetian history.** Taking advantage of the information in this book, explain St. Mark (look for winged lions, page 59), the birth of the city (page 309), how and why the city floods (page 40), and the story of the gondolas (page 246).

For fast and kid-friendly **meals** in the center, you'll find a couple of American hamburger joints between the Rialto Bridge and St. Mark's Square, great pizzerias on squares everywhere, and plenty of gelato.

SHOPPING

Long a city of aristocrats, luxury goods, and merchants, Venice was built to entice. While no one claims it's great for bargains, it has a shopping charm that makes paying strangely enjoyable. Carnevale masks, lace, glass, antique paper products, designer clothing, fancy accessories, and paintings are all popular with tourists visiting Venice.

Shops are generally open from 9:00 to 13:00 and from 15:00 to 19:30. In touristy Venice, more shops are open on Sunday than the Italian norm. If you're buying a substantial amount from nearly any shop, bargain. It's accepted and almost expected. Offer less and offer to pay cash; merchants are very conscious of the bite taken by credit-card companies. Anything not made locally is pricey to bring in and therefore generally more expensive than elsewhere in Italy. The shops near St. Mark's Square charge the most.

For ordinary items (not high-priced tourist baubles), the best all-purpose department store is the Coin store on the St. Mark's Square side of the Rialto Bridge. (From the bridge, head north toward Ferrovia, the train station.)

Shopping Streets

Here's the best route to kick off your Venetian shopping spree:

St. Mark's Square: Walk the entire colonnaded square past pricey jewelry, glass, lace, and clothing stores, continuing down the...

Mercerie: This is the main street between St. Mark's Square and the Rialto, noted for its high rent, high prices, fancy windows, and designer labels. Then, go over the...

Rialto Bridge: The streets at either side are a cancan of shopping temptations. (From here you can follow the Rialto to Frari Church Walk, page 191.) Continue down the street to...

Ruga Vecchia San Giovanni: Away from the intensity of the tourist center, you'll enter a neighborhood with plenty of inviting shops, but fewer crowds and better prices.

Elsewhere in Venice: Art-lovers browse the **art galleries** between the Accademia and the Peggy Guggenheim Collection.

Venetian Glass

Popular Venetian glass is available in many forms: vases, tea sets, decanters, glasses, jewelry, lamps, mod sculptures (such as solid-glass aquariums), and on and on. Shops will ship it home for you (snap a photo of it before it's packed up). For a cheap, packable souvenir, consider the glass-bead necklaces sold at vendors' stalls throughout Venice.

If you're serious about glass, visit the small shops on **Murano Island.** Murano's glassblowing demonstrations are fun; you'll usually see a vase and a "leetle 'orse" made from molten glass.

Around St. Mark's Square, various companies offer glass-blowing demos for tour groups. **Galleria San Marco,** a tour-group staple, offers great demos just off St. Mark's Square every few minutes. They have agreed to let individual travelers flashing this book sneak in with tour groups to see the show (and sales pitch). And, if you buy anything, show this book and they'll take 20 percent off the listed price. The gallery faces the square behind the orchestra nearest the church; at #139, go through the shop and climb the stairs (daily 9:00–18:00, tel. 041-271-8650, manager Adriano).

Souvenir Ideas

The most popular souvenirs and gifts are Murano glass (see above), Burano lace (fun lace umbrellas for little girls), Carnevale masks (fine shops and local artisans all over town), art reproductions (posters, postcards, and books), prints of Venetian scenes, traditional stationery (pens and marbled paper products of all kinds), calendars with Venetian scenes, silk ties, scarves, and plenty of goofy knickknacks (Titian mousepads, gondolier T-shirts, and little plastic gondolas).

Along Venice's many shopping streets, you'll notice fly-by-night vendors selling knockoffs of famous-maker handbags (Louis Vuitton, Gucci). These vendors are willing to bargain. Buyer beware. Legitimate manufacturers are raising a stink about these street merchants, and the government is trying to rid the city of them. As authorities are frustrated in attempts to actually arrest the merchants, they are considering making it illegal to buy items

Mask Making

In the 1700s, when Venice was Europe's party town, masks were popular—sometimes even mandatory—to preserve

the anonymity of nobles doing things forbidden back home. At Carnevale (the weeks-long Mardi Gras leading up to Lent), everyone wore masks. The most popular were based on characters from the low-brow comedic theater called Commedia dell'Arte. We all know Harlequin (simple, Lone Ranger-type masks), but there were also long-nosed masks for the hypocritical plague doctor, pretty Columbina masks, and so on.

Masks are made with the simple technique of papier-mâché. You make a mold of clay, smear the inside with Vaseline (to make it easy to remove the finished mask), then create the mask with layers of paper and glue.

from them. Their hope: The threat of a huge fine will scare potential customers away from them—so unlicensed merchants will be driven out of business and off the streets.

Getting a VAT Refund

Wrapped into the purchase price of your Venetian souvenirs is a Value Added Tax (VAT), which is generally about 20 percent. If you purchase more than €155 worth of goods at a store that participates in the VAT-refund scheme, you're entitled to get most of that tax back. Personally, I've never felt that VAT refunds are worth the hassle, but if you do, here's the scoop.

If you're lucky, the merchant will subtract the tax when you make your purchase (this is more likely to occur if the store ships the goods to your home). Otherwise, you'll need to:

Get the paperwork. Have the merchant completely fill out the necessary refund document, called a "cheque." You'll have to present your passport.

Get your stamp at the border. Process your cheque(s) at your last stop in the EU with the customs agent who deals with VAT refunds. It's best to keep your purchases in your carry-on for viewing, but if they're too large or dangerous (such as knives) to carry on, then track down the proper customs agent to inspect them before you check your bag. You're not supposed to use your purchased goods before you leave. If you show up at customs wearing your

Carnevale mask, officials might look the other way—or deny you a refund.

Collect your refund. You'll need to return your stamped document to the retailer or its representative. Many merchants work with a service, such as Global Refund or Premier Tax Free, which have offices at major airports, ports, or border crossings. These services, which extract a four-percent fee, can refund your money immediately in your currency of choice or credit your card (within two billing cycles). If you have to deal directly with the retailer, mail the store your stamped documents, and then wait. It could take months.

Customs

You can take home $800 in souvenirs per person duty-free. The next $1,000 is taxed at a flat 3 percent. After that, you pay the individual item's duty rate. You can also bring in duty-free a liter of alcohol (slightly more than a standard-sized bottle of wine), a carton of cigarettes, and up to 100 cigars. As for food, anything in cans or sealed jars is acceptable. Don't bring back dried meats, cheeses, or fresh fruits and veggies. To check customs rules and duty rates, visit www.customs.gov.

NIGHTLIFE

You must experience Venice after dark. The city is quiet at night, as tour groups stay in the cheaper hotels of Mestre on the mainland, and the masses of day-trippers return to their beach resorts. By 22:00, restaurants are winding down; by 23:00, many bars are closing; and by midnight, the city is virtually shut tight. But darkness brings a special romance to Venice. As during the day, it's the city itself that is the star. Venice—even its dark and distant back lanes—is considered very safe after nightfall.

Schedule of Events

Venice has a busy schedule of events, festivals, and entertainment. Check at the TI for listings in publications such as the free *Leo* magazine (bimonthly, in Italian and English) and in the free *Un Ospite di Venezia* magazine (monthly, bilingual, also available at top-end hotels, www.aguestinvenice.com).

Sightseeing

You can stretch your sightseeing day at the Doge's Palace (open daily until 19:00 April–Oct), Accademia (open Tue–Sun until 19:15), Campanile (the bell tower on St. Mark's Square, open daily until 21:00 July–Sept), and the Peggy Guggenheim Collection (open Sat until 22:00 June–July).

Gondola Rides

Gondolas cost lots more after 20:00 but are also more romantic and relaxing under the moon. A rip-off for some, this is a traditional must for romantics. Gondoliers charge about €65–80 for a 50-minute ride during the day; from 20:00 on, figure on €80–105 (for *musica*—singer and accordionist—it's an additional €90 during day, €100 after 20:00). You can divide the cost—and the romance—

Gondolas

Two hundred years ago, there were 10,000 gondolas in Venice. Although the aristocracy preferred horses to boats through the early Middle Ages, beginning in the 14th century, when horses were outlawed from the streets of Venice, the noble class embraced gondolas as a respectable form of transportation.

The boats became *the* way to get around the lagoon's islands. To navigate over the countless shifting sandbars, the boats were flat (no keel or rudder) and the captains stood up to see.

Today, there are only 500 gondolas, used only by tourists. The boats are prettier, but they work the same way they always have. Single oars are used both to propel and to steer the boats, which are built curved a bit on one side so that an oar thrusting from that side sends the gondola in a straight line.

These sleek yet ornate boats typically are about 35 feet long and five feet wide, and weigh about 1,100 pounds. They travel about three miles an hour (same as walking) and take the same energy to row as it does to walk. They're always painted black (6 coats)—the result of a 17th-century law a doge enacted to

among up to six people per boat. Note that only two seats (the ones in back) are next to each other. If you want to haggle, you'll find softer prices on back lanes where single gondoliers hang out, rather than at the bigger departure points. Establish the price and duration before boarding, enjoy your ride, and pay only when you're finished.

Glide through nighttime Venice with your head on someone's shoulder. Follow the moon as it sails past otherwise unseen buildings. Silhouettes gaze down from bridges while window glitter spills onto the black water. You're anonymous in the city of masks, as the rhythmic thrust of your striped-shirted gondolier turns old crows into songbirds. This is extremely relaxing (and, I think, worth the extra cost to experience at night). Since you might get a narration plus conversation with your gondolier, talk with several and choose one you like who speaks English well. Women, beware...while

eliminate competition between nobles for the fanciest rig. But each has unique upholstery, trim, and detailing, such as the squiggly-shaped, carved-wood oarlock *(forcula)* and metal "hood ornament" *(ferro)*. All in all, it takes about two months to build a gondola.

The boats run about €30,000–65,000, depending on your options (air-con, cup holders, etc). Every 40 days, the boat's hull must be treated with a new coat of varnish to protect against a lagoon-dwelling creature that eats into wood. A gondola lasts about 15 years, after which it can be refinished (once) to last another 10 years.

You can see the most picturesque gondola workshop in Venice in the Accademia neighborhood (walk down the Accademia side of the canal called Rio San Trovaso; as you approach Giudecca Canal you'll see the beached gondolas on your right across the canal). The workmen, traditionally from Italy's mountainous Dolomite region (because they need to be good with wood), maintain this refreshingly alpine-feeling little corner of Venice.

There are about 400 licensed gondoliers. When one dies, the license passes to his widow. And do the gondoliers sing, as the popular image has it? My mom asked our gondolier that very question, and he replied, "Madame, there are the lovers and there are the singers. I do not sing."

gondoliers can be extremely charming, local women say that anyone who falls for one of these Romeos "has slices of ham over her eyes."

For cheap gondola thrills during the day, stick to the €0.50 one-minute ferry ride on a Grand Canal *traghetto*. At night, *vaporetti* are nearly empty, and it's a great time to cruise the Grand Canal on the slow boat #1. Or hang out on a bridge along the gondola route and wave at—or drop leftover pigeon feed on—romantics.

Dining

Locals and those spending the night in Venice fill the piazzas, restaurants, and bars. *The* local way to spend an evening is to enjoy a slow and late dinner in a romantic canalside or piazza setting (see Eating chapter, page 218). Another option is a fast-paced, stand-up dinner of *cicchetti* in a local pub (see "Pub Crawl," page 225).

St. Mark's Square

For tourists, St. Mark's Square is the highlight, with lantern light and live music echoing from the cafés. Just being here after dark is a thrill, as **dueling café orchestras** entertain (see information on page 60). Every night, enthusiastic musicians play the same songs, creating the same irresistible magic. Hang out for free behind the tables (which allows you to move easily on to the next orchestra when the musicians take a break), or spring for a seat and enjoy a fun and gorgeously set concert. If you sit a while, it can be €15 well spent (for a drink and the cover charge for music). Dancing on the square is free (and encouraged).

Streetlamp halos, live music, floodlit history, and a ceiling of stars make St. Mark's magic at midnight. You're not a tourist, you're a living part of a soft Venetian night...an alley cat with money. In the misty light, the moon has a golden hue. Shine with the old lanterns on the gondola piers, where the sloppy lagoon splashes at the Doge's Palace...reminiscing.

More Music

Baroque Concerts: Take your pick of traditional Vivaldi concerts in churches throughout town. Homegrown Vivaldi is as trendy here as Strauss is in Vienna and Mozart is in Salzburg. In fact, you'll find frilly young Vivaldis all over town hawking concert tickets. The TI has a list of this week's Baroque concerts (tick-

ets from €18, shows start at 21:00 and generally last 90 min). You'll find posters in hotels all over town. There's music most nights at Scuola San Teodoro (east side of Rialto Bridge) and San Vitale Church (north end of Accademia Bridge), among

others. Consider the venue carefully. The general rule of thumb: Musicians in wigs and tights offer better spectacle, musicians in black-and-white suits are better performers. For the latest on church concerts, check at any TI or call 041-962-9999.

If you're attending a concert at **Scuola San Rocco** (tickets €15–30), arrive 30 minutes early to enjoy the art (which you'd have to pay €5.50 to see during the day).

Another unique music experience is a Rondo Veneziano concert—classically inspired music with a modern electronic sound.

Contemporary Concerts: The Guggenheim hosts summertime concerts of contemporary music in the museum's garden on Saturday evenings (June–July, starts about 20:30, included with

€10 museum entry). For the concert schedule, ask at the museum ticket counter or visit www.guggenheim-venice.it.

Movies

Venetian cinema is rarely in the original language; expect to hear it in Italian. **Outdoor cinema** on Campo San Polo is a fun scene (July–Aug). Every September, Venice's **film festival** (with some English-language films) doubles the viewing choices and brings out the stars.

Theater

Venice's two most famous theaters are **La Fenice** (grand old opera house) and **Teatro Goldoni** (mostly Italian live theater). Opera performances take place in Venice from late November through the end of June. For the latest, see *Leo* or *Un Ospite de Venezia* magazines (both free at TI).

Pubs, Clubs, and Late-Night Spots

While a pub-crawl dinner (see page 225) is fun and colorful, most serious eating is finished early to make way for drinking.

Campo Santa Margherita, the university student zone, is likely to be lively late. This popular-with-locals square has a good restaurant, café, and bar scene—especially May through September (Bar Rosso is particularly popular).

Paradiso Perduto, on Fondamenta della Sensa (on Rio della Sensa), is notorious for being noisy late at night. When locals complain, night owls say there's got to be someplace in Venice that stays open late. It's a restaurant and bar with a huge following for its good casual food, ambience, and open mic.

Other places likely to be open after 23:00 include the **Al Todaro** *gelateria* (on the waterfront across from the Doge's Palace) and the touristy **American Bar** (under the clock tower on St. Mark's Square). To locate the following places, see the map on page 226. **Bácaro Jazz Venezia wine bar** is open late (until 3:00 in the morning, closed Wed, on St. Mark's side of Rialto Bridge in front of the central post office just north of Campo San Bartolomeo). **Desert Planet** serves up drinks and pizzas until 2:30 in the morning (3 blocks north of St. Mark's at Calle Casselleria 5281). I like the little no-name portable wooden **wine bar** tucked on a street corner along the Grand Canal (on the fish market side of the Rialto, several blocks south of the bridge); take your glass for a canalside walk and return it later.

Also open late are Irish pubs, such as the **Devil's Forest Pub** (fine prices, daily 10:00–24:00, meals served 12:00–15:30, bar snacks all the time, closed Sun in Aug, no cover or service charge, backgammon and chess boards available for €2, a block off

Campo San Bartolomeo on Calle dei Stagneri, tel. 041-520-0623) and **Inishark Pub** (until 1:30 in the morning, just west of Campo Santa Maria Formosa on Calle Mondo Nuovo). While Irish pubs are popular with locals rather than tourists, the venerable **Harry's American Bar** (serving expensive food and American cocktails to dressy tourists at the St. Mark's vaporetto stop—see the map on page 235) is just the opposite.

Venice doesn't have a good dance scene. *Discoteche* are over-priced (€22 entry) with expensive drinks (€11) and little actual dancing. Still, for a cultural experience and a throbbing techno beat, check out **Casanova** (daily 21:00–4:00 in the morning, locals won't show up until at least 23:30 or midnight, Lista di Spagna 158a, Cannaregio, tel. 041-275-0199).

TRANSPORTATION CONNECTIONS

A two-mile-long causeway (with highway and train lines) connects Venice to the mainland. Mestre, the sprawling mainland industrial base, has fewer crowds, cheaper hotels, and plenty of cheap parking lots, but no charm. Don't stop here unless you're parking your car in a lot.

Santa Lucia Train Station

Trains to Venice stop at either Venezia Mestre (on the mainland) or at the Santa Lucia station on the island of Venice itself. If your train only stops at Mestre, worry not. Shuttle trains regularly connect Mestre's station with Venice's Santa Lucia station—your train ticket to Mestre will let you ride free (6/hr, 10 min).

Venice's **Santa Lucia train station** plops you right into the old town on the Grand Canal, an easy vaporetto ride or fascinating 40-minute walk to St. Mark's Square. Upon arrival, skip the station's crowded TI, because the two TIs at St. Mark's Square are better, and it's not worth a long wait for a minimal map (buy a good one from a newsstand with no wait). Confirm your departure plan (stop by train info desk or just study the *partenze*—departure—posters on walls).

Consider storing unnecessary heavy bags, even though lines for **baggage check** may be very long (platform #14, €3/12 hrs, €5/24 hrs, daily 6:00—24:00, no lockers).

Then walk straight out of the station to the canal. The dock for **vaporetti** #1 and #82 is on your left (for downtown Venice, most recommended hotels, and Grand Canal Cruise—see page 46); the dock for #51 and #52 is on your right (for some recommended hotels). Buy a €5 ticket (or €10.50 24-hour pass) at the ticket window and hop on a boat, after confirming that it's heading downtown (direction: Rialto or San Marco). Some boats

Italy's Public Transportation

KEY: — RAIL   ···· SHIP
      ⊥ PRIVATE RAIL   --- BUS

Arrival in Venice

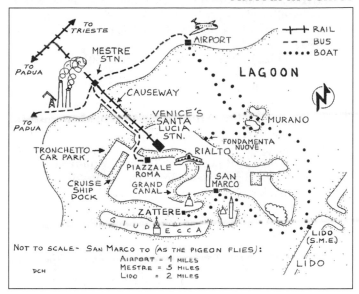

only go as far as Rialto *(solo Rialto)*, so check with the conductor.

The train station can be crowded with long lines to buy train tickets, supplements, and *cuccetta* reservations. Consider taking care of these tasks at downtown travel agencies—such as Kele & Teo Viaggi e Turismo (see page 28). The cost is the same, the lines and language barrier are smaller, and you'll save time.

Types of Trains

You'll encounter several different kinds of trains in Italy. Along with the various milk-run trains, there are the slow IR (Interregional) and *diretto* trains, the medium *espresso,* the fast IC (Intercity, €3 reservations optional), and the Eurostar bullet-train (€12 reservations required for railpass holders). Fast trains are affordable (e.g., including the express supplement, a first-class Venice-to-Florence ticket costs about €40; second-class about €28). Buying supplements on the train comes with a nasty penalty.

Schedules

Newsstands sell up-to-date regional and all-Italy timetables (€5, ask for the *orario ferroviario*). There is now a single all-Italy telephone number for train information in English (24 hrs daily, tel. 848-888-8088). On the Web, check http://bahn.hafas.de/bin /query.exe/en or www.trenitalia.com. It is now easy (and actually fun) to check schedules with the automated ticket machines at the train station.

Strikes are common. They generally last a day, and train employees will simply say, *"sciopero"* (strike). Still, sporadic trains— following no particular schedule—lumber down the tracks during most strikes.

From Venice by Train to: Padua (3–5/hr, 30 min), **Vicenza** (2/hr, 1 hr), **Verona** (1/hr, 90 min), **Ravenna** (1/hr, 3–4 hrs, transfer in Ferrara or Bologna), **Florence** (9/day, 3 hrs), **Dolomites** (8/day to Bolzano, about hrly, 4 hrs with 1 transfer; catch bus from Bolzano into mountains), **Milan** (1/hr, 3–4 hrs), **Monterosso/La Spezia/Cinque Terre** (2/day, 6 hrs, departs Venice at 10:00 and 15:00), **Rome** (8/day, 5 hrs, slower overnight), **Naples** (3/day, more with change in Rome, about 8–9 hrs), **Brindisi** (3/day, 11 hrs, change in Bologna), **Bern** (3/day, change in Milan, 8 hrs), **Munich** (2/day, 8 hrs), **Paris** (4/day, 11 hrs), and **Vienna** (3/day, 9 hrs).

Venice Airport

Venice's sleek, modern airport on the mainland, six miles north of the city, has a new wood-beam-and-glass terminal, with a TI, cash machines, car-rental agencies, and a few shops and eateries (airport info: tel. 041-260-9240). Check with your hotel or in *Un Ospite di Venezia* (the free tourist information guide from the TI and many hotels) for phone numbers and Web sites for all airlines serving Marco Polo and nearby airports.

There are three ways for you to get between the airport and downtown Venice (all covered below): speedboat, water taxi, and bus (to Venice with vaporetto connection).

If you're taking a boat from Venice to the airport, note that the dock and terminal—a 15-minute walk apart—are connected by a **free shuttle bus**. Worrying about this bus is a frequent source of stress and confusion for airport-bound travelers: When your boat arrives, there may be no shuttle bus in sight, only taxi con-men, scaring travelers—nervous about catching their flights—into hiring their cabs (for a fortune). Don't believe them. There is always a free airport bus shuttling back and forth between the dock and the nearby check-in counters. While many travelers are advised to get to the airport two or more hours before departure (even for flights within Europe), I usually arrive about an hour before take-off and manage fine.

The **Alilaguna speedboat,** while not terribly speedy (making 3–4 stops in the lagoon as it sputters along), is the simplest transportation to and from downtown Venice (€10, 2/hr, 70 min, runs 6:15–24:00 from airport, generally departs airport at about :10 and :40 after the hour; runs 4:20–22:50 from Venice starting in Zattere, the Dorsoduro hotels; continues to San Marco/Giardinetti; tel. 041-523-5775, www.alilaguna.com). Another Alilaguna line goes

Driving in Italy

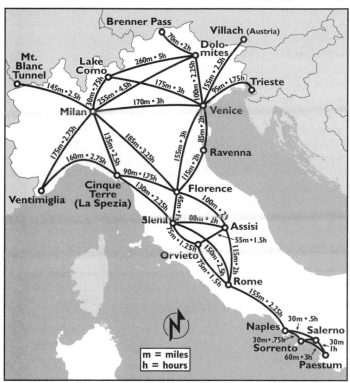

m = miles
h = hours

between the airport and Fondamenta Nuove (€5, 40 min). Pick up a free schedule (or buy tickets) at the Alilaguna kiosk at the airport (far left of the arrivals hall as you exit baggage claim) or at any vaporetto stop that has Alilaguna service. You can also purchase tickets on board.

A **water taxi** zips directly between the airport and your hotel in 30 minutes for €80. While pricey, a small group may find it a smart investment—especially for an early departure.

Buses: The blue ATVO shuttle buses connect the airport and the Piazzale Roma vaporetto stop (€3, 2/hr, 20 min, 5:30–20:40 to airport, 8:20–24:00 from airport, schedule listed in *Un Ospite di Venezia*, www.atvo.it). The cheaper orange ACTV bus #5 also links the airport with Piazzale Roma (€2, 2/hr, 30–40 min; from airport to Piazzale Roma departs Mon–Sat at 5:25 and 6:07, then every 30 minutes at :05 and :35 past the hour until 20:05; Sun 1/hr from 7:05 to 20:05 at :05 past the hour; from Piazzale Roma to airport departing generally at :10 and :40 past the hr; confirm times at TI or airport).

Those heading to Padua have a convenient SITA bus connection from the airport to Padua's bus station a few blocks from the train station and town (€3.50, 2/hr, 1 hr).

Tips for Drivers

The freeway dead-ends at Venice, near several parking lots on the edge of the island. The most central lot, San Marco, is very busy and too expensive. Follow the green lights directing you to an alternative parking lot with space, probably Tronchetto (across the causeway and on the right), which has a huge, multistoried garage (€18/day, tel. 041-520-7555). From there, avoid the travel agencies masquerading as TIs, and head directly for the vaporetto docks for the boat connection (#82) to the town center. Don't let taxi boat-men con you out of the relatively cheap €5 vaporetto ride. Parking in Mestre is easy and cheap (open-air lots €4/day, €5/day garage across from Mestre train station, easy shuttle-train connections to Venice's Santa Lucia Station—6/hr, 10 min). There are also huge and economical lots in Verona, Padua, and Vicenza.

DAY TRIPS
FROM VENICE

While Venice is just one of many towns in the Italian region of Veneto (VEN-eh-toh), few venture off the lagoon. Four important towns and possible side trips, in addition to the lakes and the Dolomites, make zipping directly from Venice to Milan (or Florence) a route strewn with temptation.

The towns of Padua, Vicenza, Verona, and Ravenna are all good stops, for various reasons. Each town gives the visitor a low-key slice of Italy that complements the urbanity of Venice, Florence, and Rome.

Visiting Verona, Padua, and Vicenza couldn't be easier: All are 30 minutes apart on the Venice–Milan line (hrly, 3 hrs). Spending a day town-hopping between Venice and Milan—with three-hour stops at Padua, Vicenza, and Verona—is exciting and efficient. Trains run frequently enough to allow flexibility and little wasted time. Of the day trips included in this book, only Ravenna, in the neighboring region of Emilia Romagna (2.5 hours from Padua or Florence), is not on the main Venice–Milan train line.

If you're Padua-bound, note that you need to reserve ahead to see the Scrovegni Chapel (see page 265). Most sights in Verona and Vicenza are closed on Monday.

PADUA
DAY TRIP

Living under Venetian rule for four centuries seemed only to sharpen Padua's independent spirit. Nicknamed "the brain of Veneto," Padua (Padova) has a prestigious university (founded 1222) that hosted Galileo, Copernicus, Dante, and Petrarch. The old town, even when packed with modern-day students, is a colonnaded time-tunnel experience. And Padua's museums and churches hold their own in Italy's artistic big league.

Even with all this, locals will tell you that Padua is a city with three "withouts": a saint without a name (since St. Anthony is merely referred to as "the Saint"), a field without grass (because the large square, Prato della Valle, is not a field, as the word *prato* implies), and a café without doors (for in days past, Caffè Pedrocchi kept its doors open all day and all night).

ORIENTATION

Padua's main tourist sights lie on a north-south axis through the heart of the city: from the train station to Scrovegni Chapel to the market squares (the center of town) to the Basilica of St. Anthony. It's roughly a 10-minute walk between each of these sights, or about 30 minutes from end to end.

Tourist Information

The main TI, in the train station, is a good place to pick up a list of sights and a map upon arrival in Padua (Mon–Sat 9:30–18:30, Sun 9:30–12:30, shorter hours in winter, tel. 049-875-2077, infostazione@turismopadova.it). Another TI is located in an alley west of Caffè Pedrocchi (daily 9:00–13:30 & 15:00–19:00, tel. 049-875-2077). A third, seasonal TI shares a square with the Basilica of St. Anthony (April–Oct Mon–Sat 9:30–13:30 &

15:00–19:00, Sun 9:30–12:00 & 15:00–18:00, closed Nov–March).

Internet Access: Oddly for a college town, Padua has few Internet cafés. Internet Point is on Via Altinate (Mon–Sat 10:00–1:00, Sun 16:00–24:00, about 300 yards east of Piazza Garibaldi and Porta Altinate at #145, tel. 049-659-292).

Arrival in Padua

The baggage deposit office (€3.90, daily 6:00–21:30, bring your passport) is outside the train station lobby, under the colonnade—exit the lobby on the far right, just past an ATM and the main TI. Inside the station lobby, near the same far right exit, is a small office marked Bus Tickets, which sells city bus tickets (€0.85, also available at the *tabacchi* shop at the far right and at newsstands). Beyond the baggage deposit is a post office (Mon–Fri 8:30–14:00, Sat 8:30–13:00, closed Sun). If you have any train business, such as reservations, note that a travel agency, Leonardi Viaggi-Turismo, is half a block up the main drag in front of the station, on the left side of the street (Mon–Fri 9:00–19:00, Sat 9:00–13:00, closed Sun, Corso del Popolo 14, tel. 049-650-455).

Buses leave from in front of the station. Buses #3, #8, #12, and #18 go through town to the Basilica of St. Anthony (called "Santo" locally), departing from platform *(corsia)* #3. Get off at the end of Via Umberto I, just before Prato della Valle. If you're not sure where to get off, ask the driver, "Santo?" Due to pedestrian and car traffic, this relatively short distance can take 20 minutes. A taxi from the station into town costs about €5.

Padua in Four Hours

Day-trippers can do a quick but enjoyable blitz of Padua—including a visit to the Scrovegni Chapel—in four hours. Your Scrovegni Chapel reservation will dictate the order of your sightseeing; see the booking procedure below.

Here's one possible plan: Take the bus from the train station to the Basilica of St. Anthony at the south end of town, then walk back through the old town, sightseeing your way back to the Scrovegni Chapel, then on to the station.

Ready, set, go...

At zero hour: Arrive at Padua train station, check bags, catch bus #3, #8, #12, or #18 to the Basilica of St. Anthony. You may want to grab a take-out lunch from one of the recommended delis near the basilica and picnic in the peaceful cloisters. Note that parts of the basilica—the Sacristy and Chapel of the Reliquaries—close during lunch.

At 30 minutes: Sightsee the basilica.

At one hour: Walk north along Via del Santo. When you hit the wall, turn left onto Via San Francesco, noting Piazza

Padua

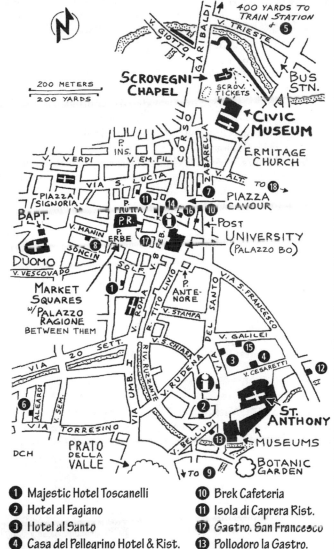

N

200 METERS
200 YARDS

400 YARDS TO
TRAIN STATION

V. GIOTTO
GARIBALDI
V. TRIESTE

SCROVEGNI CHAPEL

SCROV.
TICKETS

BUS STN.

CIVIC MUSEUM

ERMITAGE CHURCH

P. INS.

V. VERDI
V. EM. FIL.
VIA S. LUCIA

CORSO

NABARELLA
V. ALT.

TO

PIAZZA SIGNORIA

P. FRUTTA

P. R.

PIAZZA CAVOUR

BAPT.

V. MANIN

P. ERBE

SONCIN

DUOMO

V. VESCOVADO

V. & FEB.

SOLF.

V. 8 FEB.

Post UNIVERSITY (PALAZZO BO)

MARKET SQUARES w/ PALAZZO RAGIONE BETWEEN THEM

V. ROMA
R. TITO LIVIO
V. STAMPA

P. ANTENORE

VIA S. FRANCESCO

VIA DEL SANTO

V. GALILEI

V. CESARETTI

VIA 20 SETT.

RIV. RUZANTE

V. S. CHIARA

VIA UMB.

V. RUDENA

V. BELLUDI

ST. ANTHONY MUSEUMS

V. ALEARDI
V. SEM.

VIA TORRESINO

DCH

PRATO DELLA VALLE

TO

BOTANIC GARDEN

❶ Majestic Hotel Toscanelli
❷ Hotel al Fagiano
❸ Hotel al Santo
❹ Casa del Pellegrino Hotel & Rist.
❺ To Hotel Grand'Italia, Hotel Monaco & Hotel al Cason
❻ Ostello Città di Padova
❼ La Cova Rist./Pizzeria
❽ Marechiaro Pizzeria/Tratt.
❾ To Zairo Ristorante/Pizzeria
❿ Brek Cafeteria
⓫ Isola di Caprera Rist.
⓬ Gastro. San Francesco
⓭ Pollodoro la Gastro.
⓮ Caffè Pedrocchi
⓯ Pago Pago Pizzeria
⓰ PAM Supermarket
⓱ Bridge Entrance to Palazzo della Ragione
⓲ To Internet Point

Antenore's medieval sarcophagus on your left. Across the street from the piazza is a replica of Venice's gothic Ca' d'Oro (House of Gold). Continue on Via San Francesco, passing Feltrinelli International's English bookstore (Mon–Sat 9:00–13:00 & 15:30–19:30, closed Sun, under the porticos on your left) and arriving at Via VIII Febbraio.

Time to make a decision. To hit the markets first before they start to close (around 13:30), continue forward on Via San Francesco to reach Piazza delle Erbe. To continue sightseeing, turn right onto Via VIII Febbraio—the next square you'll reach has Palazzo del Bo (University), Caffè Pedrocchi, and the entrance to Palazzo della Ragione.

At 1:15 hours: Visit your choice of the two market squares, the Palazzo della Ragione, Caffè, and University. (Or go immediately to the Scrovegni Chapel, then return here for more sightseeing.)

At 1:50 hours: Walk north on Via VIII Febbraio (which becomes Via Cavour and then traffic-filled Via Garibaldi) to the Scrovegni Chapel. After Piazza Garibaldi, cross over one street to the right and head north again. The chapel is on your right, within the gardens of the old Roman Arena (don't overshoot it).

At two hours: Sightsee the Multimedia Room and Civic Museum, and get in line five minutes early for the Chapel.

At three hours: Visit the Scrovegni Chapel.

At 3:30 hours: Walk north to the train station (10–15 min) and reclaim your baggage.

At four hours: Catch your train. Ahhhh.

SIGHTS

▲▲**Basilica of St. Anthony**—Friar Anthony of Padua (1195–1231), "Christ's perfect follower and a tireless preacher of the Gospel," is buried here. For nearly 800 years, his remains and this impressive Romanesque Gothic church (building started immediately after the death of the saint in 1231) have attracted pilgrims to Padua (daily in summer 6:30–19:45, in winter 6:30–19:00, modest dress code enforced). There is a helpful information desk with Anthony-

related pamphlets in the cloisters (along with public WCs), located on the right side of the church (info desk open daily 8:30–13:00 & 14:00–18:30). To find English versions of the pamphlets—one on the saint's life and another about the basilica—head to the Chapel of the Reliquaries and offer a donation.

St. Anthony of Padua
(1195–1231)

Perhaps Christendom's most popular saint, Anthony is known as a powerful speaker, a miracle worker, and the finder of lost articles.

Born in Lisbon to a rich, well-educated family, his life changed at age 25, when he saw the mutilated bodies of some Franciscan martyrs. Their sacrifice inspired him to join the poor Franciscans and dedicate his life to Christ. He moved to Italy and lived in a cave, studying, meditating, and barely speaking to anyone.

One day, he joined his fellow monks for a service. The appointed speaker failed to show up, so Anthony was asked to say a few off-the-cuff words to the crowd. He started slowly but, filled with the Spirit, he became more confident and amazed the audience with his eloquence. Up in Assisi, St. Francis heard about Anthony and sent him on a whirlwind speaking tour.

Anthony had a strong voice, knew several languages, had encyclopedic knowledge of theology, and could speak spontaneously as the Spirit moved him. It's said he even stood on the shores of the Adriatic Sea in Rimini and enticed a school of fish to listen. Anthony also was known as a miracle worker—healing a sick horse, protecting a crowd from the rain, and making poisoned food harmless.

In 1230, Anthony retired to Padua, where he founded a monastery and initiated reforms for the poor. An illness cut off his life at age 36. Anthony once said, "Happy is the man whose words issue from the Spirit and not from himself!"

On the square in front of the church you'll find a handy **TI** (April–Oct Mon–Sat 9:30–13:30 & 15:00–19:00, Sun 9:30–12:00 & 15:00–18:00 , closed Nov–March) and a couple of friendly cafés. (A 10-min stroll north up Via del Santo will take you back into the center of town.)

Exterior of Basilica: Nod to St. Anthony, who looks down from the red-brick facade and blesses us. He holds a book, a symbol of all the knowledge he accumulated as a quiet monk before his famous preaching career.

Guarding the church is Donatello's life-size equestrian statue of the Venetian mercenary general, Gattamelata. Though it looks like a thousand other man-on-a-horse statues, it was a landmark in Italy's budding Renaissance—the first life-size, secular, equestrian statue cast out of bronze in a thousand years.

Interior: Entering the basilica, gaze down the nave, past the crowds and through the incense haze, to Donatello's glorious crucifix arising from the altar, and realize that this is one of the most important pilgrimage sites in Christendom.

Along with the crucifix, Donatello's bronze statues—Mary with Padua's six favorite saints—grace the high altar. Late in his career, the great Florentine sculptor spent a decade in Padua (c. 1444–1455), creating the altar and Gattamelata.

St. Anthony's Tomb (left side of nave): Pilgrims file slowly by the chapel containing St. Anthony's tomb. Nine marble reliefs, showing scenes and miracles from the life of the saint, circle this Renaissance masterwork from 1500.

As you enter the chapel, the first relief on the left depicts St. Anthony receiving the Franciscan habit. In the next, Anthony's compassion miraculously revives a woman who has been stabbed to death by her jealous husband. Notice the etchings of familiar Paduan architecture at the top of the sculptures; in the third panel, the building with the keel-shaped roof is Palazzo della Ragione. On the back wall of the chapel, look for the miracle of the miser's heart. Anthony dips his hand into a moneylender's side to demonstrate the absence of his heart ("for where your treasure is, there your heart will be also"), which miraculously appeared in the dead man's treasure chest.

The next relief shows Anthony holding the foot of a young man who confessed to kicking his mother. Upon hearing of this act, Anthony declared that anyone so disrespectful to his mother ought to have his foot cut off. The boy took Anthony's word literally. His hysterical mother implored Anthony's help, and Anthony's prayers to God enabled him to reattach the foot.

The pilgrims believe Anthony is their protector—a confidant and intercessor of the poor. And they believe he works miracles. The faithful place offerings, votives, and prayers to ask for help or to give thanks for miracles they believe he's performed. By putting their hand on his tomb while saying a silent prayer, pilgrims show devotion to Anthony and feel the saint's presence.

Popular Anthony is the patron saint of dozens of things: of travelers, amputees, donkeys, pregnant women, barren women, stewardesses, and pig farmers. Most pilgrims ask for his help in his role as the "finder of things"—from lost car keys to a life companion.

Chapel of the Reliquaries: This chapel sits toward the back of the basilica, in the apse. The most prized relic is in the glass case at center stage—Anthony's tongue. When Anthony's remains were exhumed thirty years after his death (1263), his body had decayed to dust, but his tongue was found miraculously unspoiled and red in color. How appropriate for the multilinguist who, full of the Spirit, couldn't stop talking about God (daily 7:00–12:45 & 14:30–19:30, shorter hours in winter, at far end of the church on the left side of the apse behind the altar).

Working clockwise around the curved chapel, start in front of the staircase at St. Anthony's holy, and holey, tunic *(tonaca)*. Using an imaginary clock, his coffin is at nine o'clock. His pillow—a comfy rock—is up the stairs. The center display case contains (top to bottom) the Saint's lower jaw *(il mento)*, his uncorrupted tongue *(lingua)*, and finally, his vocal chords *(apparato vocale*, discovered intact when his remains were examined in 1981). In the last display case, fragments of the True Cross *(la croce)* are held in a precious crucifix reliquary.

Cloisters: From the right side of the nave as you face the altar, follow signs to *chiostro;* from outside, find signs on the right side of the church.

Wander around the various cloisters. Picnic tables invite pilgrims and tourists to enjoy meals within the solitude of one of the cloisters (it's covered and suitable even when rainy, WCs in same cloister). In the far end, a fascinating little museum is filled with votives and folk art recounting miracles attributed to Anthony.

Prato della Valle—The so-called "field without grass" is 150 yards southwest of the basilica (down Via Luca Belludi). Once a Roman theater and later Anthony's preaching grounds, this square claims to be the largest in Italy. It's a pleasant, 400-yard-long, oval-shaped piazza with fountains, walkways, dozens of statues of Padua's eminent citizens, and (yes) grass.

Orto Botanico—Green thumbs appreciate this botanical garden, which contains the university's vast collection of rare plants. It was founded in 1545 by the Faculty of Medicine to cultivate medicinal plants (€4, daily April–Oct 9:00–13:00 & 15:00–18:00, March–Nov Mon–Sat 9:00–13:00, closed Sun, entrance 150 yards south of Basilica of St. Anthony; with your back to the facade, take a hard left). A visitors center—in a little cottage, past the garden's entrance then to the right—houses models of the garden's layout and computer programs that describe the history and composition of the garden in English (same hours as the garden). WCs are just outside the visitors center, in the neighboring building.

▲▲▲Scrovegni Chapel (Cappella degli Scrovegni)—Reserve in advance to see this glorious, recently renovated chapel, wallpapered with Giotto's beautifully preserved cycle of nearly 40 frescoes, depicting scenes from the lives of Jesus and Mary.

Painted by Giotto and his assistants from 1303 to 1305, and considered by many to be the first piece of modern art, this work makes it clear: Europe was breaking out of the Middle Ages. A sign of the Renaissance to come, Giotto placed real people in real scenes, expressing real human emotions. These frescoes were radical for their 3-D nature, lively colors, light sources, emotion, and humanism.

The chapel was built out of guilt for white-collar crimes. Reginaldo degli Scrovegni charged sky-high interest rates at a time when that practice was forbidden by the church. He even caught the attention of Dante, who placed him in one of the levels of hell in his *Inferno*. When Reginaldo died, the Church denied him a Christian burial. His son Enrico tried to buy forgiveness for his father's sins by building this superb chapel. After seeing Giotto's frescoes for the Franciscan monks of St. Anthony, Enrico knew he'd found the right artist to decorate the interior.

Cost and Hours: €12 entry fee for 15-minute visits includes Civic Museum and Multimedia Room (both described below); in summer after 19:00, 15-minute visits are €8 and 30-minute visits are €12 (visits don't include Civic Museum, which is closed then). The chapel is open daily 9:00–22:00 in summer, until 19:00 in off-season (people are allowed in every 15 min at :00, :15, :30, and :45 past the hour during the day, every half hour in eve, last entry 15 min before closing). The Multimedia Room has the same hours as the chapel.

Booking your Reservation: To protect the paintings from excess humidity, only 25 people are allowed in the chapel at a time for a 15-minute visit. Reservations are obligatory (booking office open Mon–Fri 9:00–19:00, Sat 9:00–18:00, closed Sun, provide telephone number where you can be reached the day before, call 049-201-0020 or reserve online at www.cappelladegliscrovegni.it).

Book your visit at least 24 hours in advance; earlier is better to guarantee a spot. It's sometimes possible to buy a ticket for the same day at the ticket office, but don't count on it. If you book in person at the ticket office, you can pay cash rather than use a credit card. Visits scheduled after 19:00 are only €8 for a standard 15-minute visit, or you can stay in the chapel for a full 30 minutes for €12. The last booking for a 30-minute visit is at 21:45.

Pick up your tickets at the ticket office at least an hour before your visit (half-hour early or up to the day before for 9:00 visits; present your booking receipt with online reservations) and be at the chapel doors (well-signed, 100 yards to the right of the ticket office as you exit) at least five minutes before your scheduled visit. The doors to the chapel are automatic, and if you're even a minute late, you'll forfeit your visit and have to rebook and repay to enter.

At your appointed time, you first enter an anteroom to watch a 15-minute video (with English subtitles) and to establish humidity levels before continuing into the chapel (no photos are allowed). Although you have only a short visit inside the chapel, it's divine. You're inside a Giotto time capsule, looking back at an artist ahead of his time.

Giotto's Frescoes in the Scrovegni Chapel: As you enter the long, narrow chapel, look down to the far end—the wall covered with Giotto's big *Last Judgment.* Christ in a bubble is flanked by crowds of saints and by scenes of heaven and hell. This is the final, climactic scene of the story told in the chapel's 38 panels—the story of Jesus and his mother Mary.

The story begins on the long north wall (with the windows) in the upper left corner. A priest scolds the man who will be Mary's father (Joachim, with the halo) and kicks him out of the Temple for the sin of being childless. In the next panel to the right, Joachim returns dejectedly to his sheep farm. Meanwhile (next panel), his wife is in the bedroom, hearing the miraculous news that their prayers have been answered—she'll give birth to Mary, the mother of Jesus.

From this humble start, the story of Mary and Jesus spirals clockwise around the chapel, from top to bottom. The top row (both north and south walls) covers Mary's life.

Jesus enters the picture in the center of the north (windowed) wall with his birth in a manger, the visit by the Magi, Presentation in the Temple, the Flight into Egypt, and so on. Spinning clockwise, you see Jesus being baptized, performing miracles, etc. Finally, Jesus is betrayed with a kiss (middle of north wall, bottom row), and is tried, humiliated, whipped, crucified, and buried. He ascends to heaven, where (on the big west wall) he reigns at the Last Judgment. The whole story unfolds beneath the blue, starry sky on the ceiling.

Some panels deserve a closer look:

Joachim Returns to the Sheepfold (north wall, upper left, second panel): Though difficult to appreciate from ground level, this oft-reproduced scene is groundbreaking. Giotto—a former shepherd himself—uses nature as a stage, setting the scene in front of a backdrop of real-life mountains, and adding down-home details like Joachim's jumping dog, frozen in mid-air.

Giotto di Bondone
(c. 1267–1337)

Though details of his life are extremely sketchy, we know that as a 12-year-old shepherd boy, Giotto was discovered painting pictures of his father's sheep on rock slabs. He became the wealthiest and most famous painter of his day. His achievement is especially remarkable, since painters at that time weren't considered anything more than craftsmen and weren't expected to be innovators.

After making a name for himself by painting the life of St. Francis frescoes in Assisi, the Florentine tackled the Scrovegni Chapel (c. 1303–1305). At age 35, he was at the height of his powers. His scenes were more realistic and human than anything done for a thousand years. Giotto didn't learn technique by dissecting corpses or studying the mathematics of 3-D perspective. But he had innate talent, and his personality shines through in the humanity of his art.

The Scrovegni frescoes break ground by introducing nature—rocks, trees, animals—as a backdrop for religious scenes. Giotto's people, with their voluminous, deeply creased robes, are as sturdy and massive as Greek statues, throwbacks to the Byzantine icon art of the Middle Ages. But these figures exude stage presence. Their gestures are simple but expressive: A head tilted down says dejection, an arm flung out is grief, clasped hands are hope. Giotto created his figures not just by drawing outlines and filling them in with single colors, but as patchworks of lighter and darker shades, pioneering modern modeling techniques. Giotto's storytelling style is straightforward, and anyone with knowledge of the episodes of Jesus' life can read the chapel like a comic book.

The Scrovegni represents a turning point in European art and culture—away from scenes of heaven and toward a more down-to-earth, human-centered view.

Betrayal of Christ, a.k.a. *Il Bacio*, "The Kiss" (north wall, bottom row, middle panel): Amid the crowded chaos of Jesus' arrest, Giotto focuses our eye on the central action, where Judas ensnares Jesus in his yellow robe (the color symbolizing envy), establishes meaningful eye contact, and kisses him.

Lamentation (south wall, bottom row, middle): Jesus has been crucified, and his followers weep and wail over the lifeless body. John spreads his arms wide and shrieks, his cries echoed by anguished angels above. Each face is a study in grief. Giotto de-emphasizes these saints' stoic response and highlights their human vulnerability.

Last Judgment (big west wall): Christ in the center is a

glorious vision, but the fun stuff is in hell (lower right). Satan is a Minotaur-headed ogre munching on sinners. Around him, demons give sinners their just desserts in a scene right out of Dante...who was Giotto's friend and fellow Florentine. Front and center is Enrico Scrovegni in a violet robe (the color symbolizing penitence), donating the chapel to the Church in exchange for forgiveness for his father's sins.

Civic Museum (Musei Civici Eremitani)—This museum, next to the Scrovegni Chapel, was an Augustinian hermit's monastery. It displays Roman and Etruscan archaeological finds, including buckets of rare coins. The ruins of a Roman amphitheater ("arena") surround the Scrovegni Chapel (also called the "Arena" Chapel), a reminder that Padua was an important Roman town.

The museum also has 13th- to 18th-century paintings by Titian, Tintoretto, Giorgione, Tiepolo, Veronese, and other Veneto artists. The highlight is a Giotto crucifix. Near the crucifix is a statue of Enrico degli Scrovegni, looking as though he's wondering how to save his father's soul (€10 includes Multimedia Room, or covered by €12 Scrovegni ticket, Tue–Sun 9:00–19:00, closed Mon, mandatory and free bag check).

Multimedia Room (Sala Multimedia)—Rows of computer screens with English info offer a virtual chapel visit. There are explanations of the individual panels, Giotto's fresco technique, close-ups of the art, and a description of the restoration. They show a 12-minute video (English headphones available) that is similar—but not identical—to the one that precedes your visit (€10 with Civic Museum, or covered by €12 Scrovegni ticket, reduced to €8 after 19:00 with 15-min visits to the Scrovegni, or €12 after 19:00 with 30-min Scrovegni visits, daily April–Oct 9:00–22:00, Nov–March 9:00–19:00, mandatory and free bag check, no photos, Piazza Eremitani, tel. 049-820-4551).

Palazzo della Ragione—This grand 13th-century palazzo commonly called *il Salone* (great hall) once held the medieval law courts. The first floor consists of a huge hall—265 feet by 90 feet—that was once adorned with frescoes by Giotto. A fire in 1312 destroyed those paintings, and the palazzo was redecorated with the 15th-century art you see today: a series of 123 frescoes depicting the signs of the zodiac, labors of the month, symbols representing characteristics of people born under each sign, and

finally, figures of saints to legitimize the power of the courts in the eyes of the church.

The hall is topped with a keel-shaped roof, which helps to support the structure without the use of columns—quite an architectural feat in its time, considering the building's dimensions. The curious stone in the right-hand corner near the entry is the "Stone of Shame," which was the seat of debtors being punished during the Middle Ages. Instead of being sentenced to death or prison (same thing back then), debtors sat upon this stone, renounced their possessions, and denounced themselves publicly before being exiled from the city (€4, more if there's an exhibition, Feb–Oct Tue–Sat 9:00–19:00, closed Sun–Mon, Nov–Jan closes 18:00, enter through City Hall across from University, up long staircase, tel. 049-820-5006).

▲▲Market Squares: Piazza delle Erbe and Piazza della Frutta—The stately Palazzo della Ragione (described above) pro-

vides a quintessentially Italian backdrop for Padua's almost exotic-feeling market, filling the surrounding squares—Piazza delle Erbe and Piazza della Frutta—each morning. Second only to the produce market in Italy's gastronomic capital of Bologna, this market has been renowned for centuries as having the freshest and greatest selection of herbs, fruits, and vegetables. Beneath the Palazzo della Ragione are various butchers, *salumerie* (delicatessens), cheese shops, bakeries, and fishmongers.

Explore this scene. Students gather here each evening, after the markets have closed, spilling out of colorful bars and cafés—drinks in hand—into the square. Their drink of choice is a *spritz,* an aperitif with Campari, Cynar (two bitter, alcoholic liquors), white wine, and sparkling water, garnished with an olive and a blood-orange wedge. **Bar Nazionale** offers outdoor seating for a ringside view of the action (at #41 under staircase of Palazzo della Ragione in Piazza delle Erbe). **Bar degli Spritz** is the students' hangout (at #36 near the middle of the palazzo at the passageway).

Get your *spritz* to take away *(da portar via),* and join the young people out on the piazza. This is a classic opportunity to enjoy a real discussion with smart, English-speaking students who see tourists not as pests but as interesting people from far away. For an instant conversation starter, ask about the current political situation in Italy or the cultural differences between the North and the South.

A typical snack stand selling all kinds of fresh, hot, and ready-to-eat seafood appetizers sets up in Piazza della Frutta between 17:00–20:30 (except Sun). Belly up to the bar with your drink and nosh on whatever's served.

Caffè Pedrocchi—This white-columned, neoclassical café is not just a café. A complex of meeting rooms and entertainment venues, it symbolizes progress. Built in 1831 during the period of Austrian rule, the Caffè Pedrocchi was inaugurated for the fourth Italian Congress of Scientists, which convened during the mid–19th century to stir up nationalistic fervor as Italy struggled to become a united nation. As a symbol of patriotic hope, it's no surprise that students plotted an uprising here in 1848. You can still see a bullet hole in the wall of the Sala Bianca, where one of the insurgents was killed. Nowadays, you get more foam than fervor, but the café is still a marvel of interior design.

Each room is decorated and furnished in a different style. The simple color scheme of the café—red, white, and green—represents the colors of the Italian flag. The Sala Verde (Green Room) is the only room where people can sit and enjoy the beautiful interior without ordering anything or having to pay—in fact, you can even bring your own food and eat it free. Otherwise, take a seat in the Red or White rooms and order from the menu of teahouse fare, including salads, sandwiches and the writer Stendhal's beloved *zabayon*, a creamy custard (June–Sept Sun, Tue, and Wed 9:00–21:00, Thu–Sat 9:00–24:00, Oct–May also Mon 9:00–21:00, entrance is at intersection of Oberdan and VIII Febbraio, between Piazza delle Erbe and Piazza Cavour, tel. 049-878-1231). On most Thursday evenings from March through November, the café hosts jazz concerts (€2 cover added to first round of drinks, reserve by phone).

Piano Nobile: This upper, noble floor, is much more elaborate. The rooms are all in different styles, such as Greek Etruscan or Egyptian, with English descriptions throughout. These rooms were intended to evoke memories of the glory of past epochs, which a united Italy had hopes of reliving.

The Piano Nobile also hosts a new, smaller museum that traces Padua's role in Italian history, from the downfall of the Venetian Republic (1797) to the founding of the Republic of Italy (1948). Exhibits, a few with English descriptions, include uniforms, medals, weaponry, old artillery, Fascist propaganda posters, and a video (in Italian) showing WWII bombardments on Padua. Pick up an English brochure as you enter (€4, Tue–Sun 9:30–12:30 & 15:30–18:00, closed Mon, access Piano Nobile from north entrance of building to right of Caffè entrance, tel. 049-820-5007).

University of Padua—The seat of this prestigious university, located in Palazzo del Bo, is adjacent to Caffè Pedrocchi. Founded in 1222 on the site of an old inn with an ox (*bue* in Italian, *bo* in dialect) painted on its sign, it's one of the first, greatest, and most progressive universities in Europe. Back when the Church controlled university curricula, a group of professors and students broke free from the University of Bologna, creating this liberal school, independent of Catholic constraints and accessible to people of alternative faiths.

A haven for free thought, it attracted intellectuals from all over Europe, including the great astronomer Copernicus, who realized here that the world didn't revolve around him. And Galileo—notorious for disagreeing with the Church's views on science—called his 18 years on the faculty here the best of his life. Students gather in ancient courtyards, surrounded by memories of illustrious alumni, including the first woman ever to receive a university degree (in 1678).

And just upstairs, Europe's first great **anatomy theater** (from the 1500s) is worth a look if you have time for a tour. Despite the Church's strict ban on autopsies, students would pack this theater to watch professors dissect human cadavers. If the Church came a-knockin', the table could be flipped, allowing the corpse to fall into a river below and be replaced with an animal instead (€3, guided tours 3/day except Sun; Mon, Wed, and Fri at 15:15, 16:15, and 17:15; Tue, Thu, and Sat at 9:15, 10:15, and 11:15). Only 30 may enter at a time, and school groups often book the entire visit. To confirm tour times and availability, call 049-827-3047 or stop by the university bookstore, located inside Palazzo del Bo on the right side of courtyard. If the tour isn't booked, buy tickets from the bookstore 15 minutes before the visit. The tours take 45 minutes and include stops at the anatomy theater, Aula Magna (grand meeting hall plastered with the crests of important faculty), and Galileo's *cattedra* (lectern).

▲**Baptistery**—If you're an art lover but can't get in to see the Scrovegni Chapel, Padua's Baptistery is a good alternative. Located next to the Duomo, the Baptistery is decorated with Giusto de' Menabuoi's brilliant frescoes—the life of Jesus is depicted on the walls, and Christ in majesty with all the saints (yes, all of them) is on the octagonal ceiling (€2.50, audioguide-€1, daily 10:00–18:00).

SLEEPING

In the Center

$$$ **Majestic Hotel Toscanelli** is a fancy hotel with 32 pleasant, air-conditioned rooms, a touch of charm, and a relatively quiet location on a side street (Sb-€95–115, Db-€153–172, 10 percent discount with this book in 2006, superior rooms and suites available at extra cost, includes a wonderful breakfast, Via dell'Arco 2, about 2 blocks south of Piazza delle Erbe, tel. 049-663-244, fax 049-876-0025, www.toscanelli.com, majestic@toscanelli.com). From

---

Sleep Code

(€1 = about $1.20, country code: 39)
S = Single, **D** = Double/Twin, **T** = Triple, **Q** = Quad, **b** = bathroom, **s** = shower only. Unless otherwise noted, credit cards are accepted, English is spoken, and breakfast is included in these rates.

To help you easily sort through these listings, I've divided the rooms into three categories, based on the price for a standard double room with bath:

$$$ **Higher Priced**—Most rooms €140 or more.
$$ **Moderately Priced**—Most rooms between €100–140.
$ **Lower Priced**—Most rooms €100 or less.

Piazza Erbe, head up Via dei Fabbri and take the first left, then turn right onto Via dell'Arco.

Near Basilica of St. Anthony

$ Hotel al Fagiano, located on a side street west of Piazza del Santo, has 30 bright and cheery air-conditioned rooms decorated with Rosella Fagiano's modern art canvases (Sb-€55, Db-€78, Tb-€88, breakfast €3–6 extra; with your back to the church facade, take Via Belludi, then veer right onto Via Locatelli, #45 is under portico on the right; tel. & fax 049-875-0073, www.alfagiano.it, info@albergoalfagiano.191.it).

$ Hotel al Santo, run by the Tenan family, offers 16 rooms with all the comforts a few steps from the basilica (Sb-€55-60, Db-€90, Tb-€130, Qb-€145, double-paned windows, air-con, quieter rooms off street, some rooms have views of basilica, tel. 049-875-2131, fax 049-878-8076, www.alsanto.it, alsanto@alsanto.it).

$ Casa del Pellegrino, with 160 spotless, cheap, institutional rooms, is home to the pilgrims who come to pay homage to St. Anthony in the basilica, which is right next door (S-€44, Sb-€58, D-€55, Db-€69, Tb-€78, Qb-€90, most rooms have air-con, ask for a room off the street, breakfast-€6, elevator, Via Cesarotti 21, tel. 049-823-9711, fax 049-823-9780, www.casadelpellegrino.com, info@casadelpellegrino.it).

Down by the Station

$$$ Hotel Grand'Italia is the place for four-star elegance, convenience, and prices. Housed in a palace, its 61 rooms are comfortable, and the breakfast room is bright and inviting (Db-€165 but can be more during holidays and trade fairs, air-con, elevator, Corso del Popolo 81, right outside train station on the right side of main drag, tel. 049-876-1111, fax 049-875-0850, www.hotelgranditalia .it, booking@hotelgranditalia.it).

$$ Hotel Monaco, a three-star hotel with 57 darkly-decorated rooms, is a few doors away from the Grand'Italia and plain in comparison, but a heck of lot cheaper (Sb-€75, Db-€98–112, air-con, elevator, traffic noise, Piazzale Stazione 3; as you exit the station, it's to your right and across the street; tel. 049-664-344, fax 049-664-669, www.hotelmonacopadova.it, info@hotelmonacopadova.it).

$$ Hotel al Cason, just a seven-minute walk from the station, offers a good value for its 48 spacious, clean, and comfortable rooms (Db-€98, air-con, elevator, Internet access, free parking, handy restaurant, tel. 049-662-636, fax 049-875-4217, www.hotelalcason .com, info@hotelalcason.com). As you exit the station, cross the road and turn right, following the street as it curves around to the left. Cross the busy boulevard on your right—just after the overpass bridge but before the medieval tower—to get to Via Frà P. Sarpi. Follow Via F. P. Sarpi 100 yards and find the hotel ahead, on your right, at #40.

Hostel: **$ Ostello Città di Padova** is a well-run hostel with 120 beds in four-, six-, and eight-bed rooms (€15.50 beds with sheets and breakfast; 4-person family rooms-€60, with bath-€68; membership required or pay €3 supplement/night, Internet and laundry available, reception open 7:00–9:30 & 16:00–23:00, rooms locked during afternoon but reception staffed if you need to leave bags, 23:00 curfew, bus #3, #8 or #18 from station, get off at Prato della Valle, Via Aleardi 30, tel. 049-875-2219, www.ctgveneto.it /ostello, ostellopadova@ctgveneto.it).

EATING

The university population means cheap, good food in central *osterie, trattorie,* and take-out joints. My recommended restaurants are all centrally located in the historic core.

La Cova Ristorante/Pizzeria, near Piazza Cavour, offers a pleasing range of pizza and pasta. But if you sit in the *ristorante* rather than the pizzeria, you're expected to have multiple courses (Wed–Mon 12:00–15:30 & 18:00–23:30, closed Tue, just off Piazza Cavour, Via P.F. Calvi 20, tel. 049-654-312).

Marechiaro Pizzeria/Trattoria is a popular, economical eatery just west of Piazza delle Erbe (Tue–Sun 12:00–14:30 & 18:30–22:30, closed Mon, Via D. Manin 37, tel. 049-875-8489).

Family-owned **Zairo** is a huge *ristorante*/pizzeria with reasonable prices, delicious and homemade pastas, Veneto specialties, snappy service, and local clientele (Tue–Sun 12:00–15:30 & 18:30–late, closed Mon, east side of Prato della Valle at #51, tel. 049-663-803).

Pago Pago dishes up €4-8 wood-fired Neapolitan pizzas (a local favorite), a variety of big €7 salads, and daily specials (Wed–Mon 12:00–14:30 & 19:00–22:30, pizza until 24:00, closed Tue, just 2 blocks from St. Anthony, heading north on Via del Santo take the first right onto Via G. Galilei to #59, a few steps ahead on the right, tel. 049-665-558).

Brek, tucked into a corner of Piazza Cavour 20, is an easy self-service *ristorante* with healthy and affordable choices (daily 11:30–14:30 & 18:30–22:00, tel. 049-875-3788).

Casa del Pellegrino Ristorante caters to St. Anthony pilgrims with simple, basic, and hearty meals, served in a cheery dining room, just north of the basilica (*primi*-€3-4, *secondi*-€6-12, pizza served only in evening, daily 12:00–14:00 & 19:30–21:00, Via Cesarotti 21, tel. 049-823-9711, Sun lunch by reservation only).

To dine rather than eat, consider **Isola di Caprera** for traditional Veneto cuisine (€22 menu or €37 seafood menu, cheaper à la carte options, Mon–Sat 12:00–15:00 & 19:30–22:30, closed Sun, air-con, Via Marsilio da Padova 11–15, a half block north of the eastern edge of Piazza della Frutta; to reserve, call 049-664-282 or 049-876-0244).

Take-out only: **Gastronomica San Francesco** serves up all kinds of homemade finger food, lasagna, roast meats, and vegetables by the *etto,* or 100 grams. A half kilo (about a pound) of lasagna and some vegetables make a light, portable lunch for two people; you can picnic at the nearby cloisters of the basilica. They'll set you up with to-go containers, plastic silverware, and napkins (Fri–Wed 10:00–13:30 & 17:00–20:00, closed Thu, Via San Francesco 214, tel. 049-876-2253). Facing the facade of the church, head down the left side 200 yards; the deli is on the corner at the end of the street.

Pollodoro la Gastronomica, another take-out deli near the basilica, sells roast chicken and will make sandwiches (Wed–Sat and Mon 8:30–14:00 & 17:00–20:00, Sun 8:30–14:00, closed Tue; 100 yards from basilica, Via Belludi 34; with your back to the church entrance, it's under the arches on the left; tel. 049-663-718).

If the markets are closed, stock up on picnic items at **PAM supermarket,** tucked into the corner of a tiny piazzetta east of Caffè Pedrocchi (Mon–Sat 8:00–20.00, closed Wed evenings and Sun, Piazzetta Garzeria 3, tel. 049-657-006).

TRANSPORTATION CONNECTIONS

From Padua by Train to: Venice (4/hr, 30–40 min), **Vicenza** (2/hr, 25 min), **Milan** (hrly, generally leaving at :24 past the hour, 2.5 hrs), **Verona** (2/hr, 1 hr).

VICENZA DAY TRIP

To many architects, Vicenza (vih-CHEHN-zah) is a pilgrimage site. Entire streets look like the back of a nickel. This is the city of Andrea Palladio (1508–1580), the 16th-century Renaissance architect who gave us the Palladian style that is so influential in countless British country homes.

Palladio's real name was Andrea di Pietro della Gondola, but his genius was such that one of his patrons—responsible for the architect's liberal arts education—gave him the nickname of Palladio, an allusion to Pallas Athena, Greek goddess of wisdom and the arts.

For the casual visitor, a quick stop offers plenty of Palladio—the last great artist of the Renaissance. Note that Vicenza's major sights are closed on Monday.

ORIENTATION

Tourist Information

The main TI is at Piazza Matteotti 12 (daily 9:00–13:00 & 14:00–18:00, tel. 0444-320-854, www.vicenzae.org); a second office is at Piazza dei Signori 8 (daily 10:00–14:00 & 14:30–18:30). Pick up a map and, if staying the night, an entertainment guide (in Italian, but *teatro* and *concerto* are easy enough to understand). Architecture fans will appreciate the free, English *Vicenza Città del Palladio* brochure.

Arrival in Vicenza

From the train station, it's a five-minute **walk** up wide Viale Roma to the bottom of Corso Palladio. Or it's a short **bus** ride to Piazza Matteotti and the top of Corso Palladio. For a day trip, consider catching the bus to Piazza Matteotti and doing your sightseeing on

Vicenza

- ❶ Hotel Campo Marzio
- ❷ Hotel Giardini
- ❸ Hotel Castello
- ❹ Hotel Vicenza
- ❺ L'Ostello Olimpico
- ❻ Internet Pigafetta
- ❼ Al Pestello Rest.
- ❽ Zì Teresa Rest.
- ❾ Antica Casa della Malvasia
- ❿ Rist. Pizzeria Paradiso & Trattoria Vecchia Guardia
- ⓫ La Meneghina Rest.
- ⓬ Soraru Pastry Shop
- ⓭ Self-Pause Ristorante
- ⓮ PAM Supermarket

the way back to the station. From the station, catch bus #1, #2, #4, #5, or #7 (€1, tickets sold at *tabacchi* shop in station, stop is immediately to your left as you exit the station). Validate your ticket in the machine near the back of the bus. Get off at Piazza Matteotti, a skinny, park-like square in front of a white neoclassical building. A **taxi** to Piazza Matteotti costs about €6.

You can usually **check luggage** at the train station (€3.90, daily 9:00–13:00 & 15:00–19:00; with your back to the tracks, it's at the far left end of the station, past the WCs).

Helpful Hints

Combo-Tickets: Most of Vicenza's sights are covered by a combo-ticket called the Biglietto Unico (€8, good for 3 days, sold only at the Olympic Theater). In addition to the theater, the Biglietto Unico includes the Pinacoteca (paintings in Palazzo Chiericati on Piazza Matteotti), the Santa Corona Archaeological and Natural History Museum (next to the Church of Santa Corona), and the Museum of the Risorgimento and Resistance (2 miles outside of town). The pricier €11 combo-ticket (Biglietto Cumulativo) gets you into every sight in Vicenza except for exhibits in Basilica Palladiana.

Internet Access: Internet Pigafetta has several terminals a few steps from Piazza Castello (Mon–Sat 7:00–20:00, closed Sun, Contrà Piazza Castello 15, tel. 0444-321-903).

Laundry: The self-service Euro Lavanderia Fai da Te is near the TI and a couple of blocks from Piazza Matteotti (daily 7:30–22:30; with your back to TI, turn left around corner, cross bridge, take right-middle fork of 5 streets to Contrà XX Settembre 27, and go under the arches on left).

Market Days: Vicenza hosts a Tuesday market (7:00–13:00) on Piazza dei Signori, and a larger Thursday market that also spills into Piazza Duomo, Piazza del Castello, and Viale Roma (7:00–13:00).

Tours: Guided tours of Vicenza may be offered in English in 2006; ask at the TI.

SIGHTS

Central Vicenza

▲▲Olympic Theater (Teatro Olimpico)—Palladio's last work is one of his greatest. It was commissioned by the Olympic Academy, a society of Vicenzan scholars and intellectuals (including Palladio), for the purpose of staging performances and intellectual debates. Begun in 1580, shortly before Palladio died, the theater was actually completed by a fellow architect, Scamozzi.

Modeled after the theaters of antiquity, this is a wood-and-stucco festival of classical columns, statues, and an oh-wow stage bursting with perspective tricks. Behind the stage, framed by a triumphal arch, five streets recede at different angles. The streets, depicting the idealized form of the city of Thebes, were created for the gala opening of *Oedipus Rex*, the first play ever performed in the theater and now a tradition for every season.

Many of the statues in niches on the stage are modeled after the people who funded the work—junior members are portrayed as Roman soldiers of antiquity, senior members as senators. The panels at the top show the labors of Hercules, in keeping with the classical antiquity theme that was all the rage in the 16th century. In contrast to the stunning stage, the audience's wooden benches are simple and crude (covered by €8 Biglietto Unico; dense 45-min audioguide-€3, or €5 for two; Tue–Sun 9:00–17:00, closed Mon, July–Aug until 19:00, last entry 15 min before closing, entrance to the left of TI, WC just past the ticket booth on the right, tel. 0444-222-800).

Performances: One of the oldest indoor theaters in Europe and considered one of the world's best, it's still used for performances from April through June (jazz and classical music) and from September through October (Greek tragedies and dramas, shows start at 21:00; for details, see www.vicenzae.org, info@vicenzae.org).

▲**Church of Santa Corona**—A block away from the Olympic Theater, this "Church of the Holy Crown" was built in the 13th century to house a thorn from the crown of thorns given to the Bishop of Vicenza by the French King Louis IX (free, Mon 15:00–18:00, Tue–Sun 8:30–12:00 & 15:00–18:00). It has Giovanni Bellini's fine *Baptism of Christ* (c. 1500, insert a coin for light, to the left of the altar). Study the incredible inlaid marble and mother-of-pearl work on the high altar (1670) and the inlaid wood complementing that in the stalls of the choir (1485).

Archaeological and Natural History Museum—Next door to the Church of Santa Corona, the ground floor of this humble museum features Roman antiquities (mosaics, statues, and artifacts excavated from Rome's Baths of Caracalla, plus swords) and a barbarian warrior skeleton complete with sword and helmet. Prehistoric scraps are upstairs, and there are a few English description sheets near exhibit entryways throughout (covered by €8 Biglietto Unico, Tue–Sun 9:00–17:00, closed Mon, last entry 15 min before closing, WC on second floor at end of prehistoric hall, tel. 0444-320-440).

Corso Andrea Palladio—From the Olympic Theater or Church of Santa Corona, stroll down Vicenza's main drag, Corso Andrea Palladio, and see why they call Vicenza "Venezia on terra firma." A steady string of Renaissance palaces and Palladian architecture is peopled by Vicenzans (considered by their neighbors to be as uppity as most of their colonnades) and punctuated by upper-class *gelaterie*.

After a few blocks, you'll see the commanding **Basilica Palladiana** (this was not a church, but a meeting place for local big shots). With its 270-foot-tall, 13th-century

tower, the basilica dominates the Piazza dei Signori, the town center since Roman times. It was young Palladio's proposal to redo
Vicenza's dilapidated Gothic palace of justice in the neo-Greek
style that established him as Vicenza's favorite architect. The rest
of Palladio's career was a one-man construction boom. Opposite
the basilica, the brick-columned **Loggia del Capitaniato**—home
of the Venetian governor and one of Palladio's last works—gives
you an easy chance to compare early Palladio (the basilica) with
late Palladio (the loggia).

The basilica is open to tourists (€1, more during frequent
special exhibitions—see www.vicenzae.org for specifics, Tue–Sun
9:00–13:00 & 15:00–19:00, closed Mon, tel. 0444-322-196). Even
without a ticket, climb the 15th-century stairs. Halfway up the
steps, you'll see the gargoyle-like lion's mouth (representing the
long arm of the Venetian Republic). Centuries ago, people used
to sneak notes into this mouth, anonymously reporting neighbors
suspected of carrying communicable diseases that could bring on
the plague. You can walk around the arcaded upper floor, which
contains the entrance to the huge basilica. The basilica's roof,
shaped like an upside-down keel, has a nautical feel, augmented
by the porthole windows. Set in the wall in front, the winged lion
(symbol of St. Mark and Venice) laid the course for this little town
in the 15th century.

Outside, on the Piazza dei Signori, note the two tall, **15th-
century columns** topped by Jesus and the winged lion. When
Venice took over Vicenza in the early 1400s, these columns were

added—à la St. Mark's
Square—to give the city a
Venetian feel.

Finish your stroll
along the Corso Palladio at
Piazzale Gasperi (where the
Pam supermarket is a handy
place to grab a picnic for the
train ride), dip into the park
called Giardino Salvi (for one
last Palladio loggia, closed
to visitors but viewable from
outside), and then walk five minutes down Viale Roma back to the
station. Trains leave about every hour for Milan/Verona and Venice
(less than an hour away).

Villas on the Outskirts of Vicenza

These two villas are worth a visit for architecture buffs
with more time. Both houses are furnished with period pieces
and have good English descriptions. Pick up the free English

brochure on Palladio's villas from the TI if you plan to visit.

Villa la Rotonda—Thomas Jefferson's Monticello was inspired by Palladio's Rotonda (a.k.a. Villa Almerico Capra). Started by Palladio in 1566, it was finished by his pupil, Scamozzi. The white, gently domed building, with grand colonnaded entries, seems to have popped out of the grassy slope. Palladio, who designed a number of country villas, had a knack for using setting for dramatic effect. This private—but sometimes tourable—residence is on the edge of Vicenza (€5 to enter grounds, mid-March–mid-Nov Tue–Sun 10:00–12:00 & 15:00–18:00, closed Mon, shorter hours off season, confirm hours before heading out there; €10 for interior—open only Wed 10:00–12:00 & 15:00–18:00; Via Rotonda 29, tel. 0444-321-793). To get to the villa from Vicenza's train station, hop a bus (#8, 2/hr, stop is to the left of the station as you're facing it on Viale Venezia) or take a taxi. For a quick round-trip any time of day, you can zip out by cab (about €8, 5-min ride from train station) to see the building sitting regally atop its hill, and then ride the same cab back.

Villa Valmarana ai Nani—The 17th-century "Villa of the Dwarfs" is just up the street from Villa Rotonda. This is convenient if you want to see a villa interior and you're not in Vicenza on a Wednesday, when Villa la Rotunda is open. This elegant neoclassical estate features panoramic views and 18th-century murals by Tiepolo.

The villa's name comes from the local legend of an ancient manor house owned by a nobleman whose daughter was born a dwarf. Her father surrounded her with dwarf servants so she wouldn't realize she was small. One day as she was looking out the window, she saw a handsome prince ride by on his horse. Realizing she was a dwarf, she killed herself in anguish. Her servants—so saddened by her death that they turned to stone—now line the wall of the villa like petrified sentries.

The rooms in the main house include frescoes with scenes from the Trojan War, classical myths, and Italian lyrical poems. The frescoes in the guest house *(forestiera)* are nearly all by Tiepolo's son, Giandomenico, whose themes highlight 18th-century gentrified culture—the idealized tranquility of peasants, the exotic fashion and styles of the Chinese from a Western perspective, and scenes from Carnevale (€5, 10:00–12:00 & 15:00–18:00, closed Mon, and Tue and Fri mornings; from Villa Rotonda, head a few steps downhill, then up the slope on Stradella Valmarana about 200 yards; tel. 0444-321-803).

SLEEPING

$$$ Hotel Campo Marzio, a four-star, American-style, pricey place with all comforts, faces a park on the main drag, a few minutes' walk directly in front of the station (Db-€165-182; prices depend on season and size of room—"superior" means bigger, with a few more amenities; all rooms have air-con, elevator, free bikes, free and easy parking, Viale Roma 21, tel. 0444-545-700, fax 0444-320-495, www.hotelcampomarzio.com, info@hotelcampomarzio.com).

$$ Hotel Giardini, with three stars and 17 sleek rooms, has splashy pastel colors and a refreshing feel (Sb-€83, Db-€114, these prices promised with this book through 2006, air-con, elevator, on busy street but has double-paned windows, within a block of Piazza Matteotti/Olympic Theater on Via Giuriolo 10, tel. & fax 0444-326-458, www.hotelgiardini.com, info@hotelgiardini.com).

$ Hotel Castello, on Piazza Castello, has 18 homey, quiet rooms and lots of stairs (Sb-€77, Db-€98, air-con, Internet access, new rooftop terrace; Contrà Piazza del Castello 24, down alley to the right of Ristorante agli Schioppi, 5-min walk from station, turn right after passing Hotel Campo Marzio, and head up hill to square, take the street slightly to the left as you enter the square; tel. 0444-323-585, fax 0444-323-583, www.hotelcastelloitaly.com, info@hotelcastelloitaly.it).

$ Hotel Vicenza, in an 18th-century theater, is family-owned and ideally located on a quiet street just off Piazza dei Signori. Its 34 peaceful rooms, some with small balconies, have a worn, Old World feel (D-€50, Db-€65, no breakfast, elevator, Stradella dei Nodari 5/7, tel. & fax 0444-321-512). They might be closing in 2006 for restoration, so call ahead.

Sleep Code

(€1 = about $1.20, country code: 39)
S = Single, **D** = Double/Twin, **T** = Triple, **Q** = Quad, **b** = bathroom. Unless otherwise noted, credit cards are accepted, English is spoken, and breakfast is included in these rates. Prices can be higher during trade fairs.

To help you easily sort through these listings, I've divided the rooms into three categories, based on the price for a standard double room with bath.

$$$ **Higher Priced**—Most rooms €140 or more.
$$ **Moderately Priced**—Most rooms between €100–140.
$ **Lower Priced**—Most rooms €100 or less.

$ *Hostel:* **L'Ostello Olimpico,** just a few years old, is wonderfully central on Piazza Matteotti, a few steps from the Olympic Theater (80 beds, 4- to 6-bed rooms-€16 per person, family rooms-€17.50 per person, Db-€19.50 per person, closed 9:30–15:15, curfew-23:30, breakfast-€1.85, lunch or dinner-€11, all eaten at nearby restaurant using vouchers from hostel, Internet access; bike rental-€1/hr, €8/day; laundry nearby on Contrà XX Settembre 27, best to reserve several weeks in advance by fax or e-mail, tel. 0444-540-222, fax 0444-547-762, ostello.vicenza@tin.it).

EATING

The local specialty is marinated cod, called *baccalà alla Vicentina.*

In **Al Pestello**'s casually elegant dining room, owner Fabio patiently and lovingly describes his menu of historic *cucina Vicentina* (including *baccalà*) from a menu written in dialect. The day's offerings are created from the freshest seasonal ingredients to complement an extensive list of local and national wines (expect to spend about €30 per person without wine, Mon 19:30–22:30, Tue–Sat 12:30–14:30 & 19:30–22:30, closed Sun, a block from the Church of Santa Corona at Contrà Santo Stefano 3, tel. 0444-323-721).

Zi Teresa is popular among locals for its romantic ambience and moderately priced traditional cuisine and pizzas (Thu–Tue 11:45–14:30 & 18:30–23:00, closed Wed, a couple blocks southwest of Piazza dei Signori, Contrà S. Antonio 1, at intersection with Contrà Proti, tel. 0444-321-411).

Antica Casa della Malvasia is a popular, atmospheric, cavernous trattoria serving up affordable regional favorites and homemade pastas (daily 12:00–14:30 & 19:00–24:00, Contrà delle Morette 5, just off Piazza dei Signori on a little alley directly across from the bell tower, tel. 0444-543-704). Their new attached *enoteca* offers wines (€0.80–€3.50/glass) and snacks.

Ristorante Pizzeria Paradiso offers dozens of inexpensive pasta and wood-fired pizza options and indoor/outdoor seating on a narrow square south of Piazza dei Signori and Piazza Erbe (Tue–Sun 12:00–14:30 & 18:30–22:30, closed Mon, Via Pescherie Vecchie 5, tel. 0444-322-320). When they're closed, try their sister restaurant next door, **Trattoria Vecchia Guardia** (different daily specials, Fri–Wed 12:00–14:30 & 18:30–22:30, closed Thu, Via Pescherie Vecchie 15, tel. 0444-321-231).

Cheap Eats: A cheap, self-service **Self-Pause Ristorante** is just off Piazza del Castello, in the shadow of the arch where Corso Andrea Palladio meets Viale Roma (Mon–Sat 12:00–14:30 & 19:00–22:00, Sun 19:00–22:00, Corso Andrea Palladio 10, tel. 0444-327-829). A few steps from that same arch is the **Pam**

supermarket, perfect for picnics (Mon–Sat 8:00–20:00, Wed only until 13:00, closed Sun, follow the curve of the road just outside the city wall).

Pastry: **La Meneghina** is an atmospheric pastry shop (Tue–Sun 8:00–23:00, closed Mon; full meals 12:00–14:30 & 19:30–22:00 in summer, until 21:00 in winter; on Contrà Cavour 18, a short street between Piazza dei Signori and Corso Andrea Palladio, tel. 0444-323-305). Nearby, on Piazza dei Signori, the tiny **Soraru** pastry shop has lots of sidewalk tables within tickling distance of the Palladio statue (Thu–Tue 8:30–13:00 & 15:30–20:00, closed Wed, next to basilica, at far end of square from the two tall columns, tel. 0444-320-915).

TRANSPORTATION CONNECTIONS

From Vicenza by Train to: Venice (2/hr, 1 hr), **Padua** (2/hr, 20 min), **Ravenna** (about hrly, 3–4 hrs, depending on train, with changes in Padua and Ferrara or Bologna), **Verona** (2/hr, 40 min).

VERONA DAY TRIP

Romeo and Juliet made Verona a household word. Alas, a visit here has nothing to do with those two star-crossed lovers. You can pay to visit the house that falsely claims to be Juliet's (with an almost-believable balcony and a courtyard swarming with tour groups), take part in the tradition of rubbing the breast of Juliet's statue to ensure finding a lover (or picking up the sweat of someone who can't), and even make a pilgrimage to what isn't "La Tomba di Giulietta."

Despite the fiction, the town has been an important crossroads for 2,000 years and is therefore packed with genuine history. R and J fans will take some solace in the fact that two real feuding families, the Montecchi and the Capellis, were the models for Shakespeare's Montagues and Capulets. And, if R and J had existed and were alive today, they would recognize much of their "hometown."

Verona's main attractions are its wealth of Roman ruins; the remnants of its 13th- and 14th-century political and cultural boom; its 21st-century, quiet, pedestrians-only ambience; and a world-class opera festival each July and August (schedule at www.arena.it). After Venice's festival of tourism, the Veneto's second city (in population and in artistic importance) is a cool and welcome sip of pure Italy, where dumpsters are painted by schoolchildren as class projects. If you like Italy but don't need great sights, this town is a joy.

ORIENTATION

The most enjoyable core of Verona is along Via Mazzini between Piazza Brà and Piazza Erbe, Verona's market square since Roman times. Head straight for Piazza Brà—and stroll. All sights of importance are located within an easy walk through the old town, which is defined by a bend in the river. For a good day trip to Verona, see the Arena and take my self-guided walk (see page 288).

Tourist Information

Verona has two TIs (both open Mon–Sat 9:00–19:00, Sun 9:00–15:00, www.tourism.verona.it): at the train station (tel. 045-800-0861) and at Piazza Brà (as you face the large yellow-white building, TI is across street to your right, tel. 045-806-8680, public WC on Piazza Brà). At either TI, pick up the free city map that includes a list of sights, opening hours, and walking tours. If you're staying the night, ask the TI about concerts or pick up a monthly entertainment guide (either *Carnet Verona* or *Verona Live*) for about €1 at any newsstand. Both are in Italian, but *concerto di musica classica* is darn close to English.

The **Verona Card** covers bus transportation and entrance to most of Verona's sights (€8/day or €12/3 days, sold at participating sights and at the exchange office in the train station).

Arrival in Verona

By Train: Get off at Verona's Porta Nuova station. The station is modern, but so cluttered with shops that it can be hard to get oriented. From the tracks, an underground passage leads to the main hall. As you emerge from the passage, pay toilets and phones are to your left, and an ATM is to your right. Beyond the ATM to the right is a long hall; at the end of the hall, a smaller hall branches off to the right, where you'll find the baggage check (€4 for up to 5 hrs, passport required), TI (across from baggage check, in office labeled *Centro Accoglienza e Informazioni*), train information desk (same office as TI), and another ATM (to the right of the TI).

The boring 15-minute walk from the station to Piazza Brà is on busy streets; take the **bus** instead. Buses leave from directly in front of the station. You need to buy a ticket before boarding from a *tabacchi* shop inside the station (€1, good for 1 hr; or €3.10 for an all-day ticket valid until midnight). Confirm the route at the TI, or ask someone, *"Che numero per centro?"* (kay NOO-may-roh pehr CHEN-troh). You'll probably have a choice of orange bus #11, #12, #13, or #14, leaving from Platform A. Validate your ticket by stamping it in the machine in the middle of the bus. Buses stop on Piazza Brà, the square with the can't-miss-it Roman Arena. The TI is just a few steps beyond the bus stop (located along the medieval walls). Buses return to the station from the bus stop just outside the city wall (on the right), where Corso Porta Nuova hits Piazza Brà.

Taxis pick up only at taxi stands (at Piazza Brà and train station) and cost about €6 for a ride between the train station and Piazza Brà.

By Plane: From Verona's airport, catch a shuttle bus to the train station (€4.50, buy tickets on board, daily 6:00–23:30, departs every 20 min, trip takes 15 min). If going *to* the airport, catch the shuttle just to the left of the train station entrance (€4.50, departs every 20 min daily 5:40–23:10).

Helpful Hints

Sightseeing Schedules: Many sights are closed on Monday and are free on the first Sunday of every month.

Opera: In July and August, Verona's opera festival brings crowds and higher hotel prices (tickets €17–157, upper-level seats about €25, book tickets either online at www.arena.it or by calling tel. 045-800-5151, box office open Mon–Fri 9:00–12:00 & 15:15–17:15, Sat–Sun 9:00–12:00; in opera season, it's open daily 10:00–17:45, or until 21:00 on days when there's a show).

Internet Access: Try Internet Train (Mon–Fri 11:00–22:00, Sat–Sun 14:00–20:00, Via Roma 17A, a couple of blocks off Piazza Brà toward Castelvecchio, tel. 045-801-3394), Internetfast.it (Mon–Sat 10:00–20:00, closed Sun, Via Oberdan 16B, just off Porta Borsari toward Piazza Brà, tel. 045-803-3212), or Internet Etc. (Tue–Sat 10:30–20:00, Sun–Mon 15:30–20:00, off Via Mazzini on Via Quattro Spade 3B, tel. 045-800-0222).

Post Office: The post office is at Via Cattaneo 23E (Mon–Sat 8:30–18:30, closed Sun, from Piazza Brà take Via Roma and turn right on Via Cattaneo, 100 yards down on right).

Laundry: Mr. Lava Lava self-service laundry is near Ponte Nuovo (daily 9:00–23:00, last wash at 22:00, €5/load for wash and dry, soap vendor and change machine available, follow Via Carducci and turn right onto Via Interrato to #36).

Bikes: The TI at the train station has eight free loaner bikes (passport required for deposit, Mon–Sat 9:00–17:30, Sun 9:00–14:00, maybe summer only).

Gnocchi Festival: Ask a Veronese to tell you about Papa del Gnoccho (NYO-koh). About 500 years ago, at a time when the Veronese were nearly starving, the prince handed out gnocchi (potato dumplings) to everyone. To this day, it's customary for the Veronese to eat gnocchi on Friday during Lent. Every year someone from the San Zeno neighborhood is elected Papa del Gnoccho. On the Friday before Mardi Gras, he's dressed like a king—but instead of a scepter, he holds a huge fork piercing a *gnoccho*. Lots of people wear costumes, including little kids (who dress as gnocchi). The focal point of this celebration is the Church of San Zeno.

TOURS

Walking Tours—Juliet & Co. offers 75-minute tours in English (€10/person, doesn't include entry to any sights or monuments, April–Sept daily at 17:30, meet in front of equestrian statue on Piazza Brà, tel. 045-810-3173, www.julietandco.com).

Private Guides—To hire your own Verona guide, consider knowledgeable, enthusiastic, and friendly Marina Menegoi (€100/2–3-hour tour, itinerary varies according to your interests, she also does tours of the region— including wine-tasting tours, tel. 045-801-2174, mobile 328-958-1108, milanit@libero.it); or try the Verona guide association (tel. 049-869-8601). Even if you don't want to hire a guide, Marina is happy to help out my readers with information that they might need—free of charge.

SELF-GUIDED WALK

Welcome to Verona

This walk will take you from Piazza Erbe to the major sights, ending at Piazza Brà. Allow an hour (including the tower climb and dawdling, but not the optional detours).

Piazza Erbe is a photographer's delight. Its pastel buildings corral the fountains, pigeons, and people who have congregated here since Roman times, when this was a forum. Notice the Venetian lion hovering above the square, reminding locals of their conquerors since 1405. During medieval times, the stone canopy in the center held the scales where merchants measured the weight of things they bought and sold, such as silk, wool, and wood. The fountain has bubbled here for 2,000 years. Its statue, originally Roman, had lost its head and arms. After a sculptor added a new head and arms, the statue became Verona's Madonna. She holds a small banner that reads: "I want justice and I bring peace." In recent years, there has been an ongoing battle between market-stall owners, who earn their living from the tourists, and the community, which wants the square left free to be enjoyed as the open "living space" it was meant to be. The debate continues—notice whether the recently banned stall owners have bought their way back onto the square.

From the center of Piazza Erbe, head toward the river on Via della Costa. The street is marked by an **arch** with a whale's rib suspended from it. According to legend, the rib has hung there for a thousand years, and will fall only when someone who's never lied walks under it. Give it a try.

The street soon opens up to a square, **Piazza dei Signori.** Center-stage is a white statue of the Italian poet Dante Alighieri. The pensive Dante seems to wonder why the tourists choose Juliet over him. Dante—expelled from Florence for political reasons— was granted asylum in Verona by the della Scala (a.k.a. Scaligeri) family. With the whale's rib behind you, you're facing the brick, crenellated, 13th-century della Scala residence. Behind Dante is the yellowish 15th-century Venetian Renaissance–style Portico

Verona

200 YARDS
200 METERS

★ PIAZZA ERBE

- ❶ Bus to Station
- ❷ Bus from Station
- ❸ Hotel Aurora
- ❹ To L'Ospite Apartments
- ❺ Hotel Europa
- ❻ Hotel Bologna
- ❼ Hotel Giulietta e Romeo
- ❽ Hotel Torcolo
- ❾ Locanda Catullo
- ❿ To Villa Francescatti Hostel
- ⓫ Osteria al Duca

- ⓬ Osteria Giulietta e Romeo
- ⓭ Ristorante Greppia
- ⓮ Bottega del Vino
- ⓯ De Gusto Ristorante
- ⓰ Ristorante Sant'Eufemia
- ⓱ San Matteo Church Rest.
- ⓲ Osteria le Vecete
- ⓳ Oreste dal Zovo
- ⓴ Enoteca Can Grande
- ㉑ Brek Cafeteria
- ㉒ PAM Supermarket

of the Counsel. In front of Dante—and to his right (follow the white *WC* signs) is the 12th-century Romanesque **Palazzo della Ragione.**

Enter the courtyard. The impressive staircase—which goes nowhere—is the only surviving Renaissance staircase in Verona. For a grand city view, you can climb to the top of the 13th-century **Torre dei Lamberti** (€2 for stairs, €3 for elevator, Tue–Sun 8:30–19:30, Mon 13:30–19:30, last entry 45 min before closing). The elevator saves you 245 steps—but you'll still need to climb about 45 more to get to the first viewing platform. It's not worth continuing up the endless spiral stairs to the second viewing platform.

Exit the courtyard the way you entered and turn right, continuing down the whale-rib street. Within a block, you'll find the strange and very Gothic **tombs of the della Scala family**, who were to Verona what the Medici family were to Florence. Notice the dogs' heads near the top of the tombs. On the first tomb, the dogs peer over a shield displaying a ladder. The della Scala family got rich making ladders...but money can't buy culture. When Marco Polo returned from Asia boasting of the wealthy Kublai Khan, the della Scalas wanted to be associated with this powerful Khan by name. But misunderstanding Khan as *cane* (dog), one Scaligero changed his name to Can Grande (big dog), and another to Can Signore (lord dog).

Continue straight for one long block and turn left on San Pietro Martire (you'll need to step into the street to check the road sign). After one block, you'll reach Verona's largest church, the brick **Church of Sant'Anastasia.** Consider visiting this church's interior—featuring surly stone hunchbacks and a Pisanello fresco (see church description on page 293)—before continuing the walk...or just peek in over the screen to get a sense of its size.

Facing the church, go right and walk along the length of it. Take a left on Via Sottoriva. In a block, you'll reach a small river-front park that usually has a few modern-day Romeos and Juliets gazing at each other rather than the view. Get up on the sidewalk right next to the river. You'll see the red-and-white bridge, **Ponte Pietra.** The white stones are from the original Roman bridge that stood here. After the bridge was bombed in World War II, the Veronese fished the marble chunks out of the river to rebuild it.

Head toward the Ponte Pietra. You'll also see, across the river and built into the hillside, the **Roman Theater**. Way above the theater is the fortress, **Castello San Pietro**. This is your chance to break away, cross the bridge, and visit the Roman Theater (see page 292 for details); or head up to the Castello for an expansive city view (go up the little road called Scalone Castello San Pietro at the end of the bridge, or climb the stairs to the left of the theater).

Me? I'm simply passing the bridge on the way to the next

church. Leave the riverfront park, and take the street to the right, Via Ponte Pietra, toward the bridge. One block before you reach the bridge (bridge entry clearly marked by an arch in a tower), turn left on Via Cappelletta. After two long blocks, you'll come to Via Duomo (the corner is marked by a little church). To tour another of Verona's historic churches—the **Duomo**—turn right and head up Via Duomo. (For more information about the Duomo—with Titian's *Assumption* and the foundations of a 10th-century church—see page 294.) To shortcut to the next stop, go left at the intersection, toward the Church of Sant'Anastasia.

With your back to the Church of Sant'Anastasia, walk down Corso S. Anastasia. In five minutes (at a brisk pace), you'll reach the ghostly white **Porta Borsari,** stretching across the road. This sturdy first-century Roman gate was one of the original entrances to this ancient town.

Continue straight (the name of the street changes to Corso Cavour). In a little park next to the castle is a first-century Roman triumphal arch, **Arco dei Gavi.** After being destroyed by French Revolutionary troops in 1796, it was rebuilt at this location in the 1900s.

Next to the arch is **Castelvecchio**—once the della Scala family's medieval castle, and now a sprawling art museum displaying Christian statuary, some weaponry, and fine 13th- to 17th-century paintings. For more on this building and its exhibits, see page 293.

From the castle, you have several options. For a city view, you can walk out upon the grand bridge that leads from the castle over the river. For another church visit, walk a few blocks from the castle (following the river away from town) to the 12th-century **Basilica of San Zeno Maggiore** (with a triptych by Mantegna, bronze doors displaying Bible stories for illiterate medieval parishioners, and some prayerful 14th-century graffiti; described on page 294).

But to finish the walk, the castle's drawbridge points the way to Via Roma, taking you to Piazza Brà. Here you'll have a chance to rest at a sidewalk café (Brek is cheap—see page 299) and visit the remarkable **Roman Arena** (described below).

SIGHTS AND ACTIVITIES

▲▲**Evening *Passeggiata***—For me, the highlight of Verona is the *passeggiata* (stroll)—especially in the evening—from the elegant cafés of Piazza Brà through the old town on Via Mazzini (one of Europe's many "first pedestrians-only streets") to the colorful Piazza Erbe.

Roman Arena—This elliptical 466-by-400-foot amphitheater is the third-largest in the Roman world. Dating from the first century A.D., it looks great in its pink marble. Over the centuries, crowds of up to 25,000 spectators have cheered Roman gladiator battles, medieval executions, and modern plays (including the popular opera festival that takes advantage of the famous acoustics every July and August). Climb to the top for a fine city view (€4, Tue–Sun 8:30–19:30, Mon 13:30–19:30, closes at 15:00 during opera season, hours

can vary so check TI, last entry 1 hr before closing, WC near entry, located on Piazza Brà, tel. 045-800-3204).

House of Juliet—This bogus house is a block off Piazza Erbe (detour right to Via Cappello 23). The tiny, admittedly romantic courtyard is a spectacle in itself, with Japanese posing on the balcony, Nebraskans

polishing Juliet's bronze breast, and amorous graffiti everywhere. The information boxes offer a good history (€1 for 2 people). ("While no documentation has been discovered to prove the truth of the legend, no documentation has disproved it either.") The "museum" exhibits art inspired by the love story, plus costumes and the bed from Franco Zeffirelli's film *Romeo and Juliet*—certainly not worth the €4 entry fee (Tue–Sun 8:30–19:30, Mon 13:30–19:30, tel. 045-803-4303).

Roman Theater (Teatro Romano)—Dating from the first century A.D., this ancient theater was discovered in the 19th century and restored. To reach the worthwhile museum, high up in the building above the theater, you can take the stairs or the elevator (to find the elevator, start at the stage and walk up the middle set of stairs, then continue straight on the path through the bushes).

The museum displays a model of the theater, a small Jesuit chapel, and lots of Roman artifacts (mosaic floors, busts and other statuary, clay and bronze votive figures, and other architectural fragments). You'll find helpful English information sheets in virtually every room (€3, free first Sun of month, WC to the right of theater entrance after ticket booth,

Tue–Sun 8:30–19:30, Mon 13:30–19:30, last entry 45 min before
closing, across the river near Ponte Pietra, tel. 045-800-0360). Every
summer, the theater stages Shakespeare plays—only a little more
difficult to understand in Italian than in Elizabethan English.

Giardino Giusti—If you'd enjoy a
Renaissance garden with manicured box
hedges and towering cypress trees, you
could find this worth the walk and fee.
Both the garden and its palazzo are up
for sale, if you've got the cash (€5, daily
9:00–19:30, 8:00 until sunset off-season;
cross river at Ponte Nuovo, continue 5
blocks up Via Carducci, then turn left to
Via Giardino Giusti 2).

Castelvecchio—Verona's powerful della
Scala family built this castle (1343–1356)
as both a residence and a fortress to defend against their enemies.
Today it's a museum showing off Verona in its glory days (€4, extra
for exhibitions, Mon 13:30–19:30, Tue–Sun 8:30–19:30, last entry
45 min before closing, good English descriptions on sheets throughout, ask about audioguides, WC in 3rd room past ticket booth).

The **ground floor** houses early Christian statues that were
once vibrantly colored (notice the faint traces of paint). The homier
first floor was the residential rooms of the castle (original wooden
ceilings, traces of frescoes, religious paintings).

The **second floor** takes you out of the Middle Ages and into
the Renaissance (paintings now have secular themes). Displayed
on this floor are fine ancient bronze and gold artifacts and a collection of hair-raising medieval weaponry—pikes, halberds, helmets,
breastplates, and enormous broadswords.

On the far side of the armaments exhibit, climb the skinny
stairway for a grand view.

Churches

Verona has several historic churches. Three in particular—
Sant'Anastasia, the Duomo, and San Zeno—are worth visiting, described below, and covered by the same €5 combo ticket
(combo-ticket sold at all the churches, or pay €2.50 apiece to enter,
churches also covered by Verona Card—see page 286; tel. 045-
592-813, no photos allowed, no tourists during Mass, modest dress
expected). The San Lorenzo and San Fermo churches, also covered
by the €5 combo-ticket, are not particularly worth a visit.

Church of Sant'Anastasia—This church was built from the late
13th century through the 15th century, but the builders ran out of
steam, and the facade was never finished. The highlights of the interior are the grimacing hunchbacks holding basins of holy water on

their backs (near entrance at base of columns) and Pisanello's fragmented fresco of *St. George and the Princess* (above chapel to right of altar; ask for English brochure, which describes the story of the church; April–Sept Mon–Sat 9:00–18:00, Sun 13:00–18:00, shorter hours March and Oct, open Sun afternoons only Nov–Feb).

Duomo—Started in the 12th century, this church was built over a period of centuries. Its bright interior demonstrates the tremendous leaps made in architecture over the course of its construction. (OK, so the white paint helps.) The highlights are Titian's *Assumption* and the ruins of an older church. To find the Titian, stand at the very back of the church and face the altar; the painting is to your left. Mary calmly rides a cloud—direction up—to the shock and bewilderment of the crowd below. To find the ruins of the older church, walk up toward the altar to the last wooden door on the left. (If the door's not open, ask someone for help.) Inside are the 10th-century foundations of the Church of St. Elena, turned intriguingly into a modern-day chapel (get the English descriptions at the entrance, April–Sept Mon–Sat 10:00–17:30, Sun 13:30–17:30, shorter hours March and Oct, open Sun afternoons only Nov–Feb).

Basilica of San Zeno Maggiore—This church is dedicated to the patron saint of Verona, whose remains are buried in the crypt under the main altar. In addition to being a fine example of Italian Romanesque, the basilica features Mantegna's *San Zeno Triptych* (sit on the right-side pews for the best view of Mantegna's perspective), peaceful double-columned cloisters, and a set of 48 paneled 11th-century bronze doors nicknamed "the poor man's Bible." Pretend you're an illiterate medieval peasant and do some reading. Facing the altar, on the far right of the nave you can see frescoes painted on top of other frescoes and graffiti dating from the 1300s. These were done by people who fled into the church in times of war or flooding to scratch prayers into the walls. Druidic-looking runes are actually decorated letters typical of the Gothic period, like those in illuminated manuscripts (April–Sept Mon–Sat 8:30–18:00, Sun 9:00–12:30 & 13:00–18:00, shorter hours March and Oct, open Sun afternoons only Nov–Feb).

SLEEPING

I've listed rates you'll pay in regular season. Prices soar above these in July and August (during opera season), the first week of April (during the Vinitaly wine festival), and any time of year for a trade

---

Sleep Code

(€1 = about $1.20, country code: 39)
S = Single, **D** = Double/Twin, **T** = Triple, **Q** = Quad, **b** = bathroom, **s** = shower only. Hotels accept credit cards and provide breakfast unless otherwise noted. Everyone speaks English.

To help you easily sort through these listings, I've divided the rooms into three categories, based on the price for a standard double room with bath:

$$$ **Higher Priced**—Most rooms €140 or more.
$$ **Moderately Priced**—Most rooms between
€100–140.
$ **Lower Priced**—Most rooms €100 or less.

---

fair or holiday. Hotel Aurora and Hotel Torcolo are my favorites for their family-run feeling.

Near Piazza Erbe

$$ **Hotel Aurora,** just off Piazza Erbe, has friendly family management, a terrace overlooking the piazza, and 19 fresh, air-conditioned rooms (S-€68, Sb-€120, Db-€135, Tb-€158, cheaper off-season, reserve with traveler's check or personal check for deposit, good buffet breakfast, elevator, nearby church bells ring the hour early, Piazza Erbe, tel. 045-594-717, fax 045-801-0860, www.hotelaurora .biz, info@hotelaurora.biz). Their two quads (each with 2 rooms— 1 double bed, 2 twin beds—and bathroom; €220/night) are better for families than couples because the bedrooms aren't private.

$ **L'Ospite,** a 10-minute walk from Piazza Erbe, has six cozy, immaculate, fully equipped apartments and lots of stairs. The rooms sleep up to four and include air-conditioning, breakfast, use of the washing machine, and weekly housekeeping (or as needed). Kind manager Federica Rossi can also organize excursions around the area or help you get opera tickets (about €35/person, depending on length of stay, monthly rates negotiable, on west side of Ponte Navi bridge, a few steps past San Paolo church on the left at Via XX Settembre #3, tel. 045-803-6994, mobile 329-426-2524, www .lospite.com, info@lospite.com).

Near Piazza Brà

Several fine places are in the quiet streets just off Piazza Brà, within 200 yards of the bus stop. From the square, yellow signs point you to the hotels.

$$$ **Hotel Bologna,** within a half block of the Arena, has 30 bright, classy, and well-maintained rooms; attractive public areas;

and an attached restaurant (Sb-€101, Db-€140, Tb-€175, air-con, Piazzetta Scalette Rubiani 3, tel. 045-800-6830, fax 045-801-0602, www.hotelbologna.vr.it, hotelbologna@tin.it).

$$$ Hotel Giulietta e Romeo, just behind the Arena, is on a quiet side street. Its 30 decent rooms (9 have balconies) are decorated in dark colors, but on the plus side, they have non-smoking rooms and don't take tour groups (Sb-€110, Db-€190, air-con, elevator, Internet access, bike rental-€5/half-day, laundry-€7.50/load, garage-€16/day, Vicolo Tre Marchetti 3, tel. 045-800-3554, fax 045-801-0862, www.giuliettaeromeo.com, info@giuliettaeromeo.com).

$$ Hotel Europa offers sleek, modern comfort. Nearly half of its 46 rooms are non-smoking—a rarity in Italy—and a few rooms have little balconies overlooking the *piazzetta* below (Db-€130, off-season mention this book when you reserve for a discount, air-con, elevator, Via Roma 8, tel. 045-594-744, fax 045-800-1852, www .veronahoteleuropa.com, hoteleuropavr@tiscali.it).

$ Hotel Torcolo offers 19 comfortable, lovingly maintained, non-smoking rooms in a good location near Piazza Brà (Sb-€70, Db-€100, breakfast-€7–12, breakfast is optional except during opera season, air-con, fridge in room, elevator, garage-€8–14/day; standing on Piazza Brà with your back to the gardens and the Arena over your right shoulder, head down the alley to the right of #16 and walk to Vicolo Listone 3; tel. 045-800-7512, fax 045-800-4058, www.hoteltorcolo.it, hoteltorcolo@virgilio.it, well-run by Silvia and Diana).

Between Piazza Brà and Piazza Erbe

$ Locanda Catullo is an inexpensive, quiet, and quirky place deeper in the old town, with 21 good, basic rooms up three flights of stairs. You can only reserve ahead if you're staying for three days or more, and you have to prepay the entire amount by personal check or bank transfer (they'll explain the procedure). This is a hassle, but it's the only cheap hotel in the center (S-€40, D-€55, Db-€65, Qb-€125, no breakfast; left off Via Mazzini onto Via Catullo, down an alley between 1D and 3A at Via Valerio Catullo 1; tel. 045-800-2786, fax 045-596-987, locandacatullo@tiscali.it, a leettle English spoken).

Hostel

$ Villa Francescatti is a good hostel (€13.50–15 beds with breakfast, 6-, 8-, and 10-bed rooms, some family rooms with private bathrooms, €3 extra for non-members, €8 dinners, launderette, Internet access, rooms closed from 9:00–17:00 but reception open all day, 23:30 curfew; bus #73 from train station during the day or #90 at night and Sun to Piazza Isolo stop, walk over the river beyond Ponte Nuovo at Salita Fontana del Ferro 15; tel. 045-590-360, fax 045-800-9127).

EATING

Osteria al Duca has an affordable two-course *menu* (€15) and lots more options. For dessert, try the chocolate salami. Family-run with a lively atmosphere, it's popular—go early (Mon and Wed–Sat 12:00–14:30 & 18:30–22:30, Tue 18:30–22:30 only, closed Sun, Via Arche Scaligere 2, a half block from della Scala family tombs, tel. 045-594-474). Its sister restaurant, **Osteria Giulietta e Romeo,** serves up the same menu a block away with fewer crowds (Tue–Sat 12:15–14:30 & 19:00–22:30, Mon 19:00–22:30 only, closed Sun, Corso Sant'Anastasia 27, tel. 045-800-9177).

Ristorante Sant'Eufemia feels like a splurge, with tuxedoed waiters and an elegant Old World dining room. Let owners Luca and Mamma pamper you as you dine on the freshest grilled seafood or meats prepared *alla Veronese*. Several reasonably priced *menus* (including *coperto* and *servizio*) range from €13 for a *piatto completo* (a full meal in one course) to €32 for a four-course seafood feast. Light eaters could make a whole meal from their great antipasto buffet, which has lots of vegetarian choices (Mon–Sat 12:00–14:30 & 19:00–22:00, closed Sun except July–Aug; find alley directly across from Corso Porta Borsari 27 called Corte S. Gio in Foro, then go through gate at end of the alley; tel. 045-800-6865).

Other good choices include **Ristorante Greppia** for typical *cucina Veronese* (Tue–Sun 12:00–14:30 & 19:00–22:30, closed Mon, Vicolo Samaritana 3, first left off Via Mazzini if you're coming from Piazza Erbe, tel. 045-800-4577) and the pricier, venerable **Bottega del Vino,** renowned for its extensive wine list (Wed–Mon 12:00–15:00 & 19:00–24:00, closed Tue, Via Scudo di Francia 3, second left off Via Mazzini as you're coming from Piazza Erbe, tel. 045-800-4535).

San Matteo Church, a cheaper option, offers self-service and wood-fired pizza by day and full-service meals by night in a renovated church. Look for big, creative salads and regional dishes with market-fresh produce at reasonable prices (Mon–Fri 12:00–14:30 & 19:00–23:00, pizzas until 24:00, open for dinner Sat–Sun in July–Aug only, tel. 045-800-4538). Located at Vicolo del Guasto 4, down a little alleyway between Via Catullo and Porta Borsari.

Osteria le Vecete offers an enjoyable, intimate pub setting. Choose from a dozen or so daily specials of homemade pastas and Veronese specialties, as well as simpler *bruschette* and salads—or select a few of the elaborately dressed *crostini* available in the case at the bar to go with your *vino* (kitchen open daily 12:00–15:00 & 18:30–22:30, but drinks are served between mealtimes and until late; it's buried in an alley between Via Mazzini and Corso Sant'Anastasia: from Piazza Brà, go down Via Mazzini and turn left onto Via Quattro Spade, then right onto Via Pelliciai, restaurant

The Wines of Verona

Wine connoisseurs love the high-quality wines of this area. One of the most common, Valpolicella, has two forms: the red wine Amarone and dessert wine Recioto. To produce Amarone, grapes are partially dried (*passito*) before fermentation, then aged for a minimum of four years in oak casks, resulting in a rich, velvety, full-bodied red. Recioto, which in local dialect means "ears," uses only the grapes from the top of the cluster (so they sort of look like the ears of a face). Since these grapes get the most sun, they mature the fastest and have the highest concentration of sugar. The grapes are dried for months until all moisture has gone out before pressing, and aged for one to three years.

Bardolino, from the vineyards near Verona on Lake Garda, is a light, fruity wine, similar to a French Beaujolais. It's a perfect picnic wine.

Soave, which might be Italy's best-known white wine, goes well with seafood and risotto dishes. While Soave can vary widely in quality, the best are called "Soave Classico" and come from the heart of the region, near the Soave Castle. Soave is sometimes aged in oak casks, giving it a mellow, rounded flavor.

Sample these and many others at the numerous *enoteca*s (wine-tasting bars) or any restaurant around town. The first week of every April, Verona hosts Vinitaly, the most important international convention of domestic and international wines. Vintners vie for prestigious awards for the past year's vintage. Tourists are welcome to attend at the end of the week, and are shuttled to the convention hall from Piazza Brà. Hotels book up months in advance. Check with the TI for more details.

If you're visiting the area in the fall, consider a day trip to nearby Monteforte d'Alpone, east of Verona. The town hosts a fun, raucous wine festival in September—ask at the TI for more information on this and other regional wine festivals.

is about a half block down on your left at #3; tel. 045-594-748).

De Gusto offers an all-you-can-eat €7.50 lunch buffet featuring dozens of fresh salad ingredients, plus soups, pasta salads, roasted veggies, and drinks (water, wine, beer, soda). Supplemental plates of cheese and *salumi* are €4–5, and wine upgrades cost about €2. The à la carte dinners are just as good (Mon–Sat 12:00–14:30 & 19:30–22:30, closed Sun, around the corner from Juliet's balcony at Via Stella 13A, tel. 045-803-0066).

Oreste dal Zovo, run by enthusiastic Oreste and his Chicagoan wife Beverly, is a fun, local wine-and-grappa bar. There's no formal food, but an abundance of fun and hearty bar snacks. This historic *enoteca* was once the private chapel of the archbishop of Verona, and hiding between the bottles are traces of its past—ask Beverly to tell you the story. In addition to the wines, you can pick up high-quality aged balsamic vinegars from Modena and extra-virgin olive oils (March–Dec daily 8:00–20:00, closed Mon Jan–Feb, cash only, no chairs—just a couple of benches; it's on the alley—Vicolo San Marco in Foro 7—off Porta Borsari, just a block from Piazza Erbe; tel. 045-803-4369).

On Piazza Brà: For fast food with a great view of Verona's main square, consider the self-service **Brek** (daily, breakfast and sandwiches from 9:30, full menu 11:30–15:00 & 18:30–22:00, indoor/outdoor seating, cheap salad plates, Piazza Brà 20, right on the square between the historic city gate and the equestrian statue, tel. 045-800-4561). **Enoteca Can Grande** serves great wine (such as the local *Passito Bianco*) and delicious seasonal special-ties thoughtfully paired with wines suggested by Giuliano and Corrina (Tue–Sun 10:00–24:00, always closed Mon, also closed Tue in winter; a block off Piazza Brà at Via dietro Liston 19D—if the equestrian statue jogged slightly right, he'd head straight here; tel. 045-595-022).

Picnic: **PAM supermarket** is just outside the historic gate on Piazza Brà (Mon–Sat 8:00–20:00, Sun 9:00–20:00, exit Piazza Brà through the gate and take the first right).

TRANSPORTATION CONNECTIONS

From Verona by Train to: Florence (4/day, 3 hrs, more with trans-fer in Bologna; note that all Rome-bound trains stop in Florence—listed as *Firenze* on train schedules), **Bologna** (nearly hrly, 2 hrs), **Milan** (hrly, 1.5-2 hrs), **Rome** (4/day, 5–6 hrs, more with transfer in Bologna), **Bolzano** (hrly, 1.5-2 hrs; note that Brennero-bound trains stop in Bolzano).

Parking in Verona: Drivers will find lots of cheap parking at the stadium, as well as cheap long-term parking near the train sta-tion and city walls and across the river from San Zeno. There are a few free spaces across the river from Castelvecchio. The most cen-tral lot is behind the Arena on Piazza Cittadella (guarded, €1/hr). Street parking costs €1.50 per hour (buy ticket at *tabacchi* shop to put on dashboard, spaces marked with blue lines). The town center is closed to regular traffic, but if you're staying here, you can drive to your hotel, and they'll get you permission—ask for details when you book.

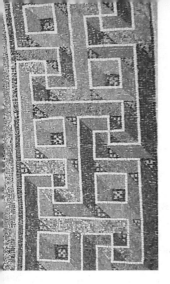

RAVENNA DAY TRIP

Ravenna is on the tourist map for one reason: Its 1,500-year-old churches, decorated with best-in-the-West Byzantine mosaics. Known in Roman times as Classe, the city was an imperial port for the large naval fleet. Briefly a capital of eastern Rome during its fall, Ravenna was taken by the barbarians. Then, in A.D. 540, the Byzantine emperor Justinian turned Ravenna into the westernmost pillar of the Byzantine empire. A pinnacle of civilization in that age, Ravenna was a light in Europe's Dark Ages. Two hundred years later, the Lombards booted the Byzantines out, and Ravenna melted into the backwaters of medieval Italy, staying out of historical sight for a thousand years.

Today the local economy booms with a big chemical industry, the discovery of offshore gas deposits, and the construction of a new ship canal. The bustling town center is Italy's best for bicyclists. Locals go about their business, while busloads of tourists slip quietly in and out of town for the best look at the glories of Byzantium this side of Istanbul.

Ravenna is only a 90-minute detour from the main Venice–Florence train line and worth the effort for those interested in old mosaics. While its sights don't merit an overnight stop, many find that the peaceful charm of this untouristy and classy town makes it a pleasant surprise in their Italian wandering.

ORIENTATION

Central Ravenna is quiet, with a pedestrian-friendly core and more bikes than cars. Keep to the sides of the streets; bikes take the center lane (subtly indicated by white brick paving) down the brick "pedestrian" streets. Listen for the outta-my-way bells.

On a quick visit to Ravenna, I'd see Basilica di San Vitale and its adjacent Mausoleum of Galla Placidia, Basilica di Sant'Apollinare Nuovo, the covered market, and Piazza del Popolo.

Tourist Information: The TI is a 15-minute walk (or a 5-minute pedal) from the train station (April–Sept Mon–Sat 8:30–19:00, Sun 10:00–16:00; Oct–March Mon– Sat 8:30–18:00, Sun 10:00–16:00; Via Salara 8, tel. 0544-35404, www.turismo .ravenna.it). For directions to the TI, see "Orientation Walk," below. Most sights close early in the winter months; pick up a schedule from the TI when you arrive.

Combo-Tickets: There are two combo-tickets for Ravenna; you'll probably want the Visit Card. Many top sights can only be seen by purchasing the €7.50 Visit Card (sold at the sights), since there are no individual admissions to these attractions. This combo-ticket includes admission to the Basilica di San Vitale, the Basilica di Sant'Apollinare Nuovo, Spirito Santo (might be under restoration in 2006), Battistero Neoniano, and Cappella Arcivescovile. From March to mid-June—when school-group tours take over and space is limited—there's a €9.50 version of this combo-ticket that includes the Mausoleum of Galla Placidia; otherwise, the mausoleum is automatically included for free.

A different €5 combo-ticket covers admissions to the National Museum and the Mausoleum of Teodorico. A €6.50 version of this combo-ticket also includes the Church of Sant'Apollinare in Classe. This ticket is only worth buying if you'll be visiting two or more of the following sights, since—unlike with the other combo-ticket mentioned above—you can buy individual admissions to these: National Museum-€4 (Tue–Sun 8:30–19:30, closed Mon, last entry 30 min before closing), Mausoleum of Teodorico-€2 (daily 8:30–19:00, last entry 30 min before closing), and Church of Sant'Apollinare in Classe-€2 (Mon–Sat 8:30–19:30, Sun 13:00–19:30, last entry 30 min before closing).

Helpful Hints

Bike Rental: Yellow bikes are available free from the TI (passport required); the bikes are parked at the TI and other locations around town. Or rent bikes from the Coop San Vitale on Piazza Farini (€1/hour, €7.75/day, Mon–Sat 7:00–20:00, closed Sun, ID required, on the left just as you exit train station, tel. 0544-37031).

Ravenna

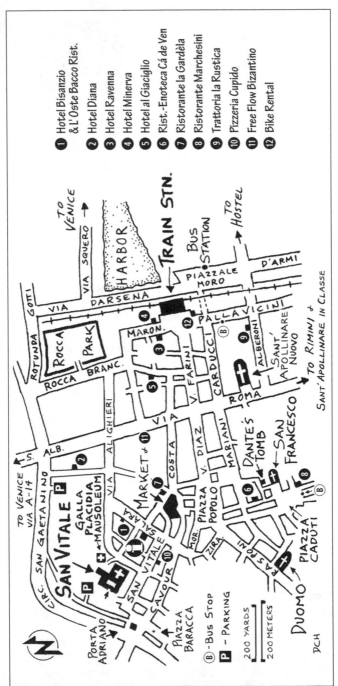

1. Hotel Bisanzio & L'Oste Bacco Rist.
2. Hotel Diana
3. Hotel Ravenna
4. Hotel Minerva
5. Hotel al Giaciglio
6. Rist.-Enoteca Cá de Ven
7. Ristorante la Gardéla
8. Ristorante Marchesini
9. Trattoria la Rustica
10. Pizzeria Cupido
11. Free Flow Bizantino
12. Bike Rental

Local Guide: For a private guide, consider Claudia Frassineti (€85/half day, mobile 335-613-2996, www.abacoguide.it, abacoguide@tiscalinet.it).

Parking: You can park for free in the lot on north end of town just west of Via di Roma, or for €3 during the day and free overnight from 20:00–8:00 at Largo Giustiniano just north of San Vitale.

SIGHTS

Orientation Walk—A visit to Ravenna can be as short as a three-hour loop from the train station. From the station, walk straight down Viale Farini to Piazza del Popolo. This square was built around 1500, during a 60-year period when the city was ruled by Venice. Under the Venetian architecture, the people of Ravenna gather here as they have for centuries.

Most sights are within a few minutes' walk of Piazza del Popolo. A right on Via IV Novembre takes you a block to the colorful covered market, Mercato Coperto (Mon–Sat 7:00–13:00, closed Sun, good for picnic fixings). The TI is a block away (head up Via Cavour and take the first right onto Via Salara 8). Ravenna's two most important sights, Basilica di San Vitale and the Mausoleum of Galla Placidia, are two blocks from Piazza del Popolo (head down San Vitale). A few blocks from Piazza del Popolo in the opposite direction is the Basilica di Sant'Apollinare Nuovo, also worth a look. From there, it's about a 10-minute walk back to the station.

▲▲**Basilica di San Vitale**—Imagine: It's A.D. 540. The city of Rome has been looted, the land is crawling with barbarians, and the infrastructure of Rome's thousand-year empire is crumbling fast. Into this chaotic world comes the emperor of the East (Justinian), bringing order and stability, briefly reassembling the

empire, and making Ravenna a beacon of civilization. His church of San Vitale—standing as a sanctuary of order in the midst of that madness—is covered with lavish mosaics: gold and glass chips the size of your fingernail. It's impressive enough to see a 1,400-year-old church. But rarer is to see one decorated in brilliant mosaics, still managing to convey the intended feeling that "this

peace and stability was brought
to you by your emperor and
God."

In a medieval frame of
mind, study the scene: High
above the altar, God is in
Heaven, portrayed as Christ
sitting on a celestial orb. He
oversees his glorious creation,
symbolized by the four rivers. And running the show
on earth is Justinian (left side), sporting both a halo and a crown
to indicate that he's leader of the Church and the state. Here,
Justinian brings together the military leaders and the church
leaders, all united by the straight line of eyes. The bald bishop of
Ravenna—the only person who was actually here—is portrayed
most realistically.

Facing the emperor (from the right side) is his wife, Theodora,
and her entourage. Decked out in jewels and pearls, the former
dancer, who became Justinian's mistress and then empress, carries
a chalice to consecrate the new church.

The walls and ceilings sparkle with colorful biblical scenes
told with a sixth-century exuberance. This was a time of transi-
tion, and many consider the mosaics of Ravenna to be both the
last ancient Roman and the first medieval European works of art.
For instance, you'll see a beardless Christ (as he was depicted by
ancient Romans) next to a bearded Christ, his standard medieval
portrayal.

The church's octagonal design—clearly Eastern—inspired
the construction of the Hagia Sofia, the mosque-turned-museum
built 10 years later in Constantinople. Charlemagne traveled here
in about A.D. 800. He was so impressed that when he returned to
his capital, Aix-la-Chapelle (present-day Aachen in Germany), he
built a church that many consider to be the first great stone building in northern Europe, modeled after this one (included in €7.50
Visit Card—see above, daily 9:00–19:00, off-season until 16:30,
last entry 15 min before closing, tel. 0544-215-193).

▲▲**Mausoleum of Galla Placidia**—Just across the courtyard
(and included in Basilica di San Vitale admission) is this tiny,
humble-looking mausoleum, with the oldest—and to many the
best—mosaics in Ravenna.

The Mausoleum of Galla Placidia (plah-CHEE-dee-ah) is
reputed to be the burial place of this daughter, sister, and mother of
emperors, who died in A.D. 450. The little light that sneaks through
the thin alabaster panels brings a glow and a twinkle to the early
Christian symbolism that fills the little room. Opposite the door is

St. Lawrence martyred on a fiery grill. He's legendary for mocking his executors, reportedly saying something like "I'm done on this side, you can turn me over now." He was famous as an example of the strength of the feisty early Christians. The four Gospels clearly labeled on the bookshelf were the source of this strength as they were persecuted by the Romans.

The dome is filled with stars. Along with Mark's lion, Luke's ox, and John's eagle, the golden cross rises from the east bringing life to all. Doves drink from fountains, symbolic of souls finding nourishment in the word of God. Cover the light of the door with your hand to see the standard Roman portrayal of Christ—beardless and as the Good Shepherd. Jesus, dressed in gold and purple like a Roman emperor, is King of Paradise—receiving the faithful (represented by lambs). The Eastern influence is apparent in the carpet-like decorative patterns (€9.50 for Visit Card March–mid-June, otherwise included in €7.50 Visit Card, daily 9:00–19:00, off-season until 16:30, last entry 45 before closing, tel. 0544-215-193).

▲▲**Basilica di Sant'Apollinare Nuovo**—This austere sixth-century church, with a typical early-Christian-basilica floor plan, has two huge and wonderfully preserved side panels. One is a procession of haloed virgins, each bringing gifts to the Madonna and the Christ Child. Opposite, Christ is on his throne with four angels, awaiting a solemn procession of 26 martyrs. Ignoring the Baroque altar from a thousand years later, we can clearly see the rectangular Roman hall of justice or basilica plan—which was adopted by churches and used throughout the Middle Ages (included in €7.50 Visit Card, daily April–Sept 9:00–19:00, March and Oct 9:30–17:30, Nov–Feb 10:00–17:00, on Via di Roma, tel. 0544-219-518).

▲**Church of Sant'Apollinare in Classe**—Featuring great Byzantine art, this church is a favorite among mosaic pilgrims (€2, included in upgraded €6.50 combo-ticket—described in "Combo-Tickets," above—with National Museum and Mausoleum of Teodorico, Mon–Sat 8:30–19:30, Sun 13:00–19:30, confirm hours Oct–March, last entry 30 min before closing, tel. 0544-473-661).

The church is two miles out of town. Catch bus #4 or #44 across the street from the train station (on the corner by the park) or from Piazza Caduti (€1, 3/hr, 15 min, reduced service Sun; with your back to the *tabacchi* shop, stop is on the corner; buy bus tickets from any *tabacchi* shop). To head back to town, walk down the same road; the stop is about 100 yards ahead on the right. The **Self-Service Sant'Apollinare in Classe** is a cheap, air-conditioned, and efficient place for lunch right on the church grounds (daily 12:00–15:00, tel. 0544-35679).

Other Sights—The **Basilica di San Francesco** is worth a look for its simple interior and flooded, mosaic-covered crypt below the main altar (daily 7:00–12:00 & 15:00–18:30). Nearby in Via Dante Alighieri, the **Tomb of Dante** is the true site of his remains. After being exiled from Florence for his political beliefs, Dante lived out the rest of his life in Ravenna. The Florentines forgave Dante posthumously and wanted to bring their famous poet's bones home to rest. To protect his relics from theft by the Florentines, Ravenna hid his bones in the neighboring Basilica di San Francesco in 1519. They lay forgotten in the church for three centuries, until they were rediscovered and replaced in his tomb in 1865. The Dante memorial—often mistaken for a tomb—in Florence's Santa Croce Church is empty (daily April–Sept 9:00–19:00, Oct–March 9:00–12:00 & 14:00–17:00).

Overrated Sight—The nearby beach town of Rimini is a crowded mess.

SLEEPING

$$$ Hotel Bisanzio is a business-class splurge in the city center (Sb-€100, Db-€124, larger Db-€170, air-con; from Piazza del Popolo take Via IV Novembre to the Mercato, turn left onto Via Cavour and take the first right, Via Salara 30; tel. 0544-217-111, fax 0544-32539, www.bisanziohotel.com, info@bizanziohotel.com).

$$ Hotel Diana, with 33 bright and tasteful rooms, is a classy, peaceful haven with a restful terrace. Though a bit outside the town center, it's still an easy walk from the Basilica di San Vitale (Sb-€57, Db-€83, fancier rooms available, free Internet access in lobby, free parking nearby, Via G. Rossi 47, tel. 0544-39164, fax 0544-30001, www.hoteldiana.ra.it, info@hoteldiana.ra.it).

$$ Hotel Ravenna, with 24 spanking-clean rooms and double-paned windows, is located across from the train station (S-€40, Sb-€48, D-€55, Db-€90, no breakfast, Viale Maroncelli 12, tel. 0544-212-204, fax 0544-212-077, www.hotelravenna.ra.it, hotelravenna@ravennablu.it).

$$ Hotel Minerva, just to the right of the train station as you exit, has 18 renovated rooms (Sb-€55, Db-€90, breakfast-€6, elevator, air-con, nearby laundry service and Internet access, Viale Maroncelli 1, tel. 0544-213-711, fax 0544-211-420, www.minerva-hotel.com, hotel.minerva@libero.it).

$ Hotel al Giaciglio, also near the station, is recently renovated and a handy choice (S-€40, D-€50, Db-€65, Via R.

Sleep Code

(€1 = about $1.20, country code: 39)
S = Single, **D** = Double/Twin, **T** = Triple, **Q** = Quad, **b** = bathroom, **s** = shower only. Unless otherwise noted, credit cards are accepted, English is spoken, and breakfast is included.

To help you easily sort through these listings, I've divided the rooms into three categories, based on the price for a standard double room with bath:

$$$ **Higher Priced**—Most rooms €100 or more.
$$ **Moderately Priced**—Most rooms between €70–100.
$ **Lower Priced**—Most rooms €100 or less.

Brancaleone 42, tel. & fax 0544-39403, www.albergoalgiaciglio .com, info@albergoalgiaciglio.com).

Hostel: $ Ostello Dante Hostel, a 15-minute walk from the station, has Internet access (with phone card), laundry service, free loaner bikes and bike rentals (€2.50/day), and a game room. There's a long lockout (10:00–17:00), but you can leave your bags if you arrive by noon (110 beds, €13.50/bed, €1 more in winter, 4–5 bed rooms, family rooms-€15/person with baths, €3/night extra for non-Italian members, includes breakfast and sheets, towels-€1, 23:30 curfew, Via Nicolodi 12, tel. & fax 0544-421-164, www .hostelravenna.com, hostelravenna@hotmail.com). From the station, follow signs for *Ostello Dante* or catch bus #1, #10, #11, or #70 from the station and get off at Via Gulli.

EATING

The atmospheric **Ristorante-Enoteca Ca' de Ven** (House of Wine) fills a 16th-century warehouse with locals enjoying quality wine and traditional cuisine. *Piadina* (peeah-DEE-nah) dominates the menu. An unleavened bread that kids are raised on here, it's served with cheese and prosciutto. Try their dessert specialty—*torta di marzipan*—made exclusively for them by a local bakery. This decadent almond-and-cocoa brownie is best with sweet red wine (Tue–Sat 12:00–14:00 & 19:00–22:00, Sun 17:30–22:15, closed Mon, 2-min walk from Piazza del Popolo on Via Cairoli which turns into Via C. Ricci, Via C. Ricci 24, tel. 0544-30163).

Locals like **Ristorante la Gardèla,** which offers reasonable prices and cuisine specialties from Italy's mountainous Emilia-Romagna region. These include *cappelletti in brodo*, a light, meat-stuffed pasta served in broth (Fri–Wed 12:00–14:30 & 19:00–22:00, closed Thu, from Piazza del Popolo follow Via IV Novembre past Piazza della Costa to corner of Via Ponte Marino 3, tel. 0544-217-147). **L'Oste Bacco** is run by the same owners with the same menu (homemade pastas from €5.50–7.50, Wed–Mon 12:15–14:30 & 19:15–22:30, closed Tue, just north of TI at Via Salara 20, tel. 0544-35363).

Ristorante Marchesini has a classy self-serve menu that includes some delicious salads and homemade pastas (Mon–Sat 12:00–14:30, Sat–Sun also 19:30–22:30 only by reservation for a fixed-price *menu*, 5-min walk from Piazza del Popolo, on corner of Piazza Caduti at Via Mazzini 6—ride elevator to first floor, tel. 0544-212-309).

Trattoria La Rustica is also worthwhile, featuring grilled meats and homemade pasta like *capelletti, garganelli,* and *tortelli* (about €20 for a 3-course dinner not including wine, Sat–Thu 12:00–14:30 & 19:00–22:30, closed Fri, located at Via Alberoni 55, tel. 0544-218-128).

Free Flow Bizantino, inside the covered market, is another self-serve place (Mon–Fri 11:45–14:30, for lunch only). Or assemble a picnic at the market and enjoy your feast in the shady gardens of the **Rocca Brancaleone** fortress (daily 8:00–20:00, closes at sunset off-season; 5-min walk from station, following Via Maroncelli until you see the walls).

For a cheap and traditional lunch or snack, try a *piadina* or *cresciolo* (calzone-like) sandwich from **Pizzeria Cupido** just up Via Cavour, past the covered market. These tasty sandwiches (€3–4.50) come stuffed with a variety of meats, cheeses, and vegetables. Try one filled with *squacquerone,* a soft regional cream cheese (daily 8:00–15:00; Mon, Thu, and Sun also open until 20:00; Via Cavour 43—through the archway, tel. 0544-37529).

TRANSPORTATION CONNECTIONS

From Ravenna by Train to: Venice (10/day, sometimes change in Ferrara, Venice's Mestre station as well, 3–4 hrs), **Florence** (about hrly, requires transfer in Bologna, 3 hrs).

VENETIAN HISTORY

CAPSULE HISTORY OF VENICE

A.D. 500–1000: Born in Mud

With Rome's infrastructure crumbling and Italy crawling with barbarians, coastal folk fled to marshy islands in the Adriatic. They sank pilings in the mud in order to build. Fishermen became sea traders.

Sights
- Gondolas and the network of canals
- Old crypt under San Zaccaria Church
- San Moisè Church
- Church on Torcello Island

1000–1500: Medieval Growth and Expansion

Well-located between northern Europe and the eastern Mediterranean, Venetian sea traders established trading outposts in Byzantine and Muslim territories to the east. At home, a stable, constitutional government ran an efficient, state-operated multinational corporation. Grand buildings reflected Venice's wealth.

Sights
- Doge's Palace
- St. Mark's Basilica
- Frari Church
- Buildings decorated in ornate Venetian Gothic style
- Doge paraphernalia and city history at Correr Museum
- Glass and lace industries
- Arsenale shipbuilding complex

1500–1600: Renaissance

Europe's richest city-state poured money into the arts...even as her power was waning. Venice established a reputation as a luxury-loving, exotic, cosmopolitan playground.

Sights
- St. Mark's Square facades and other work by Sansovino
- Palladio's classical facades on churches of San Giorgio Maggiore and Il Redentore
- Titian paintings (Accademia, Frari Church, Doge's Palace, etc.)
- Giovanni Bellini (Accademia, Frari Church, San Zaccaria Church, Correr Museum)
- Giorgione (Accademia)
- Tintoretto (Accademia, Scuola San Rocco, many churches)
- Jewish Ghetto and Jewish Museum

1600–1800: Elegant Decline

New trade routes, new European powers, and belligerent Turks drained Venice's economy and shrank its trading empire. At home, however, Venice's reputation for luxury—and now decadence—still made it a popular tourist destination for Europe's gentry.

Sights

- Ca' Rezzonico (Museum of 18th-Century Venice)
- La Salute Church
- Masks of the Carnevale tradition
- Old cafés (e.g., the Florian and the Quadri)
- La Fenice opera house
- Baroque interiors in many churches
- Canova sculpture (Correr Museum, Frari Church)
- G. B. Tiepolo paintings (Accademia, Doge's Palace, Ca' Rezzonico)
- Paintings of Canaletto, Guardi, and G. D. Tiepolo (Ca' Rezzonico)

1800–2000: Modern Venice

Conquered by Napoleon, then placed under Austrian rule, the Venetians joined Italy's Risorgimento movement, resulting in the unified, democratic nation of Italy. Since little new building was done in the city, Venice remained a museum piece for foreigners—one increasingly threatened by mainland pollution, floods, and hordes of tourists.

Sights

- Correr Museum's Risorgimento wing
- Statue of Daniele Manin
- Motorized *vaporetti* and taxis
- Train station (1954)
- Peggy Guggenheim Collection
- The Biennale International Art Exhibition
- Pollution from the mainland city of Mestre, Burger King

SAILING THE SEVEN SEAS— FROM BIRTH TO UNIFICATION WITH ITALY

In Roman times, people didn't live in the Venetian lagoon. But the region had many important mainland cities. Convoys of Roman ships would connect the major ports of Ravenna and Aquileia (then the fourth-largest Roman city) by navigating a series of lagoons they called "the Seven Seas" (hence the term we use today).

In the fifth century, when Rome fell, barbarian Visigoths and Huns ravaged the farmers of this area. Hoping the barbarians

Roman Numerals

In the U.S., you'll see Roman numerals—which originated in ancient Rome—used for copyright dates, clocks, and the Super Bowl. In Italy, you're likely to observe these numbers chiseled on statues and buildings. If you want to do some numeric detective work, here's how. In Roman numerals, as in ours, the highest numbers (thousands, hundreds) come first, followed by smaller numbers. Many numbers are made by combining numerals into sets: V = 5, so VIII = 8 (5 plus 3). Roman numerals follow a subtraction principle for multiples of fours (4, 40, 400, etc.) and nines (9, 90, 900, etc.); the number four, for example, is written as IV (1 subtracted from 5), rather than IIII. The number nine is IX (1 subtracted from 10).

Rick Steves' Venice 2006—written in Roman numerals—would translate as *Rick Steves' Venice MMVI*. Big numbers such as dates can look daunting at first. The easiest way to handle them is to read the numbers in discrete chunks. For example, Michelangelo was born in MCDLXXV. Break it down: M (1,000) + CD (100 subtracted from 500, or 400) + LXX (50 + 10 + 10, or 70) + V (5) = 1475. It was a very good year.

M = 1000	XL = 40
CM = 900	X = 10
D = 500	IX = 9
CD = 400	V = 5
C = 100	IV = 4
XC = 90	I = duh
L = 50	

didn't like water, the first "Venetians" took refuge in the lagoon. For centuries there was no "Venice" as such...just a series of about a dozen principal refugee settlements in and around the Venetian lagoon.

The lagoon is a delta littered with tiny, muddy islands created by sediment deposited by rivers. As refugees squatted on this wet and miserable land, they kept certain streams from silting, and these streams gradually became canals. A motley collection of about 120 natural islands eventually became Venice.

From the start, these former farmers harvested salt and fish for their livelihood. Later, using the trading savvy gained from the salt-and-fish business, they began trading up the rivers. With the expansion of Byzantium into Italy, there was more East–West trade, and Ravenna became the western capital of a briefly united East and West under Byzantine Emperor Justinian. As Ravenna fell, Venetians filled the void as middlemen, selling goods from the East to consumers in the West.

In the sixth century, another wave of barbarians (the Lombards) plundered the mainland. Attacking cities this time, they sent a new kind of refugee into the lagoon: shopkeepers, clergymen, artisans, and nobles.

Previously, the farmers had subsisted without much need to organize. But with the arrival of aggressive noble families, the lagoon became political. To sort out the squabbles, a local duke, or doge, was elected in 726. This began an 1,100-year period of doge rule, ending only with the arrival of Napoleon in 1797.

The doge needed a capital, and he chose the town of Rialto (the future Venice) for its easy-to-defend position. Over time, the most important trading nobles built their palaces in Rialto to be near the doge.

Because nobles settled on their own little islets, palaces are scattered all over the current city. Eventually, island communities decided to join, or literally "bridge," with others. Building bridges required shoring up the canals. Soon, paved canalside walks appeared. And by the 12th century, the government provided oil and required that streets be lit—a first in Europe.

Since feudalism didn't really work in the lagoon economy, the natural entrepreneurial energy of the nobility created the "noble merchant." Trade, which became the exclusive privilege of the upper classes, grew, thus supporting a larger, wealthier population. Suddenly, people (like both the Byzantine and Holy Roman emperors) were noticing Venice. Charlemagne, the Holy Roman Emperor (c. 800), eyed the region hungrily.

Venetians wanted to keep their freedom, but knew that they would have to choose: Byzantium or the Holy Roman Empire. Byzantium—its capital in far-away Constantinople (now called Istanbul)—was preferable. On a distant fringe of that empire, Venice would be subjugated only in name. Arranging an alignment with Byzantium also involved Church politics.

In about A.D. 800, the bishop who resided in the mainland city of Aquileia, and who was loyal to the Holy Roman Emperor, was given Venice as part of his ecclesiastical domain. This subjected the people of the lagoon to the influence of the Holy Roman Emperor. To avoid this, the Venetians accepted a rival bishop who was loyal to Byzantium.

To legitimize their split with Aquileia, the Venetians of the lagoon decided they needed just the right holy relics. This area had a strong affinity for St. Mark (he traveled here as Peter's translator), the man credited with bringing Christianity to the region. Knowing the power of actually possessing the relics of St. Mark, the Venetians managed to smuggle his remains from Egypt to Rialto in 828. Overnight, it became clear: Venice was a religious power. This underscored Venice as part of the Byzantine Empire,

Noteworthy Residents of Venice

1000–1400

Dandolo, Enrico (r. 1192–1205)—Doge during the Fourth Crusade, when Venetian crusaders looted Constantinople, helping enrich Venice.

Polo, Marco (1254–1324)—Traveler to faraway China whose journal, *The Book of Marvels,* many dismissed as fiction.

Veneziano, Paolo (1310–1358)—Painter who mastered the Byzantine gold-icon style, then added touches of Western realism.

1400s

Foscari, Francesco (1373–1457)—Doge at Venice's peak of power, whose disastrous wars against Milan and Turks started the Republic's slow fade.

Bellini, Jacopo (c. 1400–1470)—Father of painting family. His training in Renaissance Florence brought 3-D realism to Venice.

Bellini, Gentile (c. 1429–1507)—Elder son of painting family, known for straightforward, historical scenes of Venice.

Bellini, Giovanni (c. 1430–1516)—The most famous son in the painting family, whose glowing, colorful, 3-D Madonna-and-Childs started the Venetian Renaissance. Teacher of Titian and Giorgione.

Carpaccio, Vittore (c. 1460–1525)—Painter of realistic, secular scenes.

1500s

Giorgione (c. 1477–1511)—Innovative painter whose moody realism influenced Bellini (his teacher) and Titian (his friend and fellow painter).

Titian (Tiziano Vecellio, 1488–1576)—Premier Venetian Renaissance painter. Master of many styles, from teenage Madonnas to sober state portraits to exuberant mythological scenes to centerfold nudes.

Sansovino, Jacopo (1486–1570)—Renaissance architect who redid the face of Venice (especially St. Mark's Square), introducing sober, classical columns and arches to a city previously full of ornate Gothic.

Palladio, Andrea (1508–1580)—Influential architect whose classical style was much-imitated around the world, resulting in villas, government buildings, and banks that look like Greek temples.

Tintoretto (Jacopo Robusti, c. 1518–1594)—Painter of dramatic religious scenes, using strong 3-D, diagonal compositions, twisting poses, sharp contrast of light and shadow, and bright, "black velvet" colors (late Renaissance/Mannerist style).

Veronese, Paolo (1528–1588)—Painter of big, colorful canvases, capturing the exuberance and luxury of Renaissance Venice.

1600s

Monteverdi, Claudio (1567–1643)—The composer and *maestro di capella* at St. Mark's Basilica who wrote in a budding new medium—opera.

Longhena, Baldassare (1598–1682)—Architect of the Baroque-style La Salute Church.

1700s

Vivaldi, Antonio (1678–1741)—Composer of *Four Seasons* ("Dah dunt-dunt-duh dutta dah-ah-ah").

Canaletto, Antonio (1697–1768)—Painter of photo-realist Venice views.

Guardi, Francesco (1712–1793)   Painter of proto-Impressionist Venice views.

Goldoni, Carlo (1707–1793)—Comic playwright who brought refinement to Commedia dell'Arte buffoonery.

Tiepolo, Giovanni Battista (1696–1770)—Painter of mythological subjects in colorful, Rococo ceilings.

Tiepolo, Giovanni Domenico (1727–1804)—Painter son of the famous Giovanni Battista Tiepolo.

Casanova, Giovanni Giacomo (1725–1798)—Gambler, womanizer, and adventurer whose exaggerated memoirs inspired Romantics.

Canova, Antonio (1757–1822)—Neoclassical sculptor whose polished, white, beautiful statues were especially popular in Napoleon's France.

Da Ponte, Lorenzo (1749–1838)—Mozart's librettist who popularized Venice's sophisticated and decadent high society.

1800s

Manin, Daniele (1804–1857)—Rebel who led Venetian revolt (1848) against the city's Austrian rulers, eventually leading to united, democratic, modern Italy.

1900s

Guggenheim, Peggy (1898–1979)—American-born art collector, gallery owner, and friend of modern art and artists.

saving it from European control. To seal the city's oriental orientation, Venetian leaders had the grand St. Mark's Basilica built in a distinctly Eastern style.

As the home of both the doge and St. Mark, and with its easily defensible position, Venice emerged as a regional powerhouse. The miscellaneous communities in the lagoon coalesced around what is now Venice. Though technically part of the Byzantine Empire, the city was so remote that, in practice, it was virtually free.

Venetian merchants ran a profitable trading triangle: timber from Venice's mainland to Egypt for gold to Byzantium for luxury goods to Venice. As this went round and round, Venice amassed lots of capital, and its merchant fleet grew to be the biggest in the Mediterranean. Back then, a fleet was essentially the same as a navy, making Venice a military power. Cleverly, Venice agreed to defend Byzantine and Crusader ports in return for free-trade privileges. This made the eastern Mediterranean a virtual free-trade zone for a very aggressive Venetian trading community to exploit.

As Venetian nobles grew wealthy, they built lavish palaces. While their mainland counterparts fortified compounds with tall towers, Venetian merchants built palazzos—with a natural lagoon defense—that were luxurious rather than fortified. Palaces in Venice came complete with loading docks, warehouses, and, eventually, chandeliered ballrooms.

Later, Venice expanded its economy beyond trade. Picking up techniques from the East, it established strong local industries. Having mastered the art of making glass, Venice was on the cutting edge of the new science of grinding lenses for eyeglasses and telescopes. Understanding medicine as a chemical rather than an herbal business, the city developed Europe's first real pharmaceutical industry. Making Europe's first cheap paper from rags rather than from sheepskins (parchment) and offering the first patent protection (in 1474), the Venetian paper and printing industry boomed. Already clever at trading products from other countries, now Venice peddled its own stuff...more profitably than ever.

By 1104, Venice was running Europe's first industrial complex, the Arsenale. With more than 1,000 workers using an early form of assembly-line production, the Arsenale could produce about one warship a day. This put the "fear of Venice" into visiting rulers. When France's King Henry III dropped by the Arsenale, Venice entertained him with a shipbuilding spectacle: from ribs to finished product in four hours. Then the ship was completely outfitted before gliding down the exit canal.

With mountains of capital, plenty of traders with ready ships, and a sophisticated system of insurance, joint ventures, and money drafts, Venice's traveling merchants eventually became resident

Venetian History in a Seashell

In the Middle Ages, the Venetians, becoming Europe's clever middlemen for East–West trade, created a great trading empire ruled by a series of doges. By smuggling in the bones of St. Mark (San Marco, A.D. 828), Venice gained religious importance as well. With the discovery of America and new trading routes to the Orient, Venetian power ebbed. But as Venice fell, her appetite for decadence grew. Throughout the 17th and 18th centuries, Venice partied on the wealth accumulated in earlier centuries as a trading power.

merchants and bankers. By the 15th century, Venice was a commercial powerhouse—among the six biggest cities in Europe. Of its estimated 180,000 citizens, nearly 1,000 were of Rockefeller-esque wealth and power.

But Venice's power peaked. With the Ottoman defeat of the Byzantine emperor (messing up established trading partners and patterns), Vasco da Gama's voyage to India (opening up trade routes that skirted Venetian control), the rise of English and Dutch shipping in the Mediterranean, and devastating plagues, Venice began to decline.

When Napoleon rolled into Venice, he brought with him (in theory, at least) the ideals of the French Revolution. In light of French ideas of citizens' rights, the Venetian populace re-evaluated its 1,000-year aristocratic rule, and in 1797, the last doge abdicated. A period of French and Austrian rule lasted until 1866, when Venice joined the kingdom of Italy.

VENICE TIMELINE

A.D. 400–900: Rome Falls, Venice as an Isolated Sanctuary

A.D. 476 The last Roman emperor abdicates. Italy is crawling with "barbarians."

540 Byzantine Emperor Justinian reconquers Italy from the barbarians, briefly re-establishing the Roman Empire, with Ravenna as its capital.

568 Lombards invade northern Italy, driving mainlanders onto sparsely populated islands of the lagoon. The Byzantine Empire in Constantinople gives aid and protection to the refugees.

697 According to legend, the first doge, Pauluccio Anafesto, is elected at Eraclea.

726 The first documented doge, Orso Ipato, begins his rule.

Venice's Place in History

LONDON
• BRUGES
PARIS
• VIENNA
VENICE
GENOA
RAVENNA
PISA
FLORENCE   ROME
GIBRALTAR
CONS-
TANTI-
NOPLE
DCH
LEPANTO
CRETE
BLACK AREA SHOWS VENETIAN
EMPIRE AT ITS PEAK -
THE 15TH CENTURY
TO HOLY LAND
& ALEXANDRIA

800   Charlemagne controls northern Italy.

828   Venice acquires St. Mark's relics from Alexandria.
Possession of the famous relics gives Venice religious
stature, tempering the influence of the Holy Roman
Emperor.

c. 850   Tiny Venice is effectively an independent, self-ruling
country.

1000–1300: Medieval Growth as a Seafaring Trading Power

1063   The current St. Mark's Basilica houses Mark's relics,
after the original church burns down in 976.

1081   Venice sides with Byzantium against overzealous
Norman Crusaders. In return, Byzantium grants free
trade throughout the empire to Venetians.

c. 1150   Constitutional limits are placed on the doges. The
Republic is ruled by an oligarchy of wealthy families.

1204   During the Fourth Crusade, Venetian troops join
other Crusaders in attacking and looting Christian
Constantinople (partly to retaliate against Byzantine

harassment of Venetian merchants). The booty boosts Venice further.

1261 Venice's seafaring rival, Genoa, helps the Byzantines retake Constantinople. Genoa is rewarded with trading rights in the Byzantine Empire, thus sparking a century of war over markets with Venice.

1300–1400: Peak of Power

c. 1300 To avoid political coups d'état, the Venetian Senate sets constitutional limits restricting political power to only established (read: wealthy) families.

1381 Venetian ships rout Genoa's fleet at Chioggia (on the south end of the lagoon). Venice rules the waves and the sea-trade of the eastern Mediterranean.

c. 1420 After military victories in northern Italy, Venice is at the height of its power, with mainland possessions and a powerful overseas trading empire to the east. As the Turks rise in the East, a period of conflict begins, which lasts off and on until 1718.

1400–1500: Turks to the East + Jealous Enemies to the West = War

1423 Doge Francesco Foscari starts disastrous, money-draining wars against Milan. Fending off challenges from other trading rivals such as Pisa and Amalfi takes a toll. Meanwhile, the Turks chip away at Venice's trading cities on the eastern front.

1453 The Turks take Constantinople. Venice suffers major losses in its eastern markets.

1454 Venice finally makes peace with Milan. Other European powers join to prey on a weakened Venice.

1492 Columbus sails the ocean blue, heading west through the Straits of Gibraltar and establishing trade in a World that's New.

1498 Vasco da Gama circles around Africa's Cape of Good Hope, finding a new sea-trade route to eastern markets. Venice's sea-trade monopoly is threatened.

1500–Present: Venice's Slow Fade

c. 1500 Though waning in power, Venice is a Renaissance cultural capital as home to Titian, Tintoretto, Sansovino, Palladio, and others.

1509 Pig pile on Venice—a European alliance of the pope, northern Italians, and northern Europeans defeat Venice at Agnadello. Meanwhile, the Turks keep pecking away in the east.

1571   At the Battle of Lepanto, Venice and European allies score a temporary victory over the Turks. Unfortunately, it's only a moral victory, as Venice's navy suffers major damage, and the city loses more trading rights. Spain, England, and Holland, with their oceangoing vessels, emerge as superior traders in a more global economy.

1669   Crete, the last major Venetian outpost, falls to the Turks.

1718   The Turks drive Venetians from southern Greece. Venice's once-great trading empire in the eastern Mediterranean is over.

1797   Napoleon invades Venice and deposes the last doge.

1815   After the Battle of Waterloo, Europe's kings put Venice under Austrian rule. Young aristocrats visit Venice on the Grand Tour; British culture dominates.

1846   A two-mile railroad causeway links Venice to the mainland.

1848   Daniele Manin, an influential lawyer, briefly establishes an independent, democratic Venetian Republic, but the revolution is soon crushed by Austrian troops.

1866   After Prussia defeats Austria, Venice is freed to join the new, modern, democratic kingdom of Italy.

1932   A highway running parallel to the causeway is built, bringing cars to Venice's edge.

c. 1950   Unbridled industrialization on the mainland produces pollution (sulfuric acid) and threatens Venice's stone monuments.

1966   Venice suffers a disastrous flood.

c. 1985   Plans are made to control flooding with a sea barrier, but no building is undertaken.

2006   You arrive in Venice to add to the city's illustrious history.

APPENDIX

Let's Talk Telephones

Here's a primer on making phone calls. For information specific to Italy, see "Telephones" in the Introduction.

Making Calls within a European Country: About half of all European countries use area codes; the other half use a direct-dial system without area codes.

To make calls within a country that uses a direct-dial telephone system (Italy, Belgium, the Czech Republic, Denmark, France, Portugal, Norway, Spain, and Switzerland), you dial the same number whether you're calling across the country or across the street.

In countries that use area codes (such as Austria, Britain, Croatia, Finland, Germany, Hungary, Ireland, the Netherlands, Poland, Slovakia, Slovenia, and Sweden), you dial the local number when calling within a city, and you add the area code if calling long distance within the country.

Making International Calls: Always start with the international access code (011 if you're calling from the U.S. or Canada, or 00 from Europe), then dial the country code of the country you're calling (see chart below).

What you dial next depends on the phone system of the country you're calling. If the country uses area codes, drop the initial zero of the area code, then dial the rest of the number.

Countries that use direct-dial systems (no area codes) vary in how they're accessed internationally by phone. For instance, if you're making an international call to Italy, The Czech Republic, Denmark, Norway, Portugal, or Spain, simply dial the international access code, country code, and phone number. But if you're calling Belgium, France, or Switzerland, drop the initial zero of the phone number.

European Calling Chart

Just smile and dial, using this key:
AC = Area Code, LN = Local Number.

European Country	Calling long distance within ...	Calling from the U.S.A./ Canada to ...	Calling from a European country to ...
Austria	AC + LN	011 + 43 + AC (without the initial zero) + LN	00 + 43 + AC (without the initial zero) + LN
Belgium	LN	011 + 32 + LN (without initial zero)	00 + 32 + LN (without initial zero)
Britain	AC + LN	011 + 44 + AC (without initial zero) + LN	00 + 44 + AC (without initial zero) + LN
Croatia	AC + LN	011 + 385 + AC (without initial zero) + LN	00 + 385 + AC (without initial zero) + LN
Czech Republic	LN	011 + 420 + LN	00 + 420 + LN
Denmark	LN	011 + 45 + LN	00 + 45 + LN
Finland	AC + LN	011 + 358 + AC (without initial zero) + LN	00 + 358 + AC (without initial zero) + LN
France	LN	011 + 33 + LN (without initial zero)	00 + 33 + LN (without initial zero)
Germany	AC + LN	011 + 49 + AC (without initial zero) + LN	00 + 49 + AC (without initial zero) + LN
Greece	LN	011 + 30 + LN	00 + 30 + LN
Hungary	06 + AC + LN	011 + 36 + AC + LN	00 + 36 + AC + LN
Ireland	AC + LN	011 + 353 + AC (without initial zero) + LN	00 + 353 + AC (without initial zero) + LN
Italy	LN	011 + 39 + LN	00 + 39 + LN
Netherlands	AC + LN	011 + 31 + AC (without initial zero) + LN	00 + 31 + AC (without initial zero) + LN

European Country	Calling long distance within ...	Calling from the U.S.A./ Canada to ...	Calling from a European country to ...
Norway	LN	011 + 47 + LN	00 + 47 + LN
Poland	AC + LN	011 + 48 + AC (without initial zero) + LN	00 + 48 + AC (without initial zero) + LN
Portugal	LN	011 + 351 + LN	00 + 351 + LN
Slovakia	AC + LN	011 + 421 + AC (without initial zero) + LN	00 + 421 + AC (without initial zero) + LN
Slovenia	AC + LN	011 + 386 + AC (without initial zero) + LN	00 + 386 + AC (without initial zero) + LN
Spain	LN	011 + 34 + LN	00 + 34 + LN
Sweden	AC + LN	011 + 46 + AC (without initial zero) + LN	00 + 46 + AC (without initial zero) + LN
Switzerland	LN	011 + 41 + LN (without initial zero)	00 + 41 + LN (without initial zero)
Turkey	AC (if no initial zero is included, add one) + LN	011 + 90 + AC (without initial zero) + LN	00 + 90 + AC (without initial zero) + LN

- The instructions above apply whether you're calling a fixed phone or mobile phone
- The international access codes (the first numbers you dial when making an international call) are 011 if you're calling from the U.S.A./Canada, or 00 if you're calling from anywhere in Europe.
- To call the U.S.A. or Canada from Europe, dial 00, then 1 (the country code for the U.S.A. and Canada), then the area code and number. In short, 00 + 1 + AC + LN = Hi, Mom!

Country Codes

After you've dialed the international access code (00 if you're calling from Europe, 011 if calling from the U.S. or Canada), dial the code of the country you're calling.

Austria—43	Italy—39
Belgium—32	Morocco—212
Britain—44	Netherlands—31
Canada—1	Norway—47
Croatia—385	Poland—48
Czech Rep.—420	Portugal—351
Denmark—45	Slovakia—421
Estonia—372	Slovenia—386
Finland—358	Spain—34
France—33	Sweden—46
Germany—49	Switzerland—41
Gibraltar—350	Turkey—90
Greece—30	U.S.A.—1
Ireland—353	

Useful Italian Phone Numbers

Emergency (English-speaking police help): 113
Emergency (military police): 112
Road Service: 116
Directory Assistance (for €0.50, an Italian-speaking robot gives the number twice, very clearly): 12
Telephone help (in English; free directory assistance): 170

Festivals in Venice

Venice's most famous festival is **Carnevale,** the celebration Americans call Mardi Gras (Feb 17–28 in 2006, www.carnevale. venezia.it). Carnevale, which means "farewell to meat," originated centuries ago as a wild two-month-long party leading up to the austerity of Lent. In Carnevale's heyday—the 1600s and 1700s—you could do pretty much anything with anybody from any social class if you were wearing a mask. These days it's a tamer 10-day celebration, culminating in a huge dance lit with fireworks on St. Mark's Square. Sporting masks and costumes, Venetians from kids to businessmen join in the fun. Drawing the biggest crowds of the year, Carnevale has nearly been a victim of its own success, driving away many Venetians (who skip out on the craziness to go skiing in the Dolomites).

Every odd year (next in 2007), the city hosts the **Venice Biennale International Art Exhibition,** a world-class contemporary art fair spread over the Arsenale and sprawling Castello Gardens. Artists representing 65 nations from around the world offer the latest in contemporary art forms: video, computer art, performance art, and digital photography, along with painting and sculpture (generally June–Oct; vaporetto stop: Giardini/Biennale; for details, see page 45 and www.labiennale.org).

Other typically Venetian festival days filling the city's hotels with visitors and its canals with decked-out boats are: **Feast of the Ascension Day** (May 25), **Feast and Regatta of the Redeemer** (July 16), and the **Historical Regatta** (old-time boats and pageantry, Sept 3). Smaller regattas include the **Murano Regatta** (July 3) and the **Burano Regatta** (September 17).

Venice's patron saint, **St. Mark,** is commemorated every April 25. Venetian men celebrate the day by presenting roses to the women in their lives (mothers, wives, and lovers).

Every November 21 is the **Feast of Our Lady of Good Health.** On this local "Thanksgiving," a bridge is built over the Grand Canal so that the city can pile into La Salute Church and remember how Venice survived the gruesome plague of 1630. On this day, Venetians eat smoked lamb from Dalmatia (which was the cargo of the first ship admitted when the plague lifted).

Venice is always busy with special musical and artistic events. The free monthly *Un Ospite di Venezia* lists all the latest in English (free at TI or from fancy hotels). For a comprehensive list of festivals, contact the Italian tourist information office in the United States (see page 6) and visit www.turismovenezia.it.

National Holidays in Italy

These national holidays (when many sights close) are observed throughout Italy. Note that this isn't a complete list; holidays strike without warning.

Jan 1: New Year's Day
Jan 6: Epiphany
April 16: Easter Sunday (2006)
April 17: Easter Monday (2006)
April 25: Liberation Day, St. Mark's Day (Venetian patron saint)
May 1: Labor Day
May 25: Ascension Day
June 2: Anniversary of the Republic
Aug 15: Assumption of Mary
Nov 1: All Saints' Day
Nov 21: Feast of Our Lady of Good Health
Dec 8: Feast of the Immaculate Conception
Dec 25: Christmas
Dec 26: St. Stephen's Day

2006

JANUARY

S	M	T	W	T	F	S
1	2	3	4	5	6	7
8	9	10	11	12	13	14
15	16	17	18	19	20	21
22	23	24	25	26	27	28
29	30	31				

FEBRUARY

S	M	T	W	T	F	S
			1	2	3	4
5	6	7	8	9	10	11
12	13	14	15	16	17	18
19	20	21	22	23	24	25
26	27	28				

MARCH

S	M	T	W	T	F	S
			1	2	3	4
5	6	7	8	9	10	11
12	13	14	15	16	17	18
19	20	21	22	23	24	25
26	27	28	29	30	31	

APRIL

S	M	T	W	T	F	S
						1
2	3	4	5	6	7	8
9	10	11	12	13	14	15
16	17	18	19	20	21	22
23/30	24	25	26	27	28	29

MAY

S	M	T	W	T	F	S
	1	2	3	4	5	6
7	8	9	10	11	12	13
14	15	16	17	18	19	20
21	22	23	24	25	26	27
28	29	30	31			

JUNE

S	M	T	W	T	F	S
				1	2	3
4	5	6	7	8	9	10
11	12	13	14	15	16	17
18	19	20	21	22	23	24
25	26	27	28	29	30	

JULY

S	M	T	W	T	F	S
						1
2	3	4	5	6	7	8
9	10	11	12	13	14	15
16	17	18	19	20	21	22
23/30	24/31	25	26	27	28	29

AUGUST

S	M	T	W	T	F	S
		1	2	3	4	5
6	7	8	9	10	11	12
13	14	15	16	17	18	19
20	21	22	23	24	25	26
27	28	29	30	31		

SEPTEMBER

S	M	T	W	T	F	S
					1	2
3	4	5	6	7	8	9
10	11	12	13	14	15	16
17	18	19	20	21	22	23
24	25	26	27	28	29	30

OCTOBER

S	M	T	W	T	F	S
1	2	3	4	5	6	7
8	9	10	11	12	13	14
15	16	17	18	19	20	21
22	23	24	25	26	27	28
29	30	31				

NOVEMBER

S	M	T	W	T	F	S
			1	2	3	4
5	6	7	8	9	10	11
12	13	14	15	16	17	18
19	20	21	22	23	24	25
26	27	28	29	30		

DECEMBER

S	M	T	W	T	F	S
					1	2
3	4	5	6	7	8	9
10	11	12	13	14	15	16
17	18	19	20	21	22	23
24/31	25	26	27	28	29	30

Numbers and Stumblers

- Europeans write a few of their numbers differently than we do. 1 = 1, 4 = 4, 7 = 7. Learn the difference or miss your train.
- In Europe, dates appear as day/month/year, so Christmas is 25/12/06.
- Commas are decimal points and decimal points are commas. A dollar and a half is 1,50 and there are 5.280 feet in a mile.
- When pointing, use your whole hand, palm down.
- When counting with fingers, start with your thumb. If you hold up your first finger to request one item, you'll probably get two.
- What Americans call the second floor of a building is the first floor in Europe.
- Europeans keep the left "lane" open for passing on escalators and moving sidewalks. Keep to the right.

Metric Conversion (approximate)

1 inch = 25 millimeters	32 degrees F = 0 degrees C
1 foot = 0.3 meter	82 degrees F = about 28 degrees C
1 yard = 0.9 meter	1 ounce = 28 grams
1 mile = 1.6 kilometers	1 kilogram = 2.2 pounds
1 centimeter = 0.4 inch	1 quart = 0.95 liter
1 meter = 39.4 inches	1 square yard = 0.8 square meter
1 kilometer = 0.62 mile	1 acre = 0.4 hectare

Converting Temperatures: Fahrenheit and Celsius

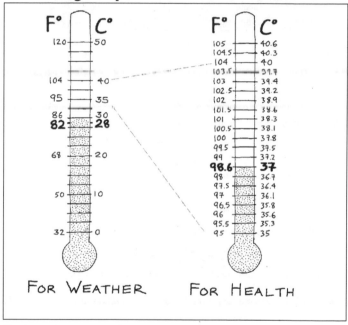

FOR WEATHER   FOR HEALTH

Europe takes its temperature using the Celsius scale, while we opt for Fahrenheit. For weather, remember that 28°C is 82°F—perfect. For health, 37°C is just right.

Venice's Climate Chart

First line, average daily low; second line, average daily high; third line, days of no rain.

J	F	M	A	M	J	J	A	S	O	N	D
33°	35°	41°	49°	56°	63°	66°	65°	61°	53°	44°	37°
42°	46°	53°	62°	70°	76°	81°	80°	75°	65°	53°	46°
25	21	24	21	23	22	24	24	25	24	21	23

Making Your Hotel Reservation

Most hotel managers know basic "hotel English." Faxing or e-mailing are the preferred methods for reserving a room. They're more accurate than telephoning and much faster than writing a letter. Use this handy form for your fax or find it online at www.ricksteves.com/reservation. Photocopy and fax away.

One-Page Fax

To: _____ @ _____
            hotel   *fax*

From: _____@ _____
            name   *fax*

Today's date: _____/_____ /_____
                    day   *month*   *year*

Dear Hotel _____ ,
Please make this reservation for me:

Name: _____

Total # of people:_____ # of rooms: _____ # of nights: _____

Arriving: _____ /_____ /_____   My time of arrival (24-hr clock): _____
            day   *month*   *year*   (I will telephone if I will be late)

Departing:_____ /_____/_____
            day   *month*   *year*

Room(s): Single _____Double _____Twin _____Triple _____ Quad_____

With: Toilet _____ Shower_____Bath _____ Sink only _____

Special needs: View_____ Quiet _____ Cheapest _____ Ground Floor _____

Please fax, mail, or e-mail confirmation of my reservation, along with the type of room reserved and the price. Please also inform me of your cancellation policy. After I hear from you, I will quickly send my credit-card information as a deposit to hold the room. Thank you.

_____
Signature

_____
Name

_____
Address

_____
City   *State*   *Zip Code*   *Country*

_____
E-mail Address

Italian Survival Phrases

Good day.	**Buon giorno.**	bwohn JOR-noh
Do you speak English?	**Parla inglese?**	PAR-lah een-GLAY-zay
Yes. / No.	**Sì. / No.**	see / noh
I (don't) understand.	**(Non) capisco.**	(nohn) kah-PEES-koh
Please.	**Per favore.**	pehr fah-VOH-ray
Thank you.	**Grazie.**	GRAHT-seeay
I'm sorry.	**Mi dispiace.**	mee dee-speeAH-chay
Excuse me.	**Mi scusi.**	mee SKOO-zee
(No) problem.	**(Non) c'è un problema.**	(nohn) cheh oon proh-BLAY-mah
Good.	**Va bene.**	vah BEHN-ay
Goodbye.	**Arrivederci.**	ah-ree-vay-DEHR-chee
one / two	**uno / due**	OO-noh / DOO-ay
three / four	**tre / quattro**	tray / KWAH-troh
five / six	**cinque / sei**	CHEENG-kway / SEHee
seven / eight	**sette / otto**	SEHT-tay / OT-toh
nine / ten	**nove / dieci**	NOV-ay / deeAY-chee
How much is it?	**Quanto costa?**	KWAHN-toh KOS-tah
Write it?	**Me lo scrive?**	may loh SKREE-vay
Is it free?	**È gratis?**	eh GRAH-tees
Is it included?	**È incluso?**	eh oon KLOO-zoh
Where can I buy / find...?	**Dove posso comprare / trovare...?**	DOH-vay POS-soh kohm-PRAH-ray / troh-VAH-ray
I'd like / We'd like...	**Vorrei / Vorremmo...**	vor-REHee / vor-RAY-moh
...a room.	**...una camera.**	OO-nah KAH-meh-rah
...a ticket to ___.	**...un biglietto per ___.**	oon beel-YEHT-toh pehr
Is it possible?	**È possibile?**	eh poh-SEE-bee-lay
Where is...?	**Dov'è...?**	DOH-veh
...the train station	**...la stazione**	lah staht-seeOH-nay
...the bus station	**...la stazione degli autobus**	lah staht-seeOH-nay DAYL-yee OW-toh-boos
...tourist information	**...informazioni per turisti**	een-for-maht-seeOH-nee pehr too-REE-stee
...the toilet	**...la toilette**	lah twah-LEHT-tay
men	**uomini, signori**	WOH-mee-nee, seen-YOH-ree
women	**donne, signore**	DON-nay, seen-YOH-ray
left / right	**sinistra / destra**	see-NEE-strah / DEHS-trah
straight	**sempre diritto**	SEHM-pray dee-REE-toh
When do you open / close?	**A che ora aprite / chiudete?**	ah kay OH-rah ah-PREE-tay / keeoo-DAY-tay
At what time?	**A che ora?**	ah kay OH-rah
Just a moment.	**Un momento.**	oon moh-MAYN-toh
now / soon / later	**adesso / presto / tardi**	ah-DEHS-soh / PREHS-toh / TAR-dee
today / tomorrow	**oggi / domani**	OH-jee / doh-MAH-nee

In the Restaurant

I'd like...	**Vorrei...**	vor-REHee
We'd like...	**Vorremmo...**	vor-RAY-moh
...to reserve...	**...prenotare...**	pray-noh-TAH-ray
...a table for one / two.	**...un tavolo per uno / due.**	oon TAH-voh-loh pehr OO-noh / DOO-ay
Non-smoking.	**Non fumare.**	nohn foo-MAH-ray
Is this seat free?	**È libero questo posto?**	eh LEE-bay-roh KWEHS-toh POH-stoh
The menu (in English), please.	**Il menù (in inglese), per favore.**	eel may-NOO (een een-GLAY-zay) pehr fah-VOH-ray
service (not) included	**servizio (non) incluso**	sehr-VEET-seeoh (nohn) een-KLOO-zoh
cover charge	**pane e coperto**	PAH-nay ay koh-PEHR-toh
to go	**da portar via**	dah POR-tar VEE-ah
with / without	**con / senza**	kohn / SEHN-sah
and / or	**e / o**	ay / oh
menu (of the day)	**menù (del giorno)**	may-NOO (dayl JOR-noh)
specialty of the house	**specialità della casa**	spay-chah-lee-TAH DEHL-lah KAH-zah
first course (pasta, soup)	**primo piatto**	PREE-moh peeAH-toh
main course (meat, fish)	**secondo piatto**	say-KOHN-doh peeAH-toh
side dishes	**contorni**	kohn-TOR-nee
bread	**pane**	PAH-nay
cheese	**formaggio**	for-MAH-joh
sandwich	**panino**	pah-NEE-noh
soup	**minestra, zuppa**	mee-NEHS-trah, TSOO-pah
salad	**insalata**	een-sah-LAH-tah
meat	**carne**	KAR-nay
chicken	**pollo**	POH-loh
fish	**pesce**	PEH-shay
seafood	**frutti di mare**	FROO-tee dee MAH-ray
fruit / vegetables	**frutta / legumi**	FROO-tah / lay-GOO-mee
dessert	**dolci**	DOHL-chee
tap water	**acqua del rubinetto**	AH-kwah dayl roo-bee-NAY-toh
mineral water	**acqua minerale**	AH-kwah mee-nay-RAH-lay
milk	**latte**	LAH-tay
(orange) juice	**succo (d'arancia)**	SOO-koh (dah-RAHN-chah)
coffee / tea	**caffè / tè**	kah-FEH / teh
wine	**vino**	VEE-noh
red / white	**rosso / bianco**	ROH-soh / beeAHN-koh
glass / bottle	**bicchiere / bottiglia**	bee-keeAY-ray / boh-TEEL-yah
beer	**birra**	BEE-rah
Cheers!	**Cin cin!**	cheen cheen
More. / Another.	**Ancora un po.' / Un altro.**	ahn-KOH-rah oon poh / oon AHL-troh
The same.	**Lo stesso.**	loh STEHS-soh
The bill, please.	**Il conto, per favore.**	eel KOHN-toh pehr fah-VOH-ray
tip	**mancia**	MAHN-chah
Delicious!	**Delizioso!**	day-leet-seeOH-zoh

For hundreds more pages of survival phrases for your trip to Italy, check out *Rick Steves' Italian Phrase Book & Dictionary* or *Rick Steves' French, Italian, and German Phrase Book*.

INDEX

RESEARCHERS

To annually update his four books on Italy, Rick relies on the help of these *fantastica* researchers:

AMANDA SCOTESE

Amanda Scotese freelances as a journalist and editor in San Francisco. Her travels in Italy include a stint selling leather jackets in Florence's San Lorenzo Market, basking in the Sicilian sun, and of course, helping out with Rick Steves' guidebooks and tours.

HEIDI SEWELL

Heidi Sewell lived in Italy for two years, learning to speak Italian and roll her own pasta. When she's not leading tours and scouring the Italian Peninsula for Back Doors worthy of Rick Steves' guidebooks, she resides in Seattle with her husband Ragen.

Start your trip at
www.ricksteves.com

Rick Steves' website is packed with over 3,000 pages of timely travel information. It's also your gateway to getting FREE monthly travel news from Rick—and more!

Free Monthly European Travel News

Fresh articles on Europe's most interesting destinations and happenings. Rick will even send you an e-mail every month (often direct from Europe) with his latest discoveries!

Timely Travel Tips

Rick Steves' best money-and-stress-saving tips on trip planning, packing, transportation, hotels, health, safety, finances, hurdling the language barrier...and more.

Travelers' Graffiti Wall

Candid advice and opinions from thousands of travelers on everything listed above, plus whatever topics are hot at the moment (discount flights, packing tips, scams...you name it).

Rick's Annual Guide to European Railpasses

The clearest, most comprehensive guide to the confusing array of railpass options out there, and how to choo-choose the railpass that best fits your itinerary and budget. Then you can order your railpass (and get a bunch of great freebies) online from us!

Great Gear at the Rick Steves Travel Store

Enjoy bargains on Rick's guidebooks, planning maps and TV series DVDs—and on his custom-designed carry-on bags, wheeled bags, day bags and light-packing accessories.

Rick Steves Tours

Every year more than 6,000 lucky travelers explore Europe on a Rick Steves tour. Learn more about our 30 different one-to-three-week itineraries, read uncensored feedback from our tour alums, and sign up for your dream trip online!

Rick on Radio and TV

Read the scripts and run clips from public television's "Rick Steves' Europe" and public radio's "Travel with Rick Steves."

Respect for Your Privacy

Ordering online from us is secure. When you buy something from us, join a tour, or subscribe to Rick's free monthly travel news e-mails, we promise to never share your name, information, or e-mail address with anyone else. You won't be spammed!

Have fun raising your Travel I.Q. at
www.ricksteves.com

Travel smart...carry on!

The latest generation of Rick Steves' carry-on travel bags is easily the best— benefiting from two decades of on-the-road attention to what really matters: maximum quality and strength; practical, flexible features; and no unnecessary frills. You won't find a better value anywhere!

Convertible, expandable, and carry-on-size:
Rick Steves' Back Door Bag $99

This is the same bag that Rick Steves lives out of for three months every summer. It's made of rugged water-resistant 1000 denier Cordura nylon, and best of all, it converts easily from a smart-looking suitcase to a handy backpack with comfortably-curved shoulder straps and a padded waistbelt.

This roomy, versatile 9" x 21" x 14" bag has a large 2600 cubic-inch main compartment, plus three outside pockets (small, medium and huge) that are perfect for often-used items. And the cinch-tight compression straps will keep your load compact and close to your back—not sagging like a sack of potatoes.

Wishing you had even more room to bring home souvenirs? Pull open the full-perimeter expando-zipper and its capacity jumps from 2600 to 3000 cubic inches. When you want to use it as a suitcase or check it as luggage (required when "expanded"), the straps and belt hide away in a zippered compartment in the back.

Attention travelers under 5'4" tall: This bag also comes in an inch-shorter version, for a compact-friendlier fit between the waistbelt and shoulder straps.

Convenient, expandable, and carry-on-size:
Rick Steves' Wheeled Bag $129

At 9" x 21" x 14" our sturdy Rick Steves' Wheeled Bag is rucksack-soft in front, but the rest is lined with a hard ABS-lexan shell to give maximum protection to your belongings. We've spared no expense on moving parts, splurging on an extra-long button-release handle and big, tough inline skate wheels for easy rolling on rough surfaces.

Wishing you had even more room to bring home souvenirs? Pull open the full-perimeter expando-zipper and its capacity jumps from 2600 to 3000 cubic inches.

Rick Steves' Wheeled Bag has exactly the same three-outside-pocket configuration as our Back Door Bag, plus a handy "add-a-bag" strap and full lining.

Our Back Door Bags and Wheeled Bags come in black, navy, blue spruce, evergreen and merlot.

For great deals on a wide selection of travel goodies, begin your next trip at the Rick Steves Travel Store!

Visit the Rick Steves Travel Store at
www.ricksteves.com

FREE-SPIRITED TOURS FROM

Rick Steves

Small Groups
Great Guides
No Grumps

Best of Europe ▪ Eastern Europe
Italy ▪ Village Italy ▪ South Italy
France ▪ Britain ▪ Ireland
Heart of France ▪ South of France
Turkey ▪ Spain/Portugal
Germany/Austria/Switzerland
Scandinavia ▪ London ▪ Paris ▪ Rome
Venice ▪ Florence…and much more!

Looking for a one, two, or three-week tour that's run in the Rick Steves style? Check out Rick Steves' educational, experiential tours of Europe.

Rick's tours are an excellent value compared to "mainstream" tours. Here's a taste of what you'll get…

- **Small groups:** With just 24-28 travelers, you'll go where typical groups of 40-50 can only dream.

- **Big buses:** You'll travel in a full-size 40-50 seat bus, with plenty of empty seats for you to spread out and be comfortable.

- **Great guides:** Our guides are hand-picked by Rick Steves for their wealth of knowledge and giddy enthusiasm for Europe.

- **No tips or kickbacks:** To keep your guide and driver 100% focused on giving you the best travel experience, we pay them well—and prohibit them from accepting tips and merchant kickbacks.

- **All sightseeing:** Your tour price includes all group sightseeing, with no hidden extra charges.

- **Central hotels:** You'll stay in Rick's favorite small, characteristic, locally-run hotels in the center of each city, within walking distance of the sights you came to see.

- **Visit www.ricksteves.com:** You'll find all our latest itineraries, dates and prices, be able to reserve online, and request a free copy of our "Rick Steves Tour Experience" DVD!

Rick Steves' Europe Through the Back Door, Inc.
130 Fourth Avenue North, PO Box 2009, Edmonds, WA 98020 USA
Phone: (425) 771-8303 ▪ Fax: (425) 771-0833 ▪ www.ricksteves.com

Rick Steves

*More **Savvy**. More **Surprising**. More **Fun**.*

COUNTRY GUIDES 2006

England
France
Germany & Austria
Great Britain
Ireland
Italy
Portugal
Scandinavia
Spain
Switzerland

CITY GUIDES 2006

Amsterdam, Bruges & Brussels
Florence & Tuscany
London
Paris
Prague & The Czech Republic
Provence & The French Riviera
Rome
Venice

BEST OF GUIDES

Best of Eastern Europe
Best of Europe

As the #1 authority on European travel, Rick gives you inside information on what to visit, where to stay, and how to get there—economically and hassle-free.

www.ricksteves.com

PHRASE BOOKS & DICTIONARIES

French
French, Italian & German
German
Italian
Portuguese
Spanish

MORE EUROPE FROM RICK STEVES

Easy Access Europe
Europe 101
Europe Through the Back Door
Postcards from Europe

RICK STEVES' EUROPE DVDs

All 43 Shows 2000-2005
Britain
Eastern Europe
France & Benelux
Germany, The Swiss Alps & Travel Skills
Ireland
Italy
Spain & Portugal

PLANNING MAPS

Britain & Ireland
Europe
France
Germany, Austria & Switzerland
Italy
Spain & Portugal

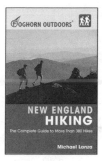

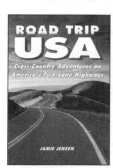

For a complete list of Rick Steves' guidebooks, see page 6.

Avalon Travel Publishing
1400 65th Street, Suite 250
Emeryville, CA 94608

AVALON
publishing group incorporated

Avalon Travel Publishing is an Imprint of Avalon Publishing Group, Inc.

Text © 2005 by Rick Steves
Maps © 2005 by Europe Through the Back Door

Printed in the United States of America by Worzalla

Portions of this book were originally published in *Rick Steves' Mona Winks* © 2001, 1998, 1996, 1993, 1988 by Rick Steves and Gene Openshaw, and in *Rick Steves' Italy* © 2005, 2004, 2003, 2002, 2001, 2000 by Rick Steves.

ISBN (10): 1-56691-735-2
ISBN (13): 978-1-56691-735-3
ISSN: 1538-1595

For the latest on Rick's lectures, guidebooks, tours, and public television series, contact Europe Through the Back Door, Box 2009, Edmonds, WA 98020, tel. 425/771-8303, fax 425/771-0833, www.ricksteves.com, rick@ricksteves.com.

Europe Through the Back Door Managing Editor: Risa Laib
ETBD Editors: Cameron Hewitt, Jennifer Hauseman, Kevin Yip
Avalon Travel Publishing Series Manager and Editor: Patrick Collins
Avalon Travel Publishing Project Editor: Madhu Prasher
Copy Editor: David R. Johnson
Indexer: Laura Welcome
Cover Design: Kari Gim, Laura Mazer
Interior Design: Laura Mazer, Amber Pirker, Jane Musser
Maps & Graphics: David C. Hoerlein, Lauren Mills, Laura VanDeventer, Mike Morgenfeld
Production & Typesetting: Patrick David Barber, Holly McGuire
Research Assistance: Amanda Scotese
Photography: Rick Steves, David C. Hoerlein, Dominic Bonuccelli, Elizabeth Openshaw, Gene Openshaw, Andrea Johnson, Karen Kant
Front Cover Photos: Front image: the Historical Regatta pageant in Grand Canal © Roberto Soncin Gerometta / Lonely Planet Images; Back image: © Glenn Beanland / Lonely Planet Images
Front Matter Color Photos: p. i, Grand Canal, Venice, Italy © Rick Steves; p. iv, Narrow Canal, Venice, Italy © Dominic Bonuccelli